Medical Law in Malta

Medical Law in Malta

Daniel Bianchi

This book was originally published as a monograph in the International Encyclopaedia of Laws/Medical Law.

Founding Editor: Roger Blanpain
General Editor: Frank Hendrickx
Volume Editor: Herman Nys; Associate Editor: Tom Goffin

Wolters Kluwer

Published by:
Kluwer Law International B.V.
PO Box 316
2400 AH Alphen aan den Rijn
The Netherlands
E-mail: lrs-sales@wolterskluwer.com
Website: www.wolterskluwer.com/en/solutions/kluwerlawinternational

Sold and distributed by:
Wolters Kluwer Legal & Regulatory U.S.
920 Links Avenue
Landisville, PA 17538
United States of America
E-mail: customer.service@wolterskluwer.com

ISBN 978-94-035-4966-8

e-Book: ISBN 978-94-035-4976-7
web-PDF: ISBN 978-94-035-4986-6

This title is available on www.kluwerlawonline.com

The Author

Dr Daniel Bianchi is a lecturer at the University of Malta's Faculty of Laws, having been appointed resident academic in healthcare law in 2012. He is also the coordinator of the 'Medicine and the Law' programme and a member of the Bioethics Research Platform at the University of Malta. Dr Bianchi moreover tutors European healthcare law at postgraduate level at the University of Edinburgh in the United Kingdom. Dr Bianchi's academic work has been published in major academic journals, including the Medical Law Review and the International Journal of Law and Psychiatry. He is regularly invited to address conferences and seminars on different topics within the field of healthcare law.

Dr Bianchi is licensed to practice law as an advocate in Malta, and he is engaged in consultancy work related to healthcare law by both public and private entities. He has also served in Malta's diplomatic corps and was posted to Malta's diplomatic mission in Tunisia.

Dr Bianchi is the national contact point of Malta at the European Association of Health Law, a member of the Malta Chamber of Advocates and a Fellow of the Royal Society of Medicine.

Academically, Dr Bianchi graduated Bachelor of Arts (BA) in Legal and Humanistic Studies and Doctor of Laws (LLD) at the University of Malta. As a Chevening scholar at the University of Edinburgh, he was awarded the degree of Master of Laws (LLM) in International Law. With the support of a Wellcome Trust studentship in Bioethics and Biolaw, he was then admitted to the degree of Master of Arts (MA) in Healthcare Ethics and Law at the University of Manchester. Supported by the Malta Government Scholarship Scheme, Dr Bianchi was awarded the degree of Doctor of Philosophy (PhD) in Bioethics and Medical Jurisprudence by the University of Manchester after defending his thesis 'Advance directives in healthcare: measures that support persons in exercising their legal capacity?'

Contact: Faculty of Laws, University of Malta, Imsida MSD2080, Malta. Email: daniel.bianchi@um.edu.mt

The Author

Table of Contents

List of Abbreviations

CEO	Chief Executive Officer
Commissioner for Mental Health	Commissioner for the Promotion of Rights of Persons with Mental Disorders
CTO	Community Treatment Order
DDI	Directorate for Disability Issues
DNR	Do Not Resuscitate Order
ECHR	Convention for the Protection of Human Rights and Fundamental Freedoms (1950) ETS 5
EU	European Union
FP	Foundation Programme
FREC	Faculty Research Ethics Committee
GDPR	Regulation (EU) 2016/679 of the European Parliament and of the Council of 27 April 2016 on the protection of natural persons with regard to the processing of personal data and on the free movement of such data, and repealing Directive 95/46/EC, OJ L 119, 4.5.2016
GIGESCA	Gender Identity, Gender Expression and Sex Characteristics Act, Chapter 540 of the Laws of Malta
IEL	International Encyclopaedia of Laws
HCPA	Health Care Professions Act, Chapter 464 of the Laws of Malta
HOTCDA	Human Organs, Tissues and Cell Donation Act, Chapter 558 of the Laws of Malta
M.D.	Doctor of Medicine and Surgery (An undergraduate degree granted by the University of Malta)
MPMTC	Malta Postgraduate Medical Training Centre
NGO	Non-governmental Organisation
SAC	Specialist Accreditation Committee
UKFP	United Kingdom's Foundation Programme

List of Abbreviations

UNCRPD	United Nations Convention on the Rights of Persons with Disabilities (Adopted 13 December 2006, entered into force 3 May 2008) 2515 UNTS 3

Preface

This monograph is the entry pertaining to Malta in the International Encyclopaedia for Medical Law. Yet, the entire body of medical law in Malta is vast, detailed and rich, containing elements that are intricate in their juridical complexity and often open to scholarly interpretation, all the while grounded in a mixed legal system. No claim can therefore be made to cover the entire breadth of medical law in Malta in this single monograph. As noted by Giovanni Comandé in the preface of the second edition of the monograph 'Medical Law in Italy', which is the Italian entry in the International Encyclopaedia for Medical Law, while 'an encyclopaedic entry is intended to be, as much as possible, neutral, destined to illustrate the state of the art, a monograph seeks to assert groundbreaking thoughts, or at least, to organize and expose the subject matter in an innovative way'. Comandé then rightly commented that he sought in his monograph to find a way of merging and balancing these two contrasting scientific approaches. That was similarly the task that guided work towards completion of the present monograph, 'Medical Law in Malta'.

In order to achieve that task, the written text largely hones in on medical law, understood as the laws underpinning the practice of medicine and the medical profession in Malta. The broader healthcare law and the many other healthcare professions are of course engaged with in the monograph, albeit often in relation to the laws governing the medical profession. This approach to frame the substance of the monograph is arguably a first for Maltese (legal) scholarship, which, if anything, has to date engaged with the laws that may touch on healthcare in a wide sense rather than specifically honing in on medical law as such. Even so, the monograph required structure and, therefore, in accordance with the instructions to the authors of entries to the International Encyclopaedia of Laws, the layout of this monograph, by and large, faithfully follows the standard outline of the International Encyclopaedia for Medical Law. Again, it is the first time that this sort of task was undertaken in relation to Maltese medical law and, in addition to furnishing a useful base framework against which to operate and narrow down the scope of research, it ultimately meant addressing important features across the spectrum of medical law in Malta without shying away from considering any given topics.

The monograph furnishes the position of the law as, to the best of the author's knowledge, it stood on 30 September 2022. The format of citations and footnotes is based on the 'House Style Guide' of Kluwer Law International.

Naxxar, Malta.
October 2022.

General Introduction

1. The book 'Medical Law in Malta' is a monograph in the International Encyclopaedia of Laws (IEL). Authors are directed by the editors of the IEL to shape each monograph around the outline of parts and chapters that are shared in common by all the monographs in a particular field. The layout of this monograph is thus based upon the standard outline of the International Encyclopaedia for Medical Law, which includes four parts. This first part involves a general background of Malta as a country, a general description of the healthcare system in Malta, and an illustration of the sources of medical law in Malta. A second part deals with the law underpinning the medical profession in Malta, a third part engages with the physician-patient relationship in Malta, and the closing part of the monograph considers the physician in relation to the healthcare system in Malta.

§1. General Background of Malta

I. Geography

2. The nation of Malta is an archipelago of islands in the centre of the Mediterranean Sea located about 93 kilometres south of Sicily in Italy and about 288 kilometres north of Libya. The archipelago as a whole has an area of about 316 square kilometres. The largest islands in the archipelago are the island of Malta, which measures about 246 square kilometres, the island of Gozo, which measures about 67 square kilometres, and the island of Comino, which measures about 3 square kilometres. While there are other islands and islets, the three largest islands are currently the only inhabited islands in Malta, and ferries are regularly available connecting those islands. Healthcare facilities are located on the islands of Malta and Gozo, while Maltese medical law is typically applicable across the nation's territories unless otherwise stipulated.

3. The capital city is Valletta, which is located on the island of Malta, on a promontory between two harbours. There are no mountains, lakes or rivers on the Maltese islands. The terrain is instead typified by valleys, hills and cliffs. The climate of

Malta is described as 'typically Mediterranean with characteristic mild, wet winters and hot, dry summers',[1] with natural water resources largely relying on rainfall.

II. Cultural Composition

4. Malta has been inhabited for thousands of years and is the site of some of the oldest free-standing stone buildings in the world. The cultural composition of Malta is underpinned by its history inasmuch as Malta was exposed to colonisation by entities with different cultural backgrounds, including the Phoenicians, the Carthaginians, the Romans, the Byzantines, the Arabs, the Normans, the Knights Hospitaller, the French and the British. Malta gained independence from the United Kingdom in 1964 and became a republic in 1974, while the last British military forces withdrew from Malta in 1979 after the closure of its military facilities on the islands. In addition to the political system described below,[2] the Maltese islands' local government now involves over sixty local councils and six regions.[3] The nation State of Malta furthermore became a Member State of the European Union (EU) in 2004. In addition to Maltese citizens and citizens of EU Member States, there are an increasing number of third-country nationals in Malta, particularly from Europe, Africa and Asia.

5. Malta's juridical culture is stipulated upon a mixed legal system that 'takes its sources from a plurality of legal systems'.[4] It has, therefore, for example, been noted elsewhere that the Maltese legal system has roots 'in the Civil Law family, but which has absorbed many features of the Common Law tradition'.[5] For instance, although the laws of Malta include five Codes in a manner akin to codification in jurisdictions embedded in a Civil Law legal system, 'the common law influence can still be seen as codification is not complete',[6] and the laws of Malta then also feature in excess of 600 chapters in Malta's statute book. The legal culture of Malta is thus not grounded in any one specific group of legal systems but is, instead, *inter alia* 'at the crossroads of civil law and common law',[7] albeit without the application of the common law doctrine of precedent or *stare decisis*.[8] Furthermore, in

1. P.J. Schembri, *Physical Geography and Ecology of the Maltese Islands: A Brief Overview*, in *Malta: Food, Agriculture, Fisheries and the Environment* 27, 31 (S Busuttil, F Lerin & L Mizzi eds, CIHEAM 1993).
2. *See* General Introduction §1.III below.
3. Local Councils Act, Ch. 363 of the Laws of Malta.
4. Kevin Aquilina, *Constitutional Law in Malta* 49 (Kluwer Law International 2018).
5. David Joseph Attard, *The Maltese legal system: Volume I* 41 (Malta University Press 2d ed. 2013).
6. Ivan Sammut, *Introduction – The Maltese Legal System and the EU*, in *The Implementation and Enforcement of European Union Law in Small Member States* 1, 4 (Ivan Sammut & Jelena Agranovska eds, Palgrave Macmillan 2021).
7. *Ibid.*
8. Code of Organization and Civil Procedure, Ch. 12 of the Laws of Malta, Art. 237. *See also* Biagio Andó, Kevin Aquilina, Jotham Scerri-Diacono & David Zammit, *Malta*, in *Mixed Jurisdictions Worldwide: The Third Legal Family* 528, 539 (Vernon Valentine Palmer ed., Cambridge University Press 2d ed. 2012).

addition to the development of Maltese autochthonous law and law drawing inspiration from other jurisdictions, the domestic legal order in Malta has increasingly been impacted by public international law and EU law. Kevin Aquilina described this hybrid legal system by illustrating 'the historical evolution of Maltese law in nine distinct phases'[9] including Roman Malta (218 BC–870 AD), Arab Malta (870–1090), Norman Malta (1090–1530), Hospitallers Malta (1530–1798), French Malta (1798–1800), British Malta (1800–1964), Independent Malta (1964–2004), European Unionised Malta (since 2004), and a revival of codification in Malta (since 2009) possibly involving some consolidation of domestic laws. Aquilina then opined that it is 'all these layers of law which make the Maltese legal system a hybrid one, that is, a healthy grafted European mixed legal system'.[10] As such, the juridical culture of Malta is exemplified by the 'uniqueness of the Maltese legal system [that] is characterised through its diverse legal sources, in particular the legislative one, which makes legislative drafting and statutory interpretation a very daunting exercise for the draftsperson, the legislator and judge'.[11] Medical law in Malta is thus to be understood in that context, duly embedded in a European mixed legal system. This is also best understood by outlining the political system in Malta while furnishing a brief outline as to how Maltese domestic law, rather than medical law, in particular,[12] is made.

III. Political System

6. Malta is a democratic republic with a written Constitution that 'constitutes a restriction on executive power [and an elected Legislature in Malta] can only enact laws if they are in consonance with the written Constitution'.[13] The executive authority is vested in the President of Malta,[14] who is the Head of State and 'shall be appointed by Resolution supported by the votes of not less than two-thirds of all the members of the House'[15] of Representatives. Legislative authority is vested in Parliament, which consists of 'the President and a House of Representatives'.[16] The members of the House are elected in a general election that is held at least every five years[17] or, otherwise, by way of a subsequent casual election or co-option to fill a vacancy in the House.[18] The President appoints as Prime Minister the member of the House of Representatives who, in his/her judgment, is best able to command the support of a majority of the members of that House,[19] which typically is the leader

9. Kevin Aquilina, *Rethinking Maltese Legal Hybridity: A Chimeric Illusion or a Healthy Grafted European Law Mixture*, 4 (2) Journal of Civil Law Studies 261, 263 (2011).
10. *Ibid.*, 283.
11. Kevin Aquilina, *Legislative Drafting and Statutory Interpretation in the Maltese Mixed Legal System*, 6 International Journal of Legislative Drafting and Law Reform 29, 41–42 (2017).
12. *See* General Introduction §3 below.
13. Tonio Borg, *A Commentary on the Constitution of Malta* 23 (Kite, 2016).
14. Constitution of Malta, Art. 78 (1).
15. *Ibid.*, Art. 48 (1).
16. *Ibid.*, Art. 51.
17. *Ibid.*, Art. 76 (2).
18. General Elections Act, Ch. 354 of the Laws of Malta, Thirteenth Schedule.
19. Constitution of Malta, Art. 80.

of the political party that won the most recent general election. Acting in accordance with the advice of the Prime Minster, the President also appoints the other Ministers from among the members of the House of Representatives,[20] and it is the Cabinet of Ministers that has 'the general direction and control of the Government of Malta and shall be collectively responsible therefor to Parliament'.[21] Since Malta's independence from the United Kingdom in 1964, either the centre-left Labour Party or the centre-right Nationalist Party have held the seat of Government in Malta. The judiciary is separate from the Government and, although there exist other tribunals that settle legal disputes in Malta, the members of the judiciary composing the superior[22] and inferior courts[23] are appointed by the President of Malta acting in accordance with a recommendation made by the Judicial Appointments Committee and, whenever a vacancy occurs in the office of judge or magistrate, 'the Minister responsible for justice shall issue a public call for applications open to persons who have the necessary qualifications to be appointed to the office of judge or magistrate'.[24] Those qualifications include being in possession of a valid warrant to practice as an advocate in Malta as well as practising that profession for a number of years as established in the Constitution.[25] The Chief Justice is also appointed by the President, albeit acting in accordance with a resolution of the House of Representatives supported by at least two-thirds of its members.[26] That being said, the judiciary in Malta has no law-making authority. It is instead Parliament that has the power to make laws in Malta.[27]

7. In accordance with the Constitution, the power of Parliament to make laws 'shall be exercised by bills passed by the House of Representatives and assented to by the President'[28] of Malta. It typically is the Minister responsible for the area covered by a proposed law who presents the bill to the House after it is approved by the Cabinet, although it is also possible for any member of the House to present a private members bill. Furthermore, bills may be preceded by a period of consultation, a Green Paper, or a White Paper. Once a law has been assented to by the President of Malta, it would then have to be published in the Government Gazette before it can enter into operation even though 'Parliament may postpone the coming into operation of any such law and may make laws with retrospective effect'.[29] A Law Commission consisting of a Law Commissioner and a body of consultants then prepares a revised edition of the statute laws of Malta,[30] which includes the different

20. *Ibid.*
21. *Ibid.*, Art. 79 (2).
22. *Ibid.*, Art. 96.
23. *Ibid.*, Art. 100.
24. *Ibid.*, Art. 96B (1).
25. *Ibid.*, Art. 96B (2).
26. *Ibid.*, Art. 96 (3).
27. *Ibid.*, Art. 65.
28. *Ibid.*, Art. 72 (1).
29. *Ibid.*, Art. 72 (4).
30. Statute Law Revision Act, 2021, Art. 3.

chapters of Malta's statute book. The Law Commission is however not the legislator.[31] Moreover, inasmuch as law-making authority arises from the Constitution of Malta, it is only in those instances when the Constitution or when law made under the authority of the Constitution acknowledges usages, ethics or other conduct to have force of law that these would then have that authority within the domestic law in Malta.[32] That being said, Parliament can and regularly does include in legislative Acts provisions that grant authority to another person or body to make subsidiary or delegated legislation. It is delegated 'because Parliament in effect delegates its law-making power to another person or body, and "subsidiary" because this legislation is subsidiary to the "primary" or "parent" Act under which this authority is created'.[33] This means that many laws in Malta are not per se made by bills arising in the House of Representatives and assented to by the President but instead arise consequent to the authority that Parliament vested on another person or body to make laws by way of, for instance, a legal notice published in the Government Gazette. This subsidiary legislation can *inter alia* be in the form of an 'order, warrant, scheme, rules, regulations, bye-laws, or other instrument'.[34] That being said, subsidiary legislation is to be laid on the table of the House of Representatives, which then has the power to annul or amend that subsidiary legislation.[35] The Minister responsible for the Law Commission may also cause to be published 'an up to date consolidated version of subsidiary legislation made under the laws included in a revised edition [of the laws of Malta] and under Acts subsequently enacted'.[36] That subsidiary legislation may then be enumerated with reference to the chapter number of the principal law from which it draws authority or, otherwise, as the Minister responsible for the Law Commission may deem proper.

IV. Population and Vital Statistics

8. Malta is the smallest Member State in the EU in terms of land mass and population. It is however also one of the most densely populated nation States in the world. The population of Malta has more than doubled in a century, from 212,258 in 1921 to 519,562 in 2021. The most recent census indicated that 480,275 people lived on the island of Malta, and 39,287 people lived on the islands of Gozo and Comino, albeit only a handful of people resided on Comino.[37] The average age at

31. *Ibid.*, Art. 4 (3).
32. *See, for instance*: Commercial Code, Ch. 13 of the Laws of Malta, Art. 3.
33. David Joseph Attard, *The Maltese Legal System: Volume I* 56 (Malta University Press 2d. ed. 2013). Original ellipses.
34. Interpretation Act, Ch. 249 of the Laws of Malta, Art. 8.
35. *Ibid.*, Art. 11.
36. Statute Law Revision Act, 2021, Art. 12 (2).
37. National Statistics Office Malta, *Census of Population and Housing 2021: Preliminary Report* 38 (2022).

that census in 2021 stood at 41.7 years,[38] while 83,102 people suffered from a long-term illness, health condition and/or disability as of 2011.[39]

9. The Health Care Standards Directorate[40] indicates that there is one large public hospital, two rehabilitation hospitals, four long-term care facilities, one oncology centre, five private hospitals, seven private medical clinics, eight radiology clinics, eight medical diagnostic laboratories and fifteen mental health licensed facilities on the island of Malta. There furthermore is a public hospital, which includes two mental health licensed facilities within its remit, one radiology clinic, two medical diagnostic laboratories and a third mental health licensed facility on the island of Gozo. Additionally, there are three tissue establishments and one blood establishment in Malta. There furthermore exist reports detailing the performance and statistics underpinning the healthcare system in Malta,[41] and while it is beyond the scope of this monograph to delve into those reports, the next sub-section briefly outlines Malta's social and cultural values before proceeding to review the healthcare system in Malta through the lens of its legal framework.

V. Social and Cultural Values

10. Malta's social and cultural values are traditionally embedded in the Roman Catholic Apostolic Religion. The Constitution of Malta, for instance, declares that the 'religion of Malta is the Roman Catholic Apostolic Religion'.[42] While the Constitution safeguards freedom of conscience and worship,[43] it also states that the 'authorities of the Roman Catholic Apostolic Church have the duty and the right to teach which principles are right and which are wrong'.[44] Malta has thus sometimes been described as a 'Roman Catholic Country',[45] which has then affected the development of medical law in Malta. That being said, it has also been opined that the 'Catholic values which were very strong in Malta in the past are being eroded and evidencing a trend towards the secularisation of the State'.[46] By way of example, the legislative authorities repealed from the Criminal Code the offence pertaining to the vilification of the Roman Catholic Apostolic Religion in 2016.[47] Another

38. *Ibid.*, 29.
39. National Statistics Office Malta, *Census of Population and Housing 2011*, 189–198 (2014). The result of the 2021 census on this matter was not available at the time of writing.
40. *See* General Introduction §2.II below.
41. Kenneth Grech, Maya Podesta, Antoinette Calleja & Neville Calleja, *Report on the Performance of the Maltese Health System, 2015* (Ministry for Energy and Health Malta 2015).
42. Constitution of Malta, Art. 2 (1).
43. *Ibid.*, Art. 40.
44. *Ibid.*, Art. 2 (2).
45. *See, for instance*: Pierre Mallia, *Problems Faced with Legislating for IVF Technology in a Roman Catholic Country*, 13 Medicine, Health Care and Philosophy 77–87 (2010); Pierre Mallia, *Developments in IVF Legislation in a Catholic Country*, 16 Medicine, Health Care and Philosophy 385–390 (2013).
46. Kevin Aquilina, *Constitutional Law in Malta* 252 (Kluwer Law International 2018).
47. Act XXXVII of 2016 – Criminal Code (Amendment) Act, 2016 [Government Gazette of Malta No. 19,610 – 19/07/2016], Art. 3.

example involves the rights of lesbian, gay, bisexual, trans and intersex people inasmuch as Malta, on some accounts, presents many of the best practices in that area.[48] As such, Malta's societal and cultural values can be understood as being ostensibly progressive while traditionally underpinned by the Roman Catholic Apostolic Religion.

11. Language is also integral to Malta's social and cultural values. The Constitution of Malta provides that the national language of Malta is the Maltese language, but it furthermore establishes the Maltese and English languages as the official languages of Malta.[49] Save as otherwise provided by Parliament, every law shall therefore be enacted in both the Maltese and the English languages. For instance, the Medicines Act states that regulations made under any provision of that Act 'may be made in the English language only'.[50] That being said, the Constitution also declares that 'if there is any conflict between the Maltese and the English texts of any law, the Maltese text shall prevail'.[51] Yet, since that provision has no retroactive effect, 'for laws enacted prior to Independence the English text prevails'.[52] The Italian language was significant to Malta until the 1930s, but its use has since dwindled.

§2. General Description of the Healthcare System

I. General Review of the Healthcare System

12. There is no statutory definition of medical law in Malta. Be that as it may, medical law, at the very least, involves the law covering the practice of medicine and medical practitioners,[53] which is then ingrained within the broader healthcare system in Malta. In order to engage with medical law, it therefore is incumbent to have a basic grasp of the healthcare system upon which it is formulated and within which it operates. This section of the monograph illustrates some of the main actors in the healthcare system, indicating the roles they play in policymaking in healthcare, in the provision of healthcare services, and in the protection of public health. That will lead on to considering the regulation of the healthcare system in the next sub-section of this part of the monograph.

13. The Ministry for Health in Malta is described as the 'main actor in the health system',[54] and it piloted the National Health Systems Strategy that aimed, in its most recent incarnation, 'to provide every individual with the opportunity to lead a healthy and active life, and to benefit from equitable access to sustainable quality

48. *See, for instance*: ILGA Europe, *Rainbow Map & Index 2022.*
49. Constitution of Malta, Art. 5.
50. Medicines Act, Ch. 458 of the Laws of Malta, Art. 112.
51. Constitution of Malta, Art. 74.
52. Tonio Borg, *A Commentary on the Constitution of Malta* 370 (Kite 2016).
53. *See* General Introduction §3 below.
54. Natasha Azzopardi-Muscat, Stefan Buttigieg, Neville Calleja & Sherry Merkur, *Malta – Health System Review*, 19 (1) Health Systems in Transition 1, 13 (2017).

health care'.[55] The legal framework underpinning the health system is spread across the Maltese statute book, but it is the Health Act that *inter alia* served to consolidate and reform the 'Government structures and entities responsible for health'.[56] These were regulated until 2013 by the Department of Health (Constitution) Ordinance, Chapter 94 of the Laws of Malta, which had established the Department of Health in Malta in 1937. Hence, the Health Bill tabled in Parliament in 2013 included, as one of its objects and reasons, providing for an updated law on the running and administration of the department involved in the provision of services connected with public health.[57] In this respect, the Health Act served as the legal basis to repeal the Department of Health (Constitution) Ordinance while also distinguishing and separating policy in health from service provision and from regulation of the healthcare system. These three branches frame, in part, the healthcare system and are considered in turn next.

14. The statutory policymaker on matters related to health and healthcare is the Government of Malta. Article 30 of the Health Act, for instance, provides that the Minister responsible for health may, subject to the provisions of that Act, 'make regulations to give effect to any provisions of this Act or to regulate or otherwise provide about *anything* in respect of the functions and the activities *which affect the provision of healthcare*'.[58] This authority to make regulations is a means to substantiate the basic framework of the healthcare system embedded in the statute book.[59] Soon after its entry into force in 2013, Article 30 of the Health Act was also nodded at by a domestic court as one source of the legitimate authority of the Minister responsible for health to effectuate changes to a clinical department at a hospital within the public healthcare system by splitting it into two different departments.[60] Yet, that authority to make regulations can be pertinent both to public and to private healthcare providers inasmuch as Article 30 of the Health Act *inter alia* clarifies that, without prejudice to the generality of that provision, the Minister responsible for health may make regulations 'to establish, in the paramount interest of health in Malta, any possible exceptions to any provision contained in any law'. Article 30 (l) of the Health Act furthermore specifies that the Minister responsible for health may make regulations 'to establish the framework of the national health policy for public and private healthcare providers'. The Health Act in Article 30 (l) moreover specifies that 'it shall be the duty of all such providers to implement this policy according to the potential and the various needs of patients attending thereat'. Even in view of this policymaking authority in healthcare, the Government has an advisory network regarding healthcare embedded in law that *inter alia* includes the Department for Policy in Health, the Health Policy and Strategy Board, the Council

---

55. Parliamentary Secretariat for Health, *A National Health Systems Strategy for Malta 2014 – 2020: Securing Our Health Systems for Future Generations* 15 (2014).
56. Health Act, Ch. 528 of the Laws of Malta, Art. 3.
57. Bill No 11 of 2013 – Health Act, 2013 [Government Gazette of Malta No. 19,102 – 25/06/2013].
58. Emphasis added.
59. *See also* General Introduction §1.III above.
60. *Fenech Onor Prof Albert v. Ministru tas-Sahha*, Civil Court First Hall – 27 December 2013 [Ref: 1893/2013/1].

of Health, and boards dealing with strategies that target a specific sector of the healthcare system. This advisory network is considered in turn next.

15. The Department for Policy in Health, which is headed by the Chief Medical Officer to the Government, is established by way of the Health Act, and its mission, in general, is 'to act as the chief adviser to the Minister [responsible for health] on all matters related to the Government's health policies'.[61] Thus, while it is not the policymaker, the Department for Policy in Health, in particular, advises the Minister responsible for health 'on the development of policy and coordination of strategic plans, on the design and implementation of action plans, and on the evaluation of outcomes in order to contribute to the sustainability of public health and healthcare services'.[62] Some examples of that Department's functions and duties embedded in subsidiary legislation that shape this advisory role include: (i) collating, analysing and publishing epidemiological data concerning the health status of the nation in order to identify and prioritise healthcare needs; (ii) carrying out needs assessment and health system planning and forecasting; (iii) developing evidence-based and financially viable strategies in consultation with stakeholders; (iv) monitoring and reporting on health system performance and health outcomes; (v) conducting health technology assessments; and (vi) advising the Minister responsible for health upon health benefits and new services to be offered by the public healthcare system after thoroughly assessing and evaluating their implication, including financial implication.[63]

16. The Department for Policy in Health moreover has the function 'to engage with relevant stakeholders to implement policies and strategies'[64] as well as 'to sustain an effective dialogue with whosoever is involved in the health system aiming for the widest consensus possible about any matter relevant to health'.[65] While this function of the Department for Policy in Health could optimise synergy between the public and private sectors in healthcare, it then is within the remit of the Health Policy and Strategy Board to evaluate and monitor policy. The latter Board, presided over by the Minister responsible for health, has the function 'to discuss and evaluate the policy, strategy developments and direction in the health sector and to monitor and follow the implementation of the health policy and strategy adopted by the Government'.[66] There consequently is a cycle whereby the Department for Policy in Health advises on matters regarding the Government's health policies, the Health Policy and Strategy Board discusses and evaluates policy, and the Government makes the policy. The cycle then continues inasmuch as the Health Policy and Strategy Board monitors and follows the implementation of the health policy and strategy adopted by the Government while the Department for Policy in Health engages with the stakeholders to implement that policy.

61. Health Act, Ch. 528 of the Laws of Malta, Art. 4 (1).
62. *Ibid*; S.L. 528.01, Functions and Responsibilities of Department for Policy in Health Regulations, r. 3 (1).
63. S.L. 528.01, Functions and Responsibilities of Department for Policy in Health Regulations, r. 3 (2).
64. *Ibid.*, r. 3 (2)(e).
65. *Ibid.*, r. 3 (2)(m).
66. Health Act, Ch. 528 of the Laws of Malta, Art. 15 (1).

17. Although policymaking is different from its implementation, some of the stakeholders that stand to implement policy have a seat on the Council of Health that has the duty to 'advise Government on any matter affecting all matters related to health in Malta'[67] whenever so requested as well as 'to advise on any matter with regards to which the law provides that the advice of the Council shall be sought'.[68] The law provides in the Medical and Kindred Professions Ordinance an instance in the context of the regulation of drugs or chemical products when the advice of the Council of Health should be sought by the Minister responsible for public health.[69] However, the latter provisions were added to the domestic legal order on the basis of the previous incarnation of the Council of Health that was established under the Department of Health (Constitution) Ordinance.[70] The Council of Health that is now established under the Health Act has, similarly to its previous incarnation under the Department of Health (Constitution) Ordinance, 'the power to appoint sub-committees and to co-opt thereon members who are not members of the said Council when discussing specific items on its agenda'.[71] Yet, the Council of Health under the Health Act is *inter alia* distinguishable from its predecessor by its statutory composition, which,[72] unlike its previous incarnation, includes among its members, in addition to representatives of the Ministry for Health, a person representing private healthcare providers, a person nominated by associations representing the patients, a trade-unionism expert in health matters, and a member of the academic staff on Health Sciences of the University of Malta. Furthermore, whereas the previous incarnation of the Council of Health under the Department of Health (Constitution) Ordinance indicated the medical practitioners who would form part of that Council based on their clinical background, the new composition under the Health Act only refers to a person specifically representing healthcare professionals in addition to a specialist in public health medicine as a member based on his/her clinical background.

18. In addition to general provisions regarding policy and policymaking underpinning the healthcare system in Malta, the law sometimes engages with policies and strategies that target a specific sector within the healthcare system. Although some of these will be mentioned later in the monograph, by way of example, at this stage, the Board of Directors for Mental Health Services is responsible for advising the Minister responsible for health 'on a high-level strategic vision for the mental health services offered by the national health system … as well as to ensure that the executive decision-making process follows the lead established by the same strategic vision'.[73] As such, the functions and duties of the Board of Directors for Mental Health Services, which is responsible and accountable for its performance

67. *Ibid.*, Art. 17 (1).
68. *Ibid.*, Art. 17 (2).
69. Medical and Kindred Professions Ordinance, Ch. 31 of the Laws of Malta, Arts 40 and 40A.
70. Department of Health (Constitution) Ordinance, Ch. 94 of the Laws of Malta, Art. 7. Repealed.
71. *Ibid.*, Art. 18 (1).
72. Health Act, Ch. 528 of the Laws of Malta, Sch. B.
73. S.L. 528.07, Board of Directors for Mental Health Services Regulations, r. 5 (1).

to the Minister responsible for health,[74] include 'advising the Minister upon strategies and objectives for the mental health services'[75] and 'the setting of targets and measurable objectives for the mental health services'.[76] The subsidiary legislation arising from the Health Act that establishes this Board furthermore furnishes a good example of the distinction between the policymaker, the service provider and clinical decision-making. This is because it separates policymaking, in the form of a high-level strategic vision, from the operation of the mental health services inasmuch as 'the administrative and management responsibility shall remain vested in the chief executive officer'[77] of the mental health licensed facility, who would be the person responsible for management of that facility[78] so that chief executive officer is then responsible 'to implement the decisions regarding the operation of the mental health services taken by the Board'.[79] It also significantly separates policymaking from clinical responsibility inasmuch as, despite the role of the Board of Directors regarding the high-level strategic vision for mental health services, 'clinical responsibility for mental health services shall remain vested in the clinical director',[80] who is the psychiatrist responsible for the clinical care provided by a mental health licensed facility.[81]

19. There will of course be some overlap between policy and the operation of the healthcare system. For instance, the Department for Policy in Health has the function 'to commission quality health services to complement the public health care services'[82] as well as the function 'to develop partnerships with non-governmental organisations and private healthcare providers'.[83] While these functions tie policy to the provision of healthcare services within the public and private healthcare sectors, the operator in both sectors is distinct from the policy maker of the healthcare system. In this respect, the next paragraphs of this section of the monograph consider the provision of services in the healthcare system.

20. The Health Act established the Department for Healthcare Services, whose mission includes ensuring 'the effective and efficient operation and delivery of healthcare services'.[84] The latter department is largely responsible, in the first instance, for the delivery and quality of the services provided by the public healthcare system. The functions and duties of the Department of Healthcare Services

---

74. *Ibid.*, r. 3 (5).
75. *Ibid.*, r. 5 (2)(b).
76. *Ibid.*, r. 5 (2)(a).
77. *Ibid.*, r. 5 (2).
78. Mental Health Act, Ch. 525 of the Laws of Malta, Art. 2.
79. S.L. 528.07, Board of Directors for Mental Health Services Regulations, r. 5 (2).
80. *Ibid.*
81. Mental Health Act, Ch. 525 of the Laws of Malta, Art. 2.
82. S.L. 528.01, Functions and Responsibilities of Department for Policy in Health Regulations, r. 3 (2)(k).
83. *Ibid.*, r. 3 (2)(n).
84. Health Act, Ch. 528 of the Laws of Malta, Art. 6 (1).

established by subsidiary legislation thus include:[85] (i) to ensure the quality of services delivered through the public health system; (ii) to oversee good governance of state healthcare services; (iii) to ensure that public health services are effective, caring and responsive to users' needs; (iv) to coordinate between public health service providers to ensure integrated and aligned service provision; (v) to implement service level agreements with public health service providers to assure the performance of public health service organisations; and (vi) to monitor the performance and outcomes of public health service providers to ensure that resources are being used in an effective and efficient manner. The Department for Healthcare Services is, therefore, not the same as the provider/s of those public healthcare services inasmuch as day-to-day operations are in practice managed by the pertinent healthcare facility. Yet, while the Health Act acknowledges 'an established framework of controlled decentralisation and autonomy involving user participation',[86] the Department for Healthcare Services has been acknowledged by the domestic courts as a party vested with the responsibility of coordinating the delivery of professional services in the public health service,[87] and it also has the function to 'advise upon the allocation of human, financial and other resources between public health service providers'.[88]

21. The Department for Healthcare Services is furthermore pertinent to all healthcare providers with the aim of having integrated and cost-efficient healthcare services meeting the developing needs of users. As such, that Department even has the following functions established by subsidiary legislation:[89] (i) to ensure that standards and regulations adopted by the Government are implemented by healthcare providers; (ii) to develop operational policies and synergies to maintain an integrated and seamless service at both community and institutional level; (iii) to set objectives and performance indicators for clinical outcomes; (iv) to advise upon innovative models of service provision and delivery through consultation with stakeholders, including unions; (v) to coordinate the professional aspects of healthcare service provision including postgraduate training and development; and (vi) to coordinate between the health and social care systems.

22. The latter function denotes the relation between the healthcare system and the social care system, which is in large part regulated under the Social Care Standards Authority Act rather than the Health Act and consequently stands to benefit from a measure of coordination between the two separate frameworks. Indeed,

---

85. S.L. 528.04, Functions and Responsibilities of the Department of Health Services Regulations. The subsidiary law in the English language refers to the Department of Health Services as opposed to the Department for Healthcare Services established by the Health Act. The Maltese language version of the subsidiary law however uses the same name of the Department as its Maltese language counterpart in the Health Act.
86. Health Act, Ch. 528 of the Laws of Malta, Art. 6 (1).
87. *Mercieca Lawrence et. v. Direttur Generali tad-Dipartiment tas-Sahha et.*, Civil Court First Hall – 28/02/2019 [Ref: 1294/2003] p. 11; *Calleja Raymond et. v. Supretendent ta' l-Isptar Mater Dei*, Civil Court First Hall – 16/06/2020 [Ref: 305/2003] p. 12.
88. S.L. 528.04, Functions and Responsibilities of the Department of Health Services Regulations, r. 3 (2)(h).
89. *Ibid.*

healthcare is inherently significant to a social welfare service that is defined in law to mean 'care services, provided in relation to the well-being of service users, whether by a person, agency or residential facility, or in the community or in a care and nursing home or in the home, as well as may be prescribed by regulations made under'[90] the Social Care Standards Authority Act. It is, for instance, under the authority of that Act that subsidiary legislation was made regulating standards for high dependency chronic care services for older persons,[91] covering long-term care. Yet, in accordance with the provisions of the Social Care Standards Authority Act, the Government of Malta 'shall determine Malta's policies and objectives in the regulation of social welfare services provided by public or private agencies or entities or any other entity or person'.[92] Thus, similarly to the healthcare system, the social care system also separates the policymaking authority, which is vested in the Government, from the service provider as well as from the regulatory authority that is then vested in the Social Care Standards Authority.

23. In addition to policymaking, advisory functions and service provision, public health is another vital component of the healthcare system if only because it underpins the regulation of the healthcare system. Although different entities[93] and several laws engage with public health,[94] there are at least three inter-linking structures that are critical to grounding public health in Malta. These inter-linking structures grounding public health in Malta are considered next in this section of the monograph before then engaging with the regulation of the healthcare system in the next sub-section of this part of the monograph.

24. First, the Department for Health Regulation was established by the Health Act in 2013, and its mission includes safeguarding public health and advising the Minister responsible for health on matters relating to public health.[95] This entails both the role of advisor to the Ministry politically responsible for health within Government and a role as an enforcing agent to safeguard public health. As to its advisory function, subsidiary legislation arising from the Health Act clarifies that the functions and duties of the Department for Health Regulation include: (i) advising Government on the public health aspects of regulation of food, medicines, blood, organs and health professionals; and (ii) advising Government on public health

90. Social Care Standards Authority Act, Ch. 582 of the Laws of Malta, Art. 2.
91. S.L. 582.09, Social Regulatory Standards for High Dependency Chronic Care Services for Older Persons Regulations.
92. Social Care Standards Authority Act, Ch. 582 of the Laws of Malta, Art. 4 (1).
93. By way of example, the Council of Health also has 'the power to recommend any such measures, enquiries or scientific investigations as, in its opinion, are useful in the interests of the public health'. *See* Health Act, Ch. 528 of the Laws of Malta, Art. 18 (2).
94. *See, for instance:* Code of Police Laws, Ch. 10 of the Laws of Malta; Notification of Cancer Act, Ch. 154 of the Laws of Malta; S.L. 452.101, Minimum Special Leave Entitlement Regulations; S.L. 460.17, Free movement of European Union nationals and their family members; Healthy Lifestyle Promotion and Care of Non-Communicable Diseases Act, Ch. 550 of the Laws of Malta (not yet in force); Cremation Act, Ch. 599 of the Laws of Malta (not yet in force).
95. Health Act, Ch. 528 of the Laws of Malta, Art. 8 (1).

aspects of emergency preparedness and coordinating emergency response programmes.[96] As to its role in regulatory enforcement, the Department for Health Regulation Regulations includes the following within its functions and duties: (a) to formulate regulations and standards in line with Government direction and to ensure their enforcement; (b) to monitor and ensure the maintenance of public health standards and regulations in licensed premises and other entities as appropriate; (c) to develop, coordinate and evaluate various environment monitoring programmes aimed at reducing health hazards and promoting environmental hazards; and (d) to safeguard the health and well-being of the public through enforcement of all national and international regulations and public health legislation.[97]

25. Second, the Head of the Department for Health Regulation is the Superintendent of Public Health,[98] which in part reaffirms the Superintendent's role prior to the Health Act under the Department of Health (Constitution) Ordinance.[99] This is also significant to public health inasmuch as the Superintendent of Public Health administers the Public Health Act in Malta[100] that then stipulates that the Superintendent 'shall be responsible for public health in Malta'.[101] Indeed, the Public Health Act is a far-reaching legislative Act aimed at promoting and protecting health, which then ties in with the functions of the Department for Health Regulation in the context of public health. For instance, the Public Health Act also stipulates that similar to the advisory role of the Department for Health Regulation outlined in the previous paragraph, the Superintendent of Public Health has an advisory function inasmuch as s/he shall 'advise the Minister [responsible for public health] on matters regarding public health in general and on matters relating to [the Public Health] Act in particular'.[102] The Public Health Act furthermore stipulates that the Superintendent of Public Health also has a measure of executive authority inasmuch as s/he: (i) shall ensure that the provisions of the Public Health Act and of regulations made there under are complied with; (ii) shall develop and implement strategies to promote and improve public health; and (iii) shall issue standards for public health.[103] While the Public Health Act thus further grounds the Superintendent of Public Health as an important component of the healthcare system, it should be recalled that Article 45 of the Public Health Act was also intended to repeal the Prevention of Disease Ordinance,[104] but that provision has not yet entered into force despite enactment in 2003. This means that the Prevention of Disease Ordinance is still formally part of the corpus of Maltese law, but the Public Health

96. S.L. 528.05, Functions and Responsibilities of the Department of Health Regulation Regulations, r. 3 (2). The subsidiary law in the English language refers to the Department of Health Regulation as opposed to the Department for Health Regulation established by the Health Act. The Maltese language version of the subsidiary law however uses the same name of the Department as its Maltese language counterpart in the Health Act.

97. *Ibid.*

98. Health Act, Ch. 528 of the Laws of Malta, Art. 8 (2).

99. Department of Health (Constitution) Ordinance, Ch. 94 of the Laws of Malta, Art. 4 (2). Repealed.

100. Public Health Act, Ch. 465 of the Laws of Malta, Art. 3.

101. *Ibid.*, Art. 4.

102. *Ibid.*

103. *Ibid.*

104. Prevention of Disease Ordinance, Ch. 36 of the Laws of Malta.

Act has, in practice, largely superseded it. It was, for example, chiefly the latter Act that provided the legal framework regarding public health to address the COVID-19 pandemic. This included, for instance, the Declaration of Public Health Emergency Order,[105] which arose from Article 14 of the Public Health Act, as well as other legislative changes to address circumstances rendered necessary due to the pandemic that engaged with the Public Health Act rather than the Prevention of Disease Ordinance.[106]

26. Third, even though the Superintendent of Public Health is, in accordance with the Public Health Act, responsible for public health in Malta, the Government of Malta is itself independently a key figure to public health in Malta. The laws that are outlined in the previous two paragraphs of this monograph may serve as an example of the role the Government can play in public health. Thus, the Department for Health Regulation has the function to formulate regulations and standards that fall within its remit but are subject to the terms 'in line with Government direction'.[107] Also, in the context of the Public Health Act, the Superintendent of Public Health has a broad authority to make, vary or revoke orders as indicated in Article 27 of that Act, but it is the Minister responsible for public health that then has the authority, after consulting the Superintendent of Public Health, to 'make regulations in general to regulate matters related to public health'.[108] This duality of orders made by the Superintendent of Public Health and regulations made by the Minister responsible for health was, for instance, used in 2020 and in 2021 when addressing the COVID-19 pandemic.[109] The role of the Government in public health is also noteworthy inasmuch as the Department for Health Regulation, headed by the Superintendent of Public Health, similarly to the other Departments established under the Health Act, are Departments of Government that are subject to Ministerial direction and control,[110] including the duties of the Heads of Department under the Public Administration Act.[111] This then leads to the Interpretation Act and the following provision that bestows broad authority to the responsible Minister:

> Where such Act confers a power on the holder of an office, and such power relates to any business of the Government, or is exercisable as part of the functions of a department of Government for which responsibility has been assigned to a Minister under the Constitution, such power shall be exercisable

105. S.L. 465.36, Declaration of a Public Health Emergency Order. Repealed.
106. *See, for instance*: L.N. 137 of 2020 – Code of Organization and Civil Procedure (Amendment of Sch. A) Regulations, 2020 [Government Gazette of Malta No. 20,382 – 03/04/2020].
107. S.L. 528.05, Functions and Responsibilities of the Department of Health Regulation Regulations, r. 3 (2)(a).
108. Public Health Act, Ch. 465 of the Laws of Malta,
109. *See, for instance:* L.N. 87 of 2021 – Closure of Places Open to the Public Order, 2021 [Government Gazette of Malta No. 20,587 – 11/03/2021]; L.N. 94 of 2021 – Enforcement of the Order relating to the Closure of Places Open to the Public Regulations, 2021 [Government Gazette of Malta No. 20,587A – 11/03/2021].
110. Public Administration Act, Ch. 595 of the Laws of Malta, Arts 3 and 8. *See also* Constitution of Malta, Art. 82; Assignment of Statutory Ministerial Responsibilities Act, Ch. 561 of the Laws of Malta.
111. *Ibid.*, Art. 18.

> by the holder of that office, and except to the extent that the holder of that office is expressly declared by any law not to be subject to the direction or control of any other person or authority, the Minister responsible for that business or department of the Government shall have power, *even where such power is expressed to be exercisable in the discretion (whether absolute or otherwise) of the holder of that office*, to give such direction in writing relative to the exercise of that power *(including a direction ordering the reversal of a decision)* as such Minister may deem fit ... [112]

27. That being said, as noted by a former Superintendent of Public Health, 'the main mission of the department is to safeguard public health; regulation is one of the means to achieve that end'.[113] Thus, whereas this sub-section briefly engaged with public health, together with the role of the policymaker, the advisory bodies, and the service provider, it is incumbent to consider the regulation of the healthcare system in the next sub-section.

II. Regulation of the Healthcare System

28. The mission of the Department for Health Regulation includes, in addition to and complimenting its role in public health,[114] the role to 'license, monitor and inspect the provision of healthcare services in order to ensure their quality and safety, and to recommend the standards to be met by healthcare providers'.[115] This sub-section of the monograph briefly illustrates those regulatory aspects while also mapping out the regulation of the healthcare system in Malta as a whole.

29. The Medical and Kindred Professions Ordinance sites licensing authority for healthcare establishments and institutions, including hospitals and clinics, in the Minister responsible for public health and no person may open or carry on any establishment or institution for those purposes unless they are in possession of a valid license issued by that Minister.[116] However, the Department for Health Regulation is a Department of Government that is subject to Ministerial control,[117] and the Health Act then formalises the functions of the Department for Health Regulation as a licensing authority within the healthcare system. Thus, subsidiary legislation arising from the Health Act non-exhaustively lists the functions and duties of

112. Interpretation Act, Ch. 249 of the Laws of Malta, Art. 6 (c). Original parentheses, emphasis added.
113. Superintendence of Public Health, *National Standards for Blood Transfusion* 5 (2012; Reviewed 2018).
114. *See* General Introduction §2.II above.
115. Health Act, Ch. 528 of the Laws of Malta, Art. 8 (1).
116. Medical and Kindred Professions Ordinance, Ch. 31 of the Laws of Malta, Art. 98. *See also* S.L. 458.23, Licensing of Private Medical Clinics, r. 4; S.L. 458.25, Licensing of Private Medical Diagnostic Laboratories, r. 4.
117. Public Administration Act, Ch. 595 of the Laws of Malta, Art. 8. *See also* Constitution of Malta, Art. 82; Assignment of Statutory Ministerial Responsibilities Act, Ch. 561 of the Laws of Malta.

that Department, which include:[118] (i) to receive and process applications for the issuing of a licence for any healthcare service, pharmacy and other services falling within public health regulations, provided by healthcare providers; and (ii) to evaluate, accredit, recognise and licence systems, policies, agencies, entities, and private healthcare providers where the safety of the institution and the service delivery are assured. It thus is the Department for Health Regulation that receives and processes applications for the issuing of a licence for several healthcare services delivered by healthcare providers, thereby making it, by way of example, the competent authority to license mental health facilities.[119]

30. Moreover, the Superintendent of Public Health, while the head of the Department for Health Regulation, is *inter alia* the licensing authority for the purpose: of the Medicines Act[120] and subsidiary legislation arising there from including the licensing of pharmacies;[121] of the Human Blood and Transplants Act[122] and subsidiary legislation arising there from; of the Medical and Kindred Professions Ordinance for the purpose of the licensing of laboratories of chemical products used in medicine or galenic preparations;[123] of the Substances used in the Illicit Manufacture of Narcotic Drugs and Psychotropic Substances Rules;[124] and of the European Reference Network Regulations.[125] The Superintendent of Public Health is also vested with authority akin to that of a licensing authority under the Human Organs, Tissues and Cell Donation Act for the purpose of authorising procurement organisations and transplantation centres,[126] while the Superintendence furthermore maintains the Human Organ and Tissue Donation Register.[127] Additionally, a professional association as an organisation consisting wholly of healthcare professionals that intends to be recognised by the Minister responsible for health in order to fulfil the functions of a professional association under the Health Care Professions Act[128] 'shall make an application to this effect, in writing, to the Superintendent of Public Health'.[129] Consequently, the Department for Health Regulation, and the Superintendent of Public Health that heads it, form a central licensing authority within the healthcare system.

---

118. S.L. 528.05, Functions and Responsibilities of the Department of Health Regulation Regulations, r. 3 (2).
119. Mental Health Act, Ch. 525 of the Laws of Malta, Art. 40.
120. Medicines Act, Ch. 458 of the Laws of Malta, Art. 3.
121. *Ibid.*, Art. 66; S.L. 458.16, Pharmacy Licence Regulations, r. 2; S.L. 458.58, Pharmacy Licence (Transfer) Regulations, r. 2. *See also* S.L. 458.55, Provision of Medicinal Products through the GenitoUrinary Clinic within the Government Health Services Rules.
122. Human Blood and Transplants Act, Ch. 483 of the Laws of Malta, Art. 3.
123. Medical and Kindred Professions Ordinance, Ch. 31 of the Laws of Malta, Art. 96.
124. S.L. 101.05, Substances used in the Illicit Manufacture of Narcotic Drugs and Psychotropic Substances Rules, r. 3. *See also* S.L. 101.06, Methadone Rules.
125. S.L. 529.09 European Reference Network Regulations, r. 2.
126. Human Organs, Tissues and Cell Donation Act, Ch. 558 of the Laws of Malta, Art. 2.
127. *Ibid.*, Art. 4.
128. *See* Part III Ch. 1 §1 below.
129. Health Care Professions Act, Ch. 464 of the Laws of Malta, Fourth Schedule, Part I [3].

31. In addition to licensing, the Department of Health Regulation Regulations clarify that it falls within the functions and duties of the Department for Health Regulation 'to monitor and ensure the maintenance of public health standards and regulations in licensed premises and other entities as appropriate'.[130] This function arising from the Health Act and its subsidiary legislation operates in tandem with the broader legal framework underpinning the healthcare system in Malta for the purpose of quality, safety and public health, including the Public Health Act and the Licensing of Private Medical Clinics Regulations.[131] That is not to say that it is a function carried out by the Superintendent of Public Health alone. For example, although the law normally refers to the Superintendent of Public Health when, for instance, indicating the competence to issue standards for public health,[132] a key office within the Department for Health Regulation for the purpose of licensing, inspection, monitoring and setting recommended standards is the Health Care Standards Directorate.[133] It then is, for instance, the latter Directorate that issued the Standards for Dental Clinics that *inter alia* drew on domestic law and EU law to lay out the essential criteria for obtaining a Dental Clinic License as well as the minimum standards for Dental Clinics.[134] Furthermore, despite its mission in the Health Act to licence, monitor and inspect the provision of healthcare services in order to ensure their quality and safety,[135] Maltese law sometimes empowers the Superintendent of Public Health to delegate at least part of its authority.[136] For example, the Medicines Act establishes the Medicines Authority[137] and provides that, in addition to any other functions pertaining to the latter Authority,[138] the Superintendent of Public Health may, by rules, delegate some of its functions as the licensing authority for the purpose of the Medicines Act to the Medicines Authority.[139] This occurs by subsidiary legislation[140] and includes, for instance, the function 'to carry out inspections of any activity, service or procedures in relation to medicinal products and to do all such things as may be necessary for the purpose of ensuring compliance with any provisions of [the Medicines] Act or made there under'[141] and 'to authorise the advertising and promotion of medicinal products'.[142] The Human Blood and Transplants Act also enables the Superintendent of Public Health to 'by

130. S.L. 528.05, Functions and Responsibilities of the Department of Health Regulation Regulations, r. 3 (2)(f).
131. S.L. 458.23, Licensing of Private Medical Clinics Regulations.
132. *See, for instance:* Public Health Act, Ch. 465 of the Laws of Malta, Art. 4 (c); Superintendence of Public Health, *National Standards for Blood Transfusion* (2012; Reviewed 2018).
133. *See, for instance*: Healthcare Standards Directorate, *Manual on How a Person Can Apply for a License to Operate a Dental Clinic: Basic Information* 2 (2019); Healthcare Standards Directorate, *Manual on How a Person Can Apply for a License to Operate a Medical Clinic: Basic Information* 2 (2019).
134. Healthcare Standards Directorate, *Standards for Dental Clinics* (2019).
135. Health Act, Ch. 528 of the Laws of Malta, Art. 8 (1).
136. *See* Public Health Act, Ch. 465 of the Laws of Malta, Art. 5.
137. Medicines Act, Ch. 458 of the Laws of Malta, Art. 4.
138. *Ibid.*, Art. 6. *See also* Art. 111.
139. *Ibid.*, Art. 3 (2)(3).
140. S.L. 458.39, Delegation to Medicines Authority Order.
141. Medicines Act, Ch. 458 of the Laws of Malta, Art. 3 (2)(n). *See, for instance:* S.L. 458.57, Pharmacovigilance Inspections Regulations.
142. *Ibid.*, Art. 3 (2)(o). *See, for instance*: S.L. 458.32, Medicinal Products (Advertising) Regulations.

rules delegate any of the functions referred to in sub-article (2) [which lists the functions of the Superintendent of Public Health as the licensing authority for the purpose of that Act] to the Medicines Authority, or to any other authority or institution it deems competent'.[143] The legislative authorities have furthermore shifted authority away from the Department for Health Regulation and the Superintendent of Public Health in the context of social care standards. Thus, while the Functions and Responsibilities of the Department of Health Regulation Regulations still include, under the functions and duties of that Department, receiving and processing applications for the issuing of a licence, by the Minister responsible for health, for any nursing home or home for the aged under Article 98 of the Medical and Kindred Professions Ordinance,[144] the words 'any nursing home or home for aged' were in fact deleted from the latter Ordinance in 2018.[145] This is because licensing and regulatory authority for social welfare services were transferred to the Social Care Standards Authority.[146]

32. The regulation of the healthcare system is additionally embedded in a wider regulatory framework spread across Maltese law, which includes the regulation of healthcare professions under the Health Care Professions Act. This *inter alia* establishes Councils with functions such as keeping the registers of the pertinent professions in healthcare while also prescribing, maintaining and supervising professional and ethical standards for the respective profession/s that fall within their individual remit, not to mention duly approving conduct as 'good conduct'[147] in terms of that Act. For the purpose of medical law, the Medical Council established by the Health Care Professions Act is particularly significant for its role in underpinning the practise of the profession of medical practitioners and dental surgeons.[148] The Health Care Professions Act also establishes the Council for Nurses and Midwives,[149] as well as the Pharmacy Council,[150] which is the relevant Council in relation to pharmacists and pharmacy technicians. The Health Care Professions Act furthermore establishes the Council for the Professions Complementary to Medicine,[151] which is the relevant Council for twenty healthcare professions listed in its Third Schedule that vary from acupuncture to physiotherapy, from dental hygiene to dental technology, and from medical laboratory science to radiography. The Council for the Professions Complementary to Medicine does not however regulate all the professions that can be or are complementary to the practise of medicine or healthcare inasmuch as other professions involved in healthcare are regulated by way of legislative Acts separate from the Health Care Professions Act. For instance, the profession of

143. Human Blood and Transplants Act, Ch. 483 of the Laws of Malta, Art. 3 (3).
144. S.L. 528.05, Functions and Responsibilities of the Department of Health Regulation Regulations, r. 3 (2)(d).
145. Act XV of 2018 – Social Care Standards Authority Act, 2018 [Government Gazette of Malta No. 19,990 – 11/05/2018], Art. 32.
146. Social Care Standards Authority Act, Ch. 582 of the Laws of Malta, Arts 14–24.
147. Health Care Professions Act, Ch. 464 of the Laws of Malta, Art. 2.
148. *Ibid.*, Art. 9.
149. *Ibid.*, Art. 21.
150. *Ibid.*, Art. 15.
151. *Ibid.*, Art. 26.

social work is regulated under the Social Work Profession Act that establishes the Malta Social Work Profession Board,[152] the profession of psychology is regulated by way of the Psychology Profession Act that establishes the Malta Psychology Profession Board,[153] the profession of counselling is regulated by the Counselling Profession Act that establishes the Council for the Counselling Profession in Malta,[154] and the profession of psychotherapy is regulated under the Psychotherapy Profession Act that establishes the Board for the Psychotherapy Profession in Malta.[155]

33. The regulatory framework of the healthcare system in Malta is, in addition to what has already been noted in this sub-section of the monograph, also stipulated upon different regulatory or quasi-regulatory entities that target specific areas within the healthcare system as indicated by the law that establishes them. While those ad hoc laws and the bodies they establish might not affect the role of the Department for Health Regulation and/or the Superintendent of Public Health as the licensing authority or the regulation of the healthcare professions per se, they can affect which entities are tasked with monitoring and inspecting the licensees and/or healthcare professionals in the performance of obligations arising from given laws. For instance, the Embryo Protection Act *inter alia* engages with medically assisted procreation in Malta, and it stipulates that '[n]o premises may be used for any activity related to medically assisted procreation unless the premises are licensed for the purpose by the Licensing Authority',[156] which is the Superintendent of Public Health according to the Human Blood and Transplants Act and regulations made there under.[157] The Embryo Protection Act also nods towards the role of the Health Care Professions Act in the context of licensing of medical practitioners and it adopts the meaning assigned to 'health care professional' under the latter Act.[158] The Embryo Protection Act, however, then establishes the Embryo Protection Authority.[159] In turn, despite the function of the licensing authority to carry out inspections of establishments, the functions of the Embryo Protection Authority extend to carrying out 'inspections in order to ensure that the standards of best practice are being respected and implemented and that all information and documentation required under [the Embryo Protection] Act are being kept appropriately and for this purpose to access clinics and any other places as necessary'.[160] Similarly, in addition to the function of the professional regulatory Councils embedded in the Health Care Professions Act to prescribe and maintain professional and ethical standards for the professions falling within their individual remit,[161] the functions of the Embryo Protection Authority include ensuring that 'high standards of ethics are maintained by all medical practitioners, paramedics and other personnel involved in procedures

152. Social Work Profession Act, Ch. 468 of the Laws of Malta, Art. 4.
153. Psychology Profession Act, Ch. 471 of the Laws of Malta, Art. 4.
154. Counselling Profession Act, Ch. 538 of the Laws of Malta, Art. 4.
155. Psychotherapy Profession Act, Ch. 587 of the Laws of Malta, Art. 4.
156. Embryo Protection Act, Ch. 524 of the Laws of Malta, Art. 22 (1).
157. Human Blood and Transplants Act, Ch. 483 of the Laws of Malta, Art. 3.
158. Embryo Protection Act, Ch. 524 of the Laws of Malta, Art. 2.
159. *Ibid.*, Art. 3.
160. *Ibid.*, Art. 4 (1)(c).
161. *See* Part I Ch. 4 below.

of medically assisted procreation and gamete donation'.[162] In this respect, in accordance with subsidiary legislation arising from the Embryo Protection Act, any officer or employee of the Embryo Protection Authority who is duly authorised by that Authority can, in a reasonable time, enter any clinic, laboratory or any other property in order to inspect them and ensure that there is no infringement of the provisions of the Embryo Protection Act, Protocols that the Embryo Protection Authority is entitled to enforce, or any decision of that Authority, as well as to access and collect data or information that the Embryo Protection Authority may require.[163] The Embryo Protection Authority Regulations also provide for some of the measures that this Authority may take in respect of any person who infringes those Regulations, any provision of the Embryo Protection Act, any decision given by the Embryo Protection Authority or any authorisation condition, or otherwise infringes any law which that Authority is entitled to enforce.[164] In view of these functions, the Embryo Protection Authority is, in practice, vested with quasi-regulatory authority, albeit not licensing authority, for the purpose of a specific area within the healthcare system, not to mention that it also has the function of ensuring, in relation to activities under the Embryo Protection Act, compliance with the obligations and requirements imposed by or under that Act as well as codes of practice established under it[165] and to maintain a statement of the general principles that it opines should be followed in carrying out its activities and its functions in relation to those activities under the Embryo Protection Act.[166]

34. There are more examples of these regulatory or quasi-regulatory entities spread across the breadth of the legal framework underpinning the healthcare system, including, at least within the context of mental healthcare, the Commissioner for the Promotion of Rights of Persons with Mental Disorders. This office is established under the Mental Health Act,[167] which regulates the provision of mental health services, care and rehabilitation whilst promoting and upholding the rights of people suffering from mental disorders.[168] A third example involves the Occupational Health and Safety Authority established in terms of the Occupational Health and Safety Authority Act inasmuch as it has the duty 'to see that the levels of occupational health and safety protection established by [the Occupational Health and Safety Authority] Act and by regulations made under this Act are maintained'.[169] The point at hand is that the Department for Health Regulation, the Superintendent of Public Health heading that Department, the councils and boards that regulate the professions involved in the healthcare system, and the broader topic-specific regulatory framework across the statute book shape the regulation of the healthcare system in Malta.

---

162. Embryo Protection Act, Ch. 524 of the Laws of Malta, Art. 4 (1)(a).
163. S.L. 524.01, Embryo Protection Authority Regulations, r. 17.
164. *Ibid.*, r. 18.
165. Embryo Protection Act, Ch. 524 of the Laws of Malta, Art. 4 (1)(e).
166. *Ibid.*, Art. 4 (1)(d); *See also* Embryo Protection Authority, *Protocol* 4 (2d ed. 2018); S.L. 524.02, Embryo Protection Authority (Protocol) Regulations (not yet in force).
167. Mental Health Act, Ch. 525 of the Laws of Malta, Art. 5.
168. *Ibid.*, Long title.
169. Occupational Health and Safety Authority Act, Ch. 424 of the Laws of Malta, Art. 5.

III. Financing of the Healthcare System

35. The previous sub-sections of this section in the General Introduction to the monograph furnished an overview of the substantive context of the healthcare system in Malta by engaging with the laws underpinning policymaking, the provision of healthcare services, pertinent advisory bodies and the regulation of the healthcare system. This sub-section instead outlines the financial aspect of the healthcare system in Malta by engaging with, in order, public healthcare, followed by private healthcare and then concluding by briefly touching on non-governmental organisations' involvement in financing healthcare.

36. The healthcare system in Malta includes a national health service, which is largely tax-financed, that 'provides a comprehensive basket of health services to all persons residing in Malta who are covered by the Maltese social security legislation and also provides for all necessary care to special groups such as irregular immigrants or foreign workers who have valid work permits'.[170] This entails that many healthcare services are free at the point of delivery within the public healthcare system, including within the context of public-private partnership/s.[171] What is covered by that basket of health services may not always be (or have been) clear, which can be of juridical significance to the financing of the healthcare system due to, for instance, EU law that requires a Member State to authorise and cover treatment appropriate to an insured person's condition that s/he intends to receive in another Member State if, among other things, 'the treatment in question is among the benefits provided for by the legislation in the Member State where the person concerned resides'.[172] In the context of Malta, the latter EU law would therefore require engagement with treatment covered by the benefits provided by Maltese law. Yet, when the Maltese authorities, soon after Malta's entry into the EU, had refused to authorise, on the basis of that EU law,[173] the treatment in another EU Member State of a patient in Malta, an application was made before the domestic courts where it was noted that there was no ad hoc law in Malta at that time outlining the treatments that were covered by the basket of health services within the public healthcare system. The domestic courts then held that absent a legislative framework stipulating what is covered by the public healthcare system, every possible treatment was ostensibly covered by that system.[174] This would have also meant that, even if treatment was not delivered in Malta, it was in the courts' view included within the healthcare benefits provided for by the Maltese public healthcare system

170. Parliamentary Secretariat for Health, *A National Health Systems Strategy for Malta 2014 – 2020: Securing Our Health Systems for Future Generations* 21 (2014).
171. *See also* Part III Ch. 3 §3.
172. Regulation (EC) No 883/2004 of the European Parliament and of the Council of 29 April 2004 on the coordination of social security systems, OJ L 166, 30.4.2004, Art. 20 (2).
173. The application was stipulated in part upon its predecessor: Regulation (EEC) No 1408/71 of the Council of 14 June 1971 on the application of social security schemes to employed persons and their families moving within the Community, OJ L 149, 5.7.1971, Art. 22.
174. *Cassar Daniel James v. Direttur tas-Sahha Istituzzjonali et.*, Civil Court First Hall – 27/11/2008 [Ref: 863/2004]; Court of Appeal (Civil, Superior) – 24/06/2011 [Ref: 863/2004/1] 31.

and, unless changes were made to the statutory framework underpinning that system, the Maltese authorities would have also had to authorise any treatment in other EU Member States if the patient/s could not receive it in Malta 'within a time limit which is medically justifiable, taking into account his/her current state of health and the probable course of his/her illness'[175] regardless whether that treatment was or *was not* delivered in Malta. This state of affairs risked negatively affecting the way that the financing of the healthcare system was managed, and it is one of the reasons why the Health Act engaged with healthcare benefits and entitlement.

37. The Department for Policy in Health established under the Health Act has the function 'to advise upon health benefits and new services to be offered by the public healthcare system',[176] but it is the Minister responsible for health who 'shall establish the healthcare benefits to be provided directly or indirectly by the public healthcare system, after considering the advice of the Advisory Committee on Healthcare Benefits'.[177] The latter Committee is also established under the Health Act and, given that the financing of those benefits arises from the national budget, it includes among its members a representative of the Minister responsible for finance[178] inasmuch as it is the latter Ministry that makes advances to the healthcare system including entities established therein.[179] It then is the duty of the Advisory Committee on Healthcare Benefits 'to recommend the healthcare benefits to be provided directly or indirectly by the public healthcare system and to maintain a publicly accessible list of such benefits regularly updated'.[180] There, in turn, is a Register 'kept by the Permanent Secretary of the Ministry for Health, which shall include all the benefits, services, interventions and treatments provided by the public healthcare system',[181] and it is also the function of the Department for Policy in Health 'to update the register of health benefits and advise government on the introduction of any new service'.[182] That being said, in the case of urgent, vitally necessary treatment, the Chief Medical Officer, who heads the Department for Policy in Health, 'may authorise the provision of such healthcare benefits and duly report to the Minister [responsible for health] and the Advisory Committee [on Healthcare Benefits] at the first available opportunity'.[183] Indeed, health entitlement policies are also administered by the Department for Policy in Health.[184]

175. Regulation (EC) No 883/2004 of the European Parliament and of the Council of 29 April 2004 on the coordination of social security systems, OJ L 166, 30.4.2004, Art. 20 (2).
176. S.L. 528.01, Functions and Responsibilities of Department for Policy in Health Regulations, r. 3 (2)(g).
177. Health Act, Ch. 528 of the Laws of Malta, Art. 21.
178. *Ibid.*, Sch. C.
179. *See, for instance:* S.L. 524.01, Embryo Protection Authority Regulations, r. 11.
180. Health Act, Ch. 528 of the Laws of Malta, Art. 23 (1).
181. *Ibid.*, Art. 25 (1).
182. S.L. 528.01, Functions and Responsibilities of Department for Policy in Health Regulations, r. 3 (2)(j).
183. Health Act, Ch. 528 of the Laws of Malta, Art. 22 (4).
184. S.L. 528.01, Functions and Responsibilities of Department for Policy in Health Regulations, r. 3 (2)(i).

38. In accordance with the Health Act, the Government Formulary List Advisory Committee is deemed to be a sub-committee of the Advisory Committee on Healthcare Benefits.[185] This is because the Government Formulary List *inter alia* includes 'conditions specific to coverage within the Government Health Services in terms of entitlement to free medicines [and] supply within the Government Health Services',[186] which can also extend to products that are not classified as medicinal products in terms of the Medicines Act.[187] The Health Act then engages with entitlement by stipulating that, without prejudice to any other provision of any other law, 'only an insured person may qualify for free healthcare benefits provided by, or on behalf of, the public healthcare system'[188] and other persons would normally have to pay the established fees unless otherwise covered as occurs,[189] for instance, in the case of applicants for international protection by way of refugee status or subsidiary protection.[190] The Health Act also defines the insured person as 'a person included in the list established by regulations made under [the Health] Act',[191] which is a law that is acknowledged in the Social Security Act[192] where all 'those who are covered by the Social Security Act, either through payment of contributions or through a mechanism of exemption from payment, are covered'.[193] In turn, the Social Security Act regulates benefits and allowances, including the provision of medical assistance,[194] which includes sickness assistance and free medical aid. In addition to clarifying when and how means-testing applies, the Social Security Act lists in its Fifth Schedule the diseases and conditions in respect of which sickness assistance may be payable and medical aid may be accorded. Rules also regulate 'every form to be used by medical practitioners or dental surgeons to issue manual prescriptions, computer generated prescriptions and eprescriptions, for medicinal products or medical aids as provided for under the Social Security Act, as well as medicinal products and medical aids granted to a patient to be discharged from a hospital'.[195] There furthermore is an Exceptional Medical Treatment Committee that deals with applications to receive 'medicinal treatment provided in cases of diseases when the medicinal treatment is not on the Government Formulary List or is not according to the Government Formulary list policies'.[196] Moreover, an established process exists whereby the Government can refer and sponsor patients to receive treatment in another country in combination with, or over and above,

185. Health Act, Ch. 528 of the Laws of Malta, Art. 22 (2).
186. S.L. 458.31, Availability of Medicinal Products within the Government Health Services Regulations, r. 5 (3).
187. *Ibid.*, r. 5 (4). *See also* S.L. 601.03, Public Procurement Regulations.
188. Health Act, Ch. 528 of the Laws of Malta, Art. 24 (1). *See also* S.L. 35.14, Hospital Fees for Foreign Patients Regulations; S.L. 35.28, Healthcare (Fees) Regulations.
189. *Ibid.*, Art. 25 (4)–(5).
190. International Protection Act, Ch. 420 of the Laws of Malta, Art. 13 (2).
191. Health Act, Ch. 528 of the Laws of Malta, Art. 2.
192. Social Security Act, Ch. 318 of the Laws of Malta, Art. 23 (1).
193. Natasha Azzopardi-Muscat, Stefan Buttigieg, Neville Calleja & Sherry Merkur, *Malta – Health system review*, 19 (1) Health Systems in Transition 1, 41 (2017).
194. Social Security Act, Ch. 318 of the Laws of Malta, Art. 19.
195. S.L. 458.24, Prescription Forms for Free Medicinal Rules, r. 1 (2).
196. S.L. 528.08, Exceptional Medicinal Treatment Committee Regulations, r. 2.

bilateral agreements with other nation States[197] or laws regarding reimbursement of cross-border healthcare.[198] It is the Department for Policy in Health that then has the function of organising highly specialised referral schemes and cross-border initiatives.[199]

39. That being said, private health expenditure is also prevalent in Malta, and it is customary to have a family physician in private health care rather than through the public healthcare system. Voluntary health insurance is regulated in Malta and is considered later in this monograph.[200] Private healthcare is paid for by patients out-of-pocket, though this can include insurance coverage, and it has been reported that the 'high private spend distorts the picture for … how much government actually spends on health, where whilst it is at an acceptable level in comparison to total government expenditure, it is considered low when compared to total (public and private) health expenditure'.[201] Private medical clinics are regulated under the Licensing of Private Medical Clinics Regulations, which stipulates that the 'tariff of fees chargeable at the clinic in respect of services, other than professional services provided at the clinic, shall be kept affixed in a conspicuous place in the clinic'[202] and the licensee is to moreover ensure that 'all patients asking for or receiving a service are informed of the fees chargeable at the clinic and can receive a copy of the relative fees charged, which copy shall be given to any person on request'.[203] In terms of professional services rendered, the Medical and Kindred Professions Ordinance stipulates that the licensee of licensed healthcare premises shall not charge, make or allow to be charged or made, any fees or other charges that are 'in excess of the fee or charge payable in respect thereof in accordance with such tariff as the Minister responsible for public health may, after consulting the Medical Council, from time to time establish'.[204] Those tariffs of fees and charges are then to be displayed by the licensee in a prominent place in the licensed premises.[205] The Ethics of the Medical Profession Regulations also stipulate that it 'shall be unlawful for any practitioner to charge a fee less than that established in the official tariff of fees unless he is satisfied that the patient does not have sufficient means to pay such

197. Katherine Footman, Cécile Knai, Rita Baeten, Ketevan Glonti & Martin McKee, *Cross-border health care in Europe* 18–21 (World Health Organization 2014); PQ 12422, *Pazjenti – Interventi barra minn Malta – Ghazla ta' kirurgu u/jew specjalist* (Legislature XII: Sitting 225 – 12/01/2015); PQ 13012, *Sptar Mater Dei – hlas ghal servizzi tas-sahha minn Pazjenti Barranin* (Legislature XII: Sitting 228 – 19/01/2015).

198. *See, for instance*: Regulation (EC) No 883/2004 of the European Parliament and of the Council of 29 April 2004 on the coordination of social security systems, OJ L 166, 30.4.2004; S.L. 528.03, Cross-border Healthcare Regulations.

199. S.L. 528.01, Functions and Responsibilities of Department for Policy in Health, r. 3 (2)(l). *See also*: *Montalto Umberto et. v. Onorevoli Ministru Ghas-Sahha et.*, Civil Court First Hall – 26/05/2022 [Ref: 100/2017].

200. *See* Part III Ch. 3 §3 below.

201. Kenneth Grech, Maya Podesta, Antoinette Calleja & Neville Calleja, *Report on the performance of the Maltese health system, 2015*, 194 (Ministry for Energy and Health Malta 2015). Original parentheses.

202. S.L. 458.23, Licensing of Private Medical Clinics, r. 6 (4).

203. *Ibid.*, r. 6 (5).

204. Medical and Kindred Professions Ordinance, Ch. 31 of the Laws of Malta, Art. 100 (1).

205. *Ibid.*, Art. 100 (2).

fee'.[206] These tariffs of fees are however not necessarily the same as the cost or fees corresponding to healthcare benefits, services, interventions and treatments that are listed in the pertinent register kept by the Permanent Secretary of the Ministry for Health[207] or in the Healthcare (Fees) Regulations,[208] which relate to the public health service. Indeed, the Tariff of Fees Payable to Medical Practitioners Order is outdated with low fees that then entail a clause within the Order itself is ostensibly applied inasmuch as the 'rates as established by this tariff are binding only whenever there has been no previous agreement between practitioner and patient'.[209] This private agreement is nevertheless under the purview of other domestic laws, as well as the Medical Council and the Medical Association of Malta. The Medical Council then directs that patients 'must be informed about fees and charges, wherever possible before asking for their consent to treatment'[210] and, if fees are charged, 'the patient must be informed if any part of the fee goes to another health care professional'[211] while failure 'of information on price variables due to existing conditions or complications is unethical'.[212]

40. In addition to the public healthcare system and private healthcare, there are also in Malta a number of non-governmental organisations (NGOs) involved in or whose activities relate to health care. These organisations rely in large part on voluntary or charitable contributions, which can then, in turn, feed into the healthcare system as a whole. For instance, certain foundations assist patients either in kind or financially when they require treatment in another country in the context of the Government's Treatment Abroad Committee and the National Highly Specialized Overseas Referrals Programme. Those foundations are regulated under the Civil Code[213] and the Voluntary Organisations Act.[214] Financing of these NGOs is becoming increasingly controlled, and, for instance, a non-enrolled voluntary organisation may not carry out a public collection,[215] which is to have a legal cause.[216] That being said, the combination of financing within the public healthcare system, the private sector, and the role of NGOs shapes the financing of the healthcare system in Malta.

206. S.L. 464.17, Ethics of the Medical Profession Regulations, r. 23 (1).
207. Health Act, Ch. 528 of the Laws of Malta, Art. 25 (1).
208. S.L. 35.28, Healthcare (Fees) Regulations.
209. S.L. 458.02, Tariff of Fees Payable to Medical Practitioners [42].
210. Medical Council of Malta, *Code of Ethics on Advertising and Financial Conduct by Medical/Dental Practitioners* 2 (2010).
211. *Ibid.*, 3.
212. Medical Council Malta, *Regulations on advertising and the provision of information to the public* 3 (2017).
213. Civil Code, Ch. 16 of the Laws of Malta, Second Schedule.
214. Voluntary Organisations Act, Ch. 492 of the Laws of Malta.
215. S.L. 492.03, Voluntary Organisation (Public Collections), r. 3 (2).
216. *Ibid.*, r. 4 (1).

§3. SOURCES OF MEDICAL LAW

41. The legal framework underpinning medical law can be more easily understood with some awareness of the sources of medical law. Yet, there is no statutory definition of medical law in Malta. The term 'medico-legal' is occasionally used in Maltese law[217] and in some academic literature[218] in Malta in the context of cases relating to medical practice, particularly when evidence is furnished before the domestic courts by a medical practitioner, but this term is different from the medical law that is instead grounded in the statute book. Indeed, as will be illustrated in this monograph, medical practice by medical practitioners is extensively covered in Maltese law beyond the scope of the term 'medico-legal' that is occasionally referred to in law. Yet, given that medical law is not codified in Malta, it traverses several fields, such as healthcare law, civil law, criminal law, public law, EU law and human rights law. It consequently means that there are a number of sources of medical law in Malta because the source of any given medical law will depend on the source of the field from which that particular medical law arises. In light of this wide breadth of sources, this section of the monograph is restricted to indicating some of the sources or features that typically underpin a substantial portion of the medical law in Malta.

42. First, medical law can be made by way of bills passed by the House of Representatives and assented to by the President of Malta. There thus are Acts of Parliament that create, add to, amend or repeal medical law. It is however also tenable that an Act of Parliament enables a person, such as a Minister, to make subsidiary legislation under the authority of the parent Act.[219] This delegated authority is frequently used to shape the finites of medical law and to regulate activities that affect medical practice. That being said, there have been instances when a particular issue of juridical and ethical import was not or could not be introduced by way of subsidiary legislation. This occurred, for instance, in the context of surrogacy, which is an offence in terms of the Embryo Protection Act inasmuch as it stipulates that whosoever 'carries out an artificial fertilization of, or transfers a human embryo into, a woman who is prepared to give up her child permanently after birth (surrogate mother)'[220] shall be guilty of an offence. A bill tabled in 2018 to amend the latter Act included a clause by which the Minister responsible for health 'shall by regulations [which is a type of subsidiary legislation] prescribe the manner in which altruistic surrogacy shall be effected and for any matter incidental and ancillary thereto'.[221] Following some debate on the matter, the latter clause was dropped from the version of the bill passed by the House of Representatives and assented to by

217. *See, for instance*: S.L. 458.02, Tariff of Fees Payable to Medical Practitioners Order [42]; S.L. 458.03, Tariff of Fees Payable to Dental Surgeons/Dentists Order [26]; S.L. 528.10, Processing of Personal Data (Secondary Processing) (Health Sector) Regulations, r. 3 (e).

218. *See, for instance*: George Gregory Buttigieg, *Optimising Maltese obstetric medico-legal dynamics: Volume I* (Lambert Academic Publishing 2020).

219. *See* General Introduction §1.III above.

220. Embryo Protection Act, Ch. 524 of the Laws of Malta, Art. 6 (f). Original parentheses.

221. Bill No 37 entitled the Embryo Protection (Amendment) Act, 2018 [Government Gazette of Malta No. 19,977 – 13 April 2018], cl. 4.

the President. It is also worthwhile noting at this stage that the House of Representatives has a Standing Committee on Health, which has the power to, 'on its own initiative, discuss policies and matters in the health sphere which have a strategic importance and are of material interest to patients, and report thereon to the House'[222] of Representatives.

43. Second, EU law is a source of medical law in Malta as a consequence of the 2003 Treaty of Accession to the EU and the European Union Act.[223] Indeed, in addition to the EU's primary law prevailing over Maltese law that would then be to the extent of its derogation 'without effect and unenforceable',[224] there are different ways that EU law can be a source of medical law depending on the EU's competence on a particular area pertinent to medical law. For instance, in the context of areas where the EU has shared competence,[225] subject to the principles of subsidiarity and proportionality,[226] the EU institutions can *inter alia* adopt directives, which then have to be transposed into domestic law, and regulations that are directly applicable in the EU's Member States.[227] These legal acts of the EU led to substantial changes to medical law in Malta shortly before and since Malta's accession to the EU either by way of legislative action in Malta as a consequence of a legal act arising from the EU or, if EU law does not *per se* require a particular domestic act, it may have a knock-on effect that leads the domestic authorities to make or change medical law because it better suits the domestic scenario in view of the wider EU law.[228] Furthermore, the EU has competence to carry out actions to support, coordinate or supplement the actions of the Member States in regard to the protection and improvement of human health.[229] While this competence does not mean that the EU can mandate new medical law at domestic level, it can be a source for Maltese legislative authorities to address medical law in Malta in order to engage with that particular competence of the EU.

44. Third, Malta is a member of the Council of Europe, the United Nations, the World Health Organization, and other international bodies as an actor in public international law. There are at least three ways that public international law is a source of Maltese medical law, mainly by way of treaties to which Malta is a party. In the first instance, given that Malta is primarily a dualist State, treaties have to normally be incorporated into national law so as to become and be enforceable as part of the laws of Malta.[230] A treaty's incorporation into Maltese law by an Act of Parliament could then *ipso jure* result in new medical law. An example of this type

222. S.L. Const. 02, Standing Orders of the House of Representatives Order, Ord. 120J (1)(a).
223. Chapter 460 of the Laws of Malta.
224. *Ibid.*, Art. 3.
225. Treaty on the Functioning of the European Union, OJ C 326, 26.10.2012, Art. 4.
226. Treaty on European Union, OJ C 326, 26.10.2012, Art. 5.
227. Treaty on the Functioning of the European Union, OJ C 326, 26.10.2012, Art. 288.
228. *See* General Introduction §2.III above.
229. Treaty on the Functioning of the European Union, OJ C 326, 26.10.2012, Art 6.
230. *See, for instance*: Ratification of Treaties Act, Ch. 304 of the Laws of Malta.

of source is the Council of Europe's Convention on preventing and combating violence against women and domestic violence.[231] In the second instance, even before the formal incorporation of a treaty into national law, it is tenable that the provisions of a treaty that has been ratified by Malta lead to changes in the medical law if only to fulfil Malta's international obligations arising from that Convention. An example of this type of source that will be addressed later in the monograph includes the United Nations' Convention on the Rights of Persons with Disabilities (UNCRPD)[232] inasmuch as, before the incorporation of some of its substantive provisions into Maltese national law,[233] it had already affected changes in the domestic law touching on medical law. A third instance involving treaties as a source of medical law occurs when the jurisprudence arising from a treaty affects the development of medical law, even if that jurisprudence is not directly binding on Malta. An example would include the Council of Europe's Convention for the Protection of Human Rights and Fundamental Freedoms,[234] which was partly incorporated into Maltese law by way of the European Convention Act.[235] While the latter Act makes provision for the enforcement of judgments delivered by the European Court of Human Rights to which Malta is a party,[236] even judgments to which Malta is not a party can and have been considered when making or changing law in Malta.

45. Fourth, professional and ethical standards underpin medical law in Malta. Suffice it to say for now that the Medical Council has the function 'to prescribe and maintain professional and ethical standards for the medical and dental professions'[237] and that the Ethics of the Medical Profession Regulations form part of the subsidiary law arising from the Health Care Professions Act.[238] While the Medical Council can take disciplinary measures when it finds a medical practitioner guilty of professional or ethical misconduct or if the medical practitioner in any other manner failed to abide by the professional and ethical standards applicable to him/her,[239] it is at this stage of the monograph significant to note that those professional and ethical standards can then be a source of medical law. Indeed, the domestic courts also engage with the professional and ethical standards of the medical profession when, for instance, establishing whether medical practitioners are liable for damages that occurred during the practice of their profession.[240] There, moreover, exists a Bioethics Consultative Committee, which is an officially appointed body under the remit of the Ministry for Health that can be and is consulted when making or changing medical law. It is furthermore noteworthy that professional and ethical standards do not operate in a vacuum, and they are not based uniquely on clinical

---

231. (2011) CETS 210.
232. (Adopted 13 December 2006, entered into force 3 May 2008) 2515 UNTS 3.
233. *See, for instance*: United Nations Convention on the Rights of Persons with Disabilities Act, Ch. 627 of the Laws of Malta.
234. (1950) ETS 5.
235. European Convention Act, Ch. 319 of the Laws of Malta, Arts 2 and 3.
236. *Ibid.*, Arts 6 and 6A.
237. Health Care Professions Act, Ch. 464 of the Laws of Malta, Art. 10 (1)(d).
238. S.L.464.17, Ethics of the Medical Profession Regulations.
239. Health Care Professions Act, Ch. 464 of the Laws of Malta, Arts 31 and 32.
240. *See* Part I Ch. 4 §1.

developments. For instance, the National Disability Strategy foresees revising codes of ethics for the medical profession 'to ensure an appropriate disability perspective, and appropriate monitoring and feedback mechanisms'[241] are put in place. This therefore ostensibly seeks to align the ethics of the medical profession with the ethos of the changes to Maltese domestic law in view of the UNCRPD.[242]

---

241. Government of Malta – Ministry for Inclusion and Social Wellbeing, *Freedom to live: Malta's 2021 – 2030 National Strategy on the Rights of Disabled Persons* 105 (2021).
242. *See, for instance*: United Nations Convention on the Rights of Persons with Disabilities Act, Ch. 627 of the Laws of Malta, Art. 5.

Part I. The Medical Profession

Chapter 1. Access to the Medical Profession

46. Access to the medical profession in this chapter is considered in three stages. Training underpinning the medical profession is considered first. This then leads to manpower planning, which engages with the coordination of training and with EU law transposed into Maltese law regarding freedom of movement and freedom of establishment. The chapter then concludes with an overview of licensing in the context of the medical profession in Malta by considering the licensing of medical practitioners and medical specialists, including general practitioners.

47. There are two points of interpretation that should be clarified at the outset: (a) The standard outline of the International Encyclopaedia for Medical Law uses the term 'physician' for the purpose of this chapter, and this term has not been changed in the outline of the monograph at hand. However, even though the term 'physician' is used in Maltese law, medicine in Malta is practised by registered and licensed medical practitioners. The Medical Council has in fact directed that its members 'refrain from using nomenclature other than that listed at law (Fifth Schedule of the HCPA), such as "Physician"'.[243] It should thus be noted that despite the titles of the sections in this monograph that reflect the IEL outline, use of the term 'physician' in this chapter of the monograph is restricted to its use in the pertinent laws of Malta to indicate those people who completed basic medical training but are not yet eligible for entry into the medical register;[244] (b) It should furthermore be noted that, unless otherwise indicated, the term 'Member State' in this chapter refers to its definition in the Health Care Professions Act meaning 'a state member of the European Union, a state within the European Economic Area, Switzerland or any other state as the Minister [responsible for health] may prescribe'.[245]

§1. Training of Physicians

48. The medical profession involves different levels of training in Malta. Training criteria draw on, in addition to autochthonous law, requirements arising in other

243. Medical Council of Malta, *Circular 01/2021: Use of 'Specialist' Nomenclature* (2021). Original ellipses, parentheses and acronyms.
244. *See* Part I Ch. 1 §1 below.
245. Health Care Professions Act, Ch. 464 of the Laws of Malta, Art. 2.

jurisdictions, especially the United Kingdom, and EU law, particularly the EU's Professionals Qualifications Directive as amended.[246] This section of the monograph illustrates the training requirements so as to gain admission to basic medical training, in order to then outline the requirements of basic medical training, the training that has to be undertaken after completion of basic medical training so as to be eligible for entry into the medical register kept by the Medical Council, and the training required to be eligible for entry into the Specialist Register kept by the Medical Council.

49. Admission into basic medical training has typically been subject to stringent requirements in Malta. The Minimum Training Conditions (Health Care Professions) Regulations, which transpose part of the EU's Professional Qualifications Directive as amended[247] into Maltese law, furthermore explicitly require admission to basic medical training to 'be contingent upon possession of a diploma or certificate providing access, for the studies in question, to universities'.[248] By way of example, training of physicians and medical practitioners in Malta is traditionally embedded, in the first instance, in the undergraduate degree of Doctor of Medicine and Surgery (MD) awarded by the University of Malta and, in order to be admitted onto that course, applicants must be in possession of academic grades as outlined in subsidiary legislation based on exams taken together in one session, which includes biology and chemistry,[249] or to otherwise be in possession of an academic degree listed in that subsidiary legislation,[250] such as in mental health nursing or in podiatry. Applicants to the MD course are also required to have a pertinent certificate in Maltese or medical Maltese. Applicants are moreover required to undergo an occupation health assessment in the first year of the MD course 'so as to ascertain that they are fit for the duties related to their proposed studies'.[251] Fitness to practice is thus an important precursor to and part of the training of a medical practitioner and, in that respect, the Medical Council, which is the regulatory authority of the medical profession, prepares guidelines with the aim of guiding medical students 'on the kinds of professional behaviour expected of them in order to be fit to practice'.[252] This includes significant aspects of the medical profession, such as relationships with patients, working with colleagues, and probity. These guidelines by the Medical Council also note that basic medical training provides an opportunity for a medical school to identify types of behaviour that are not safe and to then take action 'to help students improve their behaviour, or if this is not possible or is unsuccessful, to ensure they do not graduate as doctors or dentists'.[253] That being said, entities

246. Directive 2005/36/EC of the European Parliament and of the Council of 7 September 2005 on the recognition of professional qualifications, OJ L 255, 30.9.2005.
247. *Ibid.*, Art. 24 (1).
248. S.L. 451.04, Minimum Training Conditions (Health Care Professions) Regulations, r. 8 (1).
249. S.L. 327.135, Doctor of Medicine and Surgery – M.D. – Degree Course Regulations, r. 4 (2).
250. *Ibid.*, r. 4 (4).
251. *Ibid.*, r. 4 (7).
252. Medical Council of Malta, *Medical and dental students: Professional values and fitness to practice* 2 (2010).
253. *Ibid.*, 3.

like the Medical Council do not possess direct authority to deal with cases regarding undergraduate students' training and undergraduate students' fitness to practice. That competence instead falls on the pertinent educational institution. Consequently, the University Suitability to Practice Regulations, for instance, establish the responsibilities of students following a course at the University of Malta 'that leads to a qualification required at law for the purpose of obtaining a warrant, licence or registration to practise a regulated profession, in terms of such students' professional suitability to practise and their commitment to their chosen profession throughout their participation in the course'.[254] This applies to medical students as prospective medical practitioners, and those regulations then stipulate that even at the risk of terminating the students' participation in a course like the MD course,[255] the University of Malta shall:

> [S]trive to ensure that only such persons who demonstrate that they are likely to be suitable to practice are permitted to undertake a given course and to graduate therefrom, keeping in mind the welfare of the potential clients of such persons during their coursework and once they become warranted, licensed or registered professionals, the reputation of the University and the reputation of the respective profession.[256]

50. The requirements regarding the substantive content of basic medical training are also embedded in law. In this respect, the 'syllabi and/or programmes of study related to courses leading to an award that gives access to the professions of: (a) Medical Doctor … shall conform with the minimum training requirements established by the relative European Union Directive 2005/36/EC and with any other Maltese legislation governing the granting of permission to practise the relevant profession in Malta'.[257] In turn, the Minimum Training Conditions (Health Care Professions) Regulations demand, duly transposing EU law,[258] that basic medical training shall 'comprise a total of at least five years of study … and shall consist of at least 5 500 hours of theoretical and practical training provided by, or under the supervision of, a university'.[259] The MD course at the University of Malta is indeed, and was even before that EU law, normally five years in duration.[260] It is also possible that a student may interrupt his/her studies on that course, for instance, to undertake an intercalated year that focuses on laboratory-based research skills leading to the award of a related but separate degree.[261] In case of an intercalated

254. S.L. 327.557, University Suitability to Practice Regulations, r. 3.
255. *Ibid.*, r. 5 (1).
256. *Ibid.*, r. 4 (4)(b).
257. S.L. 327.237, Health Professions Course Syllabi and/or Programme of Study Regulations, r. 3.
258. Directive 2005/36/EC of the European Parliament and of the Council of 7 September 2005 on the recognition of professional qualifications, OJ L 255, 30.9.2005, Art. 24 (2).
259. S.L. 451.04, Minimum Training Conditions (Health Care Professions) Regulations, r. 8 (2).
260. S.L. 327.135, Doctor of Medicine and Surgery – M.D. – Degree Course Regulations, r. 5.
261. *Ibid.*, r. 5 (2).

year, the MD course shall extend over six years.[262] The Minimum Training Conditions (Health Care Professions) Regulations furthermore stipulate that basic medical training should provide knowledge and skills as listed therein, which includes 'suitable clinical experience in hospitals under appropriate supervision'.[263] Thus, continuing with the example of the MD course, this normally involves a pre-clinical phase in the first two years, when students engage with subjects that include the cardiovascular system, the musculoskeletal system, pharmacology, anatomy and microbiology. This is followed by a clinical phase in the subsequent three years when students engage with areas such as surgery, clinical skills, psychiatry, neurology and ophthalmology. Prior to sitting for any examination in the final year of the course, students must also present to the Dean of the University of Malta's Faculty of Medicine and Surgery a certificate that is signed by the concerned heads of department in that Faculty 'showing that students have completed the schedule of clinical placements prescribed for the Course satisfactorily'.[264] Furthermore, in order to be eligible to sit for the examination of the Essential Core Competences in the final year of the course, students must provide a certificate that shows they attended a minimum of 80% of a shadowing programme when students are assigned to a foundation year doctor to practice clinical and administrative skills under his/her supervision.[265]

51. In addition to the Faculty of Medicine and Surgery at the University of Malta, there is also a campus on Gozo of Queen Mary University of London's Barts and the London School of Medicine and Dentistry. This offers a Bachelor of Medicine, Bachelor of Surgery (MBBS) programme that is similar to the programme offered in the United Kingdom, albeit with clinical placements on the Maltese islands during undergraduate studies.[266] This MBBS programme is separate from the MD course offered by the University of Malta, with distinct entry requirements that, for instance, require applicants, in accordance with the practice in the United Kingdom, to undertake a University Clinical Aptitude Test (UCAT) rather than the occupation health assessment undertaken by students reading for the MD degree at the University of Malta.[267] There are of course similarities between these programmes of study, including their duration as a five-year course and that the final year involves some experience shadowing the working life of a foundation year doctor. It should furthermore be noted that the Malta Further and Higher Education Authority also licensed the EDU as a higher education institution,[268] which offers a three-year Bachelor's degree course in medicine followed by a two-year Master's

262. *Ibid.*, r. 5 (3).
263. S.L. 451.04, Minimum Training Conditions (Health Care Professions) Regulations, r. 8 (3).
264. S.L. 327.135, Doctor of Medicine and Surgery – M.D. – Degree Course Regulations, r. 11 (2).
265. *Ibid.*
266. Malta Further and Higher Education Authority, *Barts and The London School of Medicine and Dentistry*, Victoria, Gozo – Licence 2015-006.
267. Sam Coker, Queen Mary University of London, *Admissions Policy: Policy for Admissions to Undergraduate Programmes in Medicine MBBS Malta (MBBS Malta A110) and Certificate in Clinical Foundation Studies (CFFS A120) for 2022/23 entry* (2021).
268. Malta Further and Higher Education Authority, *EDU operated by Digital Education Holdings Ltd*, Kalkara, Malta – Licence 2018-010. *See also* S.L.607.03, Further and Higher Education (Licensing, Accreditation and Quality Assurance) Regulations, r. 31.

degree course in Medicine featuring theoretical teaching conducted online with practical rotations in teaching hospitals, albeit not in Malta, while ostensibly supervised by Maastricht University.[269] Be that as it may, students and graduates of a medical degree programme who are based on the Maltese islands are of course subject to Maltese law, which also means that their entry onto the medical register in Malta would be a matter for the Maltese Medical Council.

52. Graduates in Malta of basic medical training aiming to practice as a medical practitioner and to use that professional title have to then continue their training as house physicians and/or surgeons. This is because, all else being equal, medical graduates cannot lawfully take up and pursue the profession of medical practitioner *inter alia* until their name is entered into the medical register[270] and, using the example of graduates from the MD course at the University of Malta, the Health Care Professions Act stipulates that 'the Medical Council shall not enter such name unless the applicant, upon qualifying for such degree, has served as a house physician and, or surgeon in a government hospital or other hospital recognized for that purpose by the Medical Council for a period of one or two years as the Minister [responsible for health] may prescribe'.[271] Acknowledging that the Health Care Professions Act allows service as a house physician and/or surgeon to take place, in addition to a government hospital, in another hospital recognised for that purpose by the Medical Council, subsidiary legislation clarifies that 'in recognising another hospital the [Medical] Council shall take into consideration the country in which the hospital is situated and the level of supervision and structure of training offered by such hospital'.[272]

53. The Medical Council 'shall only consider the successful completion of the Foundation Programme Malta for junior doctors'[273] when determining the fulfilment of the requirement arising from the Health Care Professions Act for an applicant seeking to have his/her name entered into the medical register to have served as a house physician. The first steps in Malta within the confines of postgraduate training after basic medical training thus typically involve the Foundation Programme, which is a two-year programme that is affiliated with the United Kingdom Foundation Programme, thereby reflecting the curriculum of the latter programme. It involves a salaried position that is completed by way of rotations in different placements, including one compulsory rotation in accident and emergency, as well as supervised learning events, while under the supervision of a senior medical practitioner. Furthermore, the Medical Council keeps a list of provisional registration in order to enter, upon receipt of the pertinent application, the name of every person who holds an MD from the University of Malta or a qualification recognised by the Medical Council obtained from any other university, college or medical council 'and who is serving as a house physician and, or surgeon at a hospital recognized

---

269. Maastricht University Faculty of Health, Medicine and Life Sciences, *Review Report: EDU Medical Programme* (2021).
270. Health Care Professions Act, Ch. 464 of the Laws of Malta, Art. 7 (2)(c).
271. *Ibid.*, Art. 11 (1)(a).
272. S.L. 464.19, Medical Council (Standing Orders) Regulations, r. 36 (1). *See also* r. 36 (2)(b)
273. *Ibid.*, r. 36 (2)(a).

by the Medical Council in terms of [the Health Care Professions] Act'[274] within the confines of the Foundation Programme. As such, when the Foundation School Malta issues a call for applications, anyone intending to apply must also obtain a letter of intent from the Medical Council indicating that s/he is eligible for provisional registration. Upon completion of the Foundation programme, the Foundation School Malta awards the Foundation Programme Completion Certificate, which is required in order to proceed to specialist training leading towards entry onto the specialist register kept by the Medical Council.[275]

54. Transposing the EU's Professional Qualifications Directive,[276] the minimum duration of some categories of specialist training is embedded in law in the Health Care Professions Act[277] and, in accordance with the Minimum Training Conditions (Health Care Professions) Regulations, specialist medical training 'shall be given under the supervision of the competent authorities or bodies'.[278] It is the Specialist Accreditation Committee for medical practitioners (SAC) that then acts 'as the advisory body for training in any of the special areas of practice'[279] and 'accredit[s] post-graduate training programmes'.[280] It is furthermore the SAC that has the function of issuing certificates of completion of specialist training in the specialities listed in the Fifth Schedule of the Health Care Professions Act,[281] which largely reflects the specialities contained in the Specialist Register held by the Medical Council. Specialist medical training is to be given on a full-time basis at specific recognised establishments, and that training 'shall entail participation in the full range of medical activities of the department where the training is given, including duty on call, in such a way that the trainee specialist devotes all his professional activity to his practical and theoretical training throughout the entire working week and throughout the year, in accordance with procedures laid down by the competent authorities'.[282] The SAC then issues certificates of completion of specialist training 'upon fulfilment of criteria recommended by the relevant professional association listed in the Fourth Schedule of the Health Care Professions Act'.[283] These professional associations are organisations that *inter alia* represent 'any one or more of the specialities listed in the Fifth Schedule [of the Health Care Professions Act] or as may be prescribed'[284] and that, with regard to specialities in medicine, follow 'the guidelines issued from time to time by the European Union of Medical Specialists or the Union of European General Practitioners, as applicable'.[285] It is the professional associations, which actively participate in postgraduate education and

274. Health Care Professions Act, Ch. 464 of the Laws of Malta, Art. 11 (3).
275. *See* Part I Ch. 1 §3 below.
276. Directive 2005/36/EC of the European Parliament and of the Council of 7 September 2005 on the recognition of professional qualifications, OJ L 255, 30.9.2005, Annex V.
277. Health Care Professions Act, Ch. 464 of the Laws of Malta, Second Schedule.
278. S.L. 451.04, Minimum Training Conditions (Health Care Professions) Regulations, r. 9 (2).
279. Health Care Professions Act, Ch. 464 of the Laws of Malta, Art. 30 (6)(a)(iii).
280. *Ibid.*, Art. 30 (6)(a)(iv).
281. *Ibid.*, Art. 30 (6)(a)(i).
282. S.L. 451.04, Minimum Training Conditions (Health Care Professions) Regulations, r. 9 (3).
283. Health Care Professions Act, Ch. 464 of the Laws of Malta, Art. 30
284. *Ibid.*, Fourth Schedule, Part I [1 (e)].
285. *Ibid.*, Fourth Schedule, Part I [1 (f)].

continuing professional development,[286] that are then normally responsible for the training programmes accredited by the SAC. Thus, using the speciality of paediatrics as an example, it is the Maltese Paediatric Association that 'shall be the competent body to determine and monitor, from time to time, the curriculum for Specialist Training in Paediatrics and to recommend to the Specialist Accreditation Committee (SAC) to issue a certificate of completion of specialist training (CCST) for each paediatric trainee'.[287] While it is in the context of the training programmes leading towards entry into the specialist registers that postgraduate training takes place, the Malta Postgraduate Medical Training Centre (MPMTC) was also launched in 2008 with a view to providing training and support both to postgraduate trainers and to trainees.

55. The four tranches of training covered in this section shape the basis of training leading towards access to the medical profession by medical practitioners. These include training of students aiming to undertake medical studies, undergraduate medical studies, the training undertaken by postgraduate physicians, and training by medical practitioners on the medical register with a view towards specialisation. The Medical Council is furthermore to ensure, by encouraging continuous professional development, that medical professionals 'are able to update their knowledge, skills and competences in order to maintain a safe and effective practice and keep abreast of professional developments'.[288] There additionally exists the option to undertake postgraduate studies leading to the award of an academic postgraduate degree. The University of Malta, for instance, sometimes in conjunction with partner institutions, offers a number of academic postgraduate degree courses in different fields and/or specialities of medicine, such as family medicine,[289] clinical radiology,[290] and surgical skills.[291] Yet, aside from these academic studies leading to the award of a postgraduate academic degree that can complement one's career in the medical profession, access to the medical profession is, to an extent, related to manpower planning, which is considered in the next section.

§2. Manpower Planning

I. Coordination of Training and Employment

56. Coordination of postgraduate professional training falls within the remit of the Ministry for Health, especially given that training programmes will be subject to remuneration that commonly entails employment at a hospital within the public

286. *Ibid.*, Fourth Schedule, Part I [1 (c)].
287. Maltese Paediatric Association, *Specialist Training Programme in Paediatrics* 1 (2022).
288. S.L. 451.03, Recognition of Professional Qualifications Regulations, r. 22 (2)(b).
289. S.L. 327.368, Bye-laws for the degree of Master of Science in Family Medicine under the auspices of the Faculty of Medicine and Surgery.
290. S.L. 327.653, Bye-laws for the degree of Master of Science in Clinical Radiology – M.Sc. – Under the auspices of the Faculty of Medicine and Surgery.
291. S.L. 327.612, Master of Science in Surgical Skills – M.Sc. – Degree Course Regulations under the auspices of the Faculty of Medicine and Surgery.

health sector.[292] This signifies a tangible role for the Ministry for Health in the context of access to the medical profession inasmuch as recruitment into a training programme may operate hand in hand with employment under the auspices of that Ministry in the public service.[293] It then is the Department for Health Care Services within the Ministry for Health that has the function 'to coordinate the professional aspects of health care service provision including postgraduate training and development.[294] That Department also has the function to anticipate the needs of professional staff, including medical practitioners, and in that respect, to collaborate with third parties, including the University of Malta, the Malta College of Arts, Science and Technology, as well as other institutions 'in order to ensure the training and development of healthcare professionals and non-healthcare personnel according to their needs'.[295] Furthermore, while acknowledging the role of the Permanent Secretariat at the Ministry for Health, including its People Management Division with regard to recruitment and planning,[296] the Department for Health Care Services also has the function 'to advise upon the allocation of human, financial and other resources between public health service providers'[297] as well as 'to monitor the performance and outcomes of public health service providers to ensure that resources are being used in an effective and efficient manner'.[298] These functions entail that the Ministry for Health, including its Department for Health Care Services, is a pivotal cog in the coordination of training of medical practitioners and consequent manpower planning. It has thus also resulted in cases before the domestic courts involving the Public Service Commission and/or the Ministry for Health as respondents where applicants questioned the process of selecting and then appointing trainees that would render, after successful completion of the training programme, the successful candidate eligible for entry into the specialist register.[299]

57. While manpower planning in state-funded healthcare services can also include outsourcing or inclusion of private healthcare providers, and it is within the

---

292. S.L. 451.04, Minimum Training Conditions (Health Care Professions) Regulations, r. 9 (3).
293. *See* Constitution of Malta, Art. 110; S.L. Const. 05, Public Service Commission Appointments Regulations; Public Administration Act, Ch. 595 of the Laws of Malta.
294. S.L. 528.04, Functions and Responsibilities of Department of Health Services Regulations, r. 3 (2)(i).
295. *Ibid.*, r. 3 (2)(j).
296. *See, for instance*: S.L. Const. 05, Public Service Commission Appointments Regulations; Office of the Principal Permanent Secretary – Office of the Prime Minister, *Directive No. 9: Delegation of authority to conduct selection processes and make appointments in the Malta Public Service* (18 Sept. 2015; Version 3.3 – 25 Jan. 2018; Directive 9-2, 2 September 2022); Office of the Principal Permanent Secretary – Office of the Prime Minister, *Manual on industrial relations and the selection and appointment process under delegated authority in the Malta Public Service* (Version 5 – 2 Sept. 2022).
297. S.L. 528.04, Functions and Responsibilities of Department of Health Services Regulations, r. 3 (2)(h).
298. *Ibid.*, r. 3 (2)(n).
299. *See, for instance*: *Grixti Soler Tabib Dott Daniel et. v. Kummissjoni Dwar is-Servizz Pubbliku et.*, Civil Court First Hall – 10/04/2015 [Ref: 736/2014]; *Grixti Soler Tabib Dott Daniel et. v. Kummissjoni dwar is-Servizz Pubbliku et.*, Court of Appeal (Civil, Superior) – 12/02/2016 [Ref: 736/2014/1]; *Dalli Tabib Dottor Jeffrey v. Kummissjoni dwar is-Servizz Pubbliku et.*, Civil Court First Hall – 13/05/2021 [Ref: 880/2014].

functions of the Department of Policy in Health 'to develop partnerships with non-governmental organisations and private healthcare providers',[300] manpower planning in the private sector of healthcare is typically market-oriented albeit subject to requirements arising from domestic law. For instance, no medical practitioner 'who is also in the employment of Government, may, during those hours in which he is contracted to provide his services to Government, work in any medical clinic unless he is on approved leave of absence'.[301] This therefore touches on manpower planning in the context of medical practitioners employed by the Ministry for Health by binding them to time frames when they can and cannot work in private practice. Furthermore, while some surgical operations listed in the Licensing of Private Medical Clinics Regulations may require the presence of a registered nurse alone,[302] the licensee of a private clinic is to otherwise 'ensure that at all times in-patients are receiving treatment at the clinic, there is available resident medical coverage for such patients to the satisfaction of the Superintendent'[303] of Public Health. This requirement mandates employment of a medical practitioner in certain circumstances. That also includes instances when antenatal, intranatal or postnatal care is given at a private clinic inasmuch as the person in charge of that clinic is to ensure that 'adequate general and specialist medical cover is provided as needed',[304] that adequate arrangements 'shall exist for obtaining obstetric, paediatric, anesthetic and any other necessary help in an emergency situation',[305] and that when 'epidural anesthesia is to be offered to women in labour, this should be carried out by an anesthetist trained in this procedure'.[306]

58. Manpower planning is thus embedded in domestic law both in the public sector of healthcare and in the private sector. That being said, access to the medical profession and manpower planning in Malta can also be affected by and draw on EU laws regarding the free movement of persons and the free movement of services, especially since those laws can touch on training requirements for medical practitioners and their freedom of establishment or freedom to provide services in Malta. The impact of EU law on access to the medical profession and manpower planning in Malta is therefore briefly engaged with next while noting that it is beyond the scope of this monograph to engage with all the EU law that touches on healthcare.[307]

300. S.L. 528.01, Functions and Responsibilities of Department for Policy in Health Regulations, r. 3 (2)(n).
301. S.L. 458.23, Licensing of Private Medical Clinics Regulations, r. 12 (1).
302. *Ibid.*, Second Schedule Part I.
303. *Ibid.*, r. 8.
304. *Ibid.*, r. 10 (2)(a).
305. *Ibid.*, r. 10 (2)(b).
306. *Ibid.*, r. 10 (2)(c).
307. *See, for instance*: Herman Nys, *European Union Health Law* (Kluwer Law International 2d ed. 2021).

II. Freedom of Establishment

59. Access to the medical profession is *inter alia* dependent on entry into the medical register, which then requires a certain level of training and qualifications in medicine.[308] It is in this respect significant to manpower planning that, in accordance with its primary law, the EU provided a legal framework targeting the mutual recognition of qualifications in order to enable the free movement of workers for nationals of Member States and, in the case of the medical profession, the progressive abolition of restrictions on freedom of establishment within Member States was made 'dependent upon coordination of the conditions for their exercise [of the medical, allied and pharmaceutical professions] in the various Member States'.[309] The principle of automatic recognition of qualifications across Member States then arises from the Professional Qualifications Directive,[310] which was transposed into domestic law so that the Recognition of Professional Qualifications Regulations in Malta now demand that there:

> [S]hall be recognition of evidence of formal qualifications as doctor giving access to the professional activities of doctor with basic training and specialised doctor ... referred to in the Health Care Professions Act ... which satisfy the minimum training conditions referred to in the relevant articles of the Health Care Professions Act ... and shall for the purpose of access to, and pursuit of the professional activity, give such evidence the same effect on [Maltese] territory as the evidence of formal qualifications which it itself issues.[311]

60. In addition to the training outlined in a previous section of this monograph,[312] the Health Care Professions Act then also recognises, for the purpose of entry onto the medical register, the qualifications obtained from other Member States listed in Parts Ia,[313] Ib,[314] Ic,[315] and Id[316] of its Second Schedule as well as qualifications recognised for the purpose by a Member State obtained from a University College or Medical School that have been obtained by citizens of Malta, citizens of other Member States and their family as stipulated in EU law, or a person who has been established in a Member State.[317] Automatic recognition is also granted in the case of qualifications obtained before the accession to the EU of the person's home Member State so long as those qualifications are accompanied by a

308. *See also* Part I Ch. 1 §1 above and Part I Ch. 1 §3 below.
309. Treaty on the Functioning of the European Union, OJ C 326, 26.10.2012, Art. 53 (2).
310. Directive 2005/36/EC of the European Parliament and of the Council of 7 September 2005 on the recognition of professional qualifications, OJ L 255, 30.9.2005, Art. 21.
311. S.L. 451.03, Recognition of Professional Qualifications Regulations, r. 22 (1).
312. *See* Part I Ch. 1 §1 above.
313. Formal qualifications in basic medical training.
314. Formal qualifications of specialised doctors.
315. Training courses in specialised medicine.
316. Formal qualifications of general practitioners.
317. Health Care Professions Act, Ch. 464 of the Laws of Malta, Art. 11 (1).

certificate of acquired rights[318] or a certificate of conformity with the provisions regarding automatic recognition.[319] Third-country nationals who hold the degree of MD awarded by the University of Malta or a qualification listed in Parts Ia, Ib, Ic, Id of the Health Care Professions Act, or any other qualification recognised for the purpose at hand by the Medical Council are entered into a register kept by the Medical Council 'for a period not exceeding two years … subject to any condition as the Medical Council may deem necessary'.[320] Furthermore, pursuant to the Professional Qualifications Directive[321] as transposed into Maltese law, when the Medical Council is considering a request for authorisation to exercise the medical profession in Malta, it shall 'recognise professional traineeships carried out in another Member State provided that traineeship is in accordance with the published guidelines [of the Medical Council on the organisation and recognition of professional traineeships carried out in another Member State or in a third country] … and shall take into account professional traineeships carried out in a third country, subject to any reasonable limits, established by law, on the duration of the part of the professional traineeship which can be carried out abroad'.[322] Also, when a citizen of a Member State wishes to acquire a specialist qualification and is consequently required to fulfil prescribed training conditions, the SAC 'shall take into account, in whole or in part, periods of training completed by that person and attested by a qualification awarded by the state of which that person is a citizen, as well as any professional experience, additional training and continuing education which such person possesses'.[323]

61. When the principle of automatic recognition of qualifications does not apply, the general system for evidence of training can be applicable. Thus, in the case of persons from Member States whose qualifications do not fall within the scope of automatic recognition but who apply to enter their name into the medical register, the Medical Council will evaluate the applicant's training, and if that training 'is comparable to the Maltese requirements, the qualifications of the applicant are recognized and registration is granted'.[324] If there are substantial differences in the relevant training, but 'professional experience compensates for this difference …., the Council will recognize the qualifications and grant registration'.[325] In any other circumstance, applicants from Member States whose qualifications fall beyond the scope of automatic recognition may be asked to undertake an adaptation period or an aptitude test.[326] The latter test means 'a test of the professional knowledge, skills and competences of the applicant … with the aim of assessing the ability of the

318. *Ibid.*, Art. 43 (1).
319. *Ibid.*, Sixth Schedule.
320. *Ibid.*, Art. 11 (2).
321. Directive 2005/36/EC of the European Parliament and of the Council of 7 September 2005 on the recognition of professional qualifications, OJ L 255, 30.9.2005, Art. 55a.
322. Health Care Professions Act, Ch. 464 of the Laws of Malta, Art. 42J (1). *See also* S.L. 451.03, Recognition of Professional Qualifications Regulations, r. 31.
323. *Ibid.*, Art. 30 (7).
324. S.L. 464.19, Medical Council (Standing Orders) Regulations, Fifth Schedule.
325. *Ibid.*
326. Health Care Professions Act, Ch. 464 of the Laws of Malta, Arts 42A and 42B; S.L. 451.03, Recognition of Professional Qualifications Regulations, r. 16.

applicant to pursue a regulated profession in Malta'.[327] It typically involves the Malta Medical Council Statutory Examination with the intention of assessing 'a candidate's knowledge and capacity to be registered in Malta as a medical practitioner'.[328] There also exists the possibility of a period of adaptation, which cannot exceed three years in duration.[329] In that case, after the Medical Council determines the length of the period of adaptation, it is the MPGTC that oversees the adaptation process or, otherwise, any entity recognised for that purpose by the Medical Council.[330] Either way, the period of adaptation is conducted under the responsibility and supervision of a medical practitioner,[331] who would liaise with the MPGTC if s/he finds that the applicant requires more experience in the areas identified by the Medical Council or if there is a concern for patient safety.[332] Once the adaptation period is completed, the medical practitioner supervising the applicant and the MPGTC provide a report to the Medical Council so that it makes its decision on registration.[333]

62. In addition to the above, the Health Care Professions Act stipulates that qualifications issued by a third country are to be regarded as evidence of formal qualifications 'if the holder has three years formal experience in the profession concerned on the territory of the Member State which recognised that evidence of formal qualifications, certified by that Member State'.[334] Otherwise, the Medical Council may require third-country applicants whose qualifications in medicine have not been recognised in a Member State 'to sit for and pass a professional and linguistic proficiency test'.[335] This involves the Malta Medical Council Statutory Examination akin to that offered to applicants from Member States whose qualifications do not fall within the framework of the mutual automatic recognition of qualifications. The Health Care Professions Act also provides that, in addition to a professional and linguistic proficiency test, the Medical Council may require third-country applicants whose qualifications have not been recognised in a Member State to serve 'as a house physician and, or surgeon in a hospital recognized for the purpose by the Medical Council, for such period, being not longer than two years, as the Minister [responsible for health] may prescribe'[336] in order to be eligible for entry onto the principal medical register. That being said, the domestic courts in Malta have interpreted this provision in such a manner as to inhibit the Medical Council from applying the proviso regarding a test and service in a hospital before entry into the medical register in circumstances when the third-country applicant's

327. *Ibid.*, Art. 2.
328. Medical Council of Malta, *Medical Council Malta Statutory Examination (MCMSE): Guidance document for medical practitioners* 3 (2021).
329. Health Care Professions Act, Art. 42A (2); S.L. 451.03, Recognition of Professional Qualifications Regulations, r. 16 (1).
330. Medical Council of Malta, *Malta Adaptation Period Guidance Document* 2 (2019).
331. Health Care Professions Act, Ch. 464 of the Laws of Malta, Arts 2 and 42B (3); S.L. 451.03, Recognition of Professional Qualifications Regulations, r. 2.
332. Medical Council of Malta, *Malta Adaptation Period Guidance Document* 2 (2019).
333. *Ibid.*, 3.
334. Health Care Professions Act, Ch. 464 of the Laws of Malta, Art. 2.
335. *Ibid.*, Art. 11 (1)(c).
336. *Ibid.*

qualifications have been recognised in Malta as formal qualifications by the Malta Qualifications Recognition Information Centre[337] but not by the Medical Council per se.[338]

63. Manpower planning involving the freedom of establishment in Malta is thus, to an extent, dependent on a medical practitioner's circumstances as a citizen of a Member State or otherwise, as well as upon whether his/her qualifications fall under the remit of the automatic recognition of qualifications or otherwise. For instance, the Health Care Professions Act provides that the 'Medical Council shall recognise under the national health service, for the purposes of the exercise of the activities of general medical practitioner, the diplomas, certificates and other evidence of formal qualifications issued to a national of a Member State by other Member States'.[339] Member State nationals established in another Member State can however also pursue the medical profession on a temporary and occasional basis in Malta.[340] In that case, it is not necessary to have one's name entered into the principal medical register inasmuch as the medical practitioner would instead be eligible for 'automatic temporary registration'[341] subject to a written declaration made in advance to the Medical Council that is renewed once a year.[342] Evidence of professional qualifications and establishment in another Member State for the purpose of pursuing the medical profession, including that s/he is not prohibited from practising the medical profession, is then obtained from the medical practitioner in 'the case of first-time provision of services in Malta or if there is a material change in the situation substantiated by the documents'.[343] In addition to private healthcare service providers, this temporary registration is also used to provide temporary services at the hospital/s in the public sector, for instance, to assist in surgery or to hold outpatient clinics.[344]

64. Directive (EU) 2018/958[345] as transposed into Maltese law is also significant to the legal framework underpinning access to the medical profession inasmuch as it provides that no legislative, regulatory or administrative provisions restricting access to, or the pursuit of, a regulated profession may be introduced or, if already present, amended 'before the Ministry responsible for the said regulated profession shall have undertaken an assessment of proportionality in accordance with the rules laid down in'[346] the Proportionality Test Before Adoption of New

337. Malta Recognition of Qualifications Act, Ch. 451 of the Laws of Malta, Art. 6.
338. *Zananian Desira Isabella v. Kunsill Mediku*, First Hall Civil Court – 14/02/2017 [Ref: 740/2011] 12–13; Court of Appeal (Civil, Superior) – 02/03/2018 [Ref: 740/2011/1] 18–19.
339. Health Care Professions Act, Ch. 464 of the Laws of Malta, Art. 44A (3).
340. *Ibid.*, Art. 42 (4).
341. *Ibid.*, Art. 42 (5). *See also* S.L. 451.03, Recognition of Professional Qualifications Regulations, r. 8.
342. *Ibid.*, Art. 42 (6)(a).
343. *Ibid.*, Art. 42 (6)(b).
344. *See, for instance*: Medical Council of Malta, *Temporary Service List: Medical Practitioners.*
345. Directive (EU) 2018/958 of the European Parliament and of the Council of 28 June 2018 on a proportionality test before adoption of new regulation of professions, OJ L 173, 9.7.2018.
346. Proportionality Test Before Adoption of New Regulation of Professions Act, Ch. 612 of the Laws of Malta.

Regulation of Professions Act. This covers the medical profession, among others, and it involves a process to ensure that the introduction of or amendment to legislative, regulatory or administrative provisions restricting access to, or the pursuit of, *inter alia,* the medical profession 'are suitable for securing the attainment of the objective pursued and do not go beyond what is necessary to attain that objective'.[347] Acknowledging obligations arising from Article 168 (1) of the Treaty of the Functioning of the European Union, Directive (EU) 2018/958 and its transposing instrument into the domestic legal order in Malta, however, provides that where the provisions in question concern 'the regulation of healthcare professions and have patient safety implications, the Ministry responsible for the relative regulated profession shall take account of the objective of ensuring a high level of human health protection'.[348] In turn, it is incumbent to next consider the licensing requirements in order to access the medical profession in Malta.

§3. Licensing of Physicians

I. General Practitioners

65. The Health Care Professions Act repealed[349] the provisions in the Medical and Kindred Professions Ordinance that had, until then, regulated the licensing of the medical profession.[350] The Health Care Professions Act did not however affect the right of any member of the medical profession to continue to practice that profession if s/he had already been licensed under the Medical and Kindred Professions Ordinance[351] or to be deemed to be qualified to be registered in the appropriate register pertinent to his/her profession 'and, where appropriate, to hold the relative licence'.[352] Be that as it may, it is the Health Care Professions Act that now regulates licensing for the purpose of the medical profession in Malta, as outlined in this section of the monograph.

66. The license to practice as a medical practitioner is issued by the President of Malta,[353] and it is the Medical Council that has the function to recommend that a licence should be granted[354] or withdrawn.[355] The Health Care Professions Act stipulates that there are three conditions in order for a person to qualify for a licence to practice as a medical practitioner. First, a person must be a citizen of Malta or of a Member State or otherwise be legally entitled or authorised to work in Malta.[356]

347. *Ibid.*, Art. 6 (1).
348. *Ibid.*, Art. 6 (5).
349. Act XII of 2003 – Health Care Professions Act [Government Gazette of Malta No. 17,487 – 17/10/2003] Art. 52 (1).
350. Medical and Kindred Professions Ordinance, Ch. 31 of the Laws of Malta, Arts 3–12 (Repealed).
351. Health Care Professions Act, Ch. 464 of the Laws of Malta, Art. 52.
352. *Ibid.*, Art. 53 (1).
353. *Ibid.*, Art. 7 (1).
354. *Ibid.*, Art. 10 (1)(a).
355. *Ibid.*, Art. 10 (1)(b).
356. *Ibid.*, Art. 7 (2)(a).

To be clear, the President of Malta may, with the approval of the Minister responsible for health upon the advice of the Medical Council 'grant a temporary licence, for a period not exceeding two years, to any health care professional who is not a citizen of Malta or of a Member State, and may subject such licence to any condition he may deem appropriate'.[357]

67. The second condition to be eligible for a license to practice as a medical practitioner is that the person's name must be entered in the medical register,[358] which is kept, published and updated by the Medical Council.[359] Although the process to enter one's name onto the medical register is illustrated in the previous sections of this chapter, it should be noted in the context of licensing that there is an Appeals Committee established in terms of the Health Care Professions Act that has the function of receiving, hearing and deciding upon applications regarding a decision by the Medical Council to refuse a person's entry into the medical register.[360] It should furthermore be noted at this stage when discussing licensing that a medical practitioner's name may *inter alia* be erased from the medical register by the Medical Council either at his/her own request on account of physical or mental infirmity[361] or if, after due inquiry, the Medical Council finds that a medical practitioner is unfit to continue to practise his/her profession on account of some physical or mental infirmity.[362]

68. The third condition to be eligible for a license to practice as a medical practitioner is that the person must be of good conduct,[363] which is understood to mean conduct approved by the Medical Council.[364] In turn, the Medical Council can, after due inquiry *inter alia,* find the medical practitioner, which for this purpose includes a house physician and/or surgeon on the provisional register,[365] guilty of professional or ethical misconduct and direct one or more disciplinary measures.[366] Those measures can include that a person's name is erased from the medical register 'and, where appropriate, recommend to the President of Malta that the professional's licence be withdrawn'.[367] Less severely, a person's name may be taken off the medical register for a period of time as determined by the Medical Council 'and, where appropriate, recommend to the President of Malta that the professional's licence be

357. *Ibid.*, Art. 47.
358. *Ibid.*, Art. 7 (2)(c).
359. *Ibid.*, Art. 10 (1)(c).
360. *Ibid.*, Art. 49 (3)(a). *See also*: *Aljush Denis v. Kunsill Mediku*, Civil Court First Hall – 29/10/2020 [Ref: 349/2019].
361. *Ibid.*, Art. 38 (2).
362. *Ibid.*, Art. 38 (1). *See also* Part I Ch.. 4 §2 below.
363. *Ibid.*, Art. 7 (2)(b).
364. *Ibid.*, Art. 2.
365. *Ibid.*, Art. 7 (4).
366. *Ibid.*, Art. 32. *See also* Part I Ch. 4 §1 below.
367. *Ibid.*, Art. 32 (i).

also so suspended'.[368] Either way, a person's license to practice the medical profession issued by the President of Malta 'shall be deemed to be suspended during such period that the name of the licensed person is deleted from the register'.[369]

69. It is also significant to the licensing of the medical profession that, in accordance with Article 35 of the Health Care Professions Act, the Medical Council may, by order in writing, direct the erasure of a person's name from the medical register if it is satisfied that any entry has been fraudulently or incorrectly made. Furthermore, where the registration has been made fraudulently, the Medical Council 'may direct that no application by such person to have his name entered in the register shall be accepted before such time as the Council may direct'.[370] That being said, in a case dealing with this provision of the Health Care Professions Act, the Court of Appeal held that an entity like the Medical Council that possesses quasi-judicial functions must still observe principles of natural justice, which includes that a person has fair notice of any accusation made against him and the consequent right to be heard.[371] The ruling at hand concerned an entry into the medical register in Malta even though the medical practitioner in question had been struck off the equivalent register in the United Kingdom. The doctor's name was entered into the medical register in Malta in part because the documentation regarding his erasure from the register in the United Kingdom was not originally noted by the members of the pertinent Committee of the Medical Council regarding licensing. The Court of Appeal ruled that while the Medical Council could, in principle, make use of Article 35, it could not use the authority arising from that provision in order to retrospectively make good for the mistakes of a committee that were not attributable to the medical practitioner who had faithfully presented the necessary documentation.[372] The Court of Appeal therefore ruled that the Medical Council's recommendation to the President of Malta that the medical practitioner's license should be revoked was not justified inasmuch as it was a recommendation occasioned due to the mistake of a committee rather than the medical practitioner in question and, even if a decision by the Medical Council may be substantively correct in principle, that decision should be nullified if it is otherwise not in accordance with the principles of natural justice.[373]

70. The licence issued by the President of Malta means that a person can practise as a medical practitioner in Malta and that s/he will be entitled to use the professional title of 'medical practitioner' so long as s/he also fulfils the conditions set by the Medical Council for taking up and pursuit of that profession in Malta.[374] That licence does not however suffice to use the title 'general practitioner'. This is because family medicine is a specialisation falling within the remit of the specialist

368. *Ibid.*, Art. 32 (ii).
369. *Ibid.*, Art. 32 (2).
370. *Ibid.*, Art. 35. *See also* Part I Ch. 4 §2.
371. *Hussain Fazal Dr. v. Kunsill Mediku*, Court of Appeal (Civil, Superior) – 24/11/2017 [Ref: 183/2017/1] 12–13.
372. *Ibid.*, 18.
373. *Ibid.*, 20–21.
374. Health Care Professions Act, Ch. 464 of the Laws of Malta, Art. 3 (2).

register of medical practitioners, which is discussed in the next subsection of this monograph. As such, the Medical Council has directed that 'the title "Family Doctor" and "General Practitioner" should be used only by those doctors who have been registered in the "Family Medicine" list of the Specialist Register'.[375] Consequently, medical practitioners intending to qualify as general practitioners in Malta must undertake a specialist training programme in order to be eligible for entry into the Specialist Register of the medical profession that is kept, published and updated by the Medical Council. It is the Malta College of Family Doctors that is 'responsible for developing Specialist/ Vocational Training in Family Medicine in Malta'.[376] The specialist training programme involves a minimum of three years of training, and the 'trainee will be assigned to a GP trainer who will mentor the trainee throughout the whole training programme. There will also be mentoring by a Hospital Supervisor during the hospital rotations'.[377] Thus, in addition to training in family medicine per se, the trainee also undertakes a roster of placements within different specialist departments, such as paediatrics and orthopaedics. In this respect, it is also opportune to address the licensing of specialists in the medical profession next.

II. Medical Specialists

71. The term 'specialist' in the Health Care Professions Act means a 'health care professional whose name is entered in the appropriate part of the specialist register kept by the relevant Council in accordance with'[378] that Act. The Medical Council keeps, publishes and updates the specialist register of the medical profession,[379] and it is bound to 'keep separate registers for each of the specialities listed under the Fifth Schedule'[380] of the Health Care Professions Act. The specialist register of the medical profession, in turn, contains over fifty registers or lists of specialities, such as paediatrics, or sub-specialities, such as paediatric endocrinology and diabetes. It then is the SAC that has the function 'to issue certificates of completion of specialist training in the specialities listed in the relevant part of the Fifth Schedule'[381] of the Health Care Professions Act. A medical practitioner may however appeal a decision of the SAC to the Appeals Committee, which is established under the Health Care Professions Act, in those cases when the award of a specialist certificate is

375. Medical Council of Malta, *Circular 01/2021: Use of 'Specialist' Nomenclature* (2021). Original ellipses.
376. Edward Zammit, Mario Sammut & Gunther Abela, *Specialist Training Programme in Family Medicine – Malta* 2 (Malta College of Family Doctors 3d ed. 2017).
377. *The Specialist Training in Family Medicine Curriculum* 21 (Natalie Psaila ed., Malta College of Family Doctors 2d ed. 2021).
378. Health Care Professions Act, Ch. 464 of the Laws of Malta, Art. 2.
379. *Ibid.*, Art. 10 (1)(b).
380. *Ibid.*, Art. 11 (5).
381. *Ibid.*, Art. 30 (6)(a)(i).

refused.[382] The SAC furthermore has the function to advise the Minister responsible for health and the Medical Council 'on issues concerning specialist training and registration, and any other matter than may be referred to it'.[383]

72. There are different ways for the Medical Council to consider admission onto a specialist register following an application to that effect made by a medical practitioner. First, the Medical Council shall enter into the pertinent specialist register the name of a medical practitioner who 'is in possession of a certificate issued by the Specialist Accreditation Committee for the relevant profession which shows that he has completed the prescribed training for such speciality as may be prescribed'.[384] In practice, medical practitioners specialising in Malta after the entry into force of the Health Care Professions Act typically use this route to enter their name into the specialist register. Moreover, the Medical Council shall enter into the specialist register the name of a medical practitioner who 'is in possession of a specialist qualification listed in Part Ia and Ib of the Second Schedule'[385] of the Health Care Professions Act. This arises from the principle of automatic recognition of qualifications so that entry into the specialist register would require the qualifications awarded by the bodies listed in that Schedule, which reflects the pertinent Schedule in the Professional Qualifications Directive, that evince formal qualifications in basic medical training and the formal qualification/s of a specialised doctor.[386] The Medical Council and the SAC are thus vested with the important task of certifying, in the interest of patients and the health service, the training of medical practitioners applying to enter the specialist register across the breadth of the specialist area in question that will then be recognised across the other Member States of the EU. The Constitutional Court in Malta has, in this respect, confirmed that a medical practitioner must complete all the indicated training required to admit his/her name into the specialist register and failure to complete that training for whatever reason, including one's disability, signifies that the domestic authorities would be justified in not entering one's name into the specialist register.[387]

73. In addition to the above, the Medical Council shall also enter into the specialist register the name of a medical practitioner who 'is in possession of any specialist qualification recognized by the Specialist Accreditation Committee'[388] for the medical profession. The Health Care Professions Act then stipulates that, in the case of citizens of Malta or a Member State whose qualifications in the speciality do not satisfy the minimum prescribed qualifications for that speciality, the SAC is to deem as possession of the specialist qualification a certificate issued by the competent

---

382. *Ibid.*, Art. 49 (3)(b).
383. *Ibid.*, Art. 30 (6)(a)(ii).
384. *Ibid.*, Art. 29 (4)(a).
385. *Ibid.*, Art. 29 (4)(b).
386. S.L. 451.04, Minimum Training Conditions (Health Care Professions), r. 9 (5). *See also* Part I Ch. 1 §2.II above.
387. *Megally Naged Dottor v. Divizjoni Regolazzjoni Sahha Pubblika et.*, Civil Court First Hall (Constitutional Jurisdiction) – 12/04/2013 [Ref: 31/2009] 7; *Megally Naged Dottor v. Divizjoni Regolazzjoni Sahha Pubblika et.*, Constitutional Court – 27/02/2015 [Ref: 31/2009/1] 10.
388. Health Care Professions Act, Ch. 464 of the Laws of Malta, Art. 29 (4)(c).

authority in the Member State of which that person is a citizen or the Member State from which the person comes stating that s/he 'has been engaged in the specialised area of the profession concerned for a period which is such period of training that is prescribed for the speciality'.[389] Moreover, when the principle of automatic recognition of qualifications does not apply in view of training that began before the reference dates indicated in the Schedules appended to the Health Care Professions Act arising from the Professional Qualifications Directive, the Medical Council shall recognise evidence of formal qualifications issued by those Member States attesting the successful completion of that training and that 'is accompanied by a certificate stating that the holders have been effectively and lawfully engaged in the activities in question for at least three consecutive years during the five years preceding the award of the certificate'.[390]

74. The Health Care Professions Act furthermore provides that the SAC is to certify as holding the necessary qualifications any medical practitioner who, prior to the coming into force of that Act, 'held an appointment with the Government at consultant or senior registrar level in a government hospital or clinic'.[391] Moreover, after consulting with the relevant society and/or professional association, the SAC is to certify as holding the qualifications for registration in the specialist register of the medical profession any medical practitioner who, before the coming into force of the Health Care Professions Act, 'has practised as a specialist to the satisfaction of the Specialist Accreditation Committee'.[392] These grandfathering clauses provide for some of the senior medical specialists in Malta to date.

389. *Ibid.*
390. *Ibid.*, Art. 43 (1).
391. *Ibid.*, Art. 53 (3).
392. *Ibid.*, Art. 53 (2).

Chapter 2. The Practice of Medicine

75. Access to the medical profession, including licensing, interlinks with the practice of medicine. This chapter begins engaging with the practice of medicine by framing the pursuit of the medical profession as a medical practitioner and/or as a specialist in that profession while also briefly considering the services that can be provided by those practitioners or specialists.

76. The medical profession in Malta is one of the regulated health care professions under the Health Care Professions Act inasmuch as it features 'a professional activity or group of professional activities, access to which, the pursuit of which, or one of the modes of pursuit of which is subject, directly or indirectly, by virtue of legislative, regulatory or administrative provisions, to the possession of specific professional qualifications',[393] which are outlined in the previous chapter of this part of the monograph. A mode of pursuit of healthcare professions includes 'the use of a professional title limited by legislative, regulatory or administrative provisions to holders of a given professional title'.[394] In the case of the medical profession, a person shall only be entitled to use the professional title of 'medical practitioner' if s/he fulfils the conditions set by the Medical Council for taking up and pursuing in Malta that profession in accordance with the provisions of the Health Care Professions Act.[395]

77. The practice of medicine in the context of the Health Care Professions Act also includes 'the provision of services'.[396] In turn, the Health Care Professions Act provides that no person shall practice a healthcare profession, which includes the medical profession in addition to others such as dental surgeons and pharmacists, 'unless he fulfils the conditions for the taking up and pursuit of that health care profession in Malta, in accordance with the provisions of'[397] that Act. While recalling the exceptional circumstances outlined in the previous chapter of this part of the monograph, including the situation of house physicians and/or surgeons who are undertaking the Foundation Programme,[398] the Health Care Professions Act stipulates that '[n]o person shall practise as a medical practitioner unless he holds a licence for that purpose issued by the President of Malta'.[399] The practice of medicine by the medical profession is thus circumscribed by law as an independent profession within the healthcare professions regulated under the Health Care Professions Act.

78. Upon registration and licensing, a medical practitioner 'can practice his/her profession in Malta'.[400] This entails access to a number of activities curtailed by law

393. *Ibid.*, Art. 2.
394. *Ibid.*
395. *Ibid.*, Art. 3 (2). *See also* Medicines Act, Ch. 458 of the Laws of Malta, Art. 2.
396. *Ibid.*, Art. 2.
397. *Ibid.*, Art. 3 (1).
398. *Ibid.*, Art. 7 (3).
399. *Ibid.*, Art. 7 (1).
400. S.L. 464.19, Medical Council (Standing Orders) Regulations, Fifth Schedule.

to particular profession/s. For instance, medical practitioners are one of the professions that are authorised to have in their possession certain drugs,[401] and they are also one of the professions that can prescribe medicinal products that cannot lawfully be dispensed by a pharmacist without a medical prescription.[402] A medical practitioner can also prescribe products or substances that are not classified as medicinal products 'but which have been deemed to require a medicinal prescription for their use by the relevant competent authority'.[403] That notwithstanding, the practice of medicine may be curtailed by law. For example, a medical practitioner may prescribe to named patients medicinal preparations of the plant cannabis and synthetic cannabinoid products licensed under the Medicines Act or manufactured under good manufacturing practice, but only 'if it is considered that there is no viable alternative to such prescription due account being taken of any protocols which may be in force from time to time in respect of the prescription of medicines, of the interests of the patient and of the costs'[404] and none of those preparations may be 'indicated for smoking or in any form meant for smoking'.[405] Either way, the use and content of medical prescriptions are normally stipulated by law or otherwise, controlled by hospital internal rules for the purpose of administration to ward patients.[406] While a medical prescription is arguably ubiquitous in the practice of medicine, there are also other less evident activities in Maltese law calling on medical practitioners. By way of example, a person of full age may, in anticipation of his/her decision-making incapacity, give a mandate so that the mandatary takes care of the mandator or administers that mandator's property. Yet, before a notary public can draw up that mandate, there must be 'a *medical* declaration that circumstances so require in the best interests of that person'.[407] It is a medical practitioner who can then make that medical declaration. That being said, despite the breadth of activities at law involving the medical profession, no medical practitioner may be employed 'within the national health service unless he is in possession of a diploma, certificate or other evidence of formal qualification issued by a recognised competent authority'.[408] Persons undergoing specific training in family medicine or whose name was entered into the medical register before Malta's entry into the EU may, however, be exempted from that requirement in order to be employed as a medical practitioner in the national health service.[409]

---

401. *See, for instance*: S.L. 31.18, Drugs (Control) Regulations, r. 5; S.L. 101.02, Internal Control of Dangerous Drugs Rules, r. 13.
402. Medicines Act, Ch. 458 of the Laws of Malta, Art. 81 (1).
403. *Ibid.*, Art. 81 (2). *See also* S.L. 101.02, Internal Control of Dangerous Drugs Rules, r. 5.
404. Drug Dependence (Treatment Not Imprisonment) Act, Ch. 537 of the Laws of Malta, Art. 10 (1).
405. *Ibid.*, Art. 10 (2). *See also* Authority on the Responsible Use of Cannabis Act, Ch. 628 of the Laws of Malta.
406. *See, for instance*: S.L. 31.18, Drugs (Control) Regulations, rs 6, 9 and 10; S.L. 101.02, Internal Control of Dangerous Drugs Rules, rs 6 and 8; Medicines Act, Ch. 458 of the Laws of Malta, Arts 29 and 82; S.L. 458.24, Prescription Forms for Free Medicinals Rules; S.L. 458.49, Prescription and Dispensing Requirements Rules.
407. Civil Code, Ch. 16 of the Laws of Malta, Art. 1864A (1). Emphasis added.
408. Health Care Professions Act, Ch. 464 of the Laws of Malta, Art. 44A (1). *See also* Directive 2005/36/EC of the European Parliament and of the Council of 7 September 2005 on the recognition of professional qualifications, OJ L 255, 30.9.2005, Art 29.
409. *Ibid.*

79. The Health Care Professions Act then stipulates that no person 'shall practise as, or hold out himself to be, a specialist unless his name is entered in the respective register kept for the registration of specialists'[410] by the Medical Council. It shall also 'not be lawful for any person to assume, whether in writing or otherwise, any title or use, or be party to the use of any description implying that he is a specialist in any of the specialities of the professions regulated by [the Health Care Professions Act] unless his name [is] entered in the register kept for the registration of specialists by'[411] the Medical Council. Moreover, the Ethics of the Medical Profession Regulations provide that the word 'specialist' may 'only be used by persons who have completed their specialist training and are listed as such in the Specialist Register held by the Medical Council'.[412] While the 'Medical Council acknowledges that specialists may be required to work in an area of another speciality provided that they have proven competence in that sphere',[413] Maltese law occasionally restricts the performance of certain activities to persons included in one or more of the lists within the specialist register held by the Medical Council in order for that activity to have effect at law. For instance, the practice of medicine in the context of the Mental Health Act, which *inter alia* regulates mental health services and the rights of persons with mental disorders, revolves around medical practitioners who are included in the specialist register for psychiatry. By way of example, only a psychiatrist 'may certify a person suffering from a mental disorder as having mental capacity or lack thereof'.[414] There furthermore are instances when it is stipulated what qualifications and experience a person must have in order to practice a particular aspect of medicine. For instance, so long as practitioners involved in the practical aspects of medical radiological procedures are medical practitioners, they must then be on the specialist register held by the Medical Council as indicated in the Basic Safety Standards for Ionising Radiation Regulations,[415] subject to the categorisation of medical exposures.[416] It is also the case that some boards appointed in terms of law must include among their members medical practitioner/s listed in one or more of the lists in the specialist register held by the Medical Council. Thus, for instance, the composition of the Minors Care Review Board includes 'a person being registered in the specialist register for the pediatric field according to the Health Care Professions Act'.[417]

80. That being said, the practice of medicine in Malta after admission to the medical profession is far-reaching, and, as noted in the Ethics of the Medical Profession Regulations, the 'justification for the freedom of medicine lies in the hands

410. *Ibid.*, Art. 29 (1).
411. *Ibid.*, Art. 29 (2).
412. S.L. 464.17, Ethics of the Medical Profession Regulations, r. 8 (8)(b).
413. Medical Council of Malta, *Addendum to the Code of Ethics* (2009).
414. Mental Health Act, Ch. 525 of the Laws of Malta, Art. 24 (2).
415. S.L. 585.01, Basic Safety Standards for Ionising Radiation Regulations, Seventeenth Schedule.
416. *See also* Council Directive 2013/59/Euratom of 5 December 2013 laying down basic safety standards for protection against the dangers arising from exposure to ionising radiation, and repealing Directives 89/618/Euratom, 90/641/Euratom, 96/29/Euratom, 97/43/Euratom and 2003/122/Euratom, OJ L 13, 17.1.2014.
417. Minor Protection (Alternative Care) Act, Ch. 602 of the Laws of Malta, Art. 31 (1)(g).

of those who practise it'.[418] Even so, subject to the duty of medical practitioners to comply with the laws of Malta,[419] medical practitioners 'shall, in the practice of their profession, be subject to special supervision by'[420] the Medical Council. This entails that the Medical Council supervises the professional and ethical standards it itself can prescribe to medical practitioners, including specialists.[421] Those professional and ethical standards relate to the general conduct of medical practitioners, including the behaviour of medical practitioners towards patients under their care or being attended by them, during or consequential to the exercise of their profession, and the behaviour of medical practitioners towards other members of that profession, towards members of other health care professions and towards society.[422]

81. The practice of medicine is thus grounded in the regulation of the healthcare professions, which includes medical practitioners supervised by the Medical Council. There, however then, is a distinction between supervision and control over the lawful practice of medicine when contrasted with the illegal practice of medicine. The former practice of medicine is lawful in principle but may be vitiated by, for instance, negligence and/or non-observance of professional and/or ethical standards.[423] Instead, the illegal practice of medicine is unlawful *ab initio,* and it is engaged with next.

418. S.L. 464.17, Ethics of the Medical Profession Regulations, Sch. A [1].
419. *Ibid.*, r. 20.
420. Health Care Professions Act, Ch. 464 of the Laws of Malta, Art. 5 (1).
421. *Ibid.*, Art. 5 (2).
422. *Ibid.*, Art. 2.
423. *See* Part I Ch.Ch. 4 §1 below.

Chapter 3. Illegal Practice of Medicine

82. This chapter of the monograph illustrates four types of illegal practice of medicine: (i) practising two healthcare professions concurrently without fulfilling the indicated criteria at law; (ii) practising medicine without the necessary qualifications and licence; (iii) practices that cannot be performed by a medical practitioner; and (iv) practices that violate the professional and ethical standards of the medical profession. Given that medical practitioners are subject to and must follow the laws of Malta, several offences that may undermine the practice of medicine are furthermore considered later in this monograph.

83. It is not lawful for any healthcare professional, including medical practitioners, to practice concurrently any two or more of the healthcare professions regulated under the Health Care Professions Act unless s/he fulfils criteria required for registration of those healthcare professions while also complying by the procedure outlined in the Practice of Concurrent Professions Regulations inasmuch as they 'prescribe the circumstances in which any health care professional may practise more than one health care profession concurrently'.[424] Those circumstances include informing the 'relevant Council of any registration or pending application with another Council'[425] so that applications for dual registration and practice can be assessed by the relevant Councils using the following criteria: '(i) potential conflict of interest, (ii) patient and community implications, (iii) ability to maintain satisfactory level of continuous professional development in both professions, (iv) regulatory implications'.[426] While dual concurrent registration and practice may be limited by conditions set by the relevant Council and approved by the Minister responsible for health,[427] what constitutes the practice of concurrent professions can be indicated at law insofar as some of the duties and competencies of healthcare professions are occasionally grounded in statute. For instance, unless otherwise provided by or under the Medicines Act,[428] 'a medicinal product shall only be prepared or dispensed from a pharmacy and by a pharmacist: Provided that a pharmacist may permit medicinal products to be prepared or dispensed by a pharmacy technician under his personal supervision'.[429] Otherwise, a regulatory Council can, without dictating the exclusive scope of practice, define 'the parameters within which members of the profession … can function, so that other health care professionals and the general public can be aware of the service that such professional may legitimately provide'.[430] The Ethics of the Medical Profession Regulations also indicate that when a medical practitioner 'has reason to believe that a patient is suffering

424. Health Care Professions Act, Ch. 464 of the Laws of Malta, Art. 4.
425. S.L. 464.09, Practice of Concurrent Professions Regulations, r. 2 (2)(a).
426. *Ibid.*, r. (2)(2)(b).
427. *Ibid.*, r. 4. *See also* Medical Council Malta, *Annual report 2005*, 15.
428. *See, for instance*: Medicines Act, Ch. 458 of the Laws of Malta, Art. 79; S.L. 458.55, Provision of Medicinal Products through the Genito Urinary Clinic within the Government Health Services Rules.
429. *Ibid.*, Art. 76 (1). *See also* Part III Ch. 2 §1 below.
430. Council of Nurses and Midwives Malta, *The Scope of Professional Practice* (2002, Updated 2018) 4. *See also* Part III Ch. 2 §2 below.

from a condition arising from, or in connection with, dental treatment, it is the duty of the practitioner concerned to recommend to the patient to permit him to communicate with a dental practitioner'.[431] There may nevertheless be some overlap between the practice of medical practitioners and other healthcare professions that will not warrant registration with two different Councils so long as there is no take up and pursuit, including by using the professional title, of the other healthcare professions. For instance, the professional activities of a midwife include 'conducting spontaneous deliveries including where required episiotomies and in urgent cases breech deliveries'.[432] Even though those professional activities can also be conducted by a medical practitioner, it does not entail concurrent practice and, indeed, continuing on the example of midwives, their professional activities also include referring to medical practitioners when they recognise 'warning signs of abnormality in the mother or infant'[433] as well as 'carrying out treatment prescribed by doctors'.[434] As such, a midwife conducting deliveries in childbirth is not liable for practising a concurrent profession inasmuch as s/he is offering the services of a midwife, not of a medical practitioner, and is not taking up or pursuing the profession of medical practitioner.[435]

84. It is however an offence under the Health Care Professions Act for a person to practice as a medical practitioner unless s/he fulfils the conditions for taking up and pursuing that profession in Malta, and it is additionally an offence under that Act for persons to use the title of medical practitioner unless they fulfil the conditions set by the Medical Council for taking up and pursuit in Malta of that profession.[436] Similarly, it is an offence under the Health Care Professions Act for a person to practice as or to hold themselves out to be a specialist unless his/her name is entered into the specialist register held by the Medical Council, and it is an offence under that Act for persons to assume any title or use, or be party to the use, of any description implying that they are specialist/s in any of the specialities regulated under that Act unless their name is entered into the specialist register held by the Medical Council.[437] On a first conviction, a person would be subject to a fine, whereas subsequent convictions can also include terms of imprisonment.[438] Moreover, where 'the facts of an offence constitute a more serious offence under the Criminal Code or any other law, the provisions of that Code or other law shall apply in respect of that offence'.[439] By way of example, when a man posed as a medical practitioner in Malta's largest hospital with the intention of touching women's bodies under the pretence of performing a physical examination, in addition to acting in violation of the Health Care Professions Act, he was furthermore charged with the

431. S.L. 464.17, Ethics of the Medical Profession Regulations, r. 26 (1). *See also* Part III Ch. 1 §2 below.
432. Health Care Professions Act, Ch. 464 of the Laws of Malta, Art. 23 (5)(f).
433. *Ibid.*, Art. 23 (5)(g).
434. *Ibid.*, Art. 23 (5)(j). *See also* Part III Ch. 2 §2 below.
435. *See also* S.L. 458.04, Midwives Regulations.
436. Health Care Professions Act, Ch. 464 of the Laws of Malta, Art. 3.
437. *Ibid.*, Art. 29.
438. *Ibid.*, Art. 39.
439. *Ibid.*, Art. 40.

following offences under the Criminal Code: (i) Assuming a public function and performing an act thereof without being entitled thereto in violation of Article 84 of the Criminal Code; (ii) Knowingly making a false declaration or statement or giving false information in any document intended for any public authority so as to gain any advantage or benefit for himself or others in violation of Article 188 of the Criminal Code; and (iii) Committing a violent indecent assault on women in consequence of a fraudulent device used in violation of Articles 207 and 201 (b) of the Criminal Code.[440]

85. A registered and licensed medical practitioner can nevertheless be liable for illegal practices in Malta inasmuch as s/he is bound not to perform particular practices specifically because s/he is a medical practitioner. Some of these practices are illustrated later in this monograph, particularly when discussing the physician-patient relationship. By way of example, it is unlawful for a professional, which includes a medical practitioner, to '(i) offer and, or perform conversion practices on any person irrespective of whether compensation is received in exchange; or (ii) make referral to any other person to perform conversion practices on any person'.[441] Conversion practices in this context refer 'to any treatment, practice or sustained effort that aims to change, repress and, or eliminate a person's sexual orientation, gender identity and, or gender expression',[442] as defined in the Affirmation of Sexual Orientation, Gender Identity and Gender Expression Act. The definition of conversation practice in the latter Act does not however cover certain healthcare services, and it, for instance, excludes 'any healthcare services related to the treatment of a mental disorder'[443] albeit that the definition of mental disorder for the purpose of this offence under the Affirmation of Sexual Orientation, Gender Identity and Gender Expression Act excludes 'any form of pathologisation of sexual orientation, gender identity and, or gender expression as may be classified under the International Classification of Diseases or other similar internationally recognised classifications'.[444] Those types of circumstances related to healthcare services aside, a medical practitioner would be performing an illegal practice, as a professional consequent to his/her qualifications and licence to practice as a medical practitioner, if s/he conducts conversion practices or refers someone to another person to perform conversation practices. As a second example of an illegal practice if conducted by a medical practitioner, there are instances in Maltese law when a medical practitioner may issue a prescription only after obtaining prior authorisation from pertinent authorities, for instance, from the Superintendent of Public Health[445] and if a medical practitioner is:

440. *Il-Pulizija v. Precht Michael Camilo*, Court of Magistrates (Criminal Judicature) – 23/01/2015 [Ref: 76/2015].
441. Affirmation of Sexual Orientation, Gender Identity and Gender Expression Act, Ch. 567 of the Laws of Malta, Art. 3 (b).
442. *Ibid.*, Art. 2.
443. *Ibid.*
444. *Ibid.*
445. S.L. 31.18, Drugs (Control) Regulations, r. 13 (1).

> [S]upplying or prescribing any specified drug [under the Drugs (Control) Regulations] to or for either himself or any other person other than, or more than, is properly required for medical or dental treatment of himself or that other person … the President [of Malta] may refer the matter to the Medical Council, and, if the Council so recommends, the President may prohibit the said medical practitioner … from supplying, prescribing, procuring or possessing such drug, for such period as the President may deem fit, and it shall then be unlawful for that medical practitioner … to supply, prescribe, procure or possess any such drug during such period.[446]

Furthermore, medical practitioners are also bound to 'abide by the obligations set out in the Dangerous Drugs Ordinance and any regulations made thereunder',[447] and any breach of those provisions shall, in accordance with the Ethics of the Medical Profession Regulations, 'render the practitioner liable to his name being erased from the register'.[448]

86. There moreover are certain professional practices that a medical practitioner cannot participate in given that it would be an offence against the ethical and professional standards adopted by the Medical Council. It is, for instance, an offence *inter alia* subject to disciplinary action by the Medical Council,[449] including erasure from the medical register, for a medical practitioner to deal 'in the commerce of drugs, medicinal and other remedies by medical practitioners, dental surgeons and veterinary surgeons'.[450] Standards of this nature, which can tie in with the broader statutory framework,[451] may also affect a medical practitioner's possibilities of establishment or provision of services in other Member States. Indeed, the Medical Council has the function 'to forward to any Member State concerned all information regarding measures taken in respect of healthcare professional[s] as well as regarding any criminal penalty imposed on such professionals'.[452] Furthermore, the National Commission for Further and Higher Education shall inform the competent authorities of all other Member States about professionals, including medical practitioners, subject to the automatic recognition of qualifications and 'other professionals exercising activities that have patient safety implications, where the professional is pursuing a profession regulated in Malta',[453] whose pursuit of their profession in Malta 'has been restricted or prohibited, even temporarily, by national authorities or courts'.[454]

---

446. *Ibid.*, r. 13 (10). *See also* S.L. 101.02, Internal Control of Dangerous Drugs Rules, r. 14.
447. S.L. 464.17, Ethics of the Medical Profession Regulations, r. 19.
448. *Ibid.*
449. Health Care Professions Act, Ch. 464 of the Laws of Malta, Art. 32. *See also* Part I Ch. 4 §4.I below.
450. S.L. 464.17, Ethics of the Medical Profession Regulations, r. 4 (f).
451. *See, for instance*: Medicines Act, Ch. 458 of the Laws of Malta, Art. 77; S.L. 458.16, Pharmacy Licence Regulations, r. 3.
452. Health Care Professions Act, Ch. 464 of the Laws of Malta, Art. 10 (1)(h). *See* Art. 36 (1).
453. S.L. 451.03, Recognition of Professional Qualifications Regulations, r. 5A (1)(k).
454. *Ibid.*, r. 5A (1).

Chapter 4. Control over the Practice of Medicine

87. The chapter regarding control over the practice of medicine is split into four sections focusing on the medical profession that grounds this part of the monograph. Beginning with an outline of the process to establish the liability or otherwise of a member of the medical profession through the domestic courts, consideration is then given to the mechanisms of quality assurance in the context of that profession. This then leads on to an illustration of review boards underpinning the practice of medicine in order to then conclude by addressing disciplinary organisations, focusing in particular on the Medical Council of Malta.

§1. PROFESSIONAL LIABILITY

I. Civil Liability

88. A medical practitioner may be found liable by the courts of civil jurisdiction in Malta and can be ordered to pay compensation for damages in his/her practice of medicine. Drawing on the laws of Malta and the jurisprudence of the domestic courts, there are in practice seven stages so as to establish civil liability in the context of therapeutic or diagnostic medical practice: (i) Establishing that the medical practitioner is not *ipso jure* exempt from civil liability; (ii) determining whether there exists or existed a contractual relationship between the medical practitioner and the claimant/s or whether civil liability is instead established extra-contractually in tort; (iii) gathering proof or evidence from referees as expert witnesses; (iv) ascertaining facts including, for instance, that an event occurred that was not meant to occur or, otherwise, that an event did not take place that was meant to have taken place; (v) establishing that the claimant suffered damages; (vi) confirming that there exists a causal nexus between the damages suffered by the claimant and an event that is attributable to the medical practitioner's juridical relationship with the claimant while exercising his/her profession; (vii) determining whether, irrespective of the event and the damages that have been established to have occurred together with the causal nexus linking them, the medical practitioner acted in accordance with what can be expected of a person practising as a medical practitioner or as a specialist in the medical profession. This subsection considers each of these features in turn.

89. There are instances when a medical practitioner is *ipso jure* exempted from civil liability. In those cases, a medical practitioner cannot typically be found to be liable under civil law by the domestic courts. By way of example, the Medicines Authority 'may temporarily authorise the distribution of an unauthorised medicinal product in response to the suspected or confirmed spread of pathogenic agents, toxins, chemical agents or nuclear radiation any of which could cause harm'.[455] Transposing EU law into domestic law,[456] the Medicines Act then provides that health professionals, including medical practitioners, '*are not subject to civil or administrative liability* for any consequences resulting … from the use of an unauthorised medicinal product, when such use is recommended or required by the [Medicines Authority] in response to the suspected or confirmed spread of pathogenic agents, toxins, chemical agents or nuclear radiation any of which could cause harm'.[457] A second example of exemption from liability involves a Good Samaritan law providing that, notwithstanding Articles 1031 to 1033 of the Civil Code regarding civil liability, 'any person who causes damages in the performance of a rescue or in the course of assisting another person whose life or personal safety is in clear danger, *shall not be liable* for any damage caused in the course of the rescue or of giving assistance to the person who he rescued or assisted or tried to rescue or assist, to that person's property or to third parties or third party property'.[458] The latter provision does not however apply to 'acts performed with malice or gross negligence',[459] and persons will consequently still be liable for those acts performed with malice or gross negligence. While the law at hand does not engage with contractual relationships between medical practitioners and their patients, the member of Parliament introducing the Bill in its Second Reading included, among the examples of people that this law is intended to cover, medical practitioners who are not on duty but who may be in position to render assistance to another person whose life or personal safety is in clear danger.[460]

90. Assuming that a medical practitioner is not *ipso jure* exempt from liability, the next stage to establish civil liability involves ascertaining whether liability is or should be stipulated in contract or in tort. The legal basis of civil liability of medical practitioners in Malta was traditionally grounded by the domestic courts in tort or quasi-tort.[461] In this respect, the Civil Code provides that every person 'shall be liable for the damage which occurs through his fault'[462] and a person 'shall be deemed to be in fault if, in his own acts, he does not use the prudence, diligence, and attention of a *bonus paterfamilias*'.[463] Furthermore, any person 'who, with or

455. Medicines Act, Ch. 458 of the Laws of Malta, Art. 19 (3)(b).
456. Directive 2004/27/EC of the European Parliament and of the Council of 31 March 2004 amending Directive 2001/83/EC on the Community Code relating to medicinal products for human use, OJ L 136, 30.4.2004, Art. 1 (4).
457. Medicines Act, Ch. 458 of the Laws of Malta, Art. 19 (3)(b). Emphasis added.
458. Civil Code, Ch. 16 of the Laws of Malta, Art. 1033A. Emphasis added.
459. *Ibid.*
460. House of Representatives Malta – Office of the Clerk, *Dibattiti tal-Kamra Tad-Deputati (Rapport Uffiċjali u Rivedut),* 13th Legislature: Sitting No. 137 (4 July 2018), Hon. Claudio Grech, 736.
461. *See, for instance*: *Victor Savona pro et. noe v. Dr Peter Asphar et.*, Court Of Appeal (Civil, Superior) – 02/04/1951 [Kollezzjoni ta' Decizjonijiet tal-Qrati Superjuri ta' Malta Vol. 35-A (1951) Pt. I, P. 55]; *Josephine Borg et. v. Dottor Anthony Fiorini*, Civil Court First Hall – 18/07/1994 [Kollezzjoni ta' Decizjonijiet tal-Qrati Superjuri ta' Malta Vol. 78 (1994) Pt. 3 P. 103]; *Zerafa Frankie et. v. Avramov Olga et.*, Court of Appeal (Civil, Superior) – 30/05/2008 [Ref: 1000/2002/1].
462. Civil Code, Ch. 16 of the Laws of Malta, Art. 1031.
463. *Ibid.*, Art. 1032 (1). Original emphasis.

without intent to injure, voluntarily or through negligence, imprudence, or want of attention, is guilty of any act or omission constituting a breach of the duty imposed by law, shall be liable for any damage resulting therefrom'.[464] The Court of Appeal however ruled that, despite rulings by the domestic courts in Malta that had historically examined the civil liability of medical practitioners through the lens of tort or quasi-tort, it was more logical to examine the juridical relationship between a patient and a medical practitioner in the context of contract, which applied equally to medical practitioners seeing patients in their own private practice as well as to medical practitioners seeing patients in their work within the public health service.[465] By this rationale, once a medical practitioner agrees to care for a patient, a contractual relationship is established that can open to civil liability in contract should there be a failure to fulfil contractual obligations.[466] In turn, the Civil Code states that where 'any person fails to discharge an obligation which he has contracted, he shall be liable in damages'.[467] Since that 2008 ruling of the Court of Appeal, the domestic courts in Malta have often engaged with the civil liability of medical practitioners in the context of contract,[468] and it is therefore incumbent to briefly outline some of the differences between civil liability in tort and civil liability in contract.

91. When a claim for liability is based on a contractual relationship, the application presupposes a contractual obligation upon which liability is established. Liability in tort is instead stipulated upon a fact that establishes the juridical cause for liability.[469] There is also a difference between the two-year period of prescription to file an application for damages in tort[470] and the five-year period of prescription to file an application for damages in contract.[471] Furthermore, the onus of proof differs between liability in tort, when it falls upon the claimant to establish that the medical practitioner is at fault, and liability in contract when, so long as the claimant establishes the existence of the contractual relationship and the causal nexus between the damages claimed and that contractual relationship, the onus of proof then is on the medical practitioner to establish that s/he is not liable by, for instance,

464. *Ibid.*, Art. 1033.
465. *Gauci Rose et. v. Felice Donald et.*, Court of Appeal (Civil, Superior) – 31/10/2008 [Ref: 1311/1999/1] 17.
466. *Ibid. See also*: *Grech Simon v. Humphreys Dominic*, Civil Court First Hall – 02/06/2017 [Ref: 2224/1998/1] 16.
467. Civil Code, Ch. 16 of the Laws of Malta, Art. 1125.
468. *See, for instance: Ellul Tessie et. v. Camilleri Dr Astrid*, Court of Appeal (Civil, Superior) – 28/05/2010 [Ref: 2653/1999/1] 21; *Busuttil Linda et. v. Muscat Dr Josie et.*, Court of Appeal – 27 June 2014 [Ref: 2429/1998/1] 23; *Abela Phyllis sive Pina et. v. Tabone Dr Mario*, Court of Appeal (Civil, Superior) – 25/06/2019 [Ref: 880/1998/2] 13–18; *Fenech Carmen v. Vella Dr Ivan et.*, Civil Court First Hall – 31/10/2019 [Ref: 1952/1997/1] 21; *Brincat Andrew et. v. Tabib Ewlieni Tal-Gvern et.*, Court of Appeal (Civil, Superior) – 27/10/2021 [Ref: 225/1989/2] 26–27.
469. *Mary Vassallo v. John Mizzi et.*, Civil Court First Hall – 09/04/1949 [Kollezzjoni ta' Decizjonijiet tal-Qrati Superjuri ta' Malta Vol. 33E (1949) Pt. 2, P. 379, 381].
470. Civil Code, Ch. 16 of the Laws of Malta, Art. 2153.
471. *Ibid.*, Art. 2156. *See also*: *Galea Grezzju et. v. Vella Paul Dentist Dottor et.*, Civil Court First Hall – 29/09/2016 [Ref: 92/2013]; Fenech *Carmen v. Vella Dr Ivan et.*, Civil Court First Hall – 31/10/2019 [Ref: 1952/1997/1] 20.

demonstrating that s/he provided appropriate care with the requisite degree of diligence.[472] Also, the computation of damages will largely include moral or psychological harm within limits set in law when liability is grounded in tort,[473] but the Court of Appeal has held that those limits do not apply when liability is grounded in contract, meaning that the possibility of awarding damages for moral or psychological harm is more extensive when liability is grounded in contract than in tort.[474]

92. That being said, while the Court of Appeal has continued commenting that it has been accepted that the relationship between patients and medical practitioners is contractual in nature,[475] some members of the judiciary note in their rulings that, given that the Civil Code provides no specific norms for the medical profession, it is the general principles of liability under Articles 1031 to 1033 of the Civil Code that should apply in the context of the civil liability of medical practitioners.[476] This is significant, for instance, in the context of emergency admissions before a first consultation is possible, but it may furthermore be the case that, even if there is a contractual relationship, it will not negate other juridical relationships. For example, a patient may have a direct contractual relationship with a private hospital or clinic, but civil liability may still be established extra-contractually in tort by the patient against medical practitioners as employees of the hospital if there is no direct contractual relationship between the patient and those medical practitioners.[477] It consequently is prudent, in the first instance, to determine whether civil liability is being established on the basis of tort or quasi-tort or, otherwise, on the basis of contract.

93. Regardless of its legal basis, in cases considering the possible civil liability of medical practitioners, 'the Court often also requires the assistance of a Court appointed expert or referee as he is officially known'.[478] For instance, in a case regarding the claimed liability of a neurosurgeon, a third-party neurosurgeon may be appointed as a referee to provide proof of a technical nature. In this regard, the Code of Organization and Civil Procedure provides that the 'proof by means of a referee or referees is ordered on the demand of the parties or one of them, or by the

472. *Maggur Briffa Alfred et. v. The Golden Shepherd Group Limited noe et.*, Civil Court First Hall – 31/10/2013 [Ref: 2651/2000/1] 26; *Gauci Vincent et. v. Tabib Ewlieni tal-Gvern et.*, Court of Appeal (Civil, Superior) – 28/06/2019 [Ref: 774/2002/1] 15–16.
473. Civil Code, Ch. 16 of the Laws of Malta, Art. 1045.
474. *Brincat Andrew et. v. Tabib Ewlieni tal-Gvern*, Court of Appeal (Civil, Superior) – 27/10/2021 [Ref: 225/1989/2] 36–37.
475. *Gauci Vincent et. v. Tabib Ewlieni tal-Gvern et.*, Court of Appeal (Civil, Superior) – 28/06/2019 [Ref: 774/2002/1] 15.
476. *See, for instance*: *Cachia John et. v. Busuttil Tabib Dr Tancred et. noe*, Civil Court First Hall – 27/11/2012 [Ref: 983/1987/1] 16; *Ellul Etienne v. Tabib Principali tas-Sahha et.*, Civil Court First Hall – 14/06/2019 [Ref: 31/2016] 23.
477. *Jones Anthony sive Tony v. Pullicino Francis Dr noe*, Civil Court First Hall – 27/06/2008 [Ref: 1287/1991/1] 7; *Maggur Briffa Alfred et. v. The Golden Shepherd Group Limited noe et.*, Civil Court First Hall – 31/10/2013 [Ref: 2651/2000/1] 25–26.
478. George Gregory Buttigieg, *Optimising Maltese obstetric medico-legal dynamics: Volume I* 85 (Lambert Academic Publishing 2020).

court of its own motion'.[479] While the 'court is not bound to adopt the report of the referees against its own conviction',[480] the report of the referee/s can be relied on *tale quale* by the court unless it finds grave and serious reasons to substitute its judgment with that of the court-appointed referees,[481] for instance, if the court instructs the court-appointed referee to examine a party but that referee either altogether fails to him/herself examine a party or otherwise delegates that examination without authorisation from the court to another practitioner.[482] It then is important for the parties to cross-examine referees,[483] and it is also 'lawful for the court, on the demand of any of the parties, to proceed to the appointment of additional referees'.[484] This is because it is by way of these methods embedded in law that parties can engage with the proof provided by the referees.[485] Either way, while the courts can weigh the proof presented by the referees and can also ostensibly not adopt the report of the referees if its reasons and conclusions are considered to be unreasonable by the presiding member/s of the judiciary, the referees do not deliver the final judgment regarding civil liability. This is instead considered by the court in the remaining four stages to establish liability.

94. Thus, the next stage involves ascertaining facts in order to, for instance, determine that an event occurred that was not meant to occur or, otherwise, that an event did not take place that was meant to have taken place. In the context of contract, this stage is not *stricto jure* necessary once there is evidence of the existence of a contractual relationship.[486] However, the courts typically establish the facts in order to determine civil liability if only to then establish the causal link between that (contractual) relationship and the damages. Irrespective of tort or contract, the onus of proof at this stage lies on the claimant,[487] and the Code of Organization and Civil Procedure dictates that, saving 'any other provision of the law, the burden of proving a fact shall, in all cases, rest on the party alleging it'.[488] Examples drawn from cases arising in the Maltese courts of instances when the occurrence of a particular event was in question include the alleged perforation of an organ during the course of an operation,[489] failing to provide information necessary in order for the patient

479. Code of Organization and Civil Procedure, Ch. 12 of the Laws of Malta, Art. 644.
480. *Ibid.*, Art. 681.
481. *Agius Mark noe v. Briffa Joseph*, Civil Court First Hall – 28/06/2002 [Ref: 1221/1997/1] 5.
482. *See, for instance*: *Bartolo Nathalie v. Pullicino Orlando Onor. Dr Jeffrey et.*, Civil Court First Hall – 27/01/2022 [Ref: 302/2011] 11. *See also*, albeit in the context of criminal procedure: *Il-Pulizija v. Grasso Claude*, Court of Criminal Appeal (Inferior) – 28/01/2022 [Ref: 373/2017/1] 3–5.
483. Code of Organization and Civil Procedure, Ch. 12 of the Laws of Malta, Art. 680.
484. *Ibid.*, Art. 678.
485. *Agius Joanna et. v. Cutajar Carmel sive Lino*, Court of Appeal (Civil, Superior) – 30/05/2003 [Ref: 1374/1993/1] 14.
486. *D'Agostino Christian et. noe v. It-Tabib Ewlieni tal-Gvern*, Civil Court First Hall – 29/01/2014 [Ref: 1007/2006] 6.
487. *Mercieca Lawrence et. v. Direttur Generali tad-Dipartiment tas-Sahha et.*, Civil Court First Hall – 28/02/2019 [Ref: 1294/2003] 21.
488. Code of Organization and Civil Procedure, Ch. 12 of the Laws of Malta, Art. 562.
489. *Ellul Tessie et. v. Camilleri Dr Astrid*, Civil Court First Hall – 29/04/2008; Court of Appeal (Civil, Superior) – 28/05/2010 [Ref: 2653/1999/1].

to furnish a lawful informed consent to treatment,[490] medical practitioners in hospital failing to take into account the indication by a referring general practitioner that a patient may be allergic to penicillin,[491] or otherwise failing to provide timely post-operative care.[492] As such, the event in question is not the same as the damage suffered. For instance, in a case that resulted in the partial amputation and ensuing damage to a person's finger, while the damage was largely not in question, it was less clear at what stage an event involving medical practitioner/s did not take place that could have avoided the damage to the finger. In that case, it was concluded that one medical practitioner in particular should have referred the patient for admission to hospital and that this failure by that medical practitioner to keep the patient under observation contributed towards the finger's deterioration and damage.[493] Consequently, ascertaining facts can be significant to a claim of civil liability because, should the claimant fail to prove the occurrence of the event in question, it may then affect the evidence of a causal link between the contractual or other relationship and the actual damages at hand.

95. Establishing a causal nexus with the claimed damage/s is therefore the next stage for the purpose of establishing civil liability. The onus of proving this causal nexus rests with the claimant. If it is, for instance, claimed that a medical practitioner failed by way of *omission*, the claimant would have to demonstrate, in addition to the omission, that the damages are a likely consequence of that omission. The court would then have to be in a position of moral certainty, determined on the balance of probabilities[494] that the medical practitioner is liable in civil law due to that omission. Should the claimant fail to demonstrate the causal nexus between the damage/s and the omission, it is likely that the court will not rule in favour of the claimant. For instance, in a case where the referee reported that the patient was not properly informed about the therapeutic part of an otherwise diagnostic procedure, the court did not have the moral certainty that this omission of information eventuated the damage resulting from the therapeutic intervention. The court instead had the moral certainty that it was not demonstrated that the medical practitioner was liable even though it acknowledged that the medical practitioner should have provided the pertinent information and omitted to do so.[495] The claimant may otherwise demonstrate that the damage was caused due to the *actions* of the medical practitioner. This is a question of fact that often relies on the evidence provided by the referee/s. If it cannot be demonstrated, then the causal nexus would not have

490. *Fenech Carmen v. Vella Dr Ivan et.*, Civil Court First Hall – 31/10/2019 [Ref: 1952/1997/1].

491. *Cassar Emanuel v. Tabib Principal tal-Gvern*, Civil Court First Hall – 01/03/2022 [Ref: 1032/2017].

492. *Victor Savona pro et. noe v. Dr Peter Asphar et.*, Court Of Appeal (Civil, Superior) – 02/04/1951 [Kollezzjoni ta' Decizjonijiet tal-Qrati Superjuri ta' Malta Vol. 35-A (1951) Pt I, P 55].

493. *Pace Alfrida v. Tabib Ewlieni tal-Gvern et.*, Civil Court First Hall – 07/02/2003 [Ref: 894/1993/1] 10.

494. *Paul Vassallo et. v. Carmelo Pace*, Court of Appeal (Civil, Superior) – 05/03/1986 [Kollezzjoni ta' Decizjonijiet tal-Qrati Superjuri ta' Malta Vol. 70 (1986) Pt 2, P 143, 149].

495. *Rossi Sue v. Muscat Joseph D. sive Josie Dr*, Civil Court First Hall – 25/06/2008 [Ref: 1492/1994/1] 30–32.

been determined, and the medical practitioner's liability would consequently probably not have been established. Thus, for instance, in a case regarding damage to a woman's eye after an ophthalmic procedure, in part given that the referee reported that the procedure could not be considered to be a direct cause of the complication to the woman's eye even though it arose a short time after that procedure, the claim of civil liability was not established.[496] As such, in order for civil liability to ensue, the causal nexus linking the medical practitioner's actions or omissions with the damages must be established even if there was a demonstrable instance of medical malpractice, negligence or non-performance of obligations. Thus, for example, in a case where a medical practitioner issued certificates that a minor was not medically fit to attend school without however necessarily informing her parents, the Court of Appeal ruled that, while that conduct was negligent, it was not the cause of the damages that were occasioned to the minor consequent to the criminal behaviour of another person[497] whose actions were not dependent on the medical certificates or foreseeable by the medical practitioner, which meant that the causal nexus could not be established for the medical practitioner's civil liability to ensue.[498] That being said, as explained by Madam Justice Schembri Orland in the First Hall of the Civil Court, the exception to the norm that the claimant must demonstrate the causal nexus linking the act or omission with the damages occurs in terms of res ipsa loquitur when the act or omission itself is a manifestation of culpability.[499] In that case, the onus of proof would ostensibly fall on the medical practitioners to exonerate themselves. Though acknowledged by the Maltese courts,[500] its use is however not widespread in the context of the civil liability of medical practitioners in Malta, and the onus typically rests on the claimant to demonstrate the causal nexus linking the act or omission of the medical practitioner with the damages.

96. Given this requirement to establish the causal nexus, it is also likely, though it is not mandatory for the purpose of liability in civil law, that the claimant will indicate damages and, indeed, the onus of proof ostensibly lies on the claimant to identify damages. Those damages are not the same as the event that led to them. For instance, in a case where the claimant contended that there was evidence that her colon was perforated during the course of a procedure, the damage would have ensued, at least had the causal nexus been established, when the colostomy could not be reversed, leading to a state of permanent colostomy rather than the (unproven) perforation of the colon itself.[501] Also, in a case where a person underwent an operation on the basis of a mistaken diagnosis from which liability ensued,

496. *Fenech Carmen v. Vella Dr Ivan et.*, Civil Court First Hall – 31/10/2019 [Ref: 1952/1997/1] 31–35.
497. *Il-Pulizija v. Taylor Anthony*, Court of Criminal Appeal (Inferior) – 24/09/2001 [Ref: 65/2001/1].
498. *Xuereb Maria Elvira noe v. Taylor Anthony et.*, Court of Appeal (Civil, Superior) – 25/10/2013 [Ref: 329/2000/1] 21.
499. *Maggur Briffa Alfred et. v. The Golden Shepherd Group Limited noe et.*, Civil Court First Hall – 31/10/2013 [Ref: 2651/2000/1] 27.
500. *Alfred Shead v. Anthony Degiorgio et.*, Civil Court First Hall – 05/11/1984 [Kollezzjoni ta' Deciżjonijiet tal-Qrati Superjuri ta' Malta Vol. 68 (1984) Pt 3, P 140, 145].
501. *Ellul Tessie et. v. Camilleri Dr Astrid*, Civil Court First Hall – 29/04/2008; Court of Appeal (Civil, Superior) – 28/05/2010 [Ref: 2653/1999/1].

the damage/s extended past the unnecessary operation to include, for instance, post-traumatic stress disorder and chronic anxiety disorder.[502] This is significant when, so long as the medical practitioner is held liable under civil law, the damages are liquidated for the purpose of compensation. For instance, in the case of failure to fulfil contractual obligations, 'the damages due to the creditor are, generally, in respect of *the loss which he has sustained*, and the *profit of which he has been deprived*'.[503] Yet, recoverable damages are *inter alia* limited to those that 'are the *immediate and direct consequence* of the non-performance'.[504] Consequently, unless otherwise indicated, 'contractual damages may [traditionally] only be awarded if there is proved material loss',[505] and the claimant would, therefore, in addition to demonstrating the non-performance of the contractual obligation, also typically identify what the damages are so as to, in turn, demonstrate how they were foreseeable and are a consequence of non-performance. Furthermore, the liquidation of damages under tort law can cover 'the actual loss which the act shall have directly caused to the injured party, in the expenses which the latter may have been compelled to incur in consequence of the damage'[506] and the 'moral harm and, or psychological harm caused to the claimant'[507] in the case of damages arising from certain criminal offences. In the context of *lucrum cessans*, where the damages are a consequence of the culpable act or omission of the medical practitioner, the liquidation of damages can cover 'the loss of actual wages or other earnings, and in the loss of future earnings arising from any permanent incapacity, total or partial, which the act may have caused'.[508] The court will in turn have 'regard to the circumstances of the case, and, particularly, to the nature and degree of incapacity caused, and to the condition of the injured party',[509] which in practice means that the damages arising consequent to the act or omission of the medical practitioner are summed up, at least for the purpose of *lucrum cessans*, in a percentage disability that, after taking into account the claimant's working life expectancy and his/her income, leads to the liquidation of damages on the basis of a multiplier system that is well-grounded in the rulings of the domestic courts regarding civil liability.[510] In this regard, if the claimant had by 'imprudence, negligence or want of attention contributed or given occasion to the damage',[511] the court may, in its discretion, determine how, if at all, this would reflect on the liquidated amount of damages payable to the claimant inasmuch as a claimant should take reasonable measures to mitigate

502. *Jones Anthony sive Tony v. Pullicino Francis Dr noe*, Civil Court First Hall – 27/06/2008, 06/07/2018 [Ref: 1287/1991/1].
503. Civil Code, Ch. 16 of the Laws of Malta, Art. 1135. Emphasis added.
504. *Ibid.*, Art. 1137. Emphasis added.
505. Alessandro Lia, *Liability for lack of information* in *Contemporary issues in medical ethics & law: Conference proceedings 2012 – 2015* 175, 178 (Kevin Aquilina, Pierre Mallia & Bridget Ellul eds, Progress Press 2017).
506. Civil Code, Ch. 16 of the Laws of Malta, Art. 1045 (1).
507. *Ibid.*
508. *Ibid.*
509. *Ibid.*, Art. 1045 (2).
510. *Michael Butler v. Peter Christopher Heard*, Court of Appeal (Civil, Superior) – 22/12/1967 [Kollezzjoni ta' Decizjonijiet tal-Qrati Superjuri ta' Malta Vol. 51B (1967) Pt 1, Section 1, P 488].
511. Civil Code, Ch. 16 of the Laws of Malta, Art. 1051.

the loss and damages suffered. Those damages are then related to but separate from the event that eventuated liability if only since it is the damages that establish the percentage of disability or harm.

97. Given that Maltese law traditionally grounds damages in civil liability in patrimonial damages, barring the exception of moral or psychological harm arising from certain criminal offences, claimants without patrimonial damages may have little compensatory remedies in civil law even if liability is established. That being said, the courts have addressed this concern by way of two approaches depending upon whether liability is established in tort or otherwise in contract. As to the former liability, some rulings have interpreted the phrases 'any damage resulting therefrom' in Article 1033 of the Civil Code regarding culpable negligence and 'actual loss' in its Article 1045 regarding the measure of damages to include non-patrimonial damages that can be awarded by the courts *arbitrio boni viri*. Though it is not yet well-grounded in the jurisprudence of the courts and was even rejected by the Court of Appeal that instead ruled on damages using the traditional methods vested in Article 1045 of the Civil Code,[512] this developing jurisprudence regarding non-patrimonial damages stems from the premise that an individual whose psycho-physical integrity, as safeguarded under the Constitution of Malta and human rights instruments, was impinged upon should not be left without any compensatory remedy for those non-patrimonial damages separate from and possibly in addition to any patrimonial damages,[513] as well as any moral and psychological damages in the case of damages arising from certain criminal offences as indicated in Article 1045 of the Civil Code. By way of example, this approach was used in a case involving the recorded admission, before legal proceedings were undertaken, that a gauze was inadvertently left inside a woman during an episiotomy.[514] However, the courts in Malta adopted a related but different approach to non-patrimonial damages in respect of liability in contract. The Constitutional Court has thus noted that the premises arising from Article 1045 of the Civil Code in relation to moral and/or psychological damages are restricted to tort or quasi-tort and do not therefore affect damages related to other obligations.[515] This would then mean that compensatory remedies can be awarded for non-patrimonial damages arising from, for instance, one's failure to fulfil contractual obligations. Yet, while the ordinary civil law should, where possible, be interpreted in conformity with the Constitution and human rights instruments, it does not entail that moral and non-pecuniary damages arise in every instance of liability, which means that each situation may have to be individually assessed to establish whether or not moral damages actually do arise. Thus, for example, in a case regarding the loss of a child due to the failings of a hospital within the public healthcare system, the Court of Appeal held that moral

512. *Busuttil Linda et. v. Muscat Dr Josie et.*, Court of Appeal (Civil, Superior) – 27/06/2014 [Ref: 2429/1998/1] 32.

513. *Busuttil Linda et. v. Muscat Dr Josie et.*, Civil Court First Hall – 30/11/2010 [Ref: 2429/1998/1] 16–17; *Cassar Lucianne v. Dragonara Casino Limited*, Civil Court First Hall – 19/06/2012 [Ref: 753/2004] 12–16;

514. *Stanicic Dorianne et. v. Supretendent Sptar Mater Dei et.*, Civil Court First Hall – 22/06/2020 [Ref: 221/2014] 27–28.

515. *Agius Jane v. L-Avukat Generali et.*, Constitutional Court – 14/12/2015 [Ref: 33/2014/1] 14.

damages could be liquidated and awarded *arbitrio boni viri* consequent to the contractual relationship that was established once accepted at that hospital since the loss of a child, though not equivalent to patrimonial damages, nevertheless has a devastating effect on the life of the claimant parents.[516] As such, the courts' rulings evince that even damages that are not patrimonial in nature can result in compensatory remedies, especially when the claim is grounded in contract and there is evidence of moral damages.

98. In addition to a causal nexus linking damages to medical practitioners' actions or omissions within the confines of a juridical relationship in the conduct of their profession with the claimants, in order to establish the civil liability of medical practitioners, it must moreover, unless otherwise indicated, be established that they did 'not use the prudence, diligence, and attention of a *bonus paterfamilias*',[517] which is also, unless otherwise stipulated, 'the degree of diligence to be exercised in the performance of an obligation'[518] in contract. In that case, provided that the other features of liability outlined in this subsection of the monograph have been demonstrated, it would mean that the damage occurred through the medical practitioner's fault in the context of tortuous liability or, in the context of contractual liability, by way of the medical practitioner's failure to fulfil the contractual obligation to render the service that should be provided by medical practitioners who trained and presented themselves to practice that particular profession. Given that the law does not substantiate what the degree of diligence set in law entails for the purpose of medical practitioners, this has been substantiated by the domestic courts in Malta. The Court of Appeal has, for instance, ruled that domestic courts determining the civil liability of medical practitioners can expect those practitioners to have conformed with accepted standard medical practice while keeping abreast with the latest developments in their field.[519] This is an objective test to which, as noted by the Court of Appeal, the court cannot substitute its judgment with that of medical practice.[520] In this respect, adapting a ruling by the Supreme Court of the Republic of Ireland that had already been used by the courts in Malta,[521] the Court of Appeal declared it as established in Malta that,[522] in order for a medical practitioner to be found liable in civil law by way of negligence, s/he must be 'proved to be guilty of such failure as no medical practitioner of equal specialist or general status and skill would be guilty of if acting with ordinary care … [and] the course he did take was the one which no medical practitioner of like specialization and skill would have followed had he been taking the ordinary care required from a person of his

516. *Brincat Andrew et. v. Tabib Ewlieni tal-Gvern*, Court of Appeal (Civil, Superior) – 27/10/2021 [Ref: 225/1989/2] 37.
517. Civil Code, Ch. 16 of the Laws of Malta, Art. 1032 (1). Original emphasis.
518. *Ibid.*, Art. 1132 (1).
519. *Gauci Rose et. v. Felice Donald et.*, Court of Appeal (Civil, Superior) – 31/10/2008 [Ref: 1311/1999/1] 19.
520. *Ibid.*, 19–20.
521. *Ibid.*, 22–23; *Gambina Albert et. noe v. The Golden Shepherd Group Ltd*, Civil Court First Hall – 28/10/2013 [Ref: 2622/1999/1] 5; *Mercieca Lawrence et. v. Direttur Generali tad-Dipartiment tas-Sahha et.*, Civil Court First Hall – 28/02/2019 [Ref: 1294/2003] 25.
522. *Abela Phyllis sive Pina et. v. Tabone Dr* Mario, Court of Appeal (Civil, Superior) – 25/06/2019 [Ref: 880/1998/2] 15.

qualification'.[523] This is normally established based on the reports of referees and expert witnesses, which extend past differences of opinion alone, in order to establish that the medical practitioner deviated from approved medical practice. Thus, for instance, in a case where a child suffered injuries during the process leading to her birth, while the referee noted that a part obsolete method was used, he concluded that the specialist in that case 'reacted in the way most obstetricians would have',[524] which led the court to endorse that referee's conclusion that there was no evidence that medical malpractice led to the causation of the child's injury. Yet, in a case where a man suffered a permanent disability following neurosurgery, the referee's conclusion that the neurosurgeon had failed to do what is expected from him in the exercise of his profession satisfied the court that the claimants proved that the neurosurgeon failed in the exercise of his profession to use the prudence, diligence, and attention of a *bonus paterfamilias*, while also failing to keep abreast with developments in medicine and consequently not conforming with accepted standard practice.[525] The Court of Appeal furthermore ruled in a separate case regarding damages arising consequent to an angioplasty that civil liability had been established after the claimant demonstrated the causal nexus linking the damages to the actions of the respondent inasmuch as the latter respondent specialist had not demonstrated, as was incumbent on him to do, that the procedure was performed in accordance with the accepted practices of medical science.[526] However, the degree of diligence observed by medical practitioners might not exonerate them from civil liability if those medical practitioners agree to a higher degree of diligence than the minimum set in law and/or if the medical practitioners agree to render a particular result or outcome rather than delivering a medical service alone. For instance, in a case involving aesthetic surgery, while the court ruled that the surgeon had acted negligently and not in accordance with appropriate medical standards, it also ruled that the respondent surgeon had accepted that the professional standard of the surgery was framed by his guarantee regarding its outcome and, since this outcome was not achieved, that guarantee grounded that surgeon's civil liability even before engaging with the standards underpinning the surgeon's work.[527]

99. Aside from instances when a result is guaranteed, once it is established that there exists a causal nexus between the damages and the actions or omissions of the medical practitioner in the exercise of his/her profession who did not perform with the requisite degree of diligence, it is likely that, unless otherwise indicated at law, the medical practitioner's civil liability will have been established. Statutory provisions may nevertheless exonerate the medical practitioner from liability. For instance, in the context of contract, liability for damages does not ensue if the debtor, including a medical practitioner, 'was prevented from giving or doing the

523. *Dunne v. National Maternity Hospital* [1989] IR 91.

524. *Gambina Albert et. noe v. The Golden Shepherd Group Ltd*, Civil Court First Hall – 28/10/2013 [Ref: 2622/1999/1] 10.

525. *Mercieca Lawrence et. v. Direttur Generali tad-Dipartiment tas-Sahha et.*, Civil Court First Hall – 28/02/2019 [Ref: 1294/2003] 23.

526. *Gauci Vincent et. v. Tabib Ewlieni tal-Gvern et.*, Court of Appeal (Civil, Superior) – 28/06/2019 [Ref: 774/2002/1] 27.

527. *Falzon Venere v. Stella Marcello*, Civil Court First Hall – 09/07/2015 [Ref: 1201/2010] 6.

thing he undertook to give or to do, or if he did the thing he was forbidden to do, in consequence of an irresistible force or a fortuitous event'[528] and liability will also not ensue if there is a delay or non-performance of an obligation 'due to an extraneous cause not imputable to'[529] that debtor. Moreover, in the context of tort, any 'damage which is produced by a fortuitous event, or in consequence of an irresistible force, shall, in the absence of an express provision of the law to the contrary, be borne by the party on whose person or property such damage occurs'.[530] Additionally, while this subsection of the monograph engaged with instances when medical practitioners ostensibly possess the necessary skill to undertake a given work or service, the Civil Code also stipulates that any person 'who without the necessary skill undertakes any work or service shall be liable for any damage which, through his unskilfulness, he may cause to others',[531] which can in turn also engage with instances when a medical practitioner undertakes work or services that require the skills of a given specialisation that s/he does not possess. These sorts of provisions are likely to be considered by the courts when engaging with the causal nexus linking an event to the damages in the context of an application grounded in civil liability. Yet, the liability or otherwise of the medical practitioner in the diagnosis, care and treatment of a patient does not exclude the possibility of vicarious liability, which is considered next.

II. Vicarious Liability

100. It is tenable in Maltese law that liability is not vested in, or at least not exclusively vested in, the person/s who performed the treatment. This subsection engages with, in turn, instances when a medical practitioner delegates work to another party after establishing a contractual relationship with a patient, instances involving the liability in tort of the medical practitioner's employer or the liability in tort of the hospital where the treatment was performed, and instances involving the contractual liability of the hospital where the treatment was performed.

101. A medical practitioner can delegate work to another person within the confines of the law. In the context of a contractual relationship with the patients, the delegating medical practitioners would remain contractually bound to their patients. In that respect, should the medical practitioners not fulfil their contractual obligations, they could still be liable for any damages together with the person who conducted the procedure as a consequence of which damages ensue. Thus, for instance, in a case where a medical practitioner accepted a person as his patient for treatment after a first consultation but was not then present on the day of the scheduled treatment, that medical practitioner was held liable *in solidum* with the individual (who

528. Civil Code, Ch. 16 of the Laws of Malta, Art. 1134.
529. *Ibid.*, Art. 1133.
530. *Ibid.*, Art. 1029.
531. *Ibid.*, Art. 1038.

was not a medical practitioner) that provided the treatment with the patient's consent.[532] This is because the contractual relationship grounds responsibilities and obligations on the medical practitioner that cannot be discarded only because that service is performed by another person. Furthermore, the court noted in the case at hand that, had the medical practitioner not been in a position to perform the treatment in person at the scheduled time, he should have ensured that it was conducted by a person with the equivalent skill that he possessed as a medical practitioner.[533] The Ethics of the Medical Profession Regulations, though not alluded to by the court in this instance, indeed stipulate that no medical practitioner 'shall enable an unqualified person to exercise his profession, attend in any manner to any matter requiring professional knowledge and skill, issue or procure the issue of any professional document or otherwise act as if he were duly qualified or registered'.[534] The exceptions to the latter regulation are restricted to instances when a medical practitioner 'is supervising over any person so employed and retains personal responsibility for the professional services rendered in the case of: (a) the training of medical, dental or any bona fide students, or (b) the legitimate employment of nurses, midwives, physiotherapists and other persons trained to perform specialised functions to different persons'.[535] Despite this indication that medical practitioners retain personal responsibility for the professional services rendered in the legitimate employment of, for instance, other healthcare professionals, in the context of liability, the courts in Malta have not agreed that it would suffice, for the purpose of exonerating healthcare professionals from liability, to say that they were following the prescriptions of medical practitioners.[536] This is because those healthcare professionals are bound by their own obligations towards the patient, including not harming the patient and treating that patient with the professionalism expected from the independent healthcare professions distinct from the medical profession.

102. For the purpose of liability, in addition to the fulfilment of contractual obligations, it then is opportune to note that the Civil Code also stipulates that where 'a person for any work or service whatsoever employs another person who is incompetent, or whom he has not reasonable grounds to consider competent, he shall be liable for any damage which such other person may, through incompetence in the performance of such work or service, cause to others'.[537] While the latter provision does not exclude the possibility of a claim for damages being made in regard to the employee, this provision engages with the liability in tort of the employer. It can thus encapsulate instances when a medical practitioner is an employer, as well as instances when a private hospital is the employer or even instances when a medical practitioner is employed in the public health service. In the latter case, given that

532. *Busuttil Linda et. v. Muscat Dr Josie et.*, Court of Appeal (Civil, Superior) – 27/06/2014 [Ref: 2429/1998/1] 29.

533. *Busuttil Linda et. v. Muscat Dr Josie et.*, Civil Court First Hall – 30/11/2010 [Ref: 2429/1998/1] 12–13.

534. S.L. 464.17, Ethics of the Medical Profession Regulations, r. 18 (1).

535. *Ibid.*, r. 18 (2). *See also* Part III Ch. 2 §2 below.

536. *Maggur Briffa Alfred et. v. The Golden Shepherd Group Limited noe et.*, Civil Court First Hall – 31/10/2013 [Ref: 2651/2000/1] 37–38. *See also* Part III Ch. 2 §2 below.

537. Civil Code, Ch. 16 of the Laws of Malta, Art. 1037.

the Health Act stipulates that it is part of the mission of the Department for Healthcare Services 'to ensure the effective and efficient operation and delivery of healthcare services',[538] it has been noted by the courts that the Director General of that Department would be the legitimate respondent in the context of Article 1037 of the Civil Code inasmuch as it is that Director General who is responsible for employing medical practitioners in the national health service.[539] As such, the claimant may, for instance, have a contractual relationship with the treating medical practitioner in his capacity as an employee of the latter service, but s/he can also stipulate a claim against the Director General of the Department for Healthcare Services on the basis of Article 1037 albeit that some judges opine that the Chief Medical Officer to Government is the legitimate respondent.[540] In order for liability to ensue as a consequence of this provision, as noted by the courts, there must be four elements:[541] (i) the employer-employee relationship; (ii) *culpa in eligendo* inasmuch as a person is employed who is incompetent or the employer did not have reasonable grounds to consider that person to be competent; (iii) the act of the employee causing damages to the claimant; and (iv) the causal nexus linking those damages to the employee's incompetence.

103. The broader provisions of the Civil Code regarding liability in tort could also be applicable to the employers without being restricted to Article 1037 of that Code alone.[542] As such, even where there is no contractual relationship between the employer/s of medical practitioner/s and the patients, those patients could, in principle, lawfully seek compensation for damages from both the employee medical practitioner/s as well as their employers. The latter parties have indeed, in particular, been addressed as the lawful respondents in cases when fault is not attributable to any one healthcare professional but is instead attributable to the failings of the operational workings of the healthcare system or hospital as a whole. In this respect, the courts have rejected the claim made by some respondents that the employer would only be liable in the context of *culpa in eligendo* under Article 1037 of the Civil Code if a person is employed who is incompetent or if the employer did not have reasonable grounds to consider that person to be competent for the work at hand. For instance, in a case where a pair of surgeon's gloves were found tightly wrapped like a tourniquet under the bandages around a patient's foot two days after an operation, it was immaterial which member of staff was responsible for the malpractice at hand, which was unclear in this case, given that it was held that there existed an extra-contractual relationship between the claimant patient (or her heirs) and the respondent employer from which arose the fault in tort of that respondent in

538. Health Act, Ch. 528 of the Laws of Malta, Art. 6 (1).
539. *Mercieca Lawrence et. v. Direttur Generali tad-Dipartiment tas-Sahha et.*, Civil Court First Hall – 28/02/2019 [Ref: 1294/2003] 11.
540. *Stanicic Dorianne et. v. Supretendent Sptar Mater Dei et.*, Civil Court First Hall – 22/06/2020 [Ref: 221/2014] 26.
541. *Debono Nicholas sive Lino v. Kummissarju tal-Pulizija et.*, Civil Court First Hall – 28/01/2002 [Ref: 483/2000/1] 9.
542. *Spiteri Michelina et. v. It-Tabib Principal tal-Gvern et.*, Civil Court First Hall – 19/06/2003 [Ref: 2352/1997/1] 4–5; *Brincat Andrew et. v. Tabib Ewlieni tal-Gvern et.*, Civil Court First Hall – 12/04/2016 [Ref: 225/1989/1] 24–35.

view of the failings of the system underpinning the work of the hospital where the operation was conducted.[543] In a separate case involving damages arising consequent to a fall from a bed at a mental health licensed facility, while liability in tort was not explicitly mentioned in the conflicting version of events, the court noted that the patient-to-healthcare employee ratio in that case was not the one prescribed for the situation in which the patient was in, and the beds were not sufficiently secure for individuals in the situation of the patient, which led the court to rule that the damages arose as a consequence of these administrative failings for which the Director General of the Department for Health Care Services should respond in compensatory damages.[544] As such, Article 1037 of the Civil Code, regarding *culpa in eligendo*, does not operate to the exclusion of any other liability in tort against the employers of the healthcare professionals that rendered the service as a consequence of which damages arose.

104. That being said, the courts have increasingly grounded the nature of the relationship between patient and hospital in contract. The contractual relationship is ostensibly established once the hospital accepts to provide the (healthcare) service to the individual patient.[545] That relationship in contract has been engaged with by the courts both in the context of private hospitals as well as public hospitals. It would therefore mean that patients have a contractual relationship with the individual medical practitioner/s and a related but separate contractual relationship with the hospital or clinic within which the treatment is provided. Liability would then ensue depending upon whether it was the medical practitioner/s and/or the hospital that violated contractual obligations. For instance, in the context of a private hospital, while the duties incumbent on the licensee of that hospital are to an extent embedded in law,[546] the courts in Malta have also remarked that a hospital has an express or tacit contractual obligation to provide a safe environment for patients including policies to safeguard patients' well-being and, if damages arise as a consequence of a failure to fulfil that obligation, it would be the hospital that should be held liable in contract rather than, or in addition to, any individual healthcare professional.[547] In the context of a hospital within the public health service, while it is a function of the Department for Healthcare Services 'to ensure quality of services

543. *Sammut Emanuel et. v. Chief Government Medical Officer*, Civil Court First Hall – 12/12/2002 [Ref: 2804/1996/1] 27–29; *Sammut Emanuel et. v. Chief Government Medical Officer*, Court of Appeal (Civil, Superior) – 12/10/2006 [Ref: 2804/1996/1] 41–42.

544. *Borg Reuben et. pro et. noe v. Segretarju Permanenti fil-Ministeru tas-Sahha*, Civil Court First Hall – 04/12/2019 [Ref: 534/2017] 28–31.

545. *D'Agostino Christian et. noe v. It-Tabib Ewlieni tal-Gvern*, Civil Court First Hall – 29/01/2014 [Ref: 1007/2006] 6; *Brincat Andrew et. v. Tabib Ewlieni Tal-Gvern et.*, Court of Appeal (Civil, Superior) – 27/10/2021 [Ref: 225/1989/2] 26–27.

546. *See, for instance*: S.L. 458.23, Licensing of Private Medical Clinics Regulations. *See also* Part III Ch. 3 §1 below.

547. *Maggur Briffa Alfred et. v. The Golden Shepherd Group Limited noe et.*, Civil Court First Hall – 31/10/2013 [Ref: 2651/2000/1] 38–39. *See also*: *Gauci Vincent et. v. Tabib Ewlieni tal-Gvern et.*, Civil Court First Hall – 23/10/2013 [Ref: 774/2002] 17; *Gauci Vincent et. v. Tabib Ewlieni tal-Gvern et.*, Court of Appeal (Civil, Superior) – 28/06/2019 [Ref: 774/2002/1] 28.

delivered through the public health system',[548] the courts have opined that the hospital is contractually obliged to *inter alia* provide facilities and conditions that are reasonably thought to safeguard patients against harm.[549] Thus, when it was, for instance, demonstrated by claimants that they contracted an infection that was not dealt with by a hospital by using appropriate precautions and treating the patient in a timely manner, the court ruled that there was a failure to fulfil contractual obligations for which the Chief Government Medical Officer[550] (as then known) could be held liable.[551] It should furthermore be noted that contractual agreements are stipulated in law for the purpose of particular services, such as the contractual relations between residents and residential care homes.[552]

III. Criminal Liability

105. The Criminal Code is the instrument in Malta that consolidated the penal laws and the laws of criminal procedure. The professional liability of medical practitioners can extend to criminal liability by way of the provisions of that Code, and this sub-section furnishes a few examples of those offences.

106. The Criminal Code features offences that are specifically directed at some healthcare professions, such as provisions regarding the procurement of a miscarriage discussed later in the monograph,[553] as well offences where the punishment can increment if performed by a medical practitioner, for instance, in his/her capacity as a public officer.[554] It is, for example, an offence punishable by imprisonment for a term from four to eight years to, by lewd acts, defile a person who has not completed the age of sixteen years.[555] Yet, the offence is punishable with imprisonment for a longer term from six to twelve years when the offender, during his/her duties as a professional in possession of an official qualification and/or warrant to practice as *inter alia* a medical practitioner, commits the offence in circumstances when that offender wilfully or recklessly endangered the life of the minor, or the

548. S.L. 528.04, Functions and Responsibilities of the Department of Health Services Regulations, r. 3 (2)(a).
549. *Cassar Pullicino Louis LL.D v. Direttur Psikjatra Monte Carmeli et.*, Civil Court First Hall – 25/10/2016 [Ref: 12/1993/1] 19–20; *Bouharis Abdelkrim et. v. Director General (Health Care Services)*, Civil Court First Hall – 28/03/2019 [Ref: 205/2009] 6–7.
550. The Health Act refers to the Chief Medical Officer to Government. Liability may now, in accordance with the Health Act, be vested in other entities but the circumstances of the case at hand preceded the Health Act. *See* General Introduction §2 above.
551. *Bouharis Abdelkrim et. v. Director General (Health Care Services)*, Civil Court First Hall – 28/03/2019 [Ref: 205/2009] 9.
552. *See, for instance*: S.L. 582.02, Social Regulatory Standards on Residential Services for Persons with Disability Regulations; S.L. 582.06, Social Regulatory Standards for Residential Services offered to Individuals with Problems Related to Substance Abuse and other Dependencies; S.L. 528.09, Social Regulatory Standards for High Dependency Chronic Care Services for Older Persons Regulations; S.L. 582.15, Social Regulatory Standards for Residential Services for Senior Citizens Regulations.
553. *See* Part II Ch. 3 §1 below.
554. *See, for instance*: Criminal Code, Ch. 9 of the Laws of Malta, Arts 141 and 202 (a).
555. *Ibid.*, Art. 203 (1).

offence involves violence or grievous bodily harm to that minor, or the offence is committed with the involvement of a criminal organisation within the meaning of Article 83A of the Criminal Code.[556] That being said, the Criminal Code also provides for instances when certain procedures, which typically constitute criminal offences if committed, are exempt from criminal liability if medically justified. For instance, consistently with obligations arising from the Convention on Preventing and Combating Violence Against Women and Domestic Violence that Malta ratified in 2014,[557] the Criminal Code provides for the criminal offence of female genital mutilation.[558] Performing this operation or intervention, which includes the excision, infibulation or mutilation of the genitalia,[559] is not justifiable and is punishable in terms of the Criminal Code. However, that offence only arises in case of 'non-medical reasons',[560] which signifies that the operation or intervention is not punishable as a criminal offence if carried out for medical reasons.

107. In addition to topic-specific provisions, criminal liability against medical practitioners can ensue from a variety of other provisions. Thus, criminal liability can, for instance, ensue in the exercise of one's profession as a medical practitioner if a crime is committed with intention or *dolo*. This is not common in practice, but some examples where medical practitioners, other healthcare professionals, healthcare workers or care workers in Malta have been found criminally liable include instances involving non-consensual acts of a sexual nature,[561] unlawful exaction and obtaining money by false pretences,[562] wilfully causing grievous bodily harm,[563] and wilfully causing an elder or dependent adult to suffer under circumstances likely to produce bodily harm or death.[564] Yet, it is also tenable for a criminal offence to arise when there is no *dolo* inasmuch as the crime is committed as a consequence of criminal negligence or *culpa*.

108. A medical practitioner can, for instance, be held criminally liable in terms of Article 225 of the Criminal Code if 'through imprudence, carelessness, unskilfulness in his art or profession, or non-observance of regulations',[565] s/he causes the death of any person or, otherwise, if bodily harm is occasioned to that person.[566]

556. *Ibid.*, Art. 203 (1)(d).
557. Convention on Preventing and Combating Violence Against Women and Domestic Violence (2011) CETS 210, Art. 38.
558. Criminal Code, Ch. 9 of the Laws of Malta, Art. 251E.
559. *Ibid.*, Art. 251E (5).
560. *Ibid.*, Art. 251E (1).
561. *Ibid.*, Art. 207. *See, for instance*: *Il-Pulizija v. Omissis*, Court of Criminal Appeal (Inferior) – 21/06/2007 [Ref: 372/2006]; *Il-Pulizija v. Debono Lawrence*, Court of Magistrates (Criminal Judicature) – 18/08/2015 [Ref: 1/2015].
562. *Ibid.*, Arts 112 and 308. *See, for instance*: *Il-Pulizija v. Omissis*, Court of Magistrates (Criminal Judicature) – 26/04/2005 [Ref: 3/2005].
563. *Ibid.*, Art. 216. *See, for instance*: *Il-Pulizija v. Spiteri Charlton*, Court of Magistrates (Criminal Judicature) – 15/06/2020 [520/2018].
564. *Ibid.*, Art. 257A. *See, for instance*: *Il-Pulizija v. George-Michael Spiteri*, Court of Magistrates (Criminal Judicature) – 26/10/2017 [Ref: 618/2015].
565. Criminal Code, Ch. 9 of the Laws of Malta, Art. 225.
566. *Ibid.*, Art. 226.

Liability in criminal law must however be established 'beyond reasonable doubt'[567] so that the court is sure of the guilt of the accused.[568] That involves different stages. In the context of the provisions at hand regarding criminal negligence, it must, for instance, be established that there is a causal nexus linking the patient's death or bodily harm to the medical practitioners' imprudence, carelessness, unskilfulness in their profession or non-observance of regulations. Thus, in a case involving the prescription of a drug to manage a patient who died soon thereafter, it was sufficient for the purpose of freeing the medical practitioners from liability to establish that there was no causal nexus linking that prescription to the patient's demise and that, according to the court, the medical practitioners did everything in their power to save the life of that patient.[569] In addition to that causal nexus, a further element that must be considered in order to establish criminal liability in *culpa* on the basis of Article 225 of the Criminal Code regards the care and precautions taken by the accused medical practitioner. Indeed, as was noted by the courts in Malta when commenting upon proceedings of involuntary homicide against a surgeon, if that surgeon took 'all necessary care and precautions as was his to take in such circumstances, then he is not criminally responsible'.[570] This standard applies equally to all medical practitioners in the context of criminal negligence inasmuch as that liability is established against the backdrop of the tenets of the medical profession and an ordinary person who trained and presented himself to exercise that profession.[571] As such, when an artery was mistaken by surgeon/s for a vein intended for harvesting, the court concluded 'that all diligence needed by their profession was exercised [by the surgeons] and there could be no other way that they could have performed a better job',[572] therefore finding that the surgeon/s should not be held criminally liable. Instead, criminal negligence can ostensibly be established if it is shown that the damage was preventable but had not been foreseen due to the medical practitioners' voluntary choices while not intending to cause damage, even though it could have been foreseeable by persons diligently exercising their profession. In order to establish a medical practitioner's criminal liability that is involuntary in nature, the Court of Magistrates has therefore noted that there must at least subsist three elements: (i) the causal nexus connecting the (ii) negligent, imprudent and careless voluntary choices in the work of the medical practitioner to the (iii) damages that could have been preventable.[573]

109. Healthcare professionals other than medical practitioners, such as nurses, have been held criminally liable on the basis of Article 225 of the Criminal Code

567. *Paul Vassallo et. v. Carmelo Pace*, Court of Appeal (Civil, Superior) – 05/03/1986 [Kollezzjoni ta' Decizjonijiet tal-Qrati Superjuri ta' Malta Vol. 70 (1986) Pt 2, P 143, p 149].
568. *Il-Pulizija v. Joseph Peralta*, Court of Criminal Appeal (Inferior) – 25/04/1957 [Kollezzjoni ta' Decizjonijiet tal-Qrati Superjuri ta' Malta Vol. 41F (1957) Pt 4, P 1386, 1387].
569. *Il-Pulizija v. Desira Elaine*, Court of Magistrates (Criminal Judicature) – 18/12/2014 [Ref: 1123/2009] 51–52.
570. *A v. B*, Court of Magistrates (Criminal Judicature) – 14/10/2013 [Ref: 1306/2011] 8.
571. *Il-Pulizija v. Alexander-Roger Manche*, Court of Magistrates (Criminal Judicature) – 6 August 2013 [Ref: 1305/2011] 20.
572. *A v. B*, Court of Magistrates (Criminal Judicature) – 14/10/2013 [Ref: 1306/2011] 13.
573. *Il-Pulizija v. Alexander-Roger Manche*, Court of Magistrates (Criminal Judicature) – 6 August 2013 [Ref: 1305/2011] 22.

discussed in the previous paragraph in instances when patients committed suicide despite the healthcare professionals' presence and constant watch duty over those patients. The courts on this matter take cognizance of the regulations established by the hospital's protocols, and if healthcare professionals fail to observe those protocols, they may be liable in terms of 'non-observance of regulations' under Article 225 of the Criminal Code.[574] Furthermore, given that criminal negligence arising consequent to the latter provision can also be subjective, the courts have affirmed that a nurse's duty in the circumstances of constant-watch duty includes ensuring 'that a high-risk patient is kept out of harm's way at all times, no interludes, no pause, no exception'[575] and when the nurse does not do this, s/he would have failed 'to exercise the diligence expected of her'[576] resulting in a 'dereliction of the duty of care [and failing] … to foresee the foreseeable thereby failing to exercise the diligence expected of her'.[577] Even were the nurse not tasked with monitoring duties when s/he notices the incident occur, such as the patient being out of sight when under constant watch, it would not dispel his/her duty to act by at least informing the person tasked with monitoring duties if s/he saw that something was not right[578] and, absent those actions, the nurse would have 'failed her duties and the duty of care towards [the patient] by failing to act with the required diligence when she was duty bound to and consequently contributed towards his demise'.[579] While the courts take into account inadequate practices and structural shortcomings of the operative system of the hospital as a whole when considering the healthcare professionals' guilt or punishment,[580] the courts have thus ultimately questioned where healthcare professionals were located and what they were doing when the incident leading to the suicide occurred in order to establish whether they were observing regulations and/or exercising the diligence expected of them while also establishing the causal nexus with the patient's death.[581]

110. Similarly, criminal liability of healthcare professionals and healthcare aides was established on the basis of Article 225 of the Criminal Code in a case involving a patient's death after ingesting solid food when there were instructions at the hospital that he should not be given that sort of food. Engaging with the latter provision and with the hospital's procedures, the court at first instance ruled that a staff nurse negligently failed to use the diligence expected of him in the exercise of his profession and in his duty of care towards a patient under his custody by not verifying whether the food served to the patient was the one that had been instructed, by not confirming that the food was sufficiently mashed, by not confirming that his

574. *Il-Pulizija (Spt. Elton Taliana) v. Calleja Anthony*, Court of Magistrates (Criminal Judicature) – 21/10/2011 [Ref: 108/2003] 13.
575. *Il-Pulizija v. Yulia Toteva*, Court of Magistrates (Criminal Judicature) – 09/12/2019 [Ref: 298/2017] 38.
576. *Ibid.*
577. *Ibid.*
578. *Il-Pulizija v. Toteva Yulia*, Court of Criminal Appeal (Inferior) – 24/11/2020 [Ref: 343/2019/1] 15
579. *Ibid.*, 14.
580. *Ibid.*, 16; *Il-Pulizija v. Bondin Maria, Bonnici Carol, Sant David*, Court of Criminal Appeal (Inferior) – 06/01/2021 [Ref: 105/2019] 14.
581. *Il-Pulizija v. Calleja Anthony*, Court of Criminal Appeal (Inferior) – 08/10/2012 [Ref: 448/2011] 16.

patient had finished eating and by permitting a tray with solid food to remain in the patient's vicinity while unsupervised, when that patient was to be supervised during meal time, without at least instructing its removal.[582] Concurring with the first instance court, the appellate court then noted that the liability of healthcare professionals is established against the backdrop of the standard expected from a person exercising the given healthcare profession and that both the nurse and the nursing aide in this case should then have been aware of the patient's special needs during meal times as indicated in his medical file.[583] The courts thus held that the consequences of their behaviour were or should have been easily foreseeable, meaning that the patient's consequent demise resulted from that nurse's *culpa* or criminal negligence, together with the negligence of a nursing aide, inasmuch as *culpa* results when the healthcare professionals' conduct falls below the standard expected of them when the damaging incident would have been foreseeable had the standard demanded of those healthcare professionals been followed.[584]

111. It is worthwhile noting for the purpose of medical law that, while some individuals ostensibly have a legal duty to care for patients arising from the exercise of their profession, the courts have recognised that criminal liability in the context of Article 211 of the Criminal Code regarding wilful homicide (by commission or omission) and Article 225 of the Criminal Code regarding involuntary homicide may also arise when persons assume a duty of care of their own choosing without obligations consequent to the exercise of any profession. Thus, a person who chooses to care for another person may be held criminally liable if, for instance, through his/her wilful act of abandonment, the person who is otherwise helpless then dies if this outcome was foreseeable when, though action to save his/her life was possible, no such action was taken. This also applies if that person who chooses to care for another individual attempts to provide treatment him/herself, when s/he lacks the pertinent ability, and/or knowingly fails to call for healthcare assistance if and when that assistance is evidently required, such as in the case of an overdose of drugs.[585] This interpretation of the Criminal Code did not introduce a concept of a duty to care or rescue in Maltese law, given that the courts were engaging with concepts such as positive indirect homicide[586] or *culpa* and criminal negligence.[587] It has however been noted that principles akin to a duty of care may be drawn from the terms 'care or custody' in Article 257A of the Criminal Code regarding the

582. *Il-Pulizija v. Maria Bondin et.*, Court of Magistrates (Criminal Judicature) – 25/03/2019 [Ref: 344/2014] 48
583. *Il-Pulizija v. Bondin Maria, Bonnici Carol, Sant David*, Court of Criminal Appeal (Inferior) – 06/01/2021 [Ref: 105/2019] 12–13.
584. *Ibid.*, 11.
585. *Ir-Repubblika ta' Malta v. Jason Decelis u Concetta Decelis*, Court of Criminal Appeal (Superior) – 25/09/2008 [Ref: 6/2004] 35; *Decelis Concetta et. v. Ministru tal-Gustizzja u l-Intern et.*, Civil Court First Hall (Constitutional Jurisdiction) – 09/12/2010 [Ref: 3/2009] 29–30.
586. *Decelis Concetta et. v. Ministru tal-Gustizzja u l-Intern et.*, Constitutional Court – 02/05/2011 [Ref: 3/2009/1] 9.
587. *Il-Pulizija v. Chircop Salvatore*, Court of Magistrates (Criminal Judicature) – 06/03/2019 [Ref: 118/2016].

offence of causing or permitting an elder or a dependent adult to suffer under circumstances likely to produce bodily harm or death,[588] which can also result if persons who have the care or custody of an elder or dependent person do not obtain healthcare assistance for the elder or dependent person when that assistance is required.[589]

112. That being said, there are provisions in Maltese law to abate concerns regarding liability when a person is in a position to assist another person by seeking healthcare services. For instance, in the context of assistance rendered to a person suffering from a drug overdose, the Drug Dependence (Treatment not Imprisonment) Act provides that no liability shall ensue for sharing or consuming prohibited drugs in a quantity for personal use with the person suffering from the overdose if one provides assistance 'by taking such person to a hospital or to a place where he can receive appropriate medical care or who seeks the assistance of the competent authorities for such purpose'.[590] Furthermore, if the person providing assistance is 'liable to prosecution for another offence directly connected with the overdose of the assisted person the punishment to which such person shall be liable on conviction shall be reduced by one degree'.[591] Also, a Good Samaritan provision was added to the criminal law regarding involuntary homicide or bodily harm by providing that, notwithstanding Articles 225 to 226A of the Criminal Code, 'a person will not be criminally liable if, confronted with a present or imminent danger to another person, he performs an act necessary to ensure the safety of that person, whether or not the act ensures the safety of the person'.[592] This provision shall not however apply 'where the means used are disproportionate to the seriousness of the threat or where the act is performed with malice or gross negligence'.[593]

§2. Quality Assurance

113. Control over the practice of medicine in Malta addressed in this chapter of the monograph also involves quality assurance that is separate from considerations of liability and other disciplinary measures. Different entities have a role in quality assurance depending upon the sector in question. Recalling that Part I of the monograph addresses the 'medical profession', this section focuses in particular on the role of the Medical Council in quality assurance while also briefly considering the wider remit of quality assurance in the healthcare and social care systems in Malta.

114. The Medical Council has several functions in the context of quality assurance over the medical profession. In particular, the Medical Council is involved in

---

588. *Il-Pulizija v. Mijalkovic Dragana*, Court of Criminal Appeal (Inferior) – 17/09/2019 [Ref: 110/2019] 101.
589. *Ibid.*, 115–120; *Il-Pulizija v. Dragana Mijalkovic*, Court of Magistrates (Criminal Judicature) – 02/04/2019 [Ref: 22/2017] 60.
590. Drug Dependence (Treatment not Imprisonment) Act, Ch. 537 of the Laws of Malta, Art. 11 (1).
591. *Ibid.*, Art. 11 (2).
592. Criminal Code, Ch. 9 of the Laws of Malta, Art. 226C.
593. *Ibid.*

quality assurance covering foundation training for graduates in medicine that is related to but separate from quality assurance vested in educational institutions.[594] Thus, provided one does not already hold qualifications that render him/her eligible to have his/her name entered onto the Medical Register after having successfully completed basic medical training by or under the supervision of a University,[595] Maltese law requires that a person, in order to be eligible for the Medical Register, also serve as a house physician and/or surgeon in a government hospital or other hospital recognised for that purpose by the Medical Council.[596] In case of the latter option, the Medical Council is to 'take into consideration the country in which the hospital is situated, the level of supervision and structure of the training offered by the hospital'.[597] If one however serves as a house physician and/or surgeon in a government hospital in Malta, the Medical Council shall only consider in determining the fulfilment of the requirement at hand 'the successful completion of the Foundation Programme Malta for junior doctors'.[598] It is the Medical Council that is then 'entrusted with the quality assurance of the Malta Foundation programme'.[599] This entails that the Medical Council 'quality assures the training and assessment processes of the Programme'.[600] It performs this function by constituting a Medical Council Quality Assurance Committee in order to undertake a 'Quality Assurance visit to the Foundation School Malta'.[601] The purpose is 'to quality assure the Foundation Programme such that its graduates are considered well prepared to be fully registered by the [Medical] Council'[602] on the Medical Register. In turn, the Medical Council uses the United Kingdom's standards as a basis for quality assurance of the Foundation Programme in Malta. This is because the Foundation School in Malta, while accountable to the MPMTC, is also affiliated with the United Kingdom's Foundation Programme (UKFP) that itself quality visits the Malta Foundation School.[603] As such, the Medical Council's quality assurance process also has the purpose to assure that graduates of the Foundation Programme (FP) in Malta 'are at par with their UK peers and to ensure that the FP Malta retains its affiliation

594. *See, for instance*: Education Act, Ch. 327 of the Laws of Malta, Art. 63; S.L. 327.557, University Suitability to Practice Regulations; S.L. 327.633, General Regulations for University Undergraduate Awards, Sch. 1; Further and Higher Education Act, Ch. 607 of the Laws of Malta, Arts 2 and 17; S.L. 607.03, Further and Higher Education (Licensing, accreditation and quality assurance) Regulations. *See also* Association of Medical Schools in Europe (AMSE), Accreditation Agency for Study Programmes in Engineering, Informatics, Natural Sciences and Mathematics (ASIIN), *Accreditation Report: Doctor of Medicine and Surgery – M.D. provided by: University of Malta, Faculty of Medicine and Surgery* (20 September 2019) – Available in the European Quality Assurance Register for Higher Education (EQAR).
595. *See* Part I Ch. 1 above.
596. Health Care Professions Act, Ch. 464 of the Laws of Malta, Art. 11.
597. S.L. 464.19, Medical Council (Standing Orders) Regulations, r. 36 (2)(b).
598. *Ibid.*, r. 36 (2)(a). *See also* r. 36 (1).
599. Medical Council Malta, *QA Report of Foundation Programme Malta* 3 (2018).
600. *Ibid.*
601. Medical Council Malta, *Annual Report 2019*, 42.
602. Medical Council Malta, *QA Report of Foundation Programme Malta* 4 (2018).
603. Kevin Cassar & Tonio Piscopo, *The Malta Foundation Programme: time to act*, 21 (1) Malta Medical Journal 5–7 (2009). *See also* The Foundation Programme Malta, *UKFPO Affiliation* <http://fpmalta.com/page/view/35>.

with the UKFP'.[604] The Medical Council moreover keeps a list of provisional registration in which shall be entered, upon an application by the person concerned, 'the name of every person who holds the degree of Doctor of Medicine and Surgery from the University of Malta or *a qualification recognized by the Medical Council* obtained from any other university, college or medical council, and who is serving as a house physician and, or surgeon at a hospital recognized by the Medical Council in terms of'[605] the Health Care Professions Act. The Malta FP is thus related to provisional registration, and other than the MD degree awarded by the University of Malta, it is the Medical Council in Malta that recognises qualifications for the purpose of provisional registration in Malta.[606]

115. Other functions of the Medical Council for the purpose of quality assurance were illustrated earlier in this monograph or are otherwise better suited to later sections of the monograph. This includes the Medical Council's functions to recommend to the President of Malta the granting[607] and the withdrawal of licenses to medical practitioners to practise their profession[608] as well as its functions with regard to the registers in respect of the medical profession, which, for instance, includes the possibility of erasure from a register if it is satisfied that any entry in any register kept by it 'has been fraudulently or incorrectly made'[609] or if it establishes that a person falling under its supervision 'is unfit to continue to practise his profession on account of some physical or mental infirmity'.[610] It also is the Medical Council that must be satisfied, after due inquiry, that one is 'no longer unfit to continue to practise his profession'[611] so as to then reinstate him/her, and the Medical Council even has a role in continuous professional development.[612] It additionally is the Medical Council that is tasked with prescribing and maintaining professional and ethical standards for the medical profession.[613] Given the breadth of the role of the Medical Council, there is also a measure of oversight over the fulfilment of its functions that is separate from action via the courts. Thus, the President of Malta, acting on the advice of the Minister responsible for health, may order an inquiry if s/he is of the opinion that the Medical Council 'has failed to carry out any of the functions conferred or imposed upon it by or under … [the Health Care Professions] Act, or has, in carrying out these functions, failed to comply with any regulation relating thereto'.[614] If this opinion is confirmed consequent to the inquiry, acting on the advice of the Minister responsible for health, the President of Malta

604. Medical Council Malta, *QA Report of Foundation Programme Malta* 4 (2018).
605. Health Care Professions Act, Ch. 464 of the Laws of Malta, Art. 11 (3). Emphasis added.
606. *See also* Part I Ch. 1 above.
607. Health Care Professions Act, Ch. 464 of the Laws of Malta, Art. 10 (1)(a). *See also* Part I Ch. 1 above.
608. *Ibid.*, Art. 10 (1)(b).
609. *Ibid.*, Art. 35.
610. *Ibid.*, Art. 38 (1). *See also* S.L. 458.08, Medical Council (Erasure of Names Procedure) Rules, r. 4 (1)(c) and 4 (2).
611. *Ibid.*, Art. 38 (4). *See also* S.L. 464.19, Medical Council (Standing Orders) Regulations, r. 50.
612. S.L. 451.03, Recognition of Professional Qualifications Regulations, r. 22 (2)(b).
613. Health Care Professions Act, Art. 10 (1)(d). *See also* Part I Ch. 4 below.
614. *Ibid.*, Art. 48 (1).

may make an order declaring the Medical Council in default.[615] This will entail that the members of the Medical Council 'shall forthwith vacate their office',[616] and it will also lead to the appointment of a *pro tempore* Council.[617]

116. Quality assurance vis-à-vis the medical profession is also embedded in the healthcare system more generally. The service provider is, for instance, obliged to employ personnel who can properly complete the work at hand and provide the requested service.[618] This obligation exists in public healthcare and in private healthcare, albeit the subject of the obligation would vary between the two. In the case of public healthcare, it is one of the functions of the Department for Healthcare Services 'to ensure quality of services delivered through the public health system'.[619] It indeed is part of the mission of the Department for Healthcare Services 'to ensure the effective and efficient operation and delivery of healthcare services with an emphasis on … quality review within an established framework of controlled decentralization and autonomy involving user participation'.[620] More broadly, subject to compliance with law, individual service providers can engage in separate quality assurance measures. Yet, given that a licence for the running of a private medical clinic or hospital is to only be granted, transferred or renewed on condition that said clinic or hospital 'is in the charge of a medical practitioner or a registered nurse',[621] it means that this healthcare professional would still fall under the supervision of the pertinent regulatory Council irrespective as to whether s/he is or is not the license holder of the private medical clinic/hospital. As to licensing vis-à-vis quality assurance, it is part of the mission of the Department for Health Regulation to 'licence, monitor and inspect the provision of healthcare services in order to ensure their quality and safety, and to recommend the standards to be met by healthcare providers'.[622] In this respect, the latter Department has the function 'to monitor and ensure the maintenance of public health standards and regulations in licensed premises and other entities as appropriate'.[623] Furthermore, clinics licensed in terms of S.L. 458.23 Licensing of Private Medical Clinic Regulations are to be inspected by persons authorised by the Minister responsible for health at least twice in every period of twelve months so as to conduct 'a systematic review of facilities and services with a view to ensuring compliance'[624] with those regulations and with the conditions of the licence.

117. Social welfare services are also embedded with quality assurance measures that relate to the medical profession inasmuch as some social regulatory standards

615. *Ibid.*, Art. 48 (2).
616. *Ibid.*, Art. 48 (3)(a).
617. *Ibid.*, Art. 48 (3)(b).
618. *See* Part I Ch. 4 §1.II above.
619. S.L. 528.04, Functions and Responsibilities of Department of Health Services Regulations, r. 3 (2)(a).
620. Health Act, Ch. 528 of the Laws of Malta, Art. 6 (1). *See also* General Introduction §2.I above.
621. S.L. 458.23, Licensing of Private Medical Clinics Regulations, r. 7 (2)(a).
622. Health Act, Ch. 528 of the Laws of Malta, Art. 8 (1). *See also* General Introduction §2.II above.
623. S.L. 528.05, Functions and Responsibilities of the Department of Health Regulation Regulations, r. 3 (2)(f).
624. S.L. 458.23, Licensing of Private Medical Clinics Regulations, r. 13 (5).

engage with the personal health and medical care of the users of those services.[625] In this respect, it is the service provider in the context of social welfare services that is first responsible for the quality of services it provides, even though the Government of Malta is bound to endeavour, through the Social Care Standards Authority, to 'assist the service providers to achieve a higher quality of service'.[626] It then is the Enforcement Office within the Social Care Standards Authority that is responsible to 'conduct the necessary monitoring and enforcement of the quality of all social welfare services and to ensure that the necessary Quality Assurance verifications are being conducted'.[627] The Enforcement Office thus has the function to ensure that social welfare services are compliant with regulations and standards issued by the Social Care Standards Authority.[628] While this does not detract from and can even complement quality assurance undertaken by the Medical Council and other entities, it can, for instance, ground quality assurance and quality control vis-à-vis if and how the service provider is ensuring timely access to identified physical and mental healthcare services or if and how the service provider is ensuring that medication is 'prescribed, prepared and administered in a documented manner that complies with local legislation and best practice'.[629]

118. There are other provisions in law engaging with quality assurance or quality control in healthcare that are related to but separate from quality assurance targeting the medical profession per se. Some of these provisions draw on EU law and include quality assurance and/or quality control in the context of medicinal products,[630] medical devices,[631] clinical trials,[632] ionising radiation,[633] organ

625. *See, for instance*: S.L. 582.09, Social Regulatory Standards for High Dependency Chronic Care Services for Older Persons Regulations, Standards 2 and 3; S.L. 582.15, Social Regulatory Standards for Residential Services for Senior Citizens Regulations, Standard 3; S.L. 582.16, Social Regulatory Standards for Residential Services for Persons Living with Dementia in Homes for Senior Citizens Regulations, Standard 2.
626. Social Care Standards Authority Act, Ch. 582 of the Laws of Malta, Art. 4 (2)(b).
627. S.L. 582.12, Enforcement Office with the Social Care Standards Authority (Establishment) Regulations, r. 2 (1).
628. *Ibid.*, r. 3 (4)(c).
629. S.L. 582.09, Social Regulatory Standards for High Dependency Chronic Care Services for Older Persons Regulations, Standard 3.
630. Medicines Act, Ch. 458 of the Laws of Malta; S.L. 458.36, Manufacture and Importation of Medicinal Products for Human Use Regulations; S.L. 458.37, Wholesale Distribution and Brokering of Medicinal Products and Active Substances Regulations; S.L. 458.42, Good Manufacturing Practice in respect of Medicinal Products and Active Substances for Human Use Regulations.
631. S.L. 427,44, Medical Devices Regulations; S.L. 427.10, Active Implantable Medical Devices Regulations; S.L. 427.16, *In Vitro* Diagnostic Medical Devices Regulations; Regulation (EU) 2017/745 of the European Parliament and of the Council of 5 April 2017 on medical devices, amending Directive 2001/83/EC, Regulation (EC) No 178/2002 and Regulation (EC) No 1223/2009 and repealing Council Directives 90/385/EEC and 93/42/EEC, OJ L 117, 5.5.2017; Regulation (EU) 2017/746 of the European Parliament and of the Council of 5 April 2017 on in vitro diagnostic medical devices and repealing Directive 98/79/EC and Commission Decision 2010/227/EU, OJ L 117, 5.5.2017.
632. S.L. 458.43, Clinical Trials Regulations; Regulation (EU) No 536/2014 of the European Parliament and of the Council of 16 April 2014 on clinical trials on medicinal products for human use, and repealing Directive 2001/20/EC, OJ L 158, 27.5.2014.
633. S.L. 585.01, Basic Safety Standards for Ionising Radiation Regulations.

transplants,[634] human blood,[635] tissues and cells.[636] Control over the practice of medicine addressed in this chapter of the part of the monograph dealing with the medical profession is however also related to that profession in the context of review boards, which are addressed in the next section.

§3. Review Boards

119. There exist in Malta boards that review the practice of medicine *inter alia* exercised by medical practitioners. These review boards are different from judicial action in the domestic courts and distinct from disciplinary measures by the regulatory councils. This section illustrates four types of review boards: (i) boards appointed in terms of the Inquiries Act; (ii) boards that are only informally appointed within the healthcare system without explicit basis in law but whose decisions may nevertheless be subject to judicial review of administrative action; (iii) the role of the Office of the Ombudsman and the Commissioner for Health; and (iv) statutorily appointed review boards that relate to healthcare and may consequently indirectly touch on the medical profession that is being engaged within this part of the monograph.

120. The Inquiries Act applies to Boards appointed or authorised by or under any law to carry out any inquiry into:

> (a) the conduct of public officers, or of officers or servants of a statutory body, or of anyone or more of such public officers or officers or servants; (b) the conduct or management of any department of Government or any statutory body; (c) any matter falling within the functions or responsibility of any such department or body, or otherwise concerning or affecting a service of the Government.[637]

In the context of healthcare, the Inquiries Act can thus relate in particular to the public health service inasmuch as it can regulate certain inquiries that include 'any investigation or other examination of the facts or circumstances of a case'.[638] Given the nature of these inquiries, the final report is not necessarily made publicly available, but it can nevertheless be engaged with by the Courts and disciplinary organisations.[639] By way of example, a board of inquiry in terms of the Inquiries Act was

634. S.L. 483.06, Organ Transplants (Quality and Safety) Regulations.
635. Human Blood and Transplants Act, Ch. 483 of the Laws of Malta; S.L. 483.02, Blood (Quality and Safety) Regulations.
636. S.L. 483.01, Tissues and Cells (Quality and Safety) Regulations; S.L. 483.04, Human Tissues and Cells (Coding, Processing, Preservation, Storage and Distribution) Regulations; S.L. 483.08, Equivalent Standards of Quality and Safety of Imported Tissues and Cells Regulations.
637. Inquiries Act, Ch. 273 of the Laws of Malta, Art. 3.
638. *Ibid.*, Art. 2.
639. *See, for instance*: S.L. Const. 03, Public Service Commission Disciplinary Regulations, r. 17 (1)(a).

appointed consequent to an error within the public health service regarding a pregnant woman's blood grouping and the board's findings including, for instance, that 'the error was a serious one as it seriously prejudiced future pregnancies'[640] were reported in the later rulings by the courts addressing a claim for compensatory damages. Once appointed, a board of inquiry is to 'carry out such functions and other duties, and in such manner and within such time, as may be specified in the instrument appointing it'.[641] That instrument can allocate investigational authority as well as decisional authority unto the board of inquiry.[642] The appointing authority has significant leeway in this respect and, in addition to the Prime Minister of Malta, a Minister may also appoint a board of inquiry for any of the purposes in points (b) and (c) quoted earlier in this paragraph 'in so far as the matter of the inquiry concerns or affects a department or statutory body or service for which he is responsible or in respect of which he has powers under any enactment'.[643] For the purpose of healthcare, that will typically be the Minister responsible for health. As such, while it did not address the Inquiries Act, the court noted that it was the Minister responsible for health that ordered an inquiry into a case involving the forced removal of a medical practitioner in the presence of his patients from a room at Malta's main hospital by other members of staff.[644] This case is noteworthy for the purpose of review boards in general since the court included, among the reasons for finding that the medical practitioner suffered inhuman and degrading treatment in terms of Article 36 of the Constitution of Malta and Article 3 of the European Convention on Human Rights (ECHR), that the inquiry was conducted by persons falling under the remit of the head of department that they were investigating and that the inquiry lacked transparency.[645] It is however unclear whether that ruling will lead to explicit procedures used to conduct inquiries.

121. A board for the purpose of the Inquiries Act includes 'any commission, committee or other body of persons and includes also a single person functioning as a Board or similar authority'.[646] That type of board regulated by the Inquiries Act would however not cover review boards that are appointed internally by private healthcare providers or even other review boards that are informally appointed in a manner separate from the requisites of the Inquiries Act, but that may nevertheless address the public health service. It was, for instance, noted in a court ruling that in the circumstances of a case when a Grievances Unit was established together with a Review Board so as to consider claims of injustice received from public officers or employees, the decisions of those entities were taken into account respectively

640. *Brincat Andrew et. v. Tabib Ewlieni tal-Gvern et.*, Civil Court First Hall – 12/04/2016 [Ref: 225/1989/1] 33. *See also*: *Brincat Andrew et. v. Tabib Ewlieni Tal-Gvern et.*, Court of Appeal (Civil, Superior) – 27/10/2021 [Ref: 225/1989/2]

641. Inquiries Act, Ch. 273 of the Laws of Malta, Art. 4 (4).

642. *See, for instance*: *Rose Anne Galea v. L-Onorevoli Prim Ministru et.*, Constitutional Court – 11/04/1995 [Kollezzjoni ta' Decizjonijiet tal-Qrati Superjuri ta' Malta Vol. 79 (1995) Pt I, T 1, P 97, 107].

643. Inquiries Act, Ch. 273 of the Laws of Malta, Art. 4 (1).

644. *Megally Dr Naged v. Onor. Ministru tas-Sahha et.*, Civil Court First Hall (Constitutional Jurisdiction) – 23/06/2022 [Ref: 31/2020] 9. *See also*: *Megally Dr Naged v. Onor Ministru tas-Sahha et.*, Constitutional Court – 08/08/2022 [Ref: 31/2020/2].

645. *Ibid.*, 13.

646. Inquiries Act, Ch. 273 of the Laws of Malta, Art. 2.

by the Ministry for Health and the Principal Permanent Secretary even though they were not entities that were formally grounded in law.[647] Nevertheless, given that the Ministry for Health and the Principal Permanent Secretary took into account the decisions of the Grievances Unit and the Review Board, it was held that it rendered those decisions into administrative acts that were open to judicial review.

122. The Commissioner for Administrative Investigations, called the Ombudsman, is a formal office that does not replace any internal complaints mechanisms or the courts and is instead established in terms of the Constitution of Malta 'to investigate actions taken by or on behalf of the Government, or by such other authority, body or person as may be provided by law … being actions taken in the exercise of their administrative functions'.[648] There then exists within the Office of the Ombudsman a Commissioner for Health, who is a Commissioner for Administrative Investigations appointed with the function to 'investigate complaints related to the health service',[649] which largely relates to the public health service, as well as to *inter alia* conduct own-initiative investigations into that health service and receive from any Committee of the House of Representatives petitions that are before that Committee for consideration regarding the health service. While this entails functions akin to a Review Board, the functions of the Commissioner for Health nevertheless exclude investigations into the medical and clinical judgment for the diagnosis of illness or for the treatment of patients, and neither is the Commissioner for Health to 'investigate any technical merits of decisions taken by health care professionals, unless there is in either case proof of maladministration by the person providing the health service in the exercise of his professional competence or professional discriminatory action'.[650] The Ombudsman may also decline to exercise his/her power 'in any case where adequate means of redress are or have been available to the complainant under any other law: Provided that the Ombudsman may conduct an investigation if satisfied that in the particular circumstances it is not reasonable to expect the complainant to resort or have resorted to such means of redress'.[651] Given these parameters, investigations have been conducted and reports made on matters that do not necessarily address how the medical profession operates, but they can touch on the 'control over the practice of medicine' addressed in this chapter. This includes preliminary inquiries and/or investigations regarding disabilities occasioned after surgery in a public hospital,[652] request/s by medical practitioner/s that third country national/s be exceptionally granted access to treatment free of charge despite not being *ipso jure* entitled to treatment without payment,[653] patients' hospitalisation on the basis that medication prescribed by medical

647. *Masini Austin v. Ministeru tas-Sahha et.*, Civil Court First Hall – 11/05/2021 [Ref: 63/2017/1].
648. Constitution of Malta, Art. 64A (1).
649. S.L. 385.01, Commissioners for Administrative Investigations (Functions) Rules, r. 22.
650. *Ibid.*, r. 23.
651. Ombudsman Act, Ch. 385 of the Laws of Malta, Art. 13 (3).
652. Office of the Ombudsman, *Cases Notes 2012* (Edition 32) 101–102.
653. Parliamentary Ombudsman Malta, *Case Notes 2017* (Edition 37) 76–77.

practitioner/s was not provided,[654] services of medical officers in homes for the elderly,[655] a non-functioning specialists accreditation committee,[656] general medical and geriatric care for patients at Malta's main mental health licensed facility,[657] as well as own initiative investigations such as that regarding long waiting times at the Accident and Emergency Department within Malta's main public hospital.[658] The Ombudsman Act also provides for the procedure to be followed after investigation, which includes the possibility that the Commissioner for Health report his/her opinion and reasons to the appropriate entity and to the pertinent Minister while making any recommendation the Commissioner thinks fit. If no action is taken that the Commissioner for Health and/or the Ombudsman consider to be adequate and appropriate, s/he may then 'send a copy of the report and recommendations to the Prime Minister, and may thereafter make such report to the House of Representatives on the matter he thinks fit'[659] while attaching thereto any comments made by or on behalf of the pertinent entity.

123. There are furthermore statutorily appointed review boards that relate to healthcare and may consequently at least indirectly touch on the medical profession, albeit not as review boards of that profession. These include, for instance, the Medicines Review Board, whose function is to 'hear an appeal submitted by the applicant of a marketing authorisation on any recommendation of the Medicines Authority in relation to the safety, quality and efficacy of a medicinal product and to provide advice and make its recommendations to the Licensing Authority in this regard'.[660] There also exists the Procurement (Health Service Concessions) Review Board that determines complaints 'from candidates against any decision of a procuring entity in relation to the procurement procedure'[661] regarding contracts concerning the provision and management of health and ancillary services that fall beyond the scope of, for instance, the Public Procurement Regulations. The Public Contracts Review Board instead has the function to *inter alia* address concerns and complaints regarding tenders for public contracts or procurement procedures, including public supply, public service or public works, for example, within the confines of healthcare.[662] Furthermore, the functions of the Minors Care Review Board *inter alia* include 'ensuring that the best interests of the minor are being safeguarded by all the persons involved in his care'[663] and 'in the case of disagreement on the care of the minor in matters of particular importance, the taking of decisions it deems as being in the best interests of the minor, after having given its reasons

654. Parliamentary Ombudsman Malta, *Case Notes 2019* (Edition 39) 101–102.
655. Parliamentary Ombudsman Malta, *Annual Report 2019* (2020) 88.
656. Parliamentary Ombudsman Malta, *Annual Report 2021* (2022) 83–84.
657. *Ibid.*
658. Ombudsman: Own-initiative investigation by the Commissioner for Health: *Long waiting times at the Accident & Emergency Department, Mater Dei Hospital* (2013).
659. Ombudsman Act, Ch. 385 of the Laws of Malta, Art. 22 (4).
660. Medicines Act, Ch. 458 of the Laws of Malta, Art. 16 (1). *See also* Art. 21.
661. S.L. 595.13, Procurement (Health Service Concessions) Review Board Regulations, r. 3.
662. S.L. 601.03, Public Procurement Regulations; S.L. 601.09, Concession Contracts Regulations.
663. Minor Protection (Alternative Care) Act, Ch. 602 of the Laws of Malta, Art. 32 (2)(g).

therefor'[664] including for the purpose of treatment.[665] None of the review boards mentioned in this paragraph, however, explicitly address the medical profession, and the next section therefore outlines disciplinary measures directed at the medical profession, particularly within the confines of professional regulation, thereby also engaging with professional codes and biomedical ethics committees.

§4. Disciplinary Organisations

I. Order of Physicians

124. The Medical Council is one of the regulatory Councils that healthcare professionals authorised to practice a healthcare profession in accordance with the Health Care Professions Act shall, in the practice of their profession, be subject to its 'special supervision'.[666] Persons falling under that supervision of the Medical Council include medical practitioners, dental surgeons and persons whose name is not entered into the Medical Register but who are lawfully working as part of the medical profession in Malta, for instance, within the confines of the Foundation School.[667] In addition to its other functions, Maltese law then also provides the Medical Council with competencies that are investigative and disciplinary in nature, separate from any internal disciplinary measures taken by hospitals, healthcare centres, professional associations, employers or any liability established by the courts. This section outlines, in turn, the instances when the Medical Council can take disciplinary measures and the procedure to be adopted to take disciplinary measures while also identifying what disciplinary measures the Medical Council can take.

125. The Medical Council has the competence to take disciplinary measures in at least four broad situations after due inquiry. This is in addition to measures taken by the Medical Council when an entry into any register it keeps has been fraudulently or incorrectly made, as well as measures taken in instances when a medical practitioner is unfit to continue to practise his/her profession on account of some physical or mental infirmity, which are not per se disciplinary in nature and are therefore considered elsewhere in this monograph.[668] First, in terms of the Health Care Professions Act, disciplinary measures can be taken by the Medical Council if a person falling under its authority 'has been convicted by any court in Malta of any crime punishable by imprisonment for a term exceeding one year or of any of the crimes mentioned in articles 198 to 205 or in articles 206 to 209 of the Criminal Code'.[669] These offences include, for instance, rape and abduction, but subsidiary legislation arising from the Health Care Professions Act also stipulates that the Medical Council 'may open an inquiry into those convictions for criminal offences

---

664. *Ibid.*, Art. 32 (2)(f).
665. *Ibid.*, Arts 53 (f) and 61 (1)(m).
666. Health Care Professions Act, Ch. 464 of the Laws of Malta, Art. 5 (1).
667. *Ibid.*, Arts 7 and 11. *See, for instance*: Medical Council Malta, Case No CC/02/2020. *See also* Part I Ch. 1 above.
668. *See* Part I Ch. 4 §2 above.
669. Health Care Professions Act, Ch. 464 of the Laws of Malta, Art. 32 (1)(a).

committed by practitioners *other than those specifically mentioned* in the[670] Health Care Professions Act'. Second, the Medical Council may take disciplinary measures against a person falling under its authority if s/he 'has been guilty of professional or ethical misconduct in any respect'[671] and, third, if 'in any other manner [s/he] has failed to abide by the professional and ethical standards applicable to him'.[672] These standards are *inter alia* incorporated in professional codes that are considered later in this chapter of the monograph. Suffice it to say for now that the Ethics of the Medical Profession Regulations pinpoints certain offences that may warrant disciplinary action by the Medical Council, including offences related to advertising or canvassing[673] as well as instances when a medical practitioner discloses information obtained in the course of his/her professional relationship without that patient's consent.[674] Fourth, the broader Maltese law can furnish competence unto the Medical Council to conduct an inquiry and make recommendations to another authority regarding disciplinary measures. By way of example, the Internal Control of Dangerous Drugs Rules provides that if 'the Minister responsible for Health has reason to suspect that a medical practitioner … is supplying or prescribing drugs to or for either himself or any other person otherwise than is properly required for the purpose of medical or dental treatment of himself or that of any other person, the Minister responsible for Health may refer the matter to the Tribunal constituted in the manner specified in the Third Schedule',[675] which refers to the Medical Council. In the latter case, even if the Medical Council makes a recommendation against the medical practitioner, it would ultimately be the Minister responsible for health who may withdraw the authority of a medical practitioner to supply, procure or possess the drugs in question as well as to give prescriptions for the purpose of the Internal Control of Dangerous Drugs Rules. That being said, the Medical Council may independently take disciplinary measures in terms of the Health Care Professions Act after due inquiry.

126. In accordance with the Medical Council (Erasure of Names Procedure) Rules, no direction regarding disciplinary measures shall be given under the Health Care Professions Act except in consequence of an inquiry held in accordance with the provisions of those Rules into the charge formulated in a notice of inquiry that is served on the person against whom the charge is made.[676] An inquiry is thus the first step of any possible disciplinary action in terms of the Health Care Professions Act. In this respect, the Medical Council shall, for instance, have the power under the Health Care Professions Act to investigate, either on the complaint of any person or of its own motion, 'any allegation of professional misconduct or breach of ethics by a health care professional falling under its supervision'.[677] Some of the

670. S.L. 464.17, Ethics of the Medical Profession Regulations, r. 3 (1). Emphasis added.
671. Health Care Professions Act, Ch. 464 of the Laws of Malta, Art. 32 (1)(b).
672. *Ibid.*, Art. 32 (1)(c).
673. S.L. 464.17, Ethics of the Medical Profession Regulations, r. 5 (2).
674. *Ibid.*, Sch. A, [12 (b)].
675. S.L. 101.02, Internal Control of Dangerous Drugs Rules, r. 14 (3). *See also* S.L. 31.18, Drugs Controls Regulations, r. 13 (10). *See also* Part I Ch. 3 above.
676. S.L. 458.08, Medical Council (Erasure of Names Procedure) Rules, r. 3.
677. Health Care Professions Act, Ch. 464 of the Laws of Malta, Art. 31 (1).

procedure to be followed, at least when a complaint or information in writing of the conduct of a medical practitioner is sent to the Medical Council, is outlined in the Medical Council (Erasure of Names Procedure) Rules. These Rules stipulate that the registrar is to first submit the complaint or information that has been received to the President of the Medical Council,[678] who is to then 'direct the registrar to notify the practitioner of the receipt of the complaint or information, stating the substance thereof … and to invite the practitioner to submit to the Council, within such date as the President [of the Medical Council] shall determine, any explanation which the practitioner may have to offer'.[679] The Medical Council has also clarified that the practitioner's version of events will be copied to the complainant.[680] That being said, if it does not appear to the President of the Medical Council that 'a question arises whether the … conduct constitutes infamous conduct in a professional respect, he shall direct the registrar to refer such complaint or information to the [Medical] Council either to decide that the complaint or information need not proceed further or to direct the registrar to notify the practitioner in accordance with'[681] the procedure at hand. Once the medical practitioner is notified of the complaint or information, then unless the Medical Council is fully satisfied with any subsequent written explanation provided by the medical practitioner, the registrar shall 'serve on the practitioner a notice of inquiry which shall – (a) specify, in the form of a charge, the matters into which the inquiry is to be held; and (b) state the day, time and place at which the inquiry is to be held'.[682] Proceedings before the Medical Council are then to be held in public though it is possible, should the Medical Council consider it expedient, that proceedings be held in private.[683] Yet, the decisions of the Medical Council are to be given in public and in writing.[684]

127. Inquiries by the Medical Council are prescribed by two related but separate periods of limitation. In the first instance, the commencement of any inquiry into misconduct or other failure in terms of Article 32 (1)(b) and (c) of the Health Care Professions Act shall be barred 'by the lapse of two years which shall run from the day from which the complainant or any of the complainants become or ought to have become aware of the facts or incidents that give rise to the complaint and in any case by the lapse of ten years from the date on which the alleged fact or incident was committed'.[685] This period of limitation may be interrupted by 'any act of the inquiry served on the party being investigated'.[686] The second period of limitation regards the time frame within which the inquiry is to be concluded. Thus, the Medical Council is to conclude the inquiry 'within a period of two years from the day on which any act of the inquiry proceedings is served on the party accused in

678. S.L. 458.08, Medical Council (Erasure of Names Procedure) Rules, r. 4 (1).
679. *Ibid.*, r. 4 (3).
680. Medical Council Malta, *Guidance on how to lodge a complaint with the Medical Council Malta* 5 (2021).
681. S.L. 458.08, Medical Council (Erasure of Names Procedure) Rules, r. 4 (3).
682. *Ibid.*, r. 5 (1).
683. *Ibid.*, r. 8.
684. *Ibid.*, r. 15 (1).
685. Health Care Professions Act, Ch. 464 of the Laws of Malta, Art. 31 (2).
686. *Ibid.*, Art. 31 (3).

respect of the fact or incident with which he is charged, except where the delay is occasioned through no fault of the relevant Council'.[687] The Medical Council is relatively free to regulate its own procedure within the stipulated limitation period provided that it acts in accordance with the law,[688] but the courts have confirmed that, barring delays occasioned through no fault of its own, the Medical Council will be acting *ultra vires* beyond the scope of its authority if it directs disciplinary measure/s consequent to Article 32 of the Health Care Professions Act after the pertinent period of limitation has expired.[689]

128. Subject to the stipulated period/s of limitation set in law, the Medical Council may, after due inquiry, direct that one or more disciplinary measures are taken against a person falling under its authority. The sternest of these measures, arising from Article 32 (1)(i) of the Health Care Professions Act, is a decision that the name of a medical practitioner 'be erased from the appropriate register and, where appropriate, [the Medical Council may] recommend to the President of Malta that the professional's licence be withdrawn'. That license is either way suspended 'during such period that the name of the licensed person is deleted from the register'.[690] The Ethics of the Medical Profession Regulations non-exhaustively identify some of the offences that may entail erasure from the registers or any other disciplinary action. These include offences in the context of a professional relationship such as 'acts of immorality, indecency or dishonesty or any other act involving the abuse of a professional relationship'[691] and 'treating or attending to patients while the practitioner is under the influence of any drink or drugs'.[692] They furthermore include offences that can but do not necessarily occur within the confines of a professional relationship, such as 'driving or being in charge of a motor vehicle when under the influence of drink or drugs, or being found drunk, or being drunk and disorderly or incapable of properly looking after oneself'[693] or otherwise signing and issuing 'any certificate, report or other document containing statements which he knows, or ought to know, to be untrue, misleading or otherwise improper'.[694] The Medical Council has, for instance, erased the name of a medical practitioner from the register in a case when that practitioner was found guilty of sexual harassment of a patient while under his care.[695]

---

687. *Ibid.*, Art. 31 (4).
688. S.L. 458.08, Medical Council (Erasure of Names Procedure) Rules, rs 20 and 22. *See also*: *Buhagiar Louis v. Kunsill Mediku Malti*, Civil Court First Hall – 09/07/2020 [Ref: 1043/2012] 8–9.
689. *Portelli Dr Frank MD FRDC v. Farrugia Dr Josella noe et.*, Civil Court First Hall – 25/04/2014 [Ref: 1110/2009] 9–13; *Portelli Dr Frank MD FRDC v. Farrugia Dr Josella noe et.*, Court of Appeal – 19/07/2019 [Ref: 1110/2009/1] 18–19; *Mercieca Franco Dr v. Il-Kunsill Mediku*, Civil Court First Hall – 13/01/2022 [Ref: 1196/2010] 5–7.
690. Health Care Professions Act, Ch. 464 of the Laws of Malta, Art. 32 (2).
691. S.L. 464.17, Ethics of the Medical Profession Regulations, r. 4 (a).
692. *Ibid.*, r. 4 (b).
693. *Ibid.*, r. 4 (c).
694. *Ibid.*, r. 17.
695. Medical Council Malta, Case No. MC/D/309/7.

129. When the Medical Council determines that a person's name should be erased from an appropriate register in terms of Article 32 of the Health Care Professions Act, it is to serve a notification of that decision on the practitioner within fourteen days of the decision being taken, and the Medical Council shall also give notice to the competent authority of each Member State within twenty-one days.[696] The medical practitioner may however appeal the decision of the Medical Council applying Article 32 of the Health Care Professions Act to erase his/her name from the appropriate register. That appeal is to be made to the Court of Appeal within twenty-one days of the service of the notification of erasure.[697] In this respect, the decision of erasure taken by the Medical Council shall only take effect upon the expiry of twenty-one days 'if no appeal is lodged, or subject to such modifications, if any on appeal, after the determination of the appeal'.[698] The court has restrictively engaged with this right of appeal arising from Article 36 of the Health Care Professions Act to mean that a practitioner may not make use of it for the purpose of anything other than appealing a decision by the Medical Council to erase a person's name from the appropriate register in circumstances consequent to Articles 32 and 38 (regarding erasure in case of physical or mental infirmity) of that Act. This excludes the possibility of appeal using Article 36 in case of, for example, a time-specific suspension from the appropriate register,[699] a partial decision of the Medical Council without actually erasing the applicant's name from the appropriate register[700] and even erasure for reasons other than those arising from Articles 32 and 38 of the Health Care Professions Act, such as failure by the medical practitioner to pay a penalty imposed by the Medical Council.[701] Practitioners could however pursue action in the courts by means other than Article 36 of the Health Care Professions Act. Thus, commenting on a case where the Medical Council temporarily suspended a medical practitioner's registration while also imposing a penalty fine on that practitioner, the Court of Appeal noted that while the Medical Council retained exclusive competence regarding disciplinary measures issued in terms of the Health Care Professions Act and notwithstanding 'any legal provisions attempting to curtail the powers of the ordinary courts, time and again it has been authoritatively decided by this Court that any allegation relating to a breach of the principles of natural justice or a decision which is legally unfounded, in that it is based on a wrongful interpretation of the law or is unreasonable, is deemed to be sufficient to empower the Courts to carry out a judicial review of the contested decision'.[702]

---

696. Health Care Professions Act, Ch. 464 of the Laws of Malta, Arts 36 (1) and 42G. *See also* S.L. 451.03, Recognition of Professional Qualifications Regulations, r. 5A.
697. *Ibid.*, Art. 36 (4).
698. *Ibid.*, Art. 36 (2).
699. *Van't Verlaat Johanna v. Kunsill Mediku Malti*, Court of Appeal (Civil, Superior) – 28/04/2017 [948/2009/1] 18.
700. *Saliba Mario Tabib Dr v. Il-Kunsill Mediku*, Court of Appeal (Civil, Superior) – 10/08/2020 [Ref: 277/2019/1] 5–8.
701. *Portelli Frank Dr v. Kunsill Mediku*, Court of Appeal (Civil, Inferior) – 27 April 2010 [Ref: 18/2009] 34–35.
702. *Van't Verlaat Johanna v. Kunsill Mediku Malti*, Court of Appeal (Civil, Superior) – 28/04/2017 [948/2009/1] 21.

130. Even so, the Medical Council may, if it thinks fit, of its own motion direct that the practitioner's name be restored to the appropriate register if the disciplinary measure of erasure is used.[703] Otherwise, the individual in question can normally apply to have his/her name restored to the appropriate register after the expiration of eleven months from the date of erasure or within a period of eleven months after making the preceding application.[704] A medical practitioner's name can however also be erased from the Medical Register in other instances when this eleven-month period will not necessarily apply. If, for example, after due inquiry, the Medical Council imposes a monetary penalty but that practitioner fails to pay that penalty within three months from the date when the penalty is imposed, then the Medical Council 'shall order that the practitioner's name … be erased from any appropriate register without further notice'.[705] In that case, the practitioner's name will be restored to the appropriate register with immediate effect when full payment of the penalty is made without having to wait for any eleven-month period to lapse.[706] Also, that eleven-month period does not apply if the practitioner's name is erased on account of physical or mental infirmity, given that this individual can at any time make a request to have his/her name reinstated and if the Medical Council is satisfied, after due inquiry, that s/he is no longer unfit to practice his/her profession, the practitioner's name will be reinstated with immediate effect.[707]

131. In addition to erasure, there are four other less stern forms of disciplinary action that the Medical Council may impose after due inquiry. First, the Medical Council may direct that the practitioner's name be taken off the appropriate register 'for such period of time as the relevant Council may determine and, where appropriate, recommend to the President of Malta that the professional's license be also so suspended'.[708] By way of example, this measure akin to suspension has been imposed by the Medical Council in a case where a medical practitioner was found guilty of professional and ethical misconduct *inter alia* due to gross neglect of duties and disregard of personal responsibilities towards a patient while also failing to set a high standard in her conduct[709] as well as in a case where a medical practitioner was found guilty of ethical misconduct related to drug abuse.[710] Second, the Medical Council may, after due inquiry, impose a penalty[711] that shall not exceed EUR 20,000.[712] Examples of when this disciplinary measure has been imposed by the Medical Council include a case where a medical practitioner was found guilty

703. Health Care Professions Act, Ch. 464 of the Laws of Malta, Art. 34. *See also* S.L. 464.19, Medical Council (Standing Orders) Regulations, r. 50.
704. *Ibid.*
705. S.L. 464.18, Medical Council (Penalties) Regulations, r. 3.
706. *Ibid.*, r. 4.
707. Health Care Professions Act, Ch. 464 of the Laws of Malta, Art. 38 (3). *See also* Part I Ch. 4 §2 above.
708. *Ibid.*, Art. 32 (1)(ii).
709. Medical Council Malta, Case No. MC/77/2008. *See also*: *Van't Verlaat Johanna v. Kunsill Mediku Malti*, Civil Court First Hall – 14/11/2019 [Ref: 948/2009/1].
710. Medical Council Malta, Case No. MC/D/310/2007.
711. Health Care Professions Act, Ch. 464 of the Laws of Malta, Art. 32 (1)(iii).
712. S.L. 464.18, Medical Council (Penalties) Regulations, r. 2.

of practising as a specialist although her name was not included in the pertinent specialist register,[713] a case where a medical practitioner used a title that he did not hold while also claiming that the services provided in his private clinic were of superior quality to those of other clinics and even offering discounts on some services in his private clinic,[714] and a case when the Medical Council decided that a medical practitioner acted unethically towards another medical practitioner.[715] Third, the Medical Council may, after due inquiry, caution the practitioner. Instances when this measure has been used include when a medical practitioner was found to have exceeded the limits of correctness in his professional attitude towards a patient,[716] when a medical practitioner was found guilty of unethical behaviour for keeping the appointment in an irregular way,[717] when a medical practitioner did not in his/her conduct and in all matters set a high standard,[718] as well as when a member of the medical profession acted disrespectfully while giving evidence in court.[719] Fourth, the Medical Council may, after due inquiry, order that the practitioner undergoes 'such period of training or practice of the profession under supervision for such period as the relevant Council may determine'.[720] This measure was, for example, used against a dental surgeon after a finding by the Medical Council of unethical behaviour for obtaining money from patients to speed up the process for new dentures.[721] On this point of training, it should also be recalled that, in addition to medical practitioners, the disciplinary functions of the Medical Council can cover the medical profession more broadly to include, for instance, a person on the two-year Foundation School whose name is on the provisional register and,[722] in that respect, the Medical Council shall *inter alia* have:

> the power to inflict any penalty applicable to medical practitioners and to order that such person shall not practise the medical profession even as a house physician and, or surgeon in a government hospital or other hospital recognized by the Medical Council for the purpose, and that his name shall not be entered in the Medical Register; and where any such order has been made, it shall, for the purpose of [the Health Care Professions] Act have effect as if the name of such person has been erased from the said Register.[723]

---

713. Medical Council Malta, Case No. MC/D/290(b).
714. Medical Council Malta, Case No. MC/D/251.
715. Medical Council Malta, Case No. MC/D/262.
716. Medical Council Malta, Case No. MC/D/2055.
717. Medical Council Malta, Case No. MC/D/241.
718. Medical Council Malta, Case Nos MC/42/2012 and MC/56/2014.
719. Medical Council Malta, Case No. CC/19/2018.
720. Health Care Professions Act, Ch. 464 of the Laws of Malta, Art. 32 (1)(v). *See also* Medical Council Malta, Case No. CC/37/2015.
721. Medical Council Malta, Case No. MC/D/285.
722. *See, for instance*: Medical Council Malta, Case Nos MC/43/2013 and MC/153/2014.
723. Health Care Professions Act, Ch. 464 of the Laws of Malta, Art. 7 (4).

132. The disciplinary role of the Medical Council relates to the professional and ethical standards inasmuch as failing to abide by those standards, together with professional and ethical misconduct in any respect, are some of the main reasons occasioning disciplinary sanction by the Medical Council. These professional and ethical standards are, to an extent, contained in professional codes that are therefore considered in the next section.

II. Professional Codes

133. Professional codes addressing the medical profession are spread across Maltese medical jurisprudence, accompanied by professional codes that engage with other healthcare professions. There are furthermore instruments that are not per se professional codes, but that contain features akin to those codes, such as a code of ethics embedded in the statute of a given entity. By way of example, the Medical Association of Malta, which is a professional association in terms of the Health Care Professions Act, is regulated by a statute[724] containing a code of ethics that directs members of that association to abide by its provisions.[725] Without setting aside that broader Maltese medical jurisprudence, this sub-section of the monograph addresses professional codes that arise in particular from the Health Care Professions Act and the Medical Council, as well as the role of the wider law vis-à-vis professional codes that relate to the medical profession.

134. The Medical Council has the function of prescribing and maintaining professional and ethical standards for the medical profession.[726] These standards are, to an extent, embedded in law by way of the Ethics of the Medical Professions Regulations, which constitute subsidiary legislation arising from the Health Care Professions Act. That subsidiary law was made consequent to the authority of the Minister responsible for health to make regulations for the better implementation of the provisions of the Health Care Professions Act by authorising the Medical Council to 'issue such guidelines to health care professionals regulated by it on such matters related to the health care profession in question as may be determined'.[727] Indeed, professional and ethical standards are defined in the Health Care Professions Act to include:

> [S]tandards relating to the general conduct of a member of a health care profession, including the behaviour of such member towards his client or the patient under his care or being attended by him, during or consequential to the

724. *Ibid.*, Fourth Schedule, Part I [1 (b)].
725. Medical Association of Malta, *Statute*, Appendix 4.
726. Health Care Professions Act, Ch. 464 of the Laws of Malta, Art. 10 (1)(d).
727. *Ibid.*, Art. 51 (1)(d). *See also* L.N. 303 of 2008 – Ethics of the Medical Profession Regulations, 2008.

exercise of his profession, and the behaviour of such member towards the other members of his profession and towards members of other health care professions and towards society.[728]

In turn, it is within the scope of the Ethics of the Medical Profession Regulations 'to inform the practitioners of the particulars of the professional and ethical standards adopted by the [Medical] Council and of certain forms of conduct which may be held by the [Medical] Council to constitute misconduct in a professional respect'.[729] As such, the Ethics of the Medical Profession Regulations, which are similar to but update and modernise the Medical Council's earlier 'General Notice for the Guidance of Practitioners',[730] constitute a base professional code for the medical profession in Malta while also non-exhaustively identifying instances of professional misconduct.

135. As indicated in the definition of the professional and ethical standards quoted in the previous paragraph, there are, in principle, three sets of subjects to whom those standards relate. The first set of subjects includes the clients or the patients under the care of the medical practitioner or being attended by him/her during or consequential to the exercise of his/her profession. The Ethics of the Medical Profession Regulations thus, for instance, include provisions regarding communication with patients,[731] and it is also stipulated that a 'doctor shall not in any circumstances do, authorise to be done or condone anything that would weaken the physical or mental resistance of a human being, except for the prevention and treatment of disease'.[732] The second set of subjects includes other members of the medical profession as well as members of the other healthcare professions. The Ethics of the Medical Profession Regulations thus, for example, feature provisions stipulating that it is sometimes the duty of medical practitioners to recommend to patients that they communicate with a dental practitioner,[733] while the Regulations also engage with circumstances when a medical practitioner consults or works with another practitioner.[734] A third set of subjects in the context of professional and ethical standards relates to society at large. The Ethics of the Medical Profession Regulations hence, for instance, address medical practitioners' signs and professional plates[735] while also considering practitioners' endorsement of products.[736]

136. The Ethics of the Medical Profession Regulations nevertheless acknowledge that the 'endless number of situations that might and do arise in the course of

728. *Ibid.*, Art. 2.
729. S.L. 464.17, Ethics of the Medical Profession Regulations, r. 1 (2).
730. Medical Council Malta, *General Notice for the Guidance of Practitioners: Ethics of the Medical Profession, Ethics of the Dental Profession* (Government Printing Press 1984).
731. S.L. 464.17, Ethics of the Medical Profession Regulations, r. 13.
732. *Ibid.*, Sch. A [9].
733. *Ibid.*, r. 26.
734. *Ibid.*, Sch. A [11]. *See also* Part III Ch. 1 §2 below.
735. *Ibid.*, r. 8.
736. *Ibid.*, r. 7.

professional life cannot be all specifically covered by any set of rules'.[737] Yet, the Medical Council sometimes furnishes topic-specific instruments that direct or guide medical practitioners on specific areas of professional life. One may here use the example of advertising, canvassing and the provision of information given that it is, in principle, a topic that is well covered by the Ethics of the Medical Profession Regulations but that is nevertheless accompanied by topic-specific instruments issued by the Medical Council. It is, for example, stated in the Ethics of the Medical Profession Regulations that '[n]o practitioner shall for the purpose of being engaged by patients or of promoting his own professional advantage: (a) advertise or canvas directly or indirectly, (b) employ or [be] professionally associated with anyone who so advertises or canvases, (c) procure or acquiesce in the publication of notices commending or drawing attention to his own professional skill, knowledge, qualifications or services or depreciating those of other practitioners'.[738] It is also clearly stipulated that the 'provision of factual information about the services offered by a practitioner shall not be deemed to be contrary to the provisions of'[739] the latter regulation regarding advertising, and there is even an outline in the subsidiary law of how factual information is to be presented.[740] There furthermore are provisions in the Ethics of the Medical Profession Regulations regarding publications, interviews, telephone directories, participation in discussion, canvassing, inducement, use of professional cards, commissions and dichotomy. In spite of this, as well as the broader Maltese law addressing advertising in the context of healthcare,[741] the Medical Council additionally furnishes topic-specific instruments regarding advertising and the provision of information. These include the 2010 Code of Ethics on Advertising and Financial Conduct by Medical/Dental Practitioners, the 2017 Regulations on advertising and the provision of information to the public, and the 2020 Code of Ethics for the use of social media by doctors and dentists. While these Codes and Regulations are not embedded in law in a manner akin to the Ethics of the Medical Profession Regulations, they can be and are acted upon by the Medical Council in its regulatory capacity[742] even though its disciplinary function on the matter may ultimately be stipulated upon the pertinent provisions in the Ethics of the Medical Profession Regulations.[743] The Medical Council can moreover feed into the law via its advisory function, including, for instance, the function, 'at the request of the Minister [responsible for health], or otherwise, to advise the Minister on any matter affecting the medical and dental professions'.[744] As such, continuing on the example of advertising and provision of information, the Medical Council was, for instance, involved in the formulation of the subsidiary

737. *Ibid.*, Sch. A [4].
738. *Ibid.*, r. 5 (1).
739. *Ibid.*, r. 5 (3).
740. *Ibid.*, r. 6.
741. *See, for instance*: Medical and Kindred Professions Ordinance, Ch. 31 of the Laws of Malta, Art. 90A; Consumer Affairs Act, Ch. 378 of the Laws of Malta; S.L. 458.32, Medicinal Products (Advertising) Regulations; Public Health Act, Ch. 465 of the Laws of Malta, Art. 27 (b).
742. *See, for instance*: Medical Council Malta, *Advertising Regulations* (Circular No: 02/2020 – 27 July 2020).
743. *See, for instance*: Medical Council Malta, Case No MC66/2009/B.
744. Health Care Professions Act, Ch. 464 of the Laws of Malta, Art. 10 (1)(j).

legislation regarding requirements as to standards and practice on programmes involving the participation of certain health professionals in the broadcasting media and requirements as to advertisements, methods of advertising and directions applicable to medicinal products and treatments.[745] Consequently, although no set of rules can cover every scenario, professional codes in Malta extend from regulations incorporated in law, other instruments that are published by that Medical Council, together with the broader law to which the Medical Council can contribute via its advisory function.

137. In addition to the Ethics of the Medical Profession Regulations, as well as further professional and ethical standards prescribed by the Medical Council, the wider Maltese law furthermore frames professional codes for the medical profession in two ways. First, specific entities can monitor and influence standards for medical practitioners in the area for which they are responsible. Thus, by way of example, the Commission on Gender-Based Violence and Domestic Violence has the function 'to monitor standards and protocols for professionals in the areas covered by the scope of [the Gender-Based Violence and Domestic Violence] Act and organise specialised training for said professionals'.[746] Certain entities may also have functions that enable them to work towards changing professional codes, even if those entities are not chiefly composed of members of the profession in question. For instance, the Commission for the Rights of Persons with Disability has the function to 'work towards the elimination of discrimination against people with disabilities',[747] and the Directorate for Disability Issues (DDI) has the function to 'identify, establish and update all national policies and strategies ... directly or indirectly related to disability issues'.[748] The 2021-2030 National Strategy on the Rights of Disabled Persons then includes an output to revise the Code of Ethics for practising medical professionals and, in this respect, the Commission for the Rights of Persons with Disability would 'through its UNCRPD Monitoring and Research Unit, review the functioning of existing and revised Codes of Ethics, and put forward recommendations, which would then be discussed with stakeholders through DDI, with a view to implementation'.[749]

138. Second, there exist other professional codes in Maltese law that do not relate exclusively to the medical profession but that members of that profession may, depending on their circumstances, nevertheless be bound by or are otherwise bound to consider as a guide. These include instruments akin to topic-specific codes, such as the Protocol established by the Embryo Protection Authority in the context

745. Medical Council Malta, *Annual Report 2007*, 16. *See also* S.L. 350.30, Requirements as to Standards and Practice on Programmes involving the Participation of Certain Health Care Professionals in the Broadcasting Media and Requirements as to Advertisements and Directions Applicable to Medicinal Products and Treatments.
746. Gender-based Violence and Domestic Violence Act, Ch. 581 of the Laws of Malta, Art. 13 (g).
747. Equal Opportunities (Persons with Disability) Act, Ch. 413 of the Laws of Malta, Art. 22 (1)(g).
748. United Nations Convention on the Rights of Persons with Disabilities Act, Ch. 627 of the Laws of Malta, Art. 5 (4)(a).
749. Government of Malta – Ministry for Inclusion and Social Wellbeing, *Freedom to live: Malta's 2021 – 2030 National Strategy on the Rights of Disabled Persons* 106 (2021).

of medically assisted procreation, brought into force by regulations made by the Minister responsible for health under the Embryo Protection Act,[750] that 'gives guidance about licensed activities and the people who carry them out'.[751] By way of example, medical practitioners using pre-implantation genetic diagnosis to combine in vitro fertilisation and genetic testing as a means of avoiding the transmission of a genetic disease are to 'follow the principles of the Ethical Guidelines'[752] listed therein for that purpose. There are however also embedded in law codes of ethics that, though not professional codes addressing the medical profession, nevertheless have to be followed by at least some members of that profession in addition to any professional code binding them. For instance, the Public Administration Act establishes a Code of Ethics, which *inter alia* addresses public employees that include public officers and employees of government agencies and government entities. Recalling that there is an extensive public health service in Malta, the Code of Ethics established in the Public Administration Act stipulates that public employees and board members 'who are members of a regulated profession and who are therefore subject to a professional code of ethics are nevertheless expected to abide by the provisions of'[753] the Code of Ethics established in terms of the Public Administration Act except when the Principal Permanent Secretary furnishes an exemption in that regard. Furthermore, a 'head of a department, specialised unit, agency or government entity may, with the approval of the Principal Permanent Secretary, make rules of ethical conduct, complementary and in addition to the Code of Ethics, relating to the circumstances particular to that organisation, and the term Code of Ethics in relation to public employees in that organisation shall include such rules'.[754] Medical practitioners who are also public employees or board members within the public administration would therefore be subject to at least two codes of ethics, one arising from the regulatory authority of the medical profession and one arising from laws grounding public administration, which should be considered complementary to one another. Any conflict between multiple codes 'should be resolved, following suitable consultation, on the basis that the professional code of ethics prevails with respect to the ethical principles and practice of the profession while the [code of ethics established by way of the Public Administration Act] prevails with respect to the ethical principles and practice of any other duty emanating from the individual's responsibilities as a public employee or board member'.[755] It then is the duty of medical practitioners who are also public employees to comply with the Code of Ethics established in the Public Administration Act,[756] and failure

750. Embryo Protection Act, Ch. 524 of the Laws of Malta, Art. 2.
751. S.L. 524.02, Embryo Protection Authority (Protocol) Regulations (not yet in force).
752. *Ibid.*, r. 11.4. *See also* Part II Ch. 3 §4 below.
753. Public Administration Act, Ch. 595 of the Laws of Malta, First Schedule [5].
754. *Ibid.*, Art. 5 (5).
755. *Ibid.*, First Schedule [5].
756. *Ibid.*, Art. 5 (3).

to do so may constitute grounds for sanctions[757] and disciplinary proceedings separate from or in addition to disciplinary action taken by the Medical Council.[758]

139. Professional codes in the context of the medical profession thus include the Ethics of the Medical Profession Regulations embedded in law, as well as other instruments and/or requirements furnished by the Medical Council grounding professional and ethical standards, together with the wider law and other instruments that may arise from law that can be binding on at least some members of the medical profession. It is also worthwhile here recalling that it is a requirement in order to practice as a medical practitioner in Malta that the person is of good conduct,[759] which in the context of the Health Care Professions Act means conduct approved by the Medical Council.[760] Yet, as noted in the Ethics of the Medical Profession Regulations, in 'addition to the requirements of the Medical Council, there are customs and ethical rules which are observed by the profession as a code of conduct'.[761] This infers a code of conduct that can be unwritten but nevertheless significant to the medical profession in a manner akin to a professional code. In this respect, the next section considers the role of biomedical ethics committees.

III. Biomedical Ethics Committee

140. Maltese medical jurisprudence includes committees that address professional and ethical standards of the medical profession, bioethics, health ethics and clinical ethics. The pediments of these committees in statutory law, however, vary, which in turn affects their functions. Furthermore, medical practitioners are sometimes directed to inform individuals on bioethical issues for the purpose of obtaining their informed consent, for instance, before applying any procedures leading to medically assisted procreation.[762] In the circumstances of the latter treatment, a case may also be referred 'to an Ethics Committee as part of the decision-making process [by the pertinent authorities] to offer or decline treatment'.[763] The remit in Maltese law of biomedical ethics committees, as the standard outline of the IEL monograph on medical law collectively terms them, is therefore worthwhile briefly engaging with before broaching the physician-patient relationship in Part II of the monograph.

141. The Medical Council has the authority to 'set up committees for the purpose of enforcing professional and ethical standards applicable to the health care

757. *Ibid.*, Art. 39 (c).
758. *Ibid.*, First Schedule [23]. *See also* S.L. Const. 03, Public Service Commission Disciplinary Regulations; Office of the Principal Permanent Secretary – Office of the Prime Minister, *Manual on Disciplinary Procedures in the Public Service* (26 July 2022).
759. Health Care Professions Act, Ch. 464 of the Laws of Malta, Art. 7 (2)(b).
760. *Ibid.*, Art. 2.
761. S.L. 464.17, Ethics of the Medical Profession Regulations, Schedule A [4].
762. Embryo Protection Act, Ch. 524 of the Laws of Malta, Art. 18 (2)(f).
763. S.L. 524.02, Embryo Protection Authority (Protocol) Regulations, r. 10.10 (not yet in force).

professions regulated by it and generally in order to better perform its functions'.[764] This authority has been used by the Medical Council to streamline its work, especially 'for the purpose of collecting the evidence in inquiries, and forwarding their opinion to the Council for its consideration and decision',[765] thereby, in principle, separating analysis of complaints from hearing of inquiries, as well as to set up committee/s *inter alia* addressing the possible registration of members of the medical profession and the Foundation School Programme. These committees can include persons with expert knowledge in special matters who are not members of the Medical Council, and in addition to standing committees, the Medical Council may also appoint special committees 'to submit recommendations to the Council regarding the matters referred to them by the Council'.[766] The Medical Council has thus, in the past, appointed the equivalent of ad hoc committee/s 'to work on the Code of Ethics, mainly updating the Standards of Professional Conduct and Medical Ethics'.[767] This is significant given that it is the Medical Council that has the function to prescribe as well as to maintain professional and ethical standards for the medical profession.[768] That notwithstanding, there is no equivalent within the structures of the Medical Council of a standing committee on bioethics.

142. There however is, in principle, a Bioethics Consultative Committee, which has been described by at least one Maltese bioethicist as the main platform at the country's disposal in the context of bioethics even if it is not grounded in statute.[769] Although this Committee cannot assume duties already assigned to the Medical Council, which includes prescribing ethical standards for the medical profession, its terms of reference have specified that the Committee is 'to liaise with the Medical Council and other boards on matters of ethics affecting Health Care practice in general, whenever this is necessary and advantageous in the public interest'. The Bioethics Consultative Committee has over the years delivered opinions and recommendations on diverse topics, including advance directives and biobanking of human tissues. The role of that Committee is chiefly advisory,[770] and its terms of reference have, for instance, historically included a role to 'advise on ethical problems that may present themselves both in state and private hospitals, as well as in medical practice in general'. Indeed, other than possible ad hoc entities dealing with specific functions such as live organ donation,[771] hospitals and clinics in Malta are not bound to have in place the equivalent of a hospital ethics committee.[772] It should

764. Health Care Professions Act, Ch. 464 of the Laws of Malta, Art. 10 (2).
765. Victor Caruana Colombo in: *Annual Report of the Medical Council of Malta 2004*, 4.
766. S.L. 464.19, Medical Council (Standing Orders) Regulations, r. 34 (1).
767. Medical Council Malta, *Annual Report 2008*, 10.
768. *See also* Part I Ch. 4 §4.II above.
769. Pierre Mallia, *Malta*, in *Handbook of Global Bioethics* 1289, 1291 – 1293 (Henk A M J ten Have & Bert Gordign eds, Springer 2014).
770. *Ibid.*; Maurice N. Cauchi, Kevin Aquilina & Bridget Ellul, *Health, Bioethics and the Law* 312 (Malta University Press 2006).
771. Human Organs, Tissues and Cell Donation Act, Ch. 558 of the Laws of Malta, Art. 13.
772. *See, for instance*: Joseph Darmanin, *A hospital ethics committee in Mater Dei Hospital* (A dissertation presented to the Faculty of Theology in part fulfilment of the requirements for the Master of Arts in Bioethics at the University of Malta in 2020).

however also be said that the Bioethics Consultative Committee does not and cannot replace the functions that a hospital ethics committee should serve.

143. A Health Ethics Committee had furthermore been formally set up under the Clinical Trials Regulations[773] in line with the EU's Clinical Trials Directive.[774] That Directive is repealed in terms of the EU's Clinical Trials Regulation, but the latter Regulation nevertheless stipulates that ethical review of a clinical trial 'shall be performed by an ethics committee in accordance with the law of the Member State concerned',[775] which in Malta relates to the Health Ethics Committee. In addition to clinical trials, the Health Ethics Committee in Malta has some other functions, including with regard to the secondary processing of personal data in the health sector. For instance, processing of personal data that is not linked to the primary purpose for which the data was originally collected is permitted when that involves accessing health records for the purpose of research activities that are in the public interest. Yet, when that processing cannot be conducted using anonymised data and the research activity is conducted within the Ministry for Health or its partners, it then is only permissible among other conditions following approval by the Health Ethics Committee.[776] It is also worthwhile recalling for the purpose of this section on biomedical ethics committees that educational institutions involved in research activities have in place research ethics committees that are related to but separate from the Health Ethics Committee, such as the University of Malta's research ethics committee and its Faculties' research ethics committees including at the Faculty of Medicine and Surgery. Moreover, other entities such as the University of Malta's Centre for Molecular Medicine and Biobanking also aim, for instance, in the context of their activities to store human and other biological samples and associated data, to do so 'with suitable informed consent and ethical approval according to best practices'.[777]

773. S.L. 458.43, Clinical Trials Regulations, r. 7.
774. Directive 2001/20/EC of the European Parliament and of the Council of 4 April 2001 on the approximation of the laws, regulations and administrative provisions of the Member States relating to the implementation of good clinical practice in the conduct of clinical trials on medicinal products for human use, OJ L 121, 1.5.2001.
775. Regulation (EU) No 536/2014 of the European Parliament and of the Council of 16 April 2014 on clinical trials on medicinal products for human use, and repealing Directive 2001/20/EC, OJ L 158, 27.5.2014, Art. 4.
776. S.L. 528.10, Processing of Personal Data (Secondary Processing) (Health Sector) Regulations, r. 4 (a).
777. S.L. 327.512, Statute for the Centre for Molecular Medicine and Biobanking, r. 4 (b).

Part II. The Physician-Patient Relationship

Chapter 1. General Description

144. The chapter at hand is divided into six sections that furnish a general description of the juridical relationship between medical practitioner and patient. The broad bases in law grounding the rights and duties of medical practitioners and patients are considered first, thereby leading to a section addressing what constitutes 'informed consent' in Maltese medical law and how it is obtained. Patients' privacy is addressed next, followed by secrecy and/or confidentiality owed by medical practitioners to patients, while also engaging with instances when that secrecy and/or confidentiality can or must not apply. The right to file a complaint is also touched upon in order to then conclude this chapter by engaging with access to medical records.

145. As a point of interpretation, it should be recalled that this monograph follows the standard outline of the International Encyclopaedia for Medical Law, which uses the term 'physician'. Despite the titles of the chapters that reflect the IEL outline, the term 'medical practitioner' is used in the substantive text of this part of the monograph in the same manner as described earlier in the written text.[778]

§1. Rights and Duties of Physicians and Patients

146. The rights and duties of medical practitioners and patients are grounded in wide-reaching laws governing the healthcare system as a whole, but they also arise from more topic-specific laws that regulate a particular sector within the healthcare system as well as from the broader Maltese medical jurisprudence. This section illustrates the broad bases in law grounding those rights and duties, thereby furnishing the pediments to underpin the later chapters of this part of the monograph that address topical issues in Maltese medical law. There are six stages to this section: (i) rights and duties before one is in terms of law a 'patient' and/or before one is a medical practitioner providing services to that patient; (ii) broad spectrum rights and duties arising from Maltese law when one is a 'patient' in terms of law; (iii) domestic law that mandates restricting or otherwise permits limiting the possibility for a patient to exercise certain rights and how that type of law affects the duties of medical practitioners; (iv) rights and duties targeting specific groups of people and how

778. *See* Part I above.

that relates to the duties of medical practitioners; (v) topic-specific duties borne by medical practitioners and how that affects the rights of patients; and (vi) rights and duties of patients and medical practitioners in light of any contractual relationship between them.

147. A first stage of grounding rights and duties in the context of healthcare in Malta occurs before one is, in terms of law, a 'patient' and/or before one is a medical practitioner providing services to that patient. Rights in this context can, for instance, include entitlement rights of persons to receive healthcare, which were considered in the 'General Introduction' to this monograph,[779] as well as duties of physicians regarding registration and licensing addressed in Part I above. There are furthermore obligations consequent on the employer to ensure the health and safety of employees as well as a duty on those workers to take care of their own safety and health.[780] In addition to these key rights and duties, there are obligations embedded in law on users of healthcare services who can but do not have to, at that point, be patients, for instance, receiving treatment. The Health Act thus provides that '*users* are expected to make use of the services available in a responsible manner and to show respect to professionals, employees and also for the property'.[781] Failure to respect this expectation can even have repercussions at law. It is, for example, a contravention against public order for any person to cause 'any physician, surgeon, obstetrician, or clergyman, to attend on or visit a person whom he falsely represents to be sick'.[782]

148. A second stage of rights and duties in Maltese law arises when a person is receiving or has received health care *as a patient*. In this respect, it is within the scope of the Health Act to provide 'for the rights of patients'[783] where the term 'patient' means 'a person who is receiving, or has received, medical attention, care, or treatment, whether in a healthcare setting or otherwise'.[784] The law here bestows rights on persons directed towards services that are medical in nature. It was, for example, consequent to the Health Act that Maltese law formally provided that it shall be the right of every patient as defined in that legislative Act to 'refuse treatment that is offered to him, provided such refusal is endorsed by his signature'.[785] A key right of patients is, in this manner, grounded in law while simultaneously grounding in law patients' responsibility for exercising that right by endorsing with their signature a refusal of treatment that is offered to them. The Health Act is furthermore the basis in law for the Charter of Patient Rights and Responsibilities that sets out 'a summary of the rights and responsibilities of patients and other relevant persons'.[786] Continuing on the example of refusal of treatment, the latter Charter

779. *See also* Part III Ch. 3 §3 below.
780. *See, for instance*: Occupational Health and Safety Authority Act, Ch. 424 of the Laws of Malta; S.L. 424.18, General Provisions for Health and Safety at Work Places Regulations.
781. Health Act, Ch. 528 of the Laws of Malta, Art. 28. Emphasis added.
782. Criminal Code, Ch. 9 of the Laws of Malta, Art. 338 (v).
783. Health Act, Ch. 528 of the Laws of Malta, Art. 3.
784. *Ibid.*, Art. 2.
785. *Ibid.*, Art. 27 (1)(f).
786. *Ibid.*, Art. 29 (2).

inter alia specifies that one has the right to 'be given all the information related to risks, benefits and consequences of refusal of any treatment or care, for one to be able to make an informed choice'.[787] Yet, whereas the Health Act does not restrict the remit of patients' rights listed under Article 27 to any one sector of the healthcare system, the Charter instead largely 'highlights the level of service one would expect when utilizing *public health services* ... The rights and responsibilities represent a commitment or definition of what should be expected by the users and the healthcare providers within the *Public Health Service*'.[788] Private facilities can and do provide their own versions of a patient's charter that, maintaining the example of refusal of treatment, would typically include a right for patients to refuse treatment at any stage while taking responsibility for refusing treatment.[789] That being said, even absent acknowledgement of the right to refuse treatment, there are other means embedded in Maltese law to safeguard persons' bodily integrity, including the obligation not to provide treatment before obtaining patients' informed consent.[790]

149. A third stage for the purpose of engaging with the rights and duties of medical practitioners and patients in Malta involves considering whether there exists domestic law that mandates restricting or otherwise permits limiting the possibility for a patient to exercise certain rights and, if so, how that affects the duties of medical practitioners. Chapter 2 of this part of the monograph will engage with instances when the law mandates or permits the restriction of a person's capacity to hold rights and duties as well as his/her capacity to exercise those rights and duties due to that person's age or impaired decision-making capacity. Additionally, other specific laws can impose particular duties touching on persons' rights. Some examples may here be drawn from the Public Health Act.[791] Thus, the Superintendent of Public Health has the broad authority under the Public Health Act to make, vary or revoke orders 'listing and categorising notifiable disease conditions'.[792] In turn, the Superintendent of Public Health may 'require a person to undergo a medical examination by a medical practitioner within such period as the Superintendent may specify if the Superintendent has reason to believe that such person is suffering from a notifiable disease or if he has an occupation which is considered capable of spreading disease'.[793] The medical practitioner who conducts that medical examination is then bound to, as soon as practicable, provide the Superintendent of Public Health with a written report of the results of that examination.[794] A person who then is aware of having a notifiable disease 'shall take all reasonable measures and precautions to prevent the transmission of the disease'.[795] In addition to other powers

787. Healthcare Standards Directorate – Ministry for Health, *Charter of Patient's Rights and Responsibilities* 12 (2016).
788. *Ibid.*, 3. Emphasis added.
789. *See, for instance:* St James Hospital (Malta), *Patient's Charter*.
790. *See* Part II Ch. 1 §2 below.
791. *See also* Prevention of Disease Ordinance, Ch. 36 of the Laws of Malta; S.L. 36.07, Typhoid Fever Regulations; S.L. 45.01, Lepers Regulations.
792. Public Health Act, Ch. 465 of the Laws of Malta, Art. 27 (a)(i).
793. *Ibid.*, Art. 28 (1). *See also* Prevention of Disease Ordinance, Ch. 36 of the Laws of Malta.
794. *Ibid.*, Art. 28 (2). *See also* Part III Ch. 3 §2 below.
795. *Ibid.*, Art. 33 (1).

s/he has, the Superintendent of Public Health may furthermore order that a person suffering from a notifiable disease submit 'to further medical examination, medical testing, immunisation, medical treatment or counselling'.[796] The Public Health Act then stipulates that whenever any part of Malta is affected by any epidemic disease, 'medical practitioners exercising their profession within the area affected by the disease, as well as other medical practitioners engaged by the Government, shall not refuse to treat persons suffering from such disease within the area'.[797] Contravening provisions of the Public Health Act can, on the report of the Superintendent of Public Health, entail criminal proceedings, conviction, punishment and a court order to ultimately comply with the law,[798] without excluding the possibility of other viable criminal action, for instance, due to the transmission of communicable diseases.[799] That being said, the COVID-19 pandemic has *inter alia* been addressed by way of the authority of the Superintendent of Public Health to make, vary or revoke orders to prescribe measures to guard against or to control dangerous epidemics or infectious diseases[800] and breaches of a number of those orders given by the Superintendent were subject to be tried in accordance with the Commissioners for Justice Act rather than by way of criminal proceedings.[801]

150. A fourth stage when addressing the rights and duties of medical practitioners and patients involves engagement with laws that ground rights and duties targeting specific groups of people, especially those whose rights and liberties may be lawfully restricted. This includes, for instance, the rights of persons with mental disorders and the rights of persons with disabilities that will be addressed later in this part of the monograph, as well as the rights of persons held in detention consequent to the criminal law, which can be here used as an example. Indeed, a suspect detained or arrested by a law enforcement or judicial authority and who is being questioned in relation to any criminal offence, as well as a person who is charged or accused of having committed a criminal offence, has a right 'to consult a medical practitioner of his choice and, if such medical practitioner is not readily available, any other medical practitioner'.[802] Furthermore, a prison under the Prisons Act is subject to the Prisons Regulations that address some of the rights and duties of prisoners as well as those of medical practitioners caring for them.[803] Thus, a prison medical service is to be organised in consultation with the Minister responsible for health that 'shall include the services of registered medical practitioners who shall have the care of the health of prisoners'.[804] One of those medical practitioners will

796. *Ibid.*, Art. 29 (1)(c).
797. *Ibid.*, Art. 35.
798. *Ibid.*, Arts 38–44.
799. Criminal Code, Ch. 9 of the Laws of Malta, Art. 244A. *See also* S.L. 09.10, Communicable Diseases and Conditions Regulations.
800. Public Health Act, Ch. 465 of the Laws of Malta, Art. 27 (c). *See also* General Introduction §2.I above.
801. *Ibid.*, Art. 44A. *See also* Commissioners for Justice Act, Ch. 291 of the Laws of Malta.
802. Criminal Code, Ch. 9 of the Laws of Malta, Art. 355AS (1). *See also* Art. 534AB (1)(h).
803. Prisons Act, Ch. 260 of the Laws of Malta, Art. 3.
804. S.L. 260.03, Prisons Regulations, r. 31 (1).

be designated by the Director of Prisons as the Medical Officer of the Prison.[805] That Medical Officer is to then 'ensure the care of the physical and mental health of the prisoners and shall also ensure that medical doctors see, under proper conditions and with such frequency as is reasonably required, all sick prisoners, those who report illness or injury, and any prisoner who may require medical attention'.[806] These obligations on the Medical Officer, for instance, include informing the Director of Prisons if s/he considers that 'a prisoner's physical or mental health has been or will be adversely affected by continued imprisonment or by any condition of imprisonment'[807] as well as reporting if s/he 'suspects any prisoner of having suicidal intention'.[808] This can entail placing that prisoner under special observation, in the prison infirmary or otherwise transferring him/her to a specialised institution.[809] Indeed, the medical services of the prisons are bound to 'seek to detect and shall treat any physical or mental illness or defect or drug-related condition which may affect a prisoner's well being in prison or which may impede a prisoner's re-settlement after release'.[810] It should furthermore be said that the Detention Service Regulations arising from the Immigration Act also include provisions regarding medical care.[811] The Detention Service Regulations, for instance, provide that every detention centre shall have reasonable access to a medical officer who is to 'pay special attention to the need to recognise medical conditions which might be found among a diverse population and the cultural sensitivity appropriate when performing his duties'.[812]

151. The fifth stage, when engaging with the rights and duties of medical practitioners and patients, reverses the approach of the fourth stage so that, rather than considering the rights of an individual or patient, consequently drawing out duties of medical practitioners arising there from, one instead focuses on the duties imposed upon medical practitioners that arise from specific laws and how that ultimately affects the rights of their patients. While a number of obligations of this nature will be addressed throughout this part of the monograph, an example that can be mentioned at this stage relates to specified drugs listed in the Second Schedule of the Drugs (Control) Regulations, such as barbital. Among other duties, a medical practitioner has an obligation not to issue a prescription for a specified drug:

> [U]nless the said medical practitioner has taken reasonably sufficient steps to ascertain that such person is not, at the time of issuing the prescription, receiving treatment from another medical practitioner in respect of addiction to any specified drug or otherwise, and that such person has not been supplied with any such drug on a prescription issued by that other medical practitioner.[813]

805. *Ibid.*, r. 31 (2).
806. *Ibid.*, r. 32 (1).
807. *Ibid.*, r. 32 (3)(a).
808. *Ibid.*, r. 31 (7).
809. *Ibid.*, r. 31 (6). *See also* Mental Health Act, Ch. 525 of the Laws of Malta, Art. 38.
810. *Ibid.*, r. 37.
811. Immigration Act, Ch. 217 of the Laws of Malta, Art. 34.
812. S.L. 217.19, Detention Service Regulations, r. 37 (2).
813. S.L. 31.18, Drugs (Control) Regulations, r. 7 (6).

Specific duties incumbent on medical practitioners are spread across the statute book, and while a sound administrative system is often imperative to buttress those duties in order to operate effectively,[814] medical practitioners' duties are also more broadly embedded in professional codes.[815] A second example can thus be drawn from the Ethics of the Medical Profession Regulations that engage with instances when a medical practitioner occupying an official position has to see and report, for instance, to an employer, on a case of illness or injury to his/her employees. In those circumstances, the medical practitioner in question is to inform the patient that s/he is entitled to ask that his/her own medical practitioner be present during the examination and the medical practitioner who is acting in an official capacity is to 'scrupulously avoid any interference with, or remarks on, the treatment or diagnosis that has been adopted'.[816] Where a difference of opinion exists, while recalling that any doubts are to be interpreted in favour of the patient,[817] the Medical Council has considered it advisable that 'an independent opinion on the case is sought from another practitioner which is acceptable to both parties'.[818] Moreover, medical practitioners are not to accept conditions of service that do not ensure their professional independence.[819] This is 'understood to mean that the practitioner must at all times act in the best interest of patients without any ulterior consideration to the relationship with his employer/body contracting his services'.[820]

152. The sixth stage involves acknowledging the possibility of a contractual relationship between the patient and the medical practitioner. It would then entail that, in addition to any other rights and duties that are *ipso jure* incumbent on the parties, rights and duties may also, in principle, arise by agreement from that contract. In this respect, it is worthwhile recalling that the domestic courts have, for the purpose of liability suits, increasingly examined the juridical relationship between a patient and a medical practitioner in the context of contract.[821] Be that as it may, patients' consent is a condition that is typically essential to the existence of a juridical relationship between patients and medical practitioners, as well as being critical to the performance of medical practitioners' duties within that juridical relationship, and it is considered next.

814. *See, for instance*: *Chetcuti Vincent v. Direttur General tal-Habs et.*, Civil Court First Hall – 06/10/2010, Court of Appeal (Civil, Superior) – 01/04/2014 [Ref: 608/1995/1].
815. *See* Part I Ch. 4 §4.II above.
816. S.L. 464.17, Ethics of the Medical Profession Regulations, Schedule A [11 (d)].
817. Medical Council Malta, *Ethical position of doctors examining patients in an official capacity* 1 (MC/145/93 – 22 March 1993).
818. *Ibid.*, 2.
819. S.L. 464.17, Ethics of the Medical Profession Regulations, Schedule A [8].
820. Medical Council Malta, *Ethical position of doctors examining patients in an official capacity* 1 (MC/145/93 – 22 March 1993).
821. *See* Part I Ch. 4 §1.I above.

§2. Informed Consent

153. Maltese medical law mandates that, unless otherwise stipulated in law, medical practitioners cannot provide treatment without first obtaining a patient's informed consent or the consent of the appropriate substitute decision-maker, for instance, if the patient lacks capacity at law to consent to treatment. This section is thus divided into two parts: the first section addresses the topic of informed consent, when individuals possess the capacity to enter into a juridical relationship with medical practitioners and to consent to or refuse treatment. The second section instead addresses the situation of persons with impaired decision-making capacity while identifying how consent is obtained in respect of those persons.

154. Three points of interpretation should be clarified at the outset. First, unless otherwise indicated, the term 'treatment' in this section includes diagnostic interventions. Second, absent informed consent, there are provisions to exempt from civil liability in tort persons who rescue or assist another person whose life or personal safety is in clear danger,[822] as well as provisions to exempt from criminal liability a person who performs an act necessary to ensure the safety of another person who is in present or imminent danger.[823] Given that these provisions were addressed in Part I of this monograph, they will not be engaged with again in this section. Third, the minor patient is not considered here since that topic is addressed in a later chapter of this part of the monograph.

I. The General Principle of Informed Consent

155. It is assumed in Maltese law that, unless otherwise provided in law or demonstrated by using means outlined in law, a person will be able and competent to make decisions.[824] This subsection is based on that initial assumption and refers exclusively to the person who possesses the capacity at law to furnish consent duly addressing topics in the following order: (i) Consent as an essential requirement so as to establish a juridical relationship between patient and medical practitioner; (ii) the obligation to obtain a patient's informed consent prior to furnishing treatment; (iii) the duty of the medical practitioner to furnish information to the patient and the responsibility of the patient to furnish information to the medical practitioner or healthcare provider; and (iv) the quantity and quality of information to be provided by the medical practitioner to the patient.

156. A person's consent is, all else being equal, required in order to establish a juridical relationship with a medical practitioner, and so long as that relationship is grounded in contract,[825] consent is one of the conditions essential for the validity of

---

822. Civil Code, Ch. 16 of the Laws of Malta, Art. 1033A. *See also* Part I Ch. 4 §1.I above.
823. Criminal Code, Ch. 9 of the Laws of Malta, Art. 226C. *See also* Part I Ch. 4 §1.II above.
824. *See, for instance*: Civil Code, Ch. 16 of the Laws of Malta, Art. 967 (1); Mental Health Act, Ch. 525 of the Laws of Malta, Art. 24 (1).
825. *See* Part I Ch. 4 §1.I above.

that contract.[826] Also, while consent to establish a juridical relationship with a medical practitioner is separate from and normally precedes consent requirements to lawfully provide treatment, requirements regarding the provision of information can commence prior to the establishment of that juridical relationship. Indeed, there 'shall be a cause of nullity of the agreement when the artifices practised by one of the parties were such that without them the other party would not have contracted'[827] in the first place. An example when this severe outcome arose in Malta involved a man who provided information posing as a medical practitioner when he was not a member of that profession in order to obtain the consent of some women to touch them under the pretence of professionally examining them.[828] Yet, even absent that type of fraudulent device, the Medical and Kindred Professions Ordinance stipulates that no person 'shall advertise or permit or suffer to be advertised in any manner whatsoever, any medical or health service or treatment, not being a service provided by Government, or any other service or treatment which is or is described as being of a medical, therapeutic or curative value or effect, or in any other way beneficial to health, without the approval of the Council of Health'.[829] While the latter law covers treatment understood to include 'any form of advice relating to the treatment or cure of maladies or ailments, or any advice relating to health'[830] and was adopted in relation to the Council of Health established under the now repealed Department of Health (Constitution) Ordinance,[831] it is noted in the Ethics of the Medical Profession Regulations when addressing advertising that the 'provision of factual information about the services offered by a practitioner to patients shall not be deemed to be contrary to the provisions of [that] regulation'[832] rooted in subsidiary law. Yet, that factual information must *inter alia* 'be honest and never exploit a patient's vulnerability or lack of medical knowledge … [and] be presented discreetly so as to facilitate informed decision making'.[833] Ultimately, a medical practitioner 'shall neither instigate nor condone any advertisement relating to his professional status of work'[834] and, even when the provision of information prior to the establishment of a juridical relationship is permissible, the Medical Council provides that 'advertisements cannot replace informed consent for any procedure or service'.[835] It is incumbent on the medical practitioner him/herself to furnish information regarding the treatment being offered to an individual, and the medical practitioner cannot excuse this responsibility solely by delegating that task to leaflets or even to his/her assistants.[836]

826. Civil Code, Ch. 16 of the Laws of Malta, Art. 966 (b).
827. *Ibid.*, Art. 981 (1).
828. *Il-Pulizija v. Precht Michael Camilo*, Court of Magistrates (Criminal Judicature) – 23/01/2015 [Ref: 76/2015]. *See also* Part I Ch. 3 above.
829. Medical and Kindred Professions Ordinance, Ch. 31 of the Laws of Malta, Art. 90A (1).
830. *Ibid.*, Art. 90A (2).
831. Department of Health (Constitution) Ordinance, Ch. 94 of the Laws of Malta.
832. S.L. 464.17, Ethics of the Medical Professions Regulations, r. 5 (3).
833. *Ibid.*, r. 6.
834. *Ibid.*, Schedule A [7].
835. Medical Council Malta, *Regulations on advertising and the provision of information to the public* 3 (2017).
836. *See, for instance*: *Rossi Sue v. Muscat Joseph D sive Josie Dr*, Civil Court First Hall – 25/06/2008 [Ref: 1492/1994/1] 30–31.

157. Assuming that a juridical relationship has been established between medical practitioner and patient unless otherwise stipulated at law, such as in the case of restrictive care provided in terms of the Mental Health Act,[837] treatment cannot be provided to that patient prior to obtaining his/her informed consent. While a patient can withdraw consent after providing it,[838] the requirement to obtain informed consent before furnishing treatment *inter alia* arises from professional regulation, including professional ethics embedded in law and codes of conduct. These are typically grounded in the Health Care Professions Act,[839] regulating several professions in healthcare, as well as similar legislative Acts such as the Psychology Profession Act.[840] Taking the Ethics of the Medical Profession Regulations as an example, whereas those Regulations make no mention of patients' informed consent, it is stipulated that a 'doctor shall by his conduct and in all matters set a high standard',[841] and the obligation to obtain informed consent is an integral element of that standard. In its capacity to take disciplinary action against medical and dental practitioners, the Medical Council has, for instance, held that practitioners who did not obtain the patient's informed consent before providing treatment did not maintain the 'high standard' demanded of the profession and were in violation of the law.[842] Thus, failing to obtain informed consent is sufficient to find medical practitioners guilty in terms of the Health Care Professions Act of professional or ethical misconduct or for failing to abide by the professional and ethical standards applicable to them.[843] In addition to professional regulation, independent legislative Acts also impose requirements not to provide treatment or care before obtaining the patients' informed consent. For instance, the Mental Health Act stipulates that a voluntary patient 'shall not be admitted [to a mental health licensed facility] unless he consents in writing to the required care or treatment'[844] and, in case of involuntary admission to a mental health licensed facility, '[p]rior to the administration of any treatment, informed consent shall be given by the patient'.[845] While it should be noted that the Health Act has since 2017 ground in law a right to consent to or refuse medical attention, care or treatment, this largely relates to persons who are 16 or 17 years of age.[846] Thus, rather than relying on the initiative of the patient to refuse treatment,[847] Maltese medical law traditionally relies on the obligation to obtain

---

837. Mental Health Act, Ch. 525 of the Laws of Malta, Art. 34.
838. *See, for instance*: Healthcare Standards Directorate – Ministry for Health, *Charter of Patient's Rights and Responsibilities* 12 (2016).
839. Healthcare Professions Act, Ch. 464 of the Laws of Malta.
840. Psychology Profession Act, Ch. 471 of the Laws of Malta.
841. S.L. 464.17, Ethics of the Medical Profession Regulations, Schedule A [5].
842. Medical Council Malta, *Annual Report 2010* (Inquiry MC/79/2007 re Dr Franco Mercieca – 19/05/2010) p. 30. *See also*: *Mercieca Franco Dr v. Kunsill Mediku*, Court of Appeal (Civil, Superior) – 28/03/2014 [Ref: 146/2010/1]; *Mercieca Franco Dr v. Il-Kunsill Mediku*, Civil Court First Hall – 13/01/2022 [Ref: 1196/2010].
843. Health Care Professions Act, Ch. 464 of the Laws of Malta, Art. 32 (1)(b)–(c).
844. Mental Health Act, Ch. 525 of the Laws of Malta, Art. 7 (2)(a).
845. *Ibid.*, Art. 14.
846. Health Act, Ch. 528 of the Laws of Malta, Art. 27 (2). *See* Part II Ch. 2 §1 below.
847. *See* Part II Ch. 1 §1 above.

informed consent before providing treatment in order to temper the 'freedom of medicine'[848] and safeguard a person's integrity.

158. Informed consent then also entails the provision of information. This is a two-way process involving the medical practitioner imparting information but also one where the patient provides pertinent information to the healthcare provider and/or participates in decision-making regarding his/her treatment. As to the former information, the Health Act states that it is the right of every patient 'to receive information concerning the state of his health and the health services and treatments available'.[849] It is also the right of every patient 'to be provided in advance with clear information on the treatment options available and to be involved in discussions and decisions about the treatment to be given'.[850] The Charter of Patient Rights and Responsibilities, which arises from the Health Act and largely relates to public health services, then acknowledges that one has the right 'to accept or refuse any treatment, examination, test or screening procedure that is offered in accordance with the law'[851] but it furthermore stipulates that a patient also has a right to 'receive all the information about his/her medical condition, the care/treatment one is receiving, together with care options within established local parameters, risks and prognosis'.[852] The Charter builds upon this by acknowledging that one has the right to 'participate in decisions about one's care'[853] accompanied by the related obligation incumbent on healthcare professionals to 'refrain from making decisions related to care and treatment without the patient's direct participation except in exceptional cases'.[854] One moreover has a right, according to the Charter at hand, to 'get support and enough information to participate in the management of one's condition'.[855] For the purpose of this part of the monograph regarding the relationship between patient and medical practitioner, it is noteworthy that the Charter also lists patients' responsibilities. In the context of informed consent, those responsibilities include that one has the responsibility to 'take an active part in discussions and decisions about one's healthcare and treatment'[856] as well as the responsibility to 'inform the healthcare provider of any changes in one's health condition'.[857] With regard to information, the Charter notes that one has the responsibility to 'provide complete and accurate information about one's health and medical history, including medications, hospital stays, herbal remedies and any other matters that pertain to one's health'[858] as well as the responsibility to 'be truthful and to describe symptoms to their best ability to healthcare providers'.[859]

848. S.L. 464.17, Ethics of the Medical Profession Regulations, Schedule A [1(b)].
849. Health Act, Ch. 528 of the Laws of Malta, Art. 27 (1)(b).
850. *Ibid.*, Art. 27 (1)(c).
851. Healthcare Standards Directorate – Ministry for Health, *Charter of Patient's Rights and Responsibilities* 12 (2016).
852. *Ibid.*, 10.
853. *Ibid.*, 12.
854. *Ibid.*
855. *Ibid.*, 10.
856. *Ibid.*, 13
857. *Ibid.*
858. *Ibid.*, 11
859. *Ibid.*

159. There are instances when the domestic law itself stipulates a minimum set of details and information that a medical practitioner must furnish to patients before treatment is provided. The Embryo Protection Act, for example, provides that, for 'the purposes of informed consent and before applying any procedure leading to medically assisted procreation, the medical practitioner in charge of the procedure shall inform in detail and in writing the prospective parent or prospective parents on'[860] material listed in that provision, which includes the complications that may arise for the woman and potential offspring as well as the probable chances of success of the procedure. Yet even absent that sort of topic-specific domestic law regarding informed consent, providing information to an individual patient is understood in Malta to be, to paraphrase the Court of Appeal, a measure by which the medical practitioner demonstrates his/her diligence in exercising his/her professional skill as a medical practitioner.[861] In this respect, it has also been noted by the domestic courts that providing information to patients about the treatment that they intend receiving is understood to be part of the basic skill set of medical practitioners that is fundamental for patients to make an informed choice regarding that treatment.[862] The quantity and quality of information to be provided is thus, unless otherwise stipulated at law, dependent upon what generally accepted medical practice indicates that medical practitioners should do. Consequently, as noted by the Court of Appeal in a case involving a claim of civil liability on the basis that a woman was not informed that pregnancy may still result despite a procedure of tubal ligation, medical practitioners are not bound to provide all the information related to a particular treatment but they are bound to provide that information that generally accepted medical practice indicates should be provided.[863] It also entails taking into account the individual patient at hand, including the emotional state of the patient and the necessity of treatment.[864] That being said, the courts in Malta have also held that healthcare professionals are bound to furnish complete and detailed information in the situation of a treatment or procedure that is aesthetic in nature.[865] This is because aesthetic value is not stipulated upon clinical skills or generally accepted medical practice but is instead stipulated upon the subjective values of the patient at hand. Consequently, medical practitioners performing aesthetic treatment should, in particular, furnish information depending on the patient's overall needs, including an illustration of the foreseeable results. Be that as it may, medical practitioners should, regardless, not limit themselves to furnishing information

---

860. Embryo Protection Act, Ch. 524 of the Laws of Malta, Art. 18 (2). *See also* S.L. 483.01, Tissues and Cells (Quality and Safety) Regulations, r. 9; S.L. 483.02, Blood (Quality and Safety) Regulations, Schedule V; S.L. 483.06, Organ Transplants (Quality and Safety) Regulations, r. 14.
861. *Abela Phyllis sive Pina et. v. Tabone Dr* Mario, Court of Appeal (Civil, Superior) – 26/06/2019 [Ref: 880/1998/2] 17.
862. *Grech Simon v. Humphreys* Dominic, Civil Court First Hall – 02/06/2017 [Ref: 2224/1998/1] 18.
863. *Zerafa Frankie et. v. Avramov Olga et.*, Court of Appeal (Civil, Superior) – 30/05/2008 [Ref: 1000/2002/1] 12.
864. *Mercieca Lawrence et. v. Direttur Generali tad-Dipartiment tas-Sahha et.*, Civil Court First Hall – 28/02/2019 [Ref: 1294/2013] 17.
865. *Sammut Vanessa v. Fenech Dr Charles B.Ch.D (Hons)*, Court of Appeal (Civil, Superior) – 01/12/2006 [Ref: 289/1998/1] 14.

to patients with the sole aim and intention of obtaining patients' consent to the outcome sought by those medical practitioners.[866]

160. On this last point, the Medical Council, in its regulatory capacity, has occasionally provided details regarding how medical practitioners should frame and engage with patients' informed choices. By way of example, noting that medical practitioners sometimes share premises and bring specialists on a periodic basis to those premises, the Medical Council suggests that any recommendation furnished by one medical practitioner that a patient consults with another medical practitioner working in the same premises should not convey a subtle coercive message or pressure since that would 'compromise the voluntary choice of the individual'.[867] Medical practitioners must instead 'be able to offer and inform patients of alternative services to those provided by colleagues with whom they share the same premises'.[868] The Medical Council also noted that medical practitioners should ensure that all 'information provided should include information about inherent risks associated'[869] with the services one provides, which should include the risk of failure of a technique if the statistic is known.

II. Impaired Decision-Making Capacity

161. Maltese law regarding people who lack or have impaired decision-making capacity traditionally relies on systems 'to quickly determine loss of capacity and appoint a suitable substitute decision maker'.[870] It consequently signifies a person making a decision to consent to treatment on behalf of another person, and much of what was said in the previous subsection about the rights and requirements of consent and information would then be vested in the substitute decision-maker. This subsection identifies the process to establish loss of capacity or impaired decision-making capacity so as to then highlight who will be the substitute decision-maker and how that substitute decision-maker consents to treatment on behalf of the patient who lacks the capacity to consent to treatment. Consideration is also given in this subsection to the way that Maltese law is changing towards supporting persons to exercise their (legal) capacity to consent to treatment rather than relying exclusively on substitute decision-making.

162. Maltese law has different provisions outlining various types of capacity with related measures to determine loss of capacity. These can affect the capacity to

866. *See, for instance*: *Galea Grezzju et. v. Vella Paul Dentist Dottor et.*, Civil Court First Hall – 14/07/2022 [Ref: 92/2013] 14.

867. Medical Council of Malta, *Code of Ethics on Advertising and Financial Conduct by Medical/Dental Practitioners* 7 (2010).

868. *Ibid.*

869. Medical Council Malta, *Regulations on advertising and the provision of information to the public* 3 (June 2017).

870. National Commission for Active Ageing, *National Strategic Policy for Active Ageing Malta 2014 – 2020*, 74 (Parliamentary Secretariat for Rights of Persons with Disability and Active Ageing 2014).

establish a medical practitioner-patient relationship and/or the capacity to consent to or refuse treatment. As to the former relationship, the capacity to contract is, for instance, regulated in the Civil Code, and any contract 'entered into by a person *who has not the use of reason* … is null'.[871] No court decree is required to declare that a person has not the use of reason though persons 'capable of contracting may not set up the nullity of the contract on the ground of the disability of those with whom they have contracted'.[872] Additionally, a person over 18 years of age 'with a mental disorder or other condition, which *renders him incapable of managing his own affairs*, or who is insane or prodigal, may be interdicted or incapacitated from doing certain acts'[873] as indicated in and by way of a court decree. Any act performed by the person who is interdicted or incapacitated 'subsequently to such decree, or even subsequently to the appointment of the temporary curator, shall be null'.[874] That being said, with the exception of mental health law, one point that is not explicitly catered for in Maltese law is the capacity to consent to and refuse treatment. Some entities, such as the Health Promotion and Disease Prevention Directorate, have based assessment of capacity to consent on a standard similar to that found in the Mental Capacity Act 2005 in England and Wales,[875] inasmuch as the standard would ostensibly depend upon whether the person is able or unable 'to comprehend and retain information related to the decision and its implications and/or [whether the person is able or] unable to use and weigh this information in a decision making process'.[876] Broader domestic jurisprudence and scholarship have, however, begun grounding the capacity to consent to or refuse treatment in terms of mental capacity or competence within the confines of Maltese law.[877] For instance, the Charter of Patient's Rights and Responsibilities acknowledges that one has the right to accept or to refuse any treatment subject to that person being 'mentally competent',[878] and Mallia *et al.*, in their work regarding advance care planning, engage with 'the patient's mental capacity (as defined under the Mental Health Act of Malta, 2012)'.[879] Indeed, the concept of mental capacity was formally defined in the

871. Civil Code, Ch. 16 of the Laws of Malta, Art. 968. Emphasis added.
872. *Ibid.*, Art. 973.
873. *Ibid.*, Art. 189. Emphasis added.
874. Code of Organization and Civil Procedure, Ch. 12 of the Laws of Malta, Art. 525 (1). *See also* Civil Code, Ch. 16 of the Laws of Malta, Art. 192.
875. Mental Capacity Act 2005 (UK ST, England & Wales 2005 – C 9) s. 3.
876. Health Promotion and Disease Prevention Directorate, *Consent for COVID-19 swab testing for persons lacking capacity to consent* (2022).
877. *See also* Human Organs, Tissues and Cell Donation Act, Ch. 558 of the Laws of Malta, Art. 14 (2).
878. Healthcare Standards Directorate – Ministry for Health, *Charter of Patient's Rights and Responsibilities* 12 (2016).
879. Pierre Mallia, Godfrey Laferla, Kevin Aquilina & Emmanuel Agius, *University of Malta Bioethics Research Programme – Consensus Statement on End of Life Ethico/Legal Issues* 3 (Erasmus+ EndCare Project 2017). Original parentheses. *See also*: *Consensus Document: Faculty of Medicine & Surgery, Faculty of Laws, Faculty of Theology, Bioethics Research Programme and Medicine & Law Programme as part of an Erasmus+ project of the Bioethics Research Programme of the Medical School, on Harmonisation of end of life care (EndCare)* 11 (Pierre Mallia ed. Erasmus+ EndCare Project 2018).

Maltese statute book by way of the Mental Health Act in 2012 as follows:[880] 'the patient's ability and competence to make different categories and types of decisions and to be considered responsible for his actions'.[881]

163. The definition of mental capacity is thus embedded in the Mental Health Act, which regulates the provision of mental health services, care and rehabilitation whilst promoting and upholding the rights of people suffering from mental disorders. It is the latter group of people who are the primary concern of the Mental Health Act, and the regulation of mental capacity in that context is designed as an exception to the general rules of adult capacity in Malta.[882] For instance, only a psychiatrist 'may certify a person suffering from a mental disorder as having mental capacity or lack thereof'.[883] When a psychiatrist deems the lack of mental capacity to be of a transient nature not exceeding 14 days, then that transient lack of mental capacity need only be documented in the patient's clinical records.[884] The certification of lack of mental capacity for a period exceeding 14 days but not exceeding 26 weeks instead requires the approval of the Commissioner for the Promotion of Rights of Persons with Mental Disorders (Commissioner for Mental Health) after an independent psychiatrist is appointed by that Commissioner to verify the first certification.[885] If the approval of the Commissioner for Mental Health includes the recommendation of an application for incapacitation or interdiction, the certification of lack of mental capacity shall cease to be valid after 26 weeks 'unless procedures for incapacity or interdiction have been initiated',[886] which will then require a court decree.

164. Regardless of how capacity/incapacity is established, unless otherwise indicated at law, informed consent will have to be obtained by medical practitioners from a substitute decision-maker when an individual lacks the capacity to furnish that informed consent. Who will take on the role of substitute decision-maker will depend on the regime that is applicable to the circumstances at hand. This can be informal in that a person will be a substitute decision-maker because they already occupy a particular position in the patient's life. By way of example, under the law of cohabitation, a cohabitant 'shall have the right to take all decisions relating to the medical care of the other cohabitant'.[887] It is also possible for a person to specifically appoint a person to act on their behalf during a period of incapacity, for instance, by way of the contract of mandate given by a person in anticipation of his/her incapacity. Indeed, this type of mandate is made in order for the mandatary 'to

880. The term 'mental capacity' was used but not defined in the following: S.L. 111.01, Personal injuries of civilians scheme, r. 2 (1), and in S.L. 217.12, Common standards and procedures for returning illegally staying third-country nationals Regulations, r. 6 (1). The term 'mental incapacity' was used but not defined in the following: Traffic Regulation Ordinance, Ch. 65 of the Laws of Malta, Art. 15E (4), and in the General Elections Act, Ch. 354 of the Laws of Malta, Art. 27 (1).
881. Mental Health Act, Ch. 525 of the Laws of Malta, Art. 2.
882. Civil Code, Ch. 16 of the Laws of Malta, Part I, Title VI, Sub-title II.
883. Mental Health Act, Ch. 525 of the Laws of Malta, Art. 24 (2).
884. *Ibid.*, Art. 24 (3).
885. *Ibid.*, Art. 24 (4)–(6).
886. *Ibid.*, Art. 24 (6).
887. Cohabitation Act, Ch. 614 of the Laws of Malta, Art. 13 (2)(d).

take care of the mandator or to administer his property'[888] upon 'the occurrence of the [mandator's] incapacity'.[889] That includes, subject to approval by the court of voluntary jurisdiction and any conditions it deems necessary,[890] taking decisions regarding healthcare treatment on behalf of the mandator.[891] On pain of nullity, the mandate given by a person in anticipation of his incapacity must be drawn up by a notary public in the presence of two witnesses after having obtained a medical declaration that circumstances so require in the best interests of that person.[892] Performance of this mandate is also dependent upon the occurrence of the incapacity and the approval of the Court of Voluntary Jurisdiction upon application made by the mandatary designated in the act.[893]

165. Independent statutory legislation is furthermore increasingly providing for the appointment of representatives chosen by the subject of the decision him/herself for a given purpose, which includes providing informed consent to receive treatment. Subsidiary legislation arising from the Social Care Standards Authority Act is thus, for example, steadily engaging with the prospect of a legally appointed representative, which 'means a person that may be nominated by the resident [of a facility regulated under that Act] to be kept informed about the resident's personal affairs and take decisions or act on the resident's behalf'.[894] The Mental Health Act also significantly features a right for persons with a mental disorder to 'have a responsible carer of their choice whenever possible',[895] which entails 'a person appointed in writing by the patient to act on his behalf'.[896] The responsible carer is then the person from whom informed consent should be obtained in terms of the Mental Health Act when a patient lacks mental capacity or is legally prevented from giving consent to treatment.[897] Indeed, informed consent is defined in the Mental Health Act as the 'decision taken by the patient *or the carer* as applicable after being informed of his rights'.[898] Thus, if and for as long as 'the patient lacks the mental capacity to understand any information regarding his rights, then such information shall be communicated within 24 hours to the responsible carer'.[899] Given the role of the responsible carer vis-à-vis informed consent, s/he is to also participate in the formulation of the patient's multidisciplinary care plan while being promptly informed and given adequate guidance on how to better support and look after the

888. Civil Code, Ch. 16 of the Laws of Malta, Art. 1864A (1).
889. *Ibid.*, Art. 1864A (2).
890. *Ibid.*
891. Priscilla Mifsud Parker, *Enduring powers of attorney* in *Chetcuti Cauchi Advocates – Publications*, 19 September 2017; Mary Rose Micallef, *Enduring power of attorneys* in *Azzopardi, Borg & Associates*, 29 June 2019; Sarah Grech & Amy Lee Micallef, *The power of attorney – an indispensable tool* in *Refalo Advocates*, 26 February 2021.
892. Civil Code, Ch. 16 of the Laws of Malta, Art. 1864A (1).
893. *Ibid.*, Art. 1864A (2).
894. *See, for instance*: S.L. 582.16, Social Regulatory Standards for Residential Services for Persons living with Dementia in Homes for Senior Citizens Regulations, r. 3.
895. Mental Health Act, Ch. 525 of the Laws of Malta, Art. 3 (1)(j).
896. *Ibid.*, Art. 4 (2).
897. *Ibid.*, Arts 7 (1), 14, 32 (b), 33 (2)(a), 33 (3)(b), and 35 (2)(b).
898. *Ibid.*, Art. 2. Emphasis added.
899. *Ibid.*, Art. 3 (2).

patient.[900] Consequently, the functions of the Commissioner for Mental Health are not limited to promoting and safeguarding the rights of persons with mental disorders but also of their responsible carers.[901] It should however be noted that, in case of involuntary admission or voluntary admission in the instance of emergency treatment, if the responsible carer cannot be traced or otherwise refuses to give his/her consent, treatment can, unless otherwise prohibited by law,[902] nevertheless be given to prevent physical harm to the patient or to others or to prevent mental deterioration.[903]

166. To be clear, in terms of the Mental Health Act, where 'any person is appointed by a decree of a Court to represent the patient, the person so appointed shall be deemed to be the responsible carer of the patient'.[904] In turn, a court decree interdicting or incapacitating a person in terms of the Code of Organization and Civil Procedure will be accompanied by the appointment of a curator in that same decree.[905] While this may relate to the administration of property, the Mental Health Act expanded the functions of the curator so that, in addition to any other function, duty or responsibility imposed by any other law, the curator for a person who lacks mental capacity in terms of the Mental Health Act and who has been incapacitated or interdicted by order of a court shall *inter alia* also be bound to:

> (a) encourage and support the person to live a normal life in the community; (b) ensure that the person is complying with any treatment prescribed for his mental and physical conditions; (c) ensure that the person, as far as possible, be self reliant in matters relating to his personal, domestic and financial affairs; [and] (d) protect the person from any neglect, abuse or exploitation.[906]

It is furthermore a function of the Commissioner for Mental Health to 'monitor and seek any information from the curator in order to ascertain that the person is not being neglected, abused or exploited'[907] and that the functions laid on the curator by the Mental Health Act are being carried out.

167. There is however a slow shift away from interdiction and incapacitation in Maltese law. Thus, for instance, a person of age, as indicated in the Civil Code, who has a mental disorder or other condition that renders him/her incapable of taking care of his/her own affairs may also be subject to guardianship.[908] A guardian appointed by order of a Guardianship Board formally has functions of a substitute decision-maker inasmuch as these functions include to 'act instead of the person to

900. *Ibid.*, Art. 4 (4).
901. *Ibid.*, Art. 6 (1)(a).
902. *Ibid.*, Arts 32–35.
903. *Ibid.*, Arts 7 (2) and 14.
904. *Ibid.*, Art. 4 (3).
905. *See, for instance*: Code of Organization and Civil Procedure, Ch. 12 of the Laws of Malta, Arts 523–524.
906. Mental Health Act, Ch. 525 of the Laws of Malta, Art. 26.
907. *Ibid.*, Art. 27 (1).
908. Civil Code, Ch. 16 of the Laws of Malta, Art. 188A (1).

whose guardianship he has been appointed in matters of a personal or of a proprietary nature during such time when the said person is considered as not being capable of doing any one or more acts of civil life as specified in the Guardianship Order'.[909] Subject to the limits of the Guardianship Order or by any other decision that the Guardianship Board may give, a guardian may also 'on behalf of a person subject to guardianship sign and do all such things as are necessary to give effect to any functions or obligations vested in the guardian'.[910] That being said, in determining whether or not the person is in need of a guardian, the Guardianship Board is bound to consider whether the needs of the person 'could be met by other means less restrictive of the person's freedom of will and action'[911] and, even if an order is made, it 'must be as least restrictive of that person's freedom of decision and action as possible in the circumstances'.[912] The guardian is furthermore importantly obliged to exercise his/her functions in such a manner that 'the will of the person subject to guardianship is respected and given effect to the maximum extent possible'[913] and 'the freedom of choice and action of the person subject to guardianship shall only be restricted when necessary and only to an extent that is proportionate to the aim pursued'.[914] As such, in relation to the topic of this section of the monograph, guardianship is not necessarily only engaged when a person lacks the capacity to consent to treatment since that person may instead require support to exercise his/her legal capacity to consent to treatment rather than a substitute decision-maker. Consequently, the demand for the appointment of a guardian or joint guardians may also be made by any person who voluntarily wishes to be made subject to guardianship.[915] As such, the law obliges the guardian to act in the best interests of the person subject to guardianship in the exercise of his/her obligations but also to *inter alia* 'take appropriate measures to provide the support that the person subject to guardianship may require in exercising his legal capacity insofar as this is possible'[916] and to 'encourage and assist the person subject to guardianship to become capable of caring for himself and for his property and of making responsible judgements in respect of matters relating to his person and property'.[917] The guardian is, moreover, in the exercise of his/her functions to 'consult with the person subject to guardianship and take into account and respect the rights, will and preferences of the person insofar as possible'.[918] Guardianship Orders are thus, for instance, referred to in the social regulatory standards arising from the Social Care Standards Authority Act,[919] and they are ultimately monitored by the Commission

909. *Ibid.*, Art. 188B (b).
910. *Ibid.*, Art. 188C (3).
911. Code of Organization and Civil Procedure, Ch. 12 of the Laws of Malta, Art. 519F (2).
912. *Ibid.*, Art. 519F (3).
913. Civil Code, Ch. 16 of the Laws of Malta, Art. 188C (1)(a).
914. *Ibid.*, Art. 188C (1)(d).
915. *Ibid.*, Art. 188A (3).
916. *Ibid.*, Art. 188C (2)(a).
917. *Ibid.*, Art. 188C (2)(d).
918. *Ibid.*, Art. 188C (2)(b).
919. *See, for instance*: S.L. 582.09, Social Regulatory Standards for High Dependency Chronic Care Services for Older Persons Regulations, r. 3; S.L. 582.13, Social Regulatory Standards for

for the Rights of Persons with Disability,[920] which also monitors facilities offering services to persons with disabilities licensed in terms of the Social Care Standards Authority Act.[921]

168. Standards regarding substitute decision-making in Malta have hence been shifting away from affixing a permanent label of incapacity on a person to consent to treatment towards increased support for persons in exercising that capacity. This is due in no small measure to obligations arising from the UNCRPD, particularly the obligation on States Parties to 'recognize that persons with disabilities enjoy legal capacity on an equal basis with others in all aspects of life'[922] and the related obligation to 'take appropriate measures to provide access by persons with disabilities to the support they may require in exercising their legal capacity'.[923] Article 25 of the UNCRPD also refers to States Parties requiring 'health professionals to provide care of the same quality to persons with disabilities as to others, including on the basis of free and informed consent'. The United Nations Convention on the Rights of Persons with Disabilities Act was enacted in Malta in 2021 to *inter alia* make provision for the possibility of civil claims alleging discrimination on the basis of disability in respect of the substantive Articles of the UNCRPD. Indeed, the rights set out in Articles 5 to 30 of the UNCRPD are reproduced in the Second Schedule of that Act and 'are enforceable subject to the Declaration and Reservations made by the Government of Malta on the signing of the Convention'.[924] Also, the General Comments that are issued by the United Nations' Committee on the Rights of Persons with Disabilities 'shall constitute interpretative guidance when interpreting the substantive Convention rights'[925] for the purpose of the UNCRPD Act. This is significant here because it means that the substantive Convention rights that relate to informed consent provided on behalf of a person with disabilities by a substitute decision-maker have a basis at law to be interpreted through the lens of those General Comments, at least for the purpose of the UNCRPD Act in Malta. In turn, it is stated in General Comment No 1 that:

> States parties' obligation to replace substitute decision-making regimes by supported decision-making requires both the abolition of substitute decision-making regimes and the development of supported decision-making

Community-Based and Outreach Services Regulations, r. 3; S.L. 582.15, Social Regulatory Standards for Residential Services for Senior Citizens Regulations, r. 3; S.L. 582.16, Social Regulatory Standards for Residential Services for Persons living with Dementia in Homes for Senior Citizens Regulations, r. 3.

920. Equal Opportunities (Persons with Disability) Act, Ch. 413 of the Laws of Malta, Art. 22 (1)(t).
921. *Ibid.*, Art. 22 (1)(u).
922. Convention on the Rights of Persons with Disabilities (Adopted 13 December 2006, entered into force 3 May 2008) 2515 UNTS 3, Art. 12 (2).
923. *Ibid.*, Art. 12 (3).
924. United Nations Convention on the Rights of Persons with Disabilities Act, Ch. 627 of the Laws of Malta, Art. 2 (1).
925. *Ibid.*, Art. 2 (2)(iii).

> alternatives. The development of supported decision-making systems in parallel with the maintenance of substitute decision-making regimes is not sufficient to comply with article 12 of the Convention.[926]

It is however within the competence of the legislator to effectuate a change of this nature. A 'Personal Autonomy Act' is reportedly being drafted by the legislative authorities.[927]

§3. Privacy

169. The concept of privacy in Malta in relation to healthcare features a 'number of distinct forms of privacy',[928] including physical privacy, decisional privacy and informational privacy. There is no central and all-encompassing law regarding privacy, and while the Constitution of Malta makes reference in Article 32 to 'respect for … private and family life', this is not enforceable given that the substantive rights included in the Constitution 'ignore the right altogether'.[929] That being said, Article 8 of the ECHR regarding the right to respect for private and family life is incorporated into Maltese law and is therefore enforceable as part of the law of Malta.[930] The right to respect for private and family life is however not absolute. Interference with the right to respect for private and family life by a public authority may *inter alia* be necessary and legitimate in a democratic society in the interests of the protection of health or morals or for the protection of the rights and freedoms of others, provided that this is done in accordance with the law. Independent instruments then address privacy specifically in relation to the scope of that particular instrument, while the law, in turn, provides for measures when any privacy rights of the person may or must be interfered with. This section engages with that approach to privacy through the lens of: (i) patients' refusal of information concerning their health, (ii) obligations incumbent on medical practitioners in relation to their patients' privacy, and (iii) instances when information and medical data can be required from patients subject to processing in conformity with data protection law.

---

926. Committee on the Rights of Persons with Disabilities, *General Comment No. 1 (2014) Article 12: Equal recognition before the law* (CRPD/C/GC/1 – 19 May 2014) para. 28.
927. Commission for the Rights of Persons with Disability (Malta), *Submission to the Committee on the Rights of Persons with Disabilities in advance of its consideration of Malta's 1st Periodic Report* (February 2018) 13–14; Committee on the Rights of Persons with Disabilities, *List of issues in relation to the initial report of Malta, Addendum – Replies of Malta to the list of issues* (CRPD/C/MLT/Q/1/Add.1 – 18 June 2018) para. 120; *Consideration of reports submitted by parties to the Convention under Article 35 (continued): initial report of Malta* (CRPD/C/SR.417 – 17 September 2018) para. 4; *Concluding observations on the initial report of Malta* (CRPD/C/MLT/CO/1 – 17 October 2018) para. 19; Government of Malta – Ministry for Inclusion and Social Wellbeing, *Freedom to Live: Malta's 2021 – 2030 National Strategy on the Rights of Disabled Persons* (2021) 71.
928. Maurice N. Cauchi, Bridget Ellul & Kevin Aquilina, *Health, Bioethics and the Law* 21 (Malta University Press 2006).
929. Tonio Borg, *A commentary on the Constitution of Malta* 127 (Kite 2016).
930. European Convention Act, Ch. 319 of the Laws of Malta.

170. One may here continue from the topic of the section of the monograph regarding 'informed consent' that preceded the present section. To the extent that one has a right to receive information about one's medical condition, it is also acknowledged in the Charter of Patient Rights and Responsibilities that one has the right to 'refuse information about one's health'[931] as well as the right to 'express the wish for personal health information not to be shared in particular ways such as with a family member'.[932] Although that Charter relates largely to public health services, a patient can also, in private healthcare, stipulate as part of the contractual agreement with a medical practitioner that s/he wishes to refuse information about his/her health. Exceptions to this norm are embedded in law. By way of example, the Superintendent of Public Health has the power to make, vary or revoke orders listing and categorising notifiable disease conditions.[933] A person who may be affected by any notifiable disease does not possess a right to refuse information from pertinent authorities that he is affected by that disease and the Superintendent of Public Health therefore 'may, in the interest of public health, give information to any person or persons who may be affected by any notifiable disease or any human pathogenic organism or contaminant'.[934] A second example can be drawn from the Venereal Diseases (Treatment) Act, wherein venereal disease means 'gonorrhoea, syphilis or chancroid'.[935] A special (medical) practitioner, as identified in that Act, 'who receives from a patient found by him to be suffering from a venereal disease information as to a person from whom the patient suspects that the disease was contracted'[936] is to send a notice to the Chief Government Medical Officer[937] unless that special practitioner is of the opinion that there is no reasonable cause to believe that the disease was contracted in the manner described by the patient. If it then appears to the Chief Government Medical Officer that the person identified by that patient is a person from whom two or more patients suspect that they have contracted a venereal disease and unless it appears to the Chief Government Medical Officer that there is no reasonable cause to believe that the disease was so contracted, s/he shall serve a notice to that person. This notice will state that, according to information received, 'there is reason to believe that that person may require treatment in respect of venereal disease … [and require] that person to attend for, and submit to, medical examination by a medical officer deputed by the said Chief Government Medical Officer for the purpose, within such period and in such a place as may be specified in the notice'.[938] The person in question has no alternative at law to refuse to receive this information. A third example may instead be drawn from the Embryo Protection Act and its regulation of donation of germ line cells for the purpose of

931. Healthcare Standards Directorate – Ministry for Health, *Charter of Patient's Rights and Responsibilities* 10 (2016).
932. *Ibid.*, 14.
933. *See also* Part II Ch. 1 §1 above and Part III Ch. 3 §2 below.
934. Public Health Act, Ch. 465 of the Laws of Malta, Art. 32.
935. Venereal Diseases (Treatment) Act, Ch. 124 of the Laws of Malta, Art. 2. *See also* Part II Ch. 1 §1 above.
936. *Ibid.*, Art. 3.
937. The Health Act, Ch. 528 of the Laws of Malta, now refers to the 'Chief Medical Officer to Government'.
938. Venereal Diseases (Treatment) Act, Ch. 124 of the Laws of Malta, Art. 5.

medically assisted procreation. This is a confidential agreement between the donor and the licensee of the tissue establishment, but if the Embryo Protection Authority 'becomes aware of serious illness it shall be obliged to disclose the information to the parent or parents and, in the case that the child has attained majority, to the child'.[939] No provision is made for the parents or the child conceived from medically assisted procreation to refuse the latter information.

171. In addition to privacy in relation to the information one is provided, it is also recognised in Malta that one has a right to privacy as a patient receiving care or treatment from a medical practitioner. This includes respect for one's private space, which can entail that it is incumbent on the medical practitioner to provide for his/her patients' privacy in line with the ethical and professional standards of the medical profession. For instance, in accordance with the Ethics of the Medical Practitioner Regulations, it 'shall be the duty of every practitioner to ensure that the windows and doors of his surgery and waiting rooms are adequately screened from public view unless such waiting or consulting rooms are situated in a pharmacy'.[940] More broadly, the Charter of Patient Rights and Responsibilities recognises that one has the right to 'expect that one's privacy is respected when receiving healthcare according to the different circumstances',[941] and individual instruments can include provisions that relate to treating patients with dignity and respect.[942] When however medical practitioners can lawfully impinge upon their patients' private space, the law typically also provides measures as checks and balances upon that authority. For instance, the Mental Health Act furnishes a right to a person with a mental disorder to free and unrestricted communication with the outside world when receiving treatment in a mental health licensed facility, as well as a right to receive visitors in private within all reasonable times. Both these rights are not absolute and can be restricted if the psychiatrist under whose care the patient is admitted or receiving treatment considers that exercising the right/s in question will be 'detrimental to the patient's health or it impinges on the rights and freedoms of other people'.[943] Yet, the psychiatrist cannot unilaterally exercise that authority to restrict patients' freedoms and must instead first obtain the approval of the Commissioner for Mental Health by completing and submitting the pertinent application contained in the Mental Health Act.[944] That being said, the broad right to privacy that is explicitly recognised in the Mental Health Act can be restricted without application to the Commissioner for Mental Health if 'there is a serious risk to the person's health or the safety of others'.[945] Even so, there are means for that restriction of privacy to fall under the purview of the Commissioner of Mental Health. It is, for instance, the

939. Embryo Protection Act, Ch. 524 of the Laws of Malta, Art. 9 (4). *See also* S.L. 524.02, Embryo Protection Authority (Protocol) Regulations, r. 12.37 (not yet in force).
940. S.L. 464.17, Ethics of the Medical Profession Regulations, r. 9.
941. Healthcare Standards Directorate – Ministry for Health, *Charter of Patient's Rights and Responsibilities* 14 (2016).
942. *See, for instance*: S.L. 524.02, Embryo Protection Authority (Protocol) Regulations, r. 29.1 (not yet in force).
943. Mental Health Act, Ch. 525 of the Laws of Malta, Art. 3 (1)(r)-(s).
944. *Ibid.*, First Schedule.
945. *Ibid.*, Art. 3 (1)(p).

duty of the chief executive officer of a mental health licensed facility to forward on a monthly basis to the Commissioner for Mental Health 'all patient incident reports occurring in that facility'.[946] These incidents include 'events which have caused serious harm to patients, staff, public or environment as well as those that through appropriate intervention or pure luck result in the avoidance of such harm or damage',[947] which consequently can entail the right to privacy being interfered with for those reasons. It then is a function of the Commissioner for Mental Health to review all patient incident reports received from mental health licensed facilities[948] while also taking any necessary action within his/her remit, which includes the possibility of reporting to the competent authorities any healthcare professional for breach of human rights or for contravening a provision of the Mental Health Act.[949]

172. A further matter addressed in Maltese law regarding privacy relates to instances when information regarding one's health and/or identity can lawfully be requested from individuals. All else being equal, the informed consent of a person is normally required to furnish that information. There are however instances when this consent may not be mandatory. By way of example, the Health Act provides that the Departments regulated therein and outlined in the General Introduction to this monograph 'may request all information from patients, relatives, personnel, and professionals, and from public and private healthcare providers, and such data shall be given to it in cases of emergency, for reasons of public health and to safeguard the vital interest of the patient or a third person'.[950] Barring those situations, the informed consent of the patient is required by way of the Health Act. There are other instances when the authorisation of the court may be required in order to prevail over the right to privacy of a person, for instance, in the situation when a person changes gender identity and information drawn from or a copy of the original act of birth is demanded. In that case, if 'the Court is satisfied that the issuing of the said certificate or information is necessary to defend or safeguard a right or a legitimate interest of the person making the demand which, after taking into consideration all relevant circumstances, the court's considerations should prevail over the right to privacy of the person to whom the certificate refers'[951] and who is not consenting to the information being divulged. This and similar cases such as paternity testing can therefore be handled on a case-by-case basis so as to ensure that there is a balance between the objective of the measure at hand vis-à-vis prevailing over privacy and the right to respect for private life of the individual.[952]

---

946. *Ibid.*, Art. 42.
947. Office of the Commissioner for Mental Health, *Mental health and wellbeing – Challenges and opportunities: Annual Report 2020*, 67–68 (2022).
948. Mental Health Act, Ch. 525 of the Laws of Malta, Art. 6 (1)(g).
949. *Ibid.*, Art. 6 (1)(m).
950. Health Act, Ch. 528 of the Laws of Malta, Art. 13 (3). *See also* General Introduction §2 above.
951. Gender Identity, Gender Expression and Sex Characteristics, Ch. 540 of the Laws of Malta, Art. 4 (7)(b).
952. *See, for instance*: *Abdilla Diana v. Mifsud Francesco Saverio sive Frank et.*, Civil Court First Hall (Constitutional Jurisdiction) – 30/10/2013 [Ref: 95/2013], Constitutional Court – 26/06/2015 [Ref: 95/2013/1]; *Mifsud v. Malta*, App. No. 62257/15 (ECtHR, 29/01/2019).

173. The Health Act also provides that a patient has a right 'to have his medical data processed in conformity with the Data Protection Act'.[953] The latter law implements and further specifies provisions of the EU's General Data Protection Regulation (GDPR) that is directly applicable in Malta, and that also attaches to Article 8 of the EU's Charter of Fundamental Rights safeguarding protection of personal data.[954] While it is beyond the scope of this monograph, engaging with medical law in Malta to broach those EU laws, which are instead addressed in the monograph on European Union Health Law,[955] it is worthwhile noting here that data protection laws in Malta then engage with patients' privacy while ostensibly conforming with the requirements of EU law.

174. Examples drawn from Maltese law of the relation between patients' privacy and requirements arising from or due to EU law in relation to data protection naturally include the Data Protection Act, which establishes the office of the Information and Data Protection Commissioner.[956] For instance, subject to the Data Protection Act not being applicable to the processing of personal data in the course of an activity that falls outside the scope of EU law[957] and all else being equal, a controller of data is to consult with as well as obtain prior authorisation from that Commissioner when the controller intends to process in the public interest genetic data, biometric data or data concerning health for statistical or research purposes, provided that the Commissioner shall also in the latter case consult with a research ethics committee or a committee of an institution recognised by that Commissioner for the purpose of Article 7 of the Data Protection Act. Subsidiary legislation arising from the Data Protection Act introduces further conditions on the processing of data concerning health for insurance purposes pursuant to Article 9 of the GDPR, thereby establishing that the 'processing of data concerning health shall be deemed to be in the substantial public interest when such processing is necessary for the purpose of the business of insurance or insurance distribution activities',[958] provided that this processing is 'subject to the suitable and specific measures designed to safeguard the fundamental rights and freedoms of data subjects'.[959] To be clear, data privacy law in Malta is not restricted to the Data Protection Act and subsidiary legislation arising therefrom. By way of example, secondary processing, understood as 'the further processing of personal data in the health sector … which is not linked to the primary purpose for which the data was originally collected',[960] is regulated under subsidiary legislation arising from the Health Act. The Processing of Personal Data (Secondary Processing)(Health Sector) Regulations thus stipulate when secondary processing of personal data in the health sector is *ipso jure* permitted and

953. Health Act, Ch. 528 of the Laws of Malta, Art. 27 (1)(e).
954. Regulation (EU) 2016/679 of the European Parliament and of the Council of 27 April 2016 on the protection of natural persons with regard to the processing of personal data and on the free movement of such data, and repealing Directive 95/46/EC, OJ L 119, 4.5.2016.
955. Herman Nys, *European Union Health Law* 197–216 (Kluwer Law International 2d ed. 2021).
956. Data Protection Act, Ch. 586 of the Laws of Malta, Art. 11.
957. *Ibid.*, Art. 4 (1)(a).
958. S.L. 586.10, Processing of Data Concerning Health for Insurance Purposes Regulations, r. 4 (1).
959. *Ibid.*, r. 4 (2).
960. S.L. 528.10, Processing of Personal Data (Secondary Processing)(Health Sector) Regulations, r. 2.

when processing is permitted subject to certain conditions, while also providing that the processing of health records for any other purpose shall require the consent of the data subject as provided in the GDPR.

175. It should, at this stage of the chapter, be said that professional secrecy is pertinent to but not the same as privacy. This is also acknowledged in the GDPR. By way of example, processing of special categories of personal data, which includes the processing of genetic data and data concerning health, shall be prohibited in terms of Article 9 of the GDPR. This prohibition is, however, *inter alia* not applicable when processing is necessary 'for the purposes of preventive or occupational medicine, for the assessment of the working capacity of the employee, medical diagnosis, the provision of health or social care or treatment or the management of health or social care systems and services on the basis of Union or Member State law or pursuant to contract with a health professional'.[961] While the Information and Data Protection Commissioner has provided some material to assist in interpreting and applying this provision in practice in Malta,[962] its application is nevertheless subject to conditions and safeguards inasmuch as that data can only be processed 'by or under the responsibility of a *professional subject to the obligation of professional secrecy* under Union or Member State law or rules established by national competent bodies or by another person also *subject to an obligation of secrecy* under Union or Member State law or rules established by national competent bodies'.[963] Similarly, processing of special categories of personal data is in principle permissible when it 'is necessary for reasons of public interest in the area of public health, such as protecting against serious cross-border threats to health or ensuring high standards of quality and safety of health care and of medicinal products or medical devices, on the basis of Union or Member State law which provides for suitable and specific measures to safeguard the rights and freedoms of the data subject, in particular *professional secrecy*'.[964] This thus also touches upon professions that include the medical profession and then distinguishes data protection from professional secrecy, which is therefore addressed in the next section of this monograph.

§4. Secrecy

176. Medical law in Malta addresses secrecy in terms of professional secrecy and confidentiality incumbent on medical practitioners towards their patients. Professional secrecy and confidentiality can, in principle, be treated as two different

961. Regulation (EU) 2016/679 of the European Parliament and of the Council of 27 April 2016 on the protection of natural persons with regard to the processing of personal data and on the free movement of such data, and repealing Directive 95/46/EC, OJ L 119, 4.5.2016, Art. 9 (2)(h).
962. *See, for instance:* Ian Deguara, *Disclosure of health data in the context of occupational medicine and assessment of working capacity* (Information and Data Protection Commissioner Malta 2020).
963. Regulation (EU) 2016/679 of the European Parliament and of the Council of 27 April 2016 on the protection of natural persons with regard to the processing of personal data and on the free movement of such data, and repealing Directive 95/46/EC, OJ L 119, 4.5.2016, Art. 9 (3). Emphasis added.
964. *Ibid.*, Art. 9 (2)(i). Emphasis added. *See also* Recital 164.

legal norms, and subsidiary legislation arising from the Embryo Protection Act indeed states that '[c]onfidentiality and secrecy are two different things'.[965] Yet, the effects at law of confidentiality and professional secrecy can have a similar minimum standard, and the Professional Secrets Act thus provides that any 'reference in an enactment, whether passed before or after the date of entry into force of this Act, to an obligation to observe secrecy or confidentiality, shall be interpreted as imposing a duty at least as strong as the duty of professional secrecy, without prejudice to any other requirements of such enactment'.[966] This signifies a duty, unless the context otherwise requires, of non-disclosure both in respect of confidentiality and professional secrecy. This section addresses confidentiality first and then turns to engage with professional secrecy.

I. Ethics of the Medical Profession and Confidentiality

177. The Ethics of the Medical Profession Regulations provide that a medical practitioner 'shall not voluntarily disclose without the consent of the patient, preferably to be given in writing, any information, including any certification, which he has obtained in the course of his professional relationship with the patient'.[967] Any conviction under the latter provision may also involve disciplinary action to be taken by the Medical Council.[968] The Ethics of the Medical Profession Regulations then furnish one basis of medical practitioners' duty of confidentiality towards their patients, meaning that a medical practitioner should not disclose any information obtained in the course of a professional relationship, regardless of whether that information is of a clinical or non-clinical nature. So as to lawfully disclose information obtained in the course of a professional relationship, a medical practitioner is to obtain the consent of the patient, which should ideally be provided in writing. Any other exception to this rule of confidentiality in the Ethics of the Medical Profession Regulations 'may only be made in terms of the requirements of local laws'.[969] Indeed, in addition to the code of ethical standards incorporated in the Ethics of the Medical Profession Regulations, it is the duty of every practitioner to 'abide by the relevant provisions of the Laws of Malta'.[970] In turn, provision is made in law for instances when the rule of confidentiality does not apply, and a distinction can be drawn in this regard between instances when domestic law mandates the disclosure of information that would otherwise be covered by medical practitioners' duties of confidentiality from instances when domestic law permits but does not necessarily mandate the disclosure of information.

178. Some instances when medical practitioners are mandated to disclose information obtained during the course of a professional relationship have already been considered earlier in this monograph, for instance, when engaging with notifiable

965. S.L. 524.02, Embryo Protection Authority (Protocol) Regulations, r. 26.33 (b) (not yet in force).
966. Professional Secrecy Act, Ch. 377 of the Laws of Malta, Art. 13.
967. S.L. 464.17, Ethics of the Medical Profession Regulations, Schedule A [12 (a)].
968. *Ibid.*, Schedule A [12 (b)].
969. *Ibid.*, Schedule A [12 (a)].
970. *Ibid.*, r. 24.

diseases under the Public Health Act,[971] and other instances will be addressed later, such as when the minor patient is considered in Chapter 2 of this part of the monograph. Suffice it to say for now that in those cases when medical practitioners are mandated to disclose information, they would normally be bound to disclose that information to a specific person or entity stipulated in law, such as a judicial or regulatory body, and would otherwise still be bound by the duty of confidentiality towards the patient in respect of any other person except the person or entity identified by law to whom the information must be lawfully disclosed. For example, the Notification of Cancer Act obliges every medical practitioner 'attending on or called in to visit a patient [to] forthwith, on becoming aware that the patient is suffering from cancer in any form, send to the Superintendent of Public Health a certificate stating the name, age, occupation and address of the patient and the type of cancer from which, in his opinion, the patient is suffering as well as the organ, tissue or site which is affected by the disease'.[972] Similarly, every medical practitioner is mandated to inform the Superintendent of Public Health on a form prescribed by law 'of every patient under his care, who in his opinion is suffering from any form of addiction to or dependence on a drug'[973] as defined in the Registration of Drug Addicts Regulations. There are furthermore occasions when a medical practitioner requires the prior authorisation of the Superintendent of Public Health before issuing a prescription for a drug and, in those cases, the Superintendent may, before granting that authorisation and subject to other requirements at law, 'request from the medical practitioner such information as the Superintendent may require, including whether according to the opinion of the medical practitioner the patient is suffering from drug dependency'.[974] Also, any medical practitioner who delivers this type of prescription is 'to inform accordingly the Superintendent [of Public Health] within twenty-four hours of his prescribing such a preparation'[975] giving details required by the Drugs (Control) Regulations. While medical practitioners are not excused by virtue of these provisions from the prohibition of disclosing that information to any person or entity except those indicated in law, it is nevertheless possible that domestic law itself requires disclosure to persons other than the Superintendent of Public Health. Thus, for instance, continuing on the example of prescribed drugs per regulation 13 of the Drugs (Control) Regulations, the Superintendent of Public Health is mandated to submit the medical practitioner's request 'to a panel of medical specialists who shall advise the Superintendent as to whether such request is to be authorised or not'[976] and it shall also be lawful for the Superintendent to circulate to all medical practitioners the names and details of persons in respect of whom the preparations at hand, as well as specified drugs listed in the Second Schedule of those Regulations, have been prescribed.[977]

971. *See* Part II Ch. 1 §§1 and 3 above.
972. Notification of Cancer Act, Ch. 154 of the Laws of Malta, Art. 3.
973. S.L. 31.21, Registration of Drug Addicts Regulations, r. 3 (1).
974. S.L. 31.18, Drugs (Control) Regulations, r. 13 (2). *See also* Part I chapters 3 and 4 above.
975. *Ibid.*, r. 13 (6).
976. *Ibid.*, r. 13 (3).
977. *Ibid.*, r. 13 (12).

179. There are also topic-specific laws establishing an obligation to disclose information regardless of any duty of confidentiality. Thus, for example, Malta ratified the Council of Europe's Convention on preventing and combating violence against women and domestic violence, which has been incorporated into Maltese law and shall be enforceable as part of the Laws of Malta.[978] That Convention binds States Parties to 'take necessary measures to ensure that the confidentiality rules imposed by internal law on certain professionals do not constitute an obstacle to the possibility, under appropriate conditions, of their reporting to the competent organisations or authorities if they have reasonable grounds to believe that a serious Act of violence covered by the scope of this Convention, has been committed and further serious acts of violence are to be expected'.[979] By way of example, Article 38 of the Convention at hand binds States Parties to take necessary legislative or other measures to ensure that female genital mutilation is criminalised. In turn, the Criminal Code provides that whosoever wilfully fails to seek to avert, by formal complaint or in another manner, female genital mutilation shall be criminally liable. This also applies to medical practitioners entailing a positive duty to act, and the Criminal Code thus specifies that 'the duty to avert such an act shall apply regardless of any duty of confidentiality'.[980] Medical practitioners would thus be well advised to be acquainted with these obligations lest the consequences of non-adherence can entail criminal liability.

180. In addition to instances when Maltese law mandates disclosure of information, there are also instances when Maltese law permits but does not mandate the disclosure of information. This can, for instance, occur when the law relies on the medical practitioner's opinion of the circumstances at hand and whether, in his/her judgment, it warrants disclosure of information. The circumstances of pregnancy and child welfare can be used as an example here. Thus, the Director (Child Protection) established in terms of the Minor Protection (Alternative Care) Act *inter alia* has the function 'of *ex officio* investigating any harm or risk thereof in relation to a minor, on which he holds a reasonable suspicion or on which he was informed, and of taking any action as may be deemed appropriate for the protection of the minor'.[981] That Director may however also intervene 'after having received a report from a medical professional that a pregnant woman has a dependency on an illicit drug or has another type of dependency which in the opinion of said medical professional causes serious prejudice to the health of that woman'.[982] The medical practitioner is thus not bound to disclose information to the Director (Child Protection) upon finding that a pregnant woman has a dependency of the nature described in the latter law. Instead, the medical practitioner's disclosure of information will be dependent upon his/her opinion that the dependency causes serious prejudice to the health of the woman.

978. Gender-based Violence and Domestic Violence Act, Ch. 581 of the Laws of Malta, Art. 22 (1).
979. Convention on Preventing and Combating Violence Against Women and Domestic Violence (2011) CETS 210, Art. 28.
980. Criminal Code, Ch. 9 of the Laws of Malta, Art. 251E (4).
981. Minor Protection (Alternative Care) Act, Ch. 602 of the Laws of Malta, Art. 5 (1).
982. *Ibid.*

181. Permissible disclosure is also considered for the purpose of medically assisted procreation.[983] The Embryo Protection Act provides for the protection of human embryos and largely regulates medically assisted procreation in Malta, which is considered later in the monograph. For the purpose of this subsection and permissible disclosure of information, it is significant that subsidiary legislation arising from the Embryo Protection Act provides that limitations 'to confidentiality should be discussed with the patient, including the extent to which information will be shared with other members of the multidisciplinary team'.[984] This arises from the Embryo Protection Authority (Protocol) Regulations and its guidance note on the welfare of the child, wherein those limitations to confidentiality are also considered. Thus, in the first instance, if 'information has been provided in confidence to a member of staff, the staff member should seek consent from the information provider to discuss it with other staff'.[985] Individuals' consent is therefore the first option to break confidentiality, but if that consent is refused, then good professional practice becomes the measure by which to determine the limitations of confidentiality. Thus, if 'the member of staff considers the matter to be crucial to a decision, they should use their discretion, based on good professional practice, in deciding whether to break that confidence'.[986] Even so, in line 'with professional guidance, patients should normally be informed of the decision to break confidence and the reasons for it, before the information is shared with other members of staff'.[987] It is also postulated in the Embryo Protection Authority (Protocol) Regulations that, while information obtained during counselling should be confidential, 'it may be disclosed in certain circumstances, for example, if it gives rise to concerns about the suitability of a person to receive treatment'.[988] The Embryo Protection Authority (Protocol) Regulations furthermore take into account the possibility of suspected abuse, neglect or harm and tissue establishments are expected to have a policy and procedures in place 'for safeguarding those who use their services',[989] which can affect obligations of confidentiality. It thus is clarified that it 'is inappropriate to give assurances of absolute confidentiality in cases where there are concerns about abuse'.[990] It is instead provided in the Embryo Protection Authority (Protocol) Regulations that 'it may be in the best interests of the individual to disclose confidential patient information'.[991] That would typically, in the first instance, be subject to the individual furnishing informed consent to disclose the information but, if this is not possible, 'it may be necessary to disclose personal or sensitive personal information, despite a duty of confidentiality or legislation that would ordinarily

983. *See also* Part II Ch. 1 §3.
984. S.L. 524.02, Embryo Protection Authority (Protocol) Regulations, r. 10.6 (not yet in force).
985. *Ibid.*, r. 10.18.
986. *Ibid.*
987. *Ibid.*
988. *Ibid.*, r. 4.11.
989. *Ibid.*, r. 26.30.
990. *Ibid.*, r. 26.33 (d).
991. *Ibid.*, r. 26.33.

prohibit disclosure'.[992] That information should however only be shared on a need-to-know basis with the Embryo Protection Authority and with the police when it is in the best interests of the patient or donor.

182. Topic-specific legislation has moreover stipulated rights and obligations regarding confidentiality in respect of the individuals that it targets. By way of example, the Mental Health Act declares that persons with mental disorders have a right to:

> [C]onfidentiality of all information about themselves, their illness and treatment in whatever form stored, which information shall not be revealed to third parties without their consent unless: (i) there is a life threatening emergency when information is urgently required to save lives; or (ii) it is in the interest of public safety; or (iii) ordered by court to do so; or (iv) whosoever is requesting such information is entitled by law to receive it.[993]

The right to confidentiality in the Mental Health Act is, therefore, akin to the confidentiality requirements in Maltese medical law more broadly, not without its limits. Indeed, in addition to the four exceptions included in the overlying quotation, that right to confidentiality is without prejudice to anything provided in the Mental Health Act itself, given that there are a number of instances in the Mental Health Act when information can be disclosed.[994] For example, when addressing the regulation of Community Treatment Orders, which relates to compulsory treatment in the community rather than in a mental health licensed facility, it is provided that '[n]o disclosure of information by healthcare professionals to third parties shall take place unless: (a) the patient consents in writing, or (b) the release of information to the responsible carer or other person is required for the ongoing care of the patient under the Community Treatment Order, or (c) for the care or safety of other persons, or (d) to any person or authority entitled by law to receive it'.[995] Additionally, the right to confidentiality in the Mental Health Act is not applicable if otherwise prevented by law.[996] As such, that right to confidentiality will not, for instance, affect obligations incumbent on medical practitioners to mandatorily report notifiable diseases, certain conditions identified in law, dependencies, or obligations arising from criminal law to, for instance, avert female genital mutilation as described earlier in this subsection.

II. Professional Secrecy

183. The Criminal Code provides in Article 257 that if 'any person, who by reason of his calling, profession or office, becomes the depositary of any secret

992. *Ibid.*, r. 26.33 (c).
993. Mental Health Act, Ch. 525 of the Laws of Malta, Art. 3 (1)(k)
994. *Ibid.*, Art. 3 (1).
995. *Ibid.*, Art. 22.
996. *Ibid.*, Art. 3 (1).

confided in him, shall, except when compelled by law to give information to a public authority, disclose such secret, he shall on conviction be' subject to a fine, imprisonment or both. The Professional Secrecy Act then clarifies that the persons who by reason of their calling, profession or office fall within the scope of the latter provision of the Criminal Code include 'members of a profession regulated by the Medical and Kindred Professions Ordinance',[997] which are now regulated under the Health Care Professions Act and include medical practitioners.[998] The Professional Secrecy Act moreover specifies that references in statutory enactments to the duty of professional secrecy or similar expressions are to 'be interpreted, unless the context otherwise requires, as references to the duty imposed by article 257 of the Criminal Code not to disclose a secret covered by that article'.[999] Furthermore, in addition to the first recipient of information, a person 'shall also be deemed to have become the depositary of a secret by reason of his calling, profession or office when he obtains such secret by reason of being an employee, or employer, a partner or assistant of a person who falls within the scope of article 257 of the Criminal Code or by reason of having acted as interpreter or translator in the communication of such secret'[1000] or even where one obtains the secret 'during the course of his employment by the State'.[1001] Engaging the provisions pertaining to professional secrecy will then also depend on the definition of 'professional secret' in terms of law, which refers in the Professional Secrets Act to information falling under any of the following categories:

> (a) information which is to be considered secret under a specific provision of any law; (b) information which is described as secret by the person communicating the information to a person falling within the scope of article 257 of the Criminal Code; (c) information which has reasonably to be considered as secret in view of – (i) the circumstances in which the information has been communicated and received, and (ii) the nature of the information, and (iii) the calling, profession or office of the person receiving the information, and of the person giving the information, where applicable.[1002]

184. The above entails that most information obtained from a medical practitioner by a patient by reason of that medical practitioner's calling, profession or office will fall within the scope of the definition of professional secret in Maltese law without the patient having to specifically request that the information obtained or furnished by reason of that practitioner's calling, profession or office be covered by professional secrecy.[1003] The obligations of professional secrecy incumbent on medical practitioners will furthermore be buttressed by obligations arising from the

997. Professional Secrets Act, Ch. 377 of the Laws of Malta, Art. 3 (1).
998. *See* Part I above.
999. Professional Secrets Act, Ch. 377 of the Laws of Malta Art. 3 (3).
1000. *Ibid.*, Art. 4 (1).
1001. *Ibid.*, Art. 4 (2).
1002. *Ibid.*, Art. 2 (3).
1003. *See, for instance*: *Buttigieg George v. Zarb Gauci Maistre Rebecca sive Becky*, Court of Appeal (Civil, Inferior) – 12/06/2020 [Ref: 199/2011/1] 14.

duty of confidentiality that they owe patients in addition to professional secrecy, not to mention that the Professional Secrets Act specifies that it does nothing that 'shall restrict or limit, or be deemed to restrict or limit, the laws or custom on the protection of privileged communication'.[1004] By way of example, an employer will be bound by professional secrecy if s/he is in receipt of a report of a medical practitioner who is employed by him/her to visit in an official capacity another employee/ patient. The medical practitioner in question will, in addition to duties of professional secrecy, also owe a duty of confidentiality towards the employee/ patient. Obligations of confidentiality will then ostensibly safeguard the employee/ patient vis-à-vis information provided to the medical practitioner that would not be relevant to the employer and that should not therefore be provided by the medical practitioner to his/her employer. Any information that is provided by the medical practitioner to the employer is nevertheless safeguarded by the laws regarding professional secrecy. That being said, while a person will 'still remain subject to the provisions of article 257 of the Criminal Code after he has ceased to exercise the relevant calling or profession, or to occupy the relevant profession',[1005] a medical practitioner would not be liable were s/he to disclose a secret that was not obtained by reason of his/her calling, profession or office inasmuch as, all else being equal, that secret falls beyond the scope of Article 257 of the Criminal Code.

185. Maltese law does not mandate that a secret remain perpetually undisclosed regardless of circumstances. A medical practitioner can, thus, for instance, lawfully disclose information if it has already legitimately entered the public domain.[1006] In that case, the medical practitioner must nevertheless not disclose secrets that have not entered the public domain, but that may relate to events that have entered the public domain. For example, if a patient reveals in the public domain that s/he has an illness but has not disclosed in the public domain how s/he contracted that illness, it would not be a defence to a charge of disclosing secret information were the medical practitioner to reveal the source of the illness to the public at large so long as the medical practitioner became the depository of the latter secret by reason of his calling, profession or office. A medical practitioner can however disclose secret information if 'authorised to do so by the person who entrusted him with the information'.[1007] However, the law is also clear that for the purpose of the latter provision, 'a person who has received secret information from another shall not be able to give a valid authorisation for the disclosure of that information by a third party'.[1008] Disclosure of secret information in those circumstances is not defensible if, for instance, the medical practitioner who has received secret information authorises a third party to disclose that information without first obtaining the authorisation of the patient from whom he obtained that information. That notwithstanding, unless the person who entrusted the secret information stipulates to the contrary, 'he shall be deemed to have authorised the communication of the secret information to

1004. Professional Secrecy Act, Ch. 377 of the Laws of Malta, Art. 12.
1005. *Ibid.*, Art. 3 (2).
1006. *Ibid.*, Art. 10.
1007. *Ibid.*, Art. 6 (1).
1008. *Ibid.*, Art. 6 (2).

employees, partners and assistants of the person to whom the information was entrusted or to any other person falling within the scope of article 257 of the Criminal Code'.[1009] In this respect, unless a patient provides otherwise, a medical practitioner can, for instance, lawfully relate secret information to another medical practitioner or healthcare professional. This is however subject to the limitation that the 'communication is necessary for the performance of services requested by the person who entrusted the information'[1010] and, absent that condition, there will be no defence, all else being equal, to the charge of unlawful disclosure of secret information. By way of example, a medical practitioner in geriatrics would normally have no reason to disclose information obtained by reason of his/her profession to a medical practitioner involved in, for instance, paediatrics and would be potentially liable in terms of Article 257 of the Criminal Code for that ostensibly unlawful disclosure of secret information provided that proceedings of that nature are commenced with the sanction of the Attorney General.

186. There will however be no offence relating to the unlawful disclosure of secret information in terms of Article 257 of the Criminal Code or the Professional Secrets Act when a person discloses 'in good faith secret information in the course of and for the purpose of obtaining advice or directions from the body regulating his profession',[1011] which in the case of the medical profession is the Medical Council. There will also be no offence of the nature being illustrated in this subsection of the monograph when a person discloses in good faith secret information to a public authority or before a court or tribunal to the extent that is proportionate and reasonably required for the specific purpose of: '(i) defending himself against any claim with regard to professional work in connection with which the secret information has been obtained by him; or (ii) initiating and maintaining judicial proceedings seeking the recovery of fees or other sums due to him or the enforcement of other lawful claims or interests'.[1012] It is furthermore not an offence against Article 257 of the Criminal Code or the Professional Secrecy Act were a person to disclose in good faith 'secret information to a competent public authority in Malta in the reasonable belief that such disclosure is reasonably necessary for the purpose of preventing, revealing, detecting or prosecuting the commission of acts that amount or are likely to amount to a criminal offence, or to prevent a miscarriage of justice'.[1013] Yet, at least for the purpose of Article 257 of the Criminal Code, a medical practitioner shall not be deemed to be compelled by law to give information to a public authority 'unless there is a statutory requirement to that effect'.[1014] Although these exceptions to the rule of professional secrecy therefore permit but do not typically mandate a person to disclose information, the Professional Secrecy Act had

1009. *Ibid.*, Art. 7 (1).
1010. *Ibid.*
1011. *Ibid.*, Art. 6A (a).
1012. *Ibid.*, Art. 6A (b).
1013. *Ibid.*, Art. 6A (c).
1014. *Ibid.*, Art. 8.

been amended by way of a legislative Act that, while chiefly targeting financial business and fighting criminality,[1015] included provisions to be read and construed as one with the Professional Secrecy Act in such a manner as to oblige a person to disclose information otherwise covered by professional secrecy when s/he is required to do so 'by a competent law enforcement or regulatory authority investigating a criminal offence or a breach of duty, or by the Security Service established by the Security Service Act'.[1016]

187. Barring the above exceptions, a court order would otherwise normally be required so as a medical practitioner lawfully discloses secret information obtained by reason of his/her calling, profession or office. A court order could thus allow and enable a medical practitioner to be questioned in civil proceedings on circumstances that may have been stated to him/her in professional confidence or that may have otherwise come to his/her knowledge in his/her professional capacity.[1017] All else being equal, a medical practitioner may not however be compelled to depose in criminal proceedings with regard to circumstances that s/he obtained from professional confidence, even if evidence is required in that regard.[1018] A court may admittedly, in terms of the Professional Secrets Act, 'authorise or make an order requiring the disclosure of secret information pursuant to an express provision of law for the specific purposes for which that provision was enacted or for the specific purpose of preventing, disclosing or detecting the commission of acts that amount or are likely to amount to a criminal offence'.[1019] Yet, absent a specific provision relating to any particular calling, profession or office, the latter provision will not modify the laws in relation to the courts' power to release, for instance, a medical practitioner from the duty of professional secrecy as a witness in court. That being said, the Professional Secrecy Act dictates that a person shall disclose information otherwise covered by professional secrecy when required to do so: 'by a magistrate in the cause and for the purposes of *in genere* proceedings; and … by a court of criminal jurisdiction in the course of a prosecution for a criminal offence'.[1020] The Criminal Code also provides that the court shall 'have power to order the production of any expert or other witness who shall appear from the *procès-verbal* to have been examined at the inquest; and for such purpose any such expert or witness shall, in all cases within the jurisdiction of the Criminal Court, be included in the list of the witnesses of the Attorney General to be, if necessary, examined'.[1021] Duly appointed medical practitioners will furthermore report to the courts in situations where the

1015. House of Representatives Malta – Office of the Clerk, *Kumitat Permanenti għall-Kunsiderazzjoni ta' Abbozzi ta' Liġi (Rapport Uffiċjali u Rivedut),* 9th Legislature: Meeting no. 160 (22 July 2002) 16–18.
1016. Professional Secrecy Act, Ch. 377 of the Laws of Malta, Art. 6B (a). *See also* Act XVII of 2002 – Special Funds (Regulation) Act, Art. 224.
1017. Code of Organization and Civil Procedure, Ch. 12 of the Laws of Malta, Art. 588 (2).
1018. Criminal Code, Ch. 9 of the Laws of Malta, Art. 642 (2).
1019. Professional Secrets Act, Ch. 377 of the Laws of Malta, Art. 9.
1020. *Ibid.*, Art. 6B (original emphasis). *See also* Act XVII of 2002 – Special Funds (Regulation) Act, Art. 224.
1021. Criminal Code, Ch. 9 of the Laws of Malta, Art. 550 (3). Original emphasis.

mental capacity and/or insanity of an individual charged with a criminal offence, either at the time of the offence or at the time of the proceedings, is in question.[1022]

§5. Complaints

188. Complaints regarding medical practitioners are to be made to the body assigned at law to receive that complaint, and different laws will be applicable depending upon the nature of the complaint and the body that is tasked with handling the case. Some entities that have already been addressed earlier in the monograph when illustrating Review Boards and Disciplinary Organisations in Malta have the power to receive complaints as well as to render decisions based upon those complaints. Given that these entities have to an extent already been covered earlier in this monograph, this section is restricted to outlining their competence to receive those complaints.

189. The Medical Council's investigative and disciplinary functions in relation to medical practitioners are buttressed in the Health Care Professions Act by its power to receive complaints from any person regarding medical practitioner/s under its purview and, provided that the complaint relates to a matter falling within its functions, to duly address that complaint. For the purpose of Article 31 of the Health Care Professions Act regarding disciplinary action taken by the regulatory Councils, any person can, in principle, make a complaint even if s/he is not an injured party.[1023] In this respect, complaints can be made on any allegation of professional misconduct or breach of ethics,[1024] which *inter alia* includes the Ethics of the Medical Profession Regulations, thereby, for instance, encapsulating complaints regarding medical practitioners' advertising and complaints were medical practitioners to disclose without their patients' consent information obtained in the course of a professional relationship with those patients. The Medical Council (Erasure of Names Procedure) Rules outline the process of inquiry to be held so that directions can be taken in relation to a medical practitioner. Those Rules then also refer to complaints being made about a medical practitioner who has been convicted by any court in Malta 'of any crime punishable by imprisonment for any term exceeding one year or of any of the crimes mentioned in articles 198 to 209 of the Criminal Code'[1025] and complaints that a medical practitioner 'is unfit to continue to practise his profession on grounds of mental or physical infirmity'[1026] as well as complaints generally relating 'to the conduct of a practitioner'.[1027] The Medical Council included in a 2021 guidance note the following examples of the type of cases that it may need to act on:

1022. *Ibid.*, Arts 402 (4), 525 (3) and 623. *See also* Mental Health Act, Ch. 525 of the Laws of Malta, Arts 36 and 37.
1023. Health Care Professions Act, Ch. 464 of the Laws of Malta, Art. 31 (5).
1024. *Ibid.*, Art. 31 (1).
1025. S.L. 458.08, Medical Council (Erasure of Names Procedure) Rules, r. 4 (1)(a). *See also* Part I Ch. 4 §4.I above.
1026. *Ibid.*, r. 4 (1)(c).
1027. *Ibid.*, r. 4 (1)(b).

(i) Medical or dental practitioners who are in breach of the Health Care Professions Act … (ii) Medical or dental practitioners behaving in an unethical or unprofessional way. (iii) Medical or dental practitioners failing to abide by the Professional and/or Ethical Standards. (iv) Serious breaches in patient confidentiality by medical or dental practitioners. (v) Medical or dental practitioners breaching the Code of Ethics on Advertising.[1028]

190. More broadly, the Health Act provides that it shall be the right of every patient 'to file a complaint about services received'.[1029] Recalling that a patient is defined in the Health Act as 'a person who is receiving, or has received, medical attention, care, or treatment, whether in a healthcare setting or otherwise',[1030] patients' right to complain can thus cover services provided by medical practitioners addressed in this part of the monograph. While not excluding the possibility of a complaint to the Medical Council, it is also the case that complaints can be made to another entity. Where and how that complaint is made will depend on the services received by the patient. The Charter of Patient Rights and Responsibilities, which largely relates to public health services, then provides for the right to forward constructive complaints. One thus has the right to 'give any feedback, suggestions and raise concerns or complaints as deemed necessary … [and this right is also extended] to significant others or carers'.[1031] This is however accompanied by a responsibility to 'discuss any misunderstandings/lack of understanding, of any kind through the appropriate channels'.[1032] Even so, complaints are to be 'taken into consideration in order to improve health services'[1033] and, in that respect, one has a right to 'be given information and advice on how to give feedback and comment or raise concerns, or complaints about the care one has received and the services one has used'.[1034] The ethos underpinning the latter system of patients' complaints is therefore to ultimately improve health services. Disciplinary measures can also ensue, and an officer in the public service is indeed to report 'to the Head of Department, by any appropriate means, any misconduct committed by an officer under his responsibility by not later than five (5) working days after he becomes aware of the offence'.[1035] Patients may however require a first point of contact that can be, by way of example, the Customer Care Department in Malta's public hospital/s. Private medical clinics should also have in place their own system to address complaints. While noting the difference from disciplinary proceedings that can but need

1028. Medical Council Malta, *Guidance on how to lodge a complaint with the Medical Council Malta* 4 (2021).
1029. Health Act, Ch. 528 of the Laws of Malta, Art. 27 (1)(h).
1030. *Ibid.*, Art. 2.
1031. Healthcare Standards Directorate – Ministry for Health, *Charter of Patient's Rights and Responsibilities* 18 (2016).
1032. *Ibid.*
1033. *Ibid.*
1034. *Ibid.*
1035. S.L. Const. 03, Public Service Commission Disciplinary Regulations, r. 5 (1). *See also* Part I Ch. 4 §4.II above.

not follow from a complaint,[1036] the process to address complaints can, in the first instance, vary from an internal investigation[1037] to a more formal inquiry, but,[1038] irrespective of the process adopted, the Health Act stipulates that a patient has a right to 'be informed of the outcome of the investigation of his complaint in a timely manner'.[1039] A decision taken under the Health Act can, in turn, be appealed to the Administrative Review Tribunal,[1040] which is a Tribunal 'competent to review administrative acts of the public administration on points of law and points of fact'.[1041] It is also worthwhile noting that the Department of Health (Constitution) Ordinance had grounded in law a Hospital Management Committee in respect of Saint Luke's Hospital, which was, until 2007, Malta's main public hospital, providing that this Committee would *inter alia* be responsible 'in the first instance to consider any complaints regarding the work within the Hospital of any members of staff'.[1042] While the Health Act repealed the latter Ordinance, it did not repeal regulations made under the provisions of that Ordinance, meaning that the Hospital Management Committee Standing Orders regarding proceedings of that committee are in principle still 'in force and have effect as if made under'[1043] the Health Act.

191. In addition to complaints made in terms of the Health Care Professions Act and the Health Act, as well as the Public Service Commission Disciplinary Regulations, different laws furnish topic-specific powers on given authorities to receive and address complaints. In practice, there is often a tiered level of complaints beginning within the confines of a given facility before proceeding to the regulatory authority. By way of example, it is the duty of the chief executive officer of a mental health licensed facility 'to investigate and take appropriate remedial action where staff is not complying with'[1044] a patient management protocol, and the clinical director of that facility is to inform the chief executive officer 'when any healthcare professional fails to comply with such protocol'.[1045] It then, however, is the function of the Commissioner for Mental Health to investigate any complaint 'alleging breach of patient's rights and take any subsequent action or make recommendations which may be required to protect the welfare of that person'.[1046] More specifically, in regard to healthcare professionals, the Commissioner for Mental Health has the function to 'investigate any complaint about any aspect of care and treatment provided by a licensed facility or a healthcare professional and take any decisions or make any recommendations that are required'.[1047] Likewise, for the purpose of

---

1036. *Ibid.*, rs 7A and 18. *See* Part I Ch. 4 §4.I above.
1037. *Ibid.*, rs 17 (1)(a) and 25.
1038. *See also* Part I Ch.. 4 §3 above.
1039. Health Act, Ch. 528 of the Laws of Malta, Art. 27 (1)(h).
1040. *Ibid.*, Art. 27 (1)(i)
1041. Administrative Justice Act, Ch. 490 of the Laws of Malta, Art. 7 (1).
1042. Department of Health (Constitution) Ordinance, Ch. 94 of the Laws of Malta, Art. 41 (1)(c). Repealed.
1043. Health Act, Ch. 528 of the Laws of Malta, Art. 31 (1). *See also* S.L. 94.07, Hospital Management Committee Standing Orders and S.L. 94.10, Advisory and Executive Board Standing Orders.
1044. Mental Health Act, Ch. 525 of the Laws of Malta, Art. 41 (c).
1045. *Ibid.*, Art. 41 (b).
1046. *Ibid.*, Art. 6 (1)(i).
1047. *Ibid.*, Art. 6 (1)(j).

social welfare services, it is, in the first instance, incumbent on the service provider to address complaints.[1048] It is, however, the Social Care Standards Authority that is tasked within the confines of social welfare services with the function of 'receiving, acknowledging, investigating and taking any necessary action in relation to any complaint against any agency or service provider or public or private entities or any other entity or person',[1049] which could therefore ostensibly include medical practitioners. Similarly, complaints in the context of medically assisted procreation are to be regulated in terms of the Embryo Protection Authority (Protocol) Regulations, which provide that the 'tissue establishment should nominate a member of staff to act as complaints officer … [responsible as] (a) the first point of contact when a person makes a formal complaint, and (b) responsible for investigating complaints and ensuring the complaints procedure operates effectively'.[1050] Whereas a complaint can be dealt with as soon as it arises without using a formal complaints procedure, the latter procedure should be in place, including a complaints register. It is also clarified that if 'a complainant is unhappy with the outcome of the investigation of their complaint, they should be informed of further action they could take'.[1051] This can include a complaint made to the Embryo Protection Authority, which is *inter alia* responsible for ensuring compliance with the obligations and requirements imposed by or under the Embryo Protection Act and regulations made thereunder.[1052] Furthermore, subsidiary legislation arising from the Human Blood and Transplants Act also engages with complaints in a manner that largely transposes relative EU law into domestic law.[1053] Additionally, there is a Commissioner for Health within the Office of the Ombudsman in Malta with the function to 'investigate complaints related to a health service',[1054] but those investigative powers have their limits vis-à-vis the medical practitioner-patient relationship being addressed in this part of the monograph and were instead addressed earlier in the monograph.[1055]

§6. ACCESS TO MEDICAL RECORDS

192. The Health Act provides that it shall be the right of every patient 'to access his medical records in accordance with the Data Protection Act, provided this is not to the detriment of his overall well-being'.[1056] For the purpose of the Health Act, unless the context otherwise requires, medical records mean 'all the documents containing data, assessments and information of any kind on a patient's situation and

1048. *See, for instance*: S.L. 582.02, Social Regulatory Standards on Residential Services for Persons with Disability; S.L. 582.03, Social Regulatory Standards on Respite Services for Persons with Disability; S.L. 582.09, Social Regulatory Standards for High Dependency Chronic Care Services for Older Persons Regulations; S.L. 582.15, Social Regulatory Standards for Residential Services for Senior Citizens.
1049. Social Care Standards Authority Act, Ch. 582 of the Laws of Malta, Art. 7 (e).
1050. S.L. 524.02, Embryo Protection Authority (Protocol) Regulations, r. 24.4 (not yet in force).
1051. *Ibid.*, r. 24.10.
1052. Embryo Protection Act, Ch. 524 of the Laws of Malta, Art. 4 (1)(e).
1053. *See, for instance*: S.L. 483.02, Blood (Quality and Safety) Regulations, Schedule IX.
1054. S.L. 385.01, Commissioner for Administrative Investigations (Functions), r. 22.
1055. *See* Part I Ch.. 4, §3 above.
1056. Health Act, Ch. 528 of the Laws of Malta, Art. 27 (1)(d).

clinical development throughout the care process'.[1057] It consequently means that the topic of 'access to medical records' overlaps with topics that were considered earlier in this chapter, especially in the sections regarding privacy and secrecy. That being said, patients' right to access their own medical records is related to but is ultimately independent of the patients' right to receive all the information about their medical condition, care or treatment and care options.[1058] The latter information may be required in order to furnish informed consent to treatment, but irrespective of how well information is presented to a patient, s/he would additionally have a right to access his/her medical record. Furthermore, access to a complete medical record does not diminish patients' rights to be provided with clear information, for instance, by the healthcare professionals caring for or treating those patients. Thus, for instance, the Health Act separates the right of patients to access their own medical records in Article 27 (1)(d) from the right of patients in Article 27 (1)(c) 'to be provided in advance with clear information on the treatment options available and to be involved in discussions and decisions about the treatment to be given'.[1059] The Charter of Patient Rights and Responsibilities, although chiefly relating to public health services, similarly notes that one has a right to receive information about his/her condition and to ask questions about one's condition, but one also additionally has a right 'to have access to information held in the patient's own file and records according to stipulated policies'[1060] and the right 'to access one's own health records in accordance with the protocol set by the health care establishment'.[1061]

193. Policies and protocols to access medical records can then be established by independent healthcare establishments. By way of example, Malta's largest hospital has a Data Protection and Retention Policy stipulating that requests 'for access to personal information by data subjects are to be made in writing using the Request for Access to Personal Data Form, and sent to the Customer Care Unit of the Mater Dei Hospital'.[1062] That being said, the policies and protocols of a health care establishment cannot, all else being equal, operate to inhibit patients' right to access their medical records and, in addition to the Health Act, the GDPR also provides that the 'data subject shall have the right to obtain from the controller confirmation as to whether or not personal data concerning him or her are being processed, and, where that is the case, access to the personal data'[1063] as well as other information and a copy of the personal data undergoing processing.[1064] In the context of public health services in Malta, it is also a right of an eligible person, as defined in the Freedom

1057. *Ibid.*, Art. 2.
1058. *See* Part II Ch. 1 §2 above.
1059. Health Act, Ch. 528 of the Laws of Malta, Art. 27 (1)(c).
1060. Healthcare Standards Directorate – Ministry for Health, *Charter of Patient's Rights and Responsibilities* 10 (2016).
1061. *Ibid.*, 14.
1062. Ministry for Health (Malta), *Mater Dei Hospital – Medical Records Department & Sir Anthony Mamo Oncology Hospital: Data Protection and Retention Policy*, 2.
1063. Regulation (EU) 2016/679 of the European Parliament and of the Council of 27 April 2016 on the protection of natural persons with regard to the processing of personal data and on the free movement of such data, and repealing Directive 95/46/EC, OJ L 119, 4.5.2016, Art. 15 (1).
1064. *Ibid.*, Art. 15 (3). *See also* Art. 15 (4).

of Information Act, to access documents held by public authorities.[1065] The latter Act furthermore obliges every relevant public authority, including the Ministry for Health and public authorities falling within its remit, to publish 'a general description of the categories of documents held by it'.[1066]

194. Medical records can, of course, be held by entities that are not public authorities, but this does not undermine patients' right to access their own medical records. Indeed, for the purpose of private medical clinics, private hospitals and day care medical clinics, it is 'the duty of the person in charge of the clinic to ensure proper keeping and storage of records and, subject to the provisions of [the Licensing of Private Medical Clinics Regulations] and to any other law relating to confidentiality of records, to limit disclosure only to persons entitled to access to such information'.[1067] Although the separation between record keeping in public healthcare and private healthcare can ostensibly create an information gap in relation to an individual's records, it is noteworthy that some medical records can also be accessed online. As noted by Agius Muscat *et al.*, in a bid to narrow the information gap relating to records between the public and private health sector, 'the Government devised the myHealth portal, which allows patients and doctors of their choice to access specific types of medical records'.[1068] This portal may even be used to enable patients to consent to have their health data made available to medical practitioners in some other Member States of the EU.[1069] It is however worthwhile noting when considering the myHealth portal that, in addition to acknowledging one's right to access his/her medical records, the Charter of Patient Rights and Responsibilities also provides that patients have the responsibility to 'ensure that health records are accurate and up-to-date … [and to] inform healthcare providers if any information on one's health records is incorrect'.[1070]

195. A noteworthy case reaching the European Court of Human Rights (ECtHR) involving access to medical files in Malta related to a situation where, upon a request by a man to be provided with a copy of his medical file in order to substantiate his application before the ECtHR, the Maltese authorities noted that they would present any documentation in relation to the medical file to the ECtHR if so requested by that court. The ECtHR ruled that the Maltese authorities' 'failure to ensure that the applicant was provided with the possibility of obtaining copies of

---

1065. Freedom of Information Act, Ch. 496 of the Laws of Malta, Art. 3.
1066. *Ibid.*, Art. 17 (1)(b).
1067. S.L. 458.23, Licensing of Private Medical Clinics Regulations, r. 11 (4).
1068. Hugo Agius Muscat, Joe Pace & Stefan Buttigieg, *Digital Health in Malta*, in *Public Health in Malta 1999 – 2019* 25, 26 (Natasha Azzopardi-Muscat, Tanya Melillo & Daniel Cauchi eds, Malta Association of Public Health Medicine 2019). *See also* Emma Psaila, *Overview of the national laws on electronic health records in the EU Member States: National Report for Malta* (Milieu Ltd & Time.lex 2014).
1069. *See, for instance*: eHealth Network, *Guidelines on the electronic exchange of health data under Cross-Border Directive 2011/24/EU – Patient Summary* (Release 3 June 2021); eHealth Network, *Guideline on the electronic exchange of health data under Cross-Border Directive 2011/24/EU – General Guidelines* (Release 3 June 2022).
1070. Healthcare Standards Directorate – Ministry for Health, *Charter of Patient's Rights and Responsibilities* 14 (2016).

documents which he needed to substantiate his application ... amounted to an unjustified interference with his right of individual petition'.[1071] That being said, the Health Act itself stipulates that the right of a patient to access his/her own medical records in accordance with the Data Protection Act is subject to the single proviso that 'this is not to the detriment of his overall well-being'.[1072] Even in that circumstance, it is a proviso intended as an exceptional measure. The Mental Health Act, for instance, provides that, without prejudice to anything provided in the Mental Health Act itself and unless prevented by law,[1073] persons with a mental disorder shall have the right to 'access to their clinical records unless, in the opinion of the responsible specialist revealing such information may cause harm to the person's health or put at risk the safety of others'.[1074] It thus is the opinion of the responsible specialist, who is the psychiatrist under whose care the patient is admitted to a mental health licensed facility or under whose care the patient is receiving treatment, that is determinative in limiting access to persons with mental disorders to their clinical records in terms of the Mental Health Act. In those circumstances, the Mental Health Act however stipulates that when 'any information is withheld, the patient or the responsible carer, may contest such decision with the Commissioner'[1075] for Mental Health. Indeed, as part of the functions of the Commissioner for Mental Health to conduct regular inspections at mental health licensed facilities to ascertain that the rights of patients and all the provisions of the Mental Health Act are being upheld, the Commissioner shall, during those visits, have 'unrestricted access to all parts of the licensed facility and *patient medical records* as well as the right to interview any patient in such facility in private'.[1076]

196. Although the GDPR touches on restrictions to the rights of the patient or data subject to access personal data such as in a medical record,[1077] the GDPR is moreover relevant to third parties, for instance, in relation to the processing of special categories of personal data that include data concerning health and genetic data. The GDPR indeed provides that processing of those special categories of personal data is prohibited unless one of the requirements to process that data is met. These requirements include that the data subject has given explicit consent to the processing of personal data, albeit that EU law or the domestic law of a Member State can provide that the prohibition to process those special categories of personal data cannot be lifted by the data subject.[1078] Processing of special categories of personal data is also not prohibited under the GDPR if it 'is necessary to protect the vital interests of the data subject or of another natural person where the data subject is physically

1071. *Feilazoo v. Malta*, App. No. 6865/19 (ECtHR, 11/03/2021) para. 124.
1072. Health Act, Ch. 528 of the Laws of Malta, Art. 27 (1)(d).
1073. *See also* Part II Ch. 2 §2 below.
1074. Mental Health Act, Ch. 525 of the Laws of Malta, Art. 3 (1)(l).
1075. *Ibid.*
1076. *Ibid.*, Art. 6 (1)(k). Emphasis added.
1077. Regulation (EU) 2016/679 of the European Parliament and of the Council of 27 April 2016 on the protection of natural persons with regard to the processing of personal data and on the free movement of such data, and repealing Directive 95/46/EC, OJ L 119, 4.5.2016, Art. 23. *See also* Data Protection Act, Ch. 586 of the Laws of Malta, Arts 5 and 6; S.L. 586.09, Restriction of the Data Protection (Obligations and Rights) Regulations, r. 4.
1078. *Ibid.*, Art. 9 (2)(a).

or legally incapable of giving consent'[1079] or in circumstances that can summarily be referred to as 'processing by a health professional for "medical purposes"'.[1080] That notwithstanding, in addition to requirements arising from the GDPR itself, the GDPR also provides that 'Member States may maintain or introduce further conditions, including limitations, with regard to the processing of genetic data, biometric data or data concerning health'.[1081]

197. Maltese law provides for a number of instances when a third party can conditionally access the medical record of another person. Some of these, such as the situation of a substitute decision-maker[1082] and secondary processing,[1083] have already been addressed in this chapter, whereas others arise consequent to transposition of EU law into domestic law, such as the regulation of donation of human tissues and cells.[1084] There are also topic-specific provisions, including, for instance, the Embryo Protection Act's regulation of donations of germ line cells and the adoption of embryos. In those circumstances, the prospective parent/s are, in general, only entitled to obtain generic information about the donor/s whose identity is to, in all cases, remain confidential. However, the Embryo Protection Act also provides that:

> [T]he medical records that may affect the health of the child and the identity of the donor or of the persons from whom an adopted embryo originated shall be accessible to the child conceived from the germ line cells of such donor upon the child reaching eighteen (18) years of age and, subject to the consent of the [Embryo Protection] Authority, the medical records that may affect the health of the child shall be accessible to the parent or parents at any earlier stage in exceptional circumstances in which the life or health of the child born from such germ line cells is at risk.[1085]

In this respect, it is the responsibility of the licensee of the tissue establishment to keep a register with updated records traceable to the donor/s and to, without delay, inform the Embryo Protection Authority of the full details of every donation.[1086] The tissue establishment is to furthermore 'establish a documented procedure for controlling access to medical records'[1087] as well as 'clear security

1079. *Ibid.*, Art. 9 (2)(c).

1080. Deirdre Madden, *Medical Law in Ireland* 97 (Kluwer Law International 4th ed. 2019). *See also* Part II Ch. 1 §3 above.

1081. Regulation (EU) 2016/679 of the European Parliament and of the Council of 27 April 2016 on the protection of natural persons with regard to the processing of personal data and on the free movement of such data, and repealing Directive 95/46/EC, OJ L 119, 4.5.2016, Art. 9 (4).

1082. *See* Part II Ch. 1 §2 above.

1083. *See* Part II Ch. 1 §3 above.

1084. S.L. 483.01, Tissues and Cells (Quality and Safety) Regulations; S.L. 483.04, Human Tissues and Cells (Coding, Processing, Preservation, Storage and Distribution) Regulations.

1085. Embryo Protection Act, Ch. 524 of the Laws of Malta, Art. 9 (4). *See also* S.L. 524.02, Embryo Protection Authority (Protocol) Regulations, r. 12.33–12.35 (not yet in force).

1086. *Ibid.*, Art. 9 (6).

1087. S.L. 524.02, Embryo Protection Authority (Protocol) Regulations, r. 29.6 (not yet in force).

procedures to prevent unauthorised access to records'.[1088] The Embryo Protection Authority (Protocol) Regulations also provide measures that the tissue establishment should take to mitigate the risks of unauthorised people inadvertently gaining access to patient-identifying information as well as laying part of the process to lawfully disclose information, for instance, with the consent of the person at hand.[1089]

198. Yet, in addition to topic-specific provisions, Maltese law furthermore provides for broader measures to access records, such as the authority of an inquiring magistrate by way of the criminal law 'to order the seizure of any papers, effects, and other objects generally, which he may think necessary for the discovery of the truth'.[1090] On this point, it is also worthwhile noting that the Medical Officer of the prison medical service is bound to keep proper medical records of each prisoner, which shall be accessible, subject to their confidentiality, to the Minister responsible for prisons, the Director of Prisons, the Corradino Correctional Facility Monitoring Board and to any properly authorised person.[1091] The Prisons Regulations however also stipulate that this information 'shall not be divulged to any person except with the consent of the prisoner himself, or on the order of the Attorney General or of a court, or with the authorisation of the Director [of Prisons], or in fulfilment of any international obligation assumed by the Government of Malta'.[1092] In the case of individuals under 18 years of age attending the Children's House in Malta, which is a child-friendly space for children who are victims and/or witnesses of significant harm to, in the first instance, give testimony, it may be established after the preliminary meeting held in terms of law that a paediatric examination should take place. In that case, the paediatric specialist 'may access records of the minor kept at public and, or private hospitals and may contact general practitioners to acquire medical information about the minor'.[1093] The subject of children is however best addressed in the next chapter.

1088. *Ibid.*, r. 29.7.
1089. *Ibid.*, r. 29.8–29.19.
1090. Criminal Code, Ch. 9 of the Laws of Malta, Art. 554 (1).
1091. S.L. 260.03, Prisons Regulations, r. 39 (1).
1092. *Ibid.*, r. 7 (4). *See also* S.L. 217.19, Detention Service Regulations, r. 37.
1093. S.L. 602.01, Children's House Regulations, r. 31.

Chapter 2. The Physician-Patient Relationship in Specific Terms

199. This chapter engages with medical law in Malta governing the situation of patients who are minors in terms of law, the situation of patients who have a mental disorder, and the situation of patients who are dying or nearing the end of life. For ease of reference, the titles of each section in this chapter reflect the titles used in the standard outline of the International Encyclopaedia for Medical Law.

§1. The Minor Patient

200. There is not in Malta one law that governs every aspect of the medical practitioner-patient relationship when that patient is a minor. There is not even a definition of 'the minor' that applies uniformly across the entire statute book. By way of example, while many laws define the minor as a person who has not attained the age of 18 years so that a person attains legal capacity to independently exercise rights and duties from that age, it is nevertheless the case that all else being equal, any 'person who has attained the age of sixteen may register to donate his organs and, or tissues and, or cells'.[1094] There are also laws that specifically target the needs of the minor patient alone in a manner separate from standard healthcare services in the public health service. It is, for instance, provided that children under the age of 18 years in alternative care separated from their parents 'shall have individualised and comprehensive assessment of their healthcare needs, beyond what is offered by universal services, for them to maximize their potential'.[1095] Thus, in addition to laws that are made specifically to address the situation of the minor patient alone, other laws instead address the situation of the minor patient on an ad hoc basis depending on the subject matter of the law at hand that does not specifically regard minors alone. Yet, while provision is made in the law to cater for minors in general, including, for instance, that minors shall have a right to a medical examination as well as to medical assistance when they are deprived of their liberty in terms of the Criminal Code such as when they are suspects or accused persons in criminal proceedings,[1096] medical law can also be equally applicable to the minor patient as to any other patient. As such, this section considers some of the main differences in law between the minor patient and any other patient, including parental or other legal authority, the establishment and effects of the medical practitioner-patient relationship when that patient is a minor, minors consenting to or refusing treatment, protective measures for minors as well as the paramount consideration of the best interests of the minor while respecting that minor's views.

1094. Human Organs, Tissues and Cell Donation Act, Ch. 558 of the Laws of Malta, Art. 6 (1).
1095. S.L. 582.07, Social Regulatory Standards for Residential Services for Children in Alternative Care, Standard 4; S.L. 582.08, Social Regulatory Standards for Office Based Services for Children in Alternative Care, Standard 5.
1096. Criminal Code, Ch. 9 of the Laws of Malta, Art 534AGH. The text of this law refers to 'children'.

201. The Civil Code stipulates that a 'minor is a person of either sex who has not yet attained the age of eighteen years',[1097] and it also provides that majority 'is fixed at the completion of the eighteenth year of age'.[1098] It is the Civil Code that then traditionally grounded the authority of the parents of a minor to make decisions in relation to minors as well as the process to be undertaken in case of disagreement between the parents or in case of disagreement between the parents and, for instance, treating healthcare professionals.[1099] The Civil Code thus provides that a 'child shall be subject to the authority of his parents for all effects as by law established'[1100] and that a 'child shall obey his parents in all that is permitted by law'.[1101] Save as otherwise provided at law, such as in circumstances of imminent danger of serious prejudice to the child when either parent may take measures that are urgent and cannot be postponed,[1102] parental authority is exercised by the common accord of both parents.[1103] Yet, with regard to third parties such as medical practitioners acting in good faith, 'each of the spouses shall be deemed to act with the consent of the other where he or she performs an act relative to parental authority relative to the person of the child'.[1104] In case of disagreement on matters of particular importance, either parent may apply to the court, which will then hear the parents as well as the child if s/he has reached the age of 14 years, in order for the court to make suggestions that it deems best in the interest of the child and the unity of the family but if 'the disagreement between the parents persists, the court shall authorise the parent whom it considers more suitable to protect the interest of the child in the particular case, to decide upon the issue'.[1105] The court may furthermore generally, 'upon good cause being shown, give such directions as regards the person ... of a minor as it may deem appropriate in the best interests of the child'.[1106]

202. Legal authority over minors may also be shifted away from their parents, or otherwise, parental authority in relation to *inter alia* healthcare treatment may be affected without necessarily involving the courts. By way of example, a report may be made in terms of the Minor Protection (Alternative Care) Act regarding harm or risk of harm accruing to the minor and,[1107] in determining what action, if any, to take, the Director (Child Protection) established under that legislative Act is to 'have regard to the possibility of agreeing to a social contract to resolve a matter concerning a minor's need for care and protection without having to make an application to

1097. Civil Code, Ch. 16 of the Laws of Malta, Art 157.
1098. *Ibid.*, Art 188.
1099. Ruth Farrugia, *Legal aspects of child and parental rights*, in *Patients' Rights, Reproductive Technology, Transplantation: Proceedings of a Symposium* 36–44 (Maurice N. Cauchi ed., The Bioethics Consultative Committee Malta 2000).
1100. Civil Code, Ch. 16 of the Laws of Malta, Art. 131 (1).
1101. *Ibid.*, Art. 132 (1).
1102. *Ibid.*, Art. 131 (5).
1103. *Ibid.*, Art. 131 (2).
1104. *Ibid.*, Art. 131 (6). *See also* Art. 66I (1)(a).
1105. *Ibid.*, Art. 131 (4).
1106. *Ibid.*, Art. 149.
1107. *See also* Part II Ch. 2 §1 below.

the Court to make a protection order'.[1108] Although the social contract cannot provide for the assignment of parental responsibilities for the minor, the Director (Child Protection) can agree to terms and conditions such as the provision of support and therapeutic interventions for the minor as well as the provision of medical and educational assistance to the minor.[1109] Even so, where a care plan is in effect, which can include matters relating to the health and well-being of the minor, and 'the consent of a parent is required for something necessary to avoid significant harm to the health or education of the minor, and such parent withholds said consent without good reason, the Director (Child Protection) or any other entity which the Minister may order by notice in the Gazette *may act without such parental consent and take any decision in the best interest of the minor*'.[1110] This decision may be challenged by any interested party via an application to the Juvenile Court requesting that it be cancelled, revoked or changed, and the care plan is furthermore subject to review by the Minors Care Review Board,[1111] which can also take decisions it deems to be in the best interests of the minor in matters of particular importance in case of disagreement on the care of that minor.[1112] Yet, in addition to emergency orders that do not require authorisation to execute,[1113] the Director (Child Protection) may furthermore request the Juvenile Court to issue a protection order for a minor whereby that Court may *inter alia* authorise 'a treatment order by which the parent or parents of the minor or the person caring for the minor *or the minor* are ordered to',[1114] for instance, receive psychiatric or psychological care or receive any other treatment or assistance that the Juvenile Court deems appropriate after having heard experts in the fields.

203. Be that as it may, parental authority shall terminate *inter alia* when the child attains the age of eighteen years, when the child marries or if the child leaves the parental home with the consent of the parents to set up a separate domestic establishment.[1115] Yet, in addition to parental authority, the provisions of the Civil Code are also relevant in regard to the capacity to contract, which is, in turn, significant if the medical practitioner-patient relationship is contractual in nature.[1116] All else being equal, a person who has not attained the age of 18 years is incapable of contracting in the cases specified by law,[1117] and any contract entered into by a person who is 'under the age of seven years is null'.[1118] Similarly, any 'obligation entered into by a child under the age of fourteen years is also null'.[1119] That being said, if the latter child has attained the age of nine years, 'the agreement shall be valid in so far as it relates to the obligations entered into by any other person in his

1108. Minor Protection (Alternative Care) Act, Ch. 602 of the Laws of Malta, Art. 12 (1).
1109. *Ibid.*, Art. 12 (3).
1110. *Ibid.*, Art. 13 (5). Emphasis added.
1111. *Ibid.*, Art. 13 (6)–(7).
1112. *Ibid.*, Art. 32 (3)(f).
1113. *Ibid.*, Art. 20.
1114. *Ibid.*, Art. 19 (1)(c). Emphasis added.
1115. Civil Code, Ch. 16 of the Laws of Malta, Art. 150.
1116. *See* Part I Ch. 4 §1.I above.
1117. Civil Code, Ch. 16 of the Laws of Malta, Art. 967 (3)(a).
1118. *Ibid.*, Art. 968.
1119. *Ibid.*, Art. 969 (1).

favour'.[1120] This also applies 'with regard to any person who has attained the age of fourteen years, but has not attained the age of eighteen years, if such person is subject to parental authority, or is provided with a curator'[1121] unless s/he is married. These provisions are, in principle, equally applicable to a contractual relationship involving a minor patient and a medical practitioner[1122] while noting that persons capable of contracting, such as the treating medical practitioner, 'may not set up the nullity of the contract on the ground of the disability of those with whom they have contracted'.[1123] That notwithstanding, consent to enter into a contractual relationship is separate from the capacity to consent to or refuse treatment.

204. The Mental Health Act was one of the first laws in Malta to separate the capacity to establish a medical practitioner-patient relationship from the capacity to consent to treatment based on the age of the patient. The Mental Health Act thus explicitly regulates the treatment of minors, defined therein as 'a person under the age of eighteen years',[1124] by stipulating that if 'a minor has sufficient maturity and understanding to consent to treatment, no treatment or care shall be given to the minor unless the minor consents to it'.[1125] To be clear, in the case when a minor patient has sufficient maturity and understanding to consent to treatment but refuses to consent to that treatment in circumstances when s/he is involuntarily admitted to a mental health licensed facility, 'treatment can be given to prevent physical harm to self or others or to prevent mental deterioration'.[1126] Barring that exception and unless otherwise provided at law, the minor patient with a mental disorder may then also, in principle, have sufficient maturity and understanding to consent to major medical or surgical procedures and,[1127] subject to other requirements set in law,[1128] to consent to therapeutic interventions considered to be invasive or irreversible treatments for mental illness as listed in the Mental Health Act such as stereotactic ablative anterior capsulotomy for severe refractory major depressive disorder.[1129] It is the opinion of the psychiatrist under whose care the minor patient is admitted or receiving treatment that is determinative in establishing whether the minor has sufficient maturity and understanding to consent to treatment and, if the minor does not have that maturity and understanding, then 'the consent of the responsible carer shall be required'[1130] and the responsible carer will likely be 'either parent by mutual consent'[1131] unless the minor patient has appointed a responsible carer. This obligation to obtain the consent of the responsible carer, though ordinarily also

1120. *Ibid.*, Art. 969 (2).
1121. *Ibid.*, Art. 970.
1122. *See, for instance*: Ann Marie Mangion, *Confidentiality and treatment of young adults – Proposals for Amendment I*, in *Contemporary issues in medical ethics & law: Conference proceedings 2012 – 2015* 25, 29–30 (Kevin Aquilina, Pierre Mallia & Bridget Ellul eds, Progress Press 2017).
1123. Civil Code, Ch. 16 of the Laws of Malta, Art. 973.
1124. Mental Health Act, Ch. 525 of the Laws of Malta, Art. 2.
1125. *Ibid.*, Art. 31 (1)(a).
1126. *Ibid.*, Art. 31 (1)(a). *See also* Part II Ch.. 2 §2 below.
1127. *Ibid.*, Art. 32.
1128. *Ibid.*, Art. 33 (2).
1129. *Ibid.*, Fourteenth Schedule.
1130. *Ibid.*, Art. 31 (1)(b).
1131. *Ibid.*, Art. 4 (2).

required for major medical or surgical procedures when a minor patient with a mental disorder lacks sufficient maturity and understanding to consent to treatment, is however not applicable for those procedures 'in an emergency where the patient's life is at risk'.[1132] Also, if the minor patient with a mental disorder does not have sufficient maturity and understanding to consent to treatment and the responsible carer refuses to give consent, 'treatment can be given to prevent physical harm to self or others or to prevent mental deterioration',[1133] and the psychiatrist under whose care the minor patient is admitted or receiving treatment can request the Commissioner of Mental Health 'to substitute the responsible carer by any other person'.[1134] That being said, irrespective of the minor's maturity and understanding, if a minor is admitted to a mental health licensed facility or if a parent with dependent minors is admitted to a mental health licensed facility, it is the responsibility of that facility to grant within reasonable limits flexible visiting hours to minimise the effects of parent-child separation 'unless the responsible specialist in consultation with the other members of the multidisciplinary team, believes that such separation is in the best interests of the minor',[1135] and/or of the parent if it is the parent who is admitted to the facility.[1136]

205. Minor patients receiving treatment that is not addressed by the Mental Health Act can nevertheless fall within the terms of the Health Act. Significantly in respect of minors' capacity to consent to or refuse treatment, Article 27 grounding patients' rights in the Health Act was amended in 2017 to provide that, without prejudice to patients' rights in Article 27 (1) and notwithstanding the provisions of any other law including laws governing the establishment of medical practitioner-patient relationship when that patient is a minor, 'a person who has attained the age of sixteen years shall have the right to consent to, or refuse, medical attention, care or treatment if the medical practitioner is of the opinion that such person has sufficient maturity and understanding to so consent or refuse'.[1137] If that is not the case, then 'the consent of the person having parental or other legal authority over such person shall be required'.[1138] It therefore is the opinion of the medical practitioner that is determinative to establish that a person has sufficient maturity and understanding to consent to or refuse treatment and would consequently not require the consent of a third party, such as a parent, to furnish medical attention, care or treatment. Indeed, it is only after a medical practitioner furnishes certification regarding patients' maturity and understanding to consent to or refuse treatment that:

> [O]ther healthcare professionals regulated *by the Health Care Professions Act* shall be considered to be authorised to participate in the medical attention, care or treatment and in the healthcare plan decided by the medical practitioner by

1132. *Ibid.*, Art. 32 (c).
1133. *Ibid.*, Art. 31 (1)(b).
1134. *Ibid.*, Art. 4 (2).
1135. *Ibid.*, Art. 28.
1136. *Ibid.*, Art. 29.
1137. Health Act, Ch. 528 of the Laws of Malta, Art. 27 (2).
1138. *Ibid.*

offering and administering those services, benefits, interventions and treatments required by the said person without the need for any further authorisation in that respect.[1139]

Furthermore, while the Health Act was amended in 2021 to note that any reference in Article 27 to treatment 'shall be deemed to include a reference to psychiatric treatment and to counselling',[1140] the opinion of a medical practitioner will also, in that case, first be required indicating that the person has sufficient maturity and understanding to consent to treatment involving counselling that is, for instance, provided by a counsellor or other profession that is not regulated by the Health Care Professions Act. That being said, adding a provision to specify what is deemed to be included as treatment for the purpose of Article 27 of the Health Act ostensibly means excluding other treatment from the purview of that provision unless specifically included by the legislator within its remit. For instance, given that the profession of psychotherapy is not regulated under the Health Care Professions Act[1141] and given that it is professions regulated by the latter Act that would not require further authorisation after the certification of a medical practitioner regarding the maturity and understanding of a minor, it means that psychotherapy provided by a psychotherapist as part of the healthcare plan decided by a medical practitioner would still require the consent of the person holding parental or other legal authority regardless of the minor's maturity and understanding inasmuch as that situation is not covered by Article 27 of the Health Act.

206. The opinion of the medical practitioner is however determinative in terms of the Health Act to establish whether treatment can still be given even if the person has sufficient maturity and understanding to refuse treatment and *is refusing treatment.* Indeed, if that is the case, Article 27 (2) of the Health Act provides that 'the treatment may still be given if the medical practitioner is of the opinion that the treatment is urgently required in the best interest of the said person'. This power vested in medical practitioners may arguably be justifiable in juridical terms in view of the obligations arising from the United Nations Convention on the Rights of the Child, to which Malta is a Party, requiring that in 'all actions concerning children … the best interests of the child shall be a primary consideration'[1142] with the child defined in that Convention as 'every human being below the age of eighteen years unless under the law applicable to the child, majority is attained earlier'.[1143] To be clear, the terms 'minor' or 'child' are not used in the Health Act, which is prudent inasmuch as there are different age brackets in the statute book in Malta to classify the juridical effects of age of minority. Neither is there an upper age limit grounding the rights arising from Article 27 (2) in the Health Act relating to sufficient maturity and understanding to consent to treatment. Yet, the latter provision read in light of the broader law relates to persons who are 16 and 17 years of age as was

1139. *Ibid.*, Art. 27 (3). Emphasis added.
1140. *Ibid.*, Art. 27 (4).
1141. Psychotherapy Profession Act, Ch. 587 of the Laws of Malta.
1142. Convention on the Rights of the Child (Adopted 20 November 1989, entered into force 2 September 1990) 1577 UNTS 3, Art. 3.
1143. *Ibid.*, Art. 1.

intended by the legislator.[1144] Any other account would, arguably unacceptably, reverse the presumption that a patient who attained the age of majority has capacity to consent to or refuse treatment and while patients would still have had a right to refuse treatment, an account of Article 27 (2) that applies to all persons over 16 years of age would bestow upon medical practitioners a veto upon the effect of every patients' right to refuse treatment rather than just the minor patient.

207. Even so, Maltese law is increasingly involving minors in decision-making or otherwise incorporating 'the voice of the child'[1145] as part of healthcare assessment without omitting safeguards and protective measures for minors in their best interests. An example of this balance can be drawn from the Minor Protection (Alternative Care) Act, which defines the minor in Article 2 as 'a child under eighteen years of age' and has the scope 'to safeguard, protect and give priority to the best interest of minors and to ensure, in the least possible time, the permanence of the care given to minors'.[1146] The Minor Protection (Alternative Care) Act then sets out by grounding in law the presumption that the minor has sufficient understanding unless the contrary becomes evident,[1147] which is important in respect of the participation of the minor and to consider his/her views.[1148] Indeed, in the case of a care plan, 'the officers and professionals who shall draw up the care plan shall, if the minor is considered as having sufficient understanding [which is presumed in the first instance], indicate the methodology used to establish the views and wishes of the minor and their recommendations thereon'.[1149] The Minor Protection (Alternative Care) Act however also imposes an obligation on any professional, including medical practitioners, to immediately submit a report when s/he has knowledge of an act causing or which may cause significant harm on a minor as defined therein or which constitutes a criminal offence on a minor or if s/he has knowledge that a minor is in need of care and protection.[1150] Reference in the latter obligation to 'significant harm' covers abuse, neglect, harassment, ill-treatment, exploitation, abandonment, exposure, trafficking, fear of violence, and female genital mutilation.[1151] It also covers minors who are victims of domestic violence in terms of the Gender-Based Violence and Domestic Violence Act, which means that a report must be made by a professional (including a medical practitioner) who has knowledge of any of the following with regard to minors:

> [A]cts or omissions including verbal, physical, sexual, psychological or economic violence causing physical and, or moral harm or suffering, including

1144. House of Representatives Malta – Office of the Clerk, *Dibattiti tal-Kamra Tad-Deputati (Rapport Uffiċjali u Rivedut)*, 12th Legislature: Sitting No. 468 (12 Jan. 2017) 357–376.
1145. *See, for instance*: S.L. 582.07, Social Regulatory Standards for Residential Services for Children in Alternative Care, r. 3; S.L. 582.08, Social Regulatory Standards for Office Based Services for Children in Alternative Care, r. 3.
1146. Minor Protection (Alternative Care) Act, Ch. 602 of the Laws of Malta, Art. 1 (2).
1147. *Ibid.*, Art. 3.
1148. *Ibid.*, Arts 12 (8), 13 (3), 17, 19 (2), 22, 23 (4), 24 (5), and 63 (3)
1149. *Ibid.*, Art. 13 (3).
1150. *Ibid.*, Art. 9 (2). *See also* Art. 21 in relation to unaccompanied minors.
1151. *Ibid.*, Art. 9 (5).

> threats of such acts or omissions, coercion, or arbitrary deprivation of liberty, that occur within the family or domestic unit, whether or not the perpetrator shares or has shared the same residence with the victim, and shall include children who are witnesses of violence within the family or domestic unit.[1152]

The obligation to report is to be exercised by making a report to the Director (Child Protection) established under the Minor Protection (Alternative Care) Act or to the Executive Police. Inasmuch as professionals, including medical practitioners, are likely to first report to another entity or institution, such as the Medical Council, the law provides that 'such entity or institution shall register such report in writing and shall, without delay, and in any case not later than twenty-four hours from the receipt of the report, refer the report to the Director (Child Protection) or the Executive Police'.[1153] Yet, were a professional to omit to submit that report, it may entail that s/he incurs a term of imprisonment, a fine or both. Even in view of the severity of the issue, Mandatory Reporting Guidelines have been produced to 'support the professional to exercise his/her discretion in deciding what is the best course of action to address reasonable suspicions or knowledge of child maltreatment that has come to them through their work'.[1154] These guidelines then separate instances that are suspect and should be reported by professionals like medical practitioners from instances when it is advisable to consult with superiors that may support child protection decisions as well from instances when no report is warranted, such as when the child has attained 18 years of age.

208. Subsidiary legislation arising from the Minor Protection (Alternative Care) Act regulating the Children's House furnishes another example of increasingly taking into account the voice and choice of the minor patient while maintaining protective measures. The Children's House caters for children under the age of 18 years who are victims and/or witnesses of significant harm, providing a child-friendly environment so that they give their testimony and subsequently receive support to meet their best interests. These children are presumed to have sufficient understanding to be forensically interviewed as well as to receive support services 'unless the contrary is established by the professionals working with the child or unless the child is too young to be communicative or it is clear that this is against the child's best interests and, or wellbeing'.[1155] That being said, the Manager (Children's House) is to *inter alia* 'liaise with the paediatric specialist so that the minor may undergo a medical examination if this is deemed necessary owing to the nature of the suspicions or knowledge of significant harm suffered by the minor'.[1156] While no mention is made of informed consent, which does not *ipso jure* undermine the professional obligation to obtain that consent, the subsidiary law states that at 'all times, the referred minor may refuse to being medically examined or to stop such

1152. Gender-based Violence and Domestic Violence Act, Ch. 581 of the Laws of Malta, Art. 2.

1153. Minor Protection (Alternative Care) Act, Ch. 602 of the Laws of Malta, Art. 9 (2).

1154. Government of Malta – Ministry for Social Justice and Solidarity, the Family and Children's Rights, *Mandatory Reporting Guidelines for Professionals in terms of the Minor Protection (Alternative Care) Act, CAP. 602 of the Laws of Malta* (Technical Committee 2020).

1155. S.L. 602.01, Children's House Regulations, r. 4.

1156. *Ibid.*, r. 7 (c).

examination and such wishes shall be respected'.[1157] Also, if the paediatric examination is deemed necessary and takes place in circumstances when a parent or legal guardian is the alleged perpetrator of the maltreatment that led to the referral, 'the Manager (Children's House) or the Director of Child Protection or the key social worker from the Directorate of Child Protection and, or a person indicated by the minor may be present in the same room instead of'[1158] that parent or legal guardian. This balance of respecting the minor's refusal of examination but nevertheless requiring consent or safeguards involving a third party in order to perform the examination is also evident in the context of therapeutic support. Indeed, parental consent is required for the purpose of therapeutic support once the investigative interview is completed. However, if the alleged perpetrator is one of the parents or legal guardians, then 'the Manager (Children's House) shall communicate the therapeutic needs of the child to the Director (Child Protection) who shall make a request for such therapy to be given to the minor without parental consent [f]or authorisation to the competent court'.[1159] That notwithstanding, the referred minor may at all times 'refuse therapy or may ask for a change in the professional and such wishes shall be respected'.[1160]

209. It should however also be recalled that medical practitioners are bound by the ethical and professional standards of their profession, which includes maintaining 'a tradition of placing the needs of the patient above all else'.[1161] The significance of that role in the context of minors can be explained through the lens of the law regulating sex assignment treatment or surgical intervention on the sex characteristics of a minor. This is regulated under the Gender Identity, Gender Expression and Sex Characteristics Act,[1162] which defines a minor as 'a person who has not as yet attained the age of sixteen years'.[1163] It is, in the first instance, 'unlawful for medical practitioners or other professionals to conduct any sex assignment treatment and, or surgical intervention on the sex characteristics of a minor which treatment and, or intervention can be deferred until the person to be treated can provide informed consent'.[1164] It consequently, for instance, means that infants born in 'a state of indeterminate sexuality'[1165] should have no sex assignment treatment and/or surgical intervention on their sex characteristics until the subjects of the decisions can themselves provide informed consent to the treatment or surgery.[1166] Yet,

1157. *Ibid.*, r. 33.
1158. *Ibid.*, r. 30.
1159. *Ibid.*, r. 35 (1).
1160. *Ibid.*, r. 36.
1161. S.L. 464.17, Ethics of the Medical Profession Regulations, Schedule A [1 (a)].
1162. *See also* Part II Ch. 3 §8 below.
1163. Gender Identity, Gender Expression and Sex Characteristics Act, Ch. 540 of the Laws of Malta, Art. 2.
1164. *Ibid.*, Art. 14 (1).
1165. *Black's Medical Dictionary* 347 (Harvey Marcovitch ed., Bloomsbury 43d ed. 2017).
1166. House of Representatives Malta – Office of the Clerk, *Kumitat Permanenti ghall-Kunsiderazzjoni ta' Abbozzi ta' Ligi (Rapport Ufficjali u Rivedut)*, 12th Legislature: Meeting no. 46 (22 March 2015) 24–27.

unless otherwise prohibited by law,[1167] that sex assignment treatment and/or surgical intervention on the sex characteristics of the minor can be lawfully conducted if the intervention cannot be deferred until the minor can provide informed consent, and it 'shall be conducted if the minor gives informed consent through the person exercising parental authority or the tutor of the minor'.[1168] To be clear, medical practitioners are not mandated to treat and indeed, when the decision for treatment is being expressed by the minor with the consent of the persons exercising parental authority or the tutor of the minor, medical practitioner/s are bound by law to '(a) ensure that the best interests of the child as expressed in the Convention on the Rights of the Child be the paramount consideration; and (b) give weight to the views of the minor having regard to the minor's age and maturity'.[1169] In that respect, medical practitioners may bear the weight of determining whether to refuse to provide treatment and/or surgical intervention if it is not in the best interests of the child. It is furthermore a violation of the law to perform a medical intervention that is driven by social factors without the consent of the minor.[1170] That being said, sex assignment treatment and/or surgical intervention on the sex characteristics of a minor may take place in exceptional circumstances when the minor is still unable to provide consent once agreement is reached between the interdisciplinary team appointed by the Minister responsible for equality and the persons exercising parental authority or the tutor of the minor.[1171] Thus, by not laying a blanket ban on sex assignment treatment on minors and/or surgical intervention on the sex characteristics of minors, Maltese law ostensibly 'aims to strike a balance between various actors while keeping the child at the centre of the focus'.[1172] In that respect, medical practitioners are constrained by law not to perform certain treatments and/or surgery as well as being bound by law to ensure the best interests of the child or minor patient as a paramount consideration.

§2. The Mental Patient

210. The term 'mental patient' used in the standard outline of the International Encyclopaedia for Medical Law is not present in Maltese law, which instead uses other terms such as 'person with a mental disorder'. Legislation addressing the medical practitioner-patient relationship when that patient has a mental disorder has already been engaged with in this monograph; for instance, in the section addressing 'informed consent' when considering the role of the Commissioner for Mental Health, the significance of mental capacity in Maltese law, the functions of the

1167. Mental Health Act, Ch. 525 of the Laws of Malta, Art. 31 (2).

1168. Gender Identity, Gender Expression and Sex Characteristics Act, Ch. 540 of the Laws of Malta, Art. 14 (1).

1169. *Ibid.*, Art. 14 (6).

1170. *Ibid.*, Art. 14 (3).

1171. *Ibid. See also* Claudia Bartolo Tabone, *Intersessualità: L' "I" Invisibile*, in *La Bioetica e i cinque sensi: Tra practica clinica e metafore* 89, 94 (Pietro Grassi & Raymond Zammit eds, Tau Editrice 2021).

1172. Tanya Ní Mhuirthile, *The legal status of intersex persons in Malta*, in *The Legal Status of Intersex Persons* 357, 366 (Jens Scherpe, Anatol Dutta & Tobias Helms eds, Intersentia 2018).

responsible carer and the institute of guardianship, as well as in the preceding section of this chapter when addressing the minor patient with a mental disorder. It is also the case that many of the laws that have been mentioned so far or that will be mentioned later in this monograph may contain ad hoc provisions addressing the situation of persons with a mental disorder. By way of example, while the office of the Ombudsman was considered in the section regarding 'review boards' in Part I of the monograph, it was not at that stage noted that:

> [W]here any letter appearing to be written by … any patient of any hospital within the meaning of the Mental Health Act, is addressed to the Ombudsman, it shall be immediately forwarded, unopened, to the Ombudsman by the person for the time being in charge of the place or institution where the writer of the letter … is a patient [and any] letter written by the Ombudsman to a … patient so described shall be immediately forwarded, unopened, to such … patient by the person for the time being in charge of the place or institution'.[1173]

Overall, while persons with a mental disorder have a right unless otherwise prevented by law, to 'receive treatment of the same quality and standard as other individuals',[1174] this right is without prejudice to anything provided in the Mental Health Act. In that respect, after illustrating the meaning of 'mental disorder' in Maltese law, this section outlines to what extent and how medical law in Malta engages with persons with mental disorders in relation to admission to a mental health licensed facility and in relation to community treatment orders, while also taking into account the broader medical law engaging with patients with a mental disorder.

211. The Mental Health Act in Malta regulates the provision of mental health services, care and rehabilitation while promoting and upholding the rights of people suffering from mental disorders. It also served as the legal basis to repeal the law that had until 2014 provided for 'the treatment and care of mentally disordered persons'[1175] and, while some subsidiary law is still formally in force despite arising from now repealed parent Acts,[1176] the Mental Health Act is presently the main law in Malta regulating mental health services. Thus, while it is by no means the only law addressing persons with mental disorders, it is the Mental Health Act that, for instance, grounds in law a comprehensive definition of mental disorder:

> [A] significant mental or behavioural dysfunction, exhibited by signs and, or symptoms indicating a disruption of mental functioning, including disturbance in one or more of the areas of thought, mood, volition, perception, cognition, orientation or memory which are present to such a degree as to be considered

1173. Ombudsman Act, Ch. 385 of the Laws of Malta, Art. 16 (2).
1174. Mental Health Act, Ch. 525 of the Laws of Malta, Art. 3 (1)(b). *See also* Art 43 (1).
1175. Mental Health Act, Ch. 262 of the Laws of Malta. Repealed.
1176. *See, for instance*: S.L. 94.02, Board of the Hospital for Mental Diseases Regulations; S.L. 94.11, Medical Officers of the Hospital for Mental Diseases Regulations; S.L. 262.02, Transfer of Hospital Patients Regulations; S.L. 262.04, Designation of Places as Hospital Order.

> pathological in accordance with internationally accepted medical and diagnostic standards and "mental illness" shall be construed accordingly, and for the purpose of any matter related to criminal proceedings, it shall include "insanity" as understood for the purpose of the Criminal Code.[1177]

Medical practitioners must thus rely on internationally accepted medical and diagnostic standards to establish what can be considered to be pathological in such a manner as to fall within the definition of mental disorder in Maltese law. An exception to this rule arises from the Gender Identity, Gender Expression and Sex Characteristics Act, which provides that the 'pathologisation of any form of sexual orientation, gender identity and, or gender expression as may be classified under the International Classification of Diseases or any other similar internationally recognised classification, shall be null and void in Malta'.[1178] Indeed, the Affirmation of Sexual Orientation, Gender Identity and Gender Expression Act, while largely adopting the definition of mental disorder drawn from the Mental Health Act, nevertheless provides for the exclusion in that definition 'of any form of pathologisation of sexual orientation, gender identity and, or gender expression as may be classified under the International Classification of Diseases or other similar internationally recognised classifications'.[1179] More recent versions of the internationally recognised classifications of diseases may have lessened the significance of these provisions in Maltese law and,[1180] either way, it is also provided that the 'nullity of such classification shall not impact negatively the provision of any healthcare service related to sex and, or gender'.[1181]

212. Grounded upon its definition of mental disorder, the Mental Health Act then regulates admission to a mental health licensed facility, which 'means a healthcare setting, whether private or public, duly licensed to provide mental health care'.[1182] As such, mental healthcare is related to but separate from other healthcare inasmuch as mental healthcare has its own topic-specific licensed healthcare setting and regulatory framework. Thus, voluntary admission to a mental health licensed facility is tenable upon two conditions being satisfied. First, the person needs inpatient treatment in a mental health licensed facility.[1183] Indeed, a person with a mental disorder might not require inpatient treatment and s/he has the right to 'receive treatment in the least restrictive environment and in the least restrictive manner'[1184]

1177. Mental Health Act, Ch. 525 of the Laws of Malta, Art. 2. Original punctuation.
1178. Gender Identity, Gender Expression and Sex Characteristics Act, Ch. 540 of the Laws of Malta, Art. 15 (2).
1179. Affirmation of Sexual Orientation, Gender Identity and Gender Expression Act, Ch. 567 of the Laws of Malta, Art. 2.
1180. World Health Organization, *International Statistical Classification of Diseases and Related Health Problems 11th Revision* (ICD-11, Adopted in May 2019 and came into effect in January 2022); American Psychiatric Association, *Diagnostic and Statistical Manual of Mental Disorders: DSM-5-TR* (5th ed. Text Revision, American Psychiatric Association Publishing 2022).
1181. Gender Identity, Gender Expression and Sex Characteristics Act, Ch. 540 of the Laws of Malta, Art. 15 (2).
1182. Mental Health Act, Ch. 525 of the Laws of Malta, Art. 2.
1183. *Ibid.*, Art. 7 (1).
1184. *Ibid.*, Art. 3 (1)(d).

as well as the right to 'receive care primarily in the community'.[1185] Second, so as to be admitted voluntarily to a mental health licensed facility, a person must also be willing to receive inpatient treatment,[1186] and that person 'shall not be admitted unless he consents in writing to the required care and treatment'.[1187] For the purpose of the Mental Health Act, treatment 'includes voluntary and involuntary treatment of a medical, nursing, social and psychological nature',[1188] but the voluntary patient 'shall not be secluded unless he consents in writing'[1189] and s/he is to have a multidisciplinary care plan formulated in consultation with him/her and/or the responsible carer within 168 hours of admission with written informed consent to be provided by that patient if significant changes are made to the care plan.[1190] In cases when the patient lacks capacity or is legally prevented from giving consent, the responsible carer shall give that consent.[1191] That being said, the voluntary patient can discharge him/herself from the mental health licensed facility provided that the nurse in charge of that patient 'may prevent self discharge for up to four hours to allow review by a medical practitioner if it is perceived that there are grounds for involuntary admission'.[1192] In this respect, the person who is voluntarily admitted to a mental health licensed facility is to be informed on admission that medical personnel may exercise that authority to prevent discharge. There is an exception to this rule inasmuch as the psychiatrist under whose care the patient is admitted may decide 'that it is not in the interest of the patient to be informed of such authority in which case such information shall be passed to the responsible carer'.[1193]

213. In order for a person to be involuntarily admitted to a mental health licensed facility or otherwise detained as an involuntary patient if s/he is already a voluntary patient in that facility, a psychiatrist whose name is entered in the Specialist Register for psychiatry held by the Medical Council must certify that there exist all three criteria for involuntary admission listed in Article 8 of the Mental Health Act. First, the person must have 'a severe mental disorder'.[1194] The Mental Health Act does not dictate what distinguishes a mental disorder as being severe or otherwise, but the Mental Health Strategy 2020–2030 issued by the Ministry for Health acknowledges 'schizophrenia, delusional and mood disorders'[1195] as severe mental illness while psychosis is specifically identified in that Strategy document under the subheading 'severe mental disorders'.[1196] That notwithstanding, a reasonable suspicion of severe mental disorder shall suffice to satisfy this first criterion 'in

1185. *Ibid.*, Art. 3 (1)(e).
1186. *Ibid.*, Art. 7 (1).
1187. *Ibid.*, Art. 7 (2)(a). *See also* Art. 3 (1)(i).
1188. *Ibid.*, Art. 2.
1189. *Ibid.*, Art. 7 (2)(b).
1190. *Ibid.*, Art. 7 (2)(e)–(f). *See also* Art. 3 (1)(h).
1191. *Ibid.*, Art. 7 (2).
1192. *Ibid.*, Art. 7 (3).
1193. *Ibid.*, Art. 7 (2)(d).
1194. *Ibid.*, Art. 8 (1)(a).
1195. Ministry for Health Malta, *Building resilience, transforming services: A mental health strategy for Malta 2020 – 2030*, 24 (2019).
1196. *Ibid.*, 20.

case of emergency when there is a serious likelihood of immediate physical harm to the person or to third parties'.[1197] Second, a psychiatrist must certify that 'due to the mental disorder, there is a serious risk of physical harm to that person or to other persons'.[1198] In addition to the mental disorder and the serious risk of physical harm, a psychiatrist must also certify a third criterion inasmuch as 'failure to admit or detain that person is likely to lead to a serious deterioration in his condition or will prevent the administration of appropriate treatment that cannot be given in the community'.[1199] While these three criteria must all be satisfied so as to render a person with a mental disorder eligible for involuntary admission to a mental health licensed facility, there are furthermore two conditions embedded in the Mental Health Act that do not have to be certified by a psychiatrist, but that could nevertheless exclude the possibility of involuntary admission. Thus, a person is not to be admitted to a mental health licensed facility 'if other less restrictive alternatives such as community care can be utilised',[1200] which means that involuntary admission would still be tenable if other less restrictive measures exist, but they cannot be utilised. Moreover, a 'person requiring custodial care only shall not be kept in a licensed facility as an involuntary patient'.[1201] Custodial care is defined in the Mental Health Act as 'non-medical care that helps a person with his or her activities of daily living and not requiring constant attention of healthcare professionals',[1202] which refers in the Mental Health Act to any professional registered with a Council under the Health Care Professions Act or under the laws regulating the professions of social work[1203] and/or psychology.[1204] Although Article 8 of the Mental Health Act regarding the criteria for involuntary admission does not exclude the possibility that a person requiring custodial care alone is kept in a mental health licensed facility as a voluntary patient, the requirements of voluntary admission would, in that case, nevertheless have to be satisfied.

214. So as to render lawful an involuntary admission to a mental health licensed facility, in addition to requiring that all three criteria of involuntary admission have been satisfied as described above and that there are no criteria that exclude the option of involuntary admission, the Mental Health Act also requires that appropriate forms are completed, submitted and, if necessary, approved. The process to be adopted will depend upon the stage that the involuntary admission has reached. A first stage involves involuntary admission for observation, which is not to exceed ten days duration from the time of admission unless an application is then made to proceed to the next stage of involuntary admission. The application for involuntary admission for observation is to be submitted to the clinical director of the mental health licensed facility, who is to forward the application form to the Commissioner for Mental Health within two days of the person being admitted, albeit that the

1197. Mental Health Act, Ch. 525 of the Laws of Malta, Art. 8 (1).
1198. *Ibid.*, Art. 8 (2).
1199. *Ibid.*, Art. 8 (1)(c)
1200. *Ibid.*, Art. 8 (3).
1201. *Ibid.*, Art. 8 (2).
1202. *Ibid.*, Art. 2.
1203. Social Work Profession Act, Ch. 468 of the Laws of Malta.
1204. Psychology Profession Act, Ch. 471 of the Laws of Malta.

Commissioner's approval is not required for admission to occur.[1205] That application is to be made by the responsible carer or by a mental welfare officer, who is a healthcare professional as defined in the Mental Health Act with experience in mental health duly appointed by the Minister responsible for health on the recommendation of the clinical director of the mental health licensed facility for the purpose of the Mental Health Act.[1206] The mental welfare officer is only to complete the application if the responsible carer fails to do so or when the responsible carer explicitly refuses consent for involuntary admission and if that mental welfare officer is satisfied, after reviewing the patient,[1207] that 'such an application ought to be made and is of the opinion that there are valid reasons for involuntary admission to a licensed facility and that care cannot be safely given in the community'.[1208] Yet, the Mental Health Act provides that even if both the responsible carer and the mental welfare officer are of the opinion that involuntary admission is not justified, 'such disagreement shall not prevent or delay the involuntary admission for observation'.[1209] This is because of the key role played by medical recommendations inasmuch as an application for involuntary admission for observation cannot be made 'unless the medical assessment has been carried out and the medical recommendation filled in'.[1210] This medical assessment is to be made by two medical practitioners, one of whom must be a psychiatrist, and, in case of discrepancy between the two assessments, a third independent assessment by a different psychiatrist is carried out so that the majority recommendation prevails.[1211] The Mental Health Act also provides that, in 'case of emergency, when there is a serious likelihood of immediate physical harm to the person or to third parties, an initial single medical assessment shall suffice for the purpose of application for involuntary admission for observation'[1212] provided that the second medical assessment by a psychiatrist is carried out within twenty-four hours of admission to the mental health licensed facility. Also, in the case of minors under 18 years of age, involuntary admission for observation shall only be permissible if a psychiatrist who has clinical experience of working with minors with mental health problems and has been appointed for that purpose by the Minister responsible for health certifies on the prescribed form in the Mental Health Act 'that community based alternatives are not available or are unlikely to be effective or have been tried and failed or are unsafe'.[1213]

215. Urgent treatment may be given to the patient during a period of involuntary admission for observation provided that a psychiatrist assesses the patient within 24 hours of admission and 'any issues of immediate concern are dealt with promptly and expediently'.[1214] However, no involuntary treatment shall be given

1205. Mental Health Act, Ch. 525 of the Laws of Malta, Art. 10 (3).
1206. *Ibid.*, Art. 2.
1207. *Ibid.*, Second Schedule.
1208. *Ibid.*, Art. 10 (2).
1209. *Ibid.*
1210. *Ibid.*, Art. 10 (1).
1211. *Ibid.*, Art. 9 (1).
1212. *Ibid.*, Art. 9 (2).
1213. *Ibid.*, Art. 30 (1).
1214. *Ibid.*, Art. 11 (1).

before the second medical assessment by a psychiatrist has been carried out 'unless it is emergency treatment meant solely to prevent physical harm to the patient or others or to prevent mental deterioration'.[1215] A patient is to then be discharged or detained as a voluntary patient after the ten-day period of observation lapses unless an application for Involuntary Admission for Treatment Order is made to the Commissioner for Mental Health. In that case, the patient can lawfully continue to be detained involuntarily until the Commissioner renders a decision, which s/he is bound to deliver within five days of receipt of the application. It is the psychiatrist under whose care the patient is admitted or treated that makes the application for an Involuntary Admission for Treatment Order if it becomes evident to the multidisciplinary team within the period of observation 'that the patient requires involuntary admission beyond the observation period for therapeutic reasons'.[1216] The applying psychiatrist must also certify that the criteria for involuntary admission still apply to the patient at hand.[1217] The application for Involuntary Admission for Treatment Order must be 'supported by a multidisciplinary care plan outlining the patient's needs, how and by whom these will be addressed, specifying expected outcomes and timeframes'.[1218] This multidisciplinary care plan, in terms of the Mental Health Act, means 'the plan setting out the relevant medical, nursing, social, psychological and rehabilitative interventions that may be necessary to holistically address the needs of the person, expected outcomes, responsibilities and timeframes to be respected when giving the care and treatment to the patient'.[1219] If the Commissioner for Mental Health approves that application for Involuntary Admission for Treatment Order, it 'shall not exceed ten weeks after the lapse of the initial period of observation'[1220] or four weeks in the case of minors.[1221]

216. An application for an extension of the Involuntary Admission for Treatment Order for a further period not exceeding five weeks as approved by the Commissioner for Mental Health, or 'four weeks or less up to a maximum period of twelve weeks from the initial date of involuntary admission'[1222] in the case of minors, can only be made once.[1223] The application for that extension must be submitted to the Commissioner for Mental Health by the responsible psychiatrist at least seven days before the initial period of involuntary admission for treatment expires and must also include that psychiatrist's opinion that the criteria for involuntary admission still apply to the patient.[1224] Before granting the extension, the Commissioner for Mental Health is to investigate 'whether the criteria for involuntary admission are still operative and whether there was any failure by any healthcare professional in not attaining the desired outcomes as a result of not abiding by

1215. *Ibid.*, Art. 9 (3).
1216. *Ibid.*, Art. 12 (1).
1217. *Ibid.*, Third Schedule.
1218. *Ibid.*, Art. 12 (1).
1219. *Ibid.*, Art. 2.
1220. *Ibid.*, Art. 12 (3).
1221. *Ibid.*, Art. 30 (2).
1222. *Ibid.*, Art. 30 (3).
1223. *Ibid.*, Art. 13 (1).
1224. *Ibid.*, Fourth Schedule.

established patient management protocols and, or the multidisciplinary care plan submitted by the team',[1225] and if so, the Commissioner is to make any recommendations he deems necessary as well as take actions against healthcare professionals as stipulated in the Mental Health Act.[1226] Any admission extending past the extension period permitted by the Commissioner for Mental Health will require an application for a Continuing Detention Order to be submitted to that Commissioner by the responsible psychiatrist, which is to be submitted at least seven days before the termination of the extended Involuntary Admission for Treatment Order or an existing continuing detention order and must also include that psychiatrist's opinion that the criteria for involuntary admission still apply to the patient.[1227] Following an independent review by another psychiatrist and if the Commissioner for Mental Health is then satisfied 'that the person still has a mental disorder that requires treatment and should continue to be detained for his own safety or that of others, and that no other less restrictive way would achieve the best possible outcome for that person and his safety and, or the protection of the public',[1228] then the Commissioner may grant a Continuing Detention Order for a maximum period of six months or, in the case of minors, three months.[1229] This period may be renewed subject to a fresh application being made to the Commissioner for Mental Health accompanied by a modified multidisciplinary care plan.

217. To be clear, the patient has a right to provide informed consent prior to the administration of any treatment, even during a period of involuntary admission in a mental health licensed facility and, in those cases where the patient lacks the mental capacity to consent to treatment, it will fall upon the responsible carer to furnish that consent. That being said, the Mental Health Act also provides that if the patient or, as the case may be, the responsible carer refuses to give consent, treatment can nevertheless be given 'to prevent physical harm to self or others or to prevent mental deterioration'[1230] and, in the case of the responsible carer refusing treatment, an application may be made to the Commissioner for Mental Health by the responsible psychiatrist to change that carer. The criteria for involuntary admission must furthermore exist throughout the period of involuntary admission in order for that involuntary admission to remain lawful. The responsible psychiatrist is indeed obliged to immediately request the Commissioner for Mental Health to release the patient from the Involuntary Admission for Treatment Order or the Continuing Detention Order if 'the patient's mental health status improves and the criteria for involuntary admission and treatment cease to exist either during the period of involuntary admission, or at the end of the approved involuntary treatment period, as the case may be'.[1231] That being said, if the application for involuntary admission has been lawfully completed and the subject of that application nevertheless refuses to be taken to the mental health licensed facility, then any of the persons who signed

1225. *Ibid.*, Art. 13 (3)(a).
1226. *Ibid.*, Art. 13 (3)(b).
1227. *Ibid.*, Fifth Schedule.
1228. *Ibid.*, Art. 13 (4).
1229. *Ibid.*, Art. 31 (4).
1230. *Ibid.*, Art. 14.
1231. *Ibid.*, Art. 15 (1).

the application shall request police assistance, which are, in turn, duty-bound to provide that assistance so that the person is taken to the mental health licensed facility.[1232] Likewise, if a person absconds without permission from a mental health licensed facility while liable to be detained there and the patient refuses to return after being recalled by the responsible psychiatrist or a delegated member of the multidisciplinary team with the help of the responsible carer, then the responsible psychiatrist is to request police assistance by issuing a Conveyance Order so that the person is returned to the mental health licensed facility.[1233]

218. The Mental Health Act nevertheless also regulates two main avenues for persons with mental disorders to receive compulsory treatment in the community rather than in a mental health licensed facility. First, the psychiatrist under whose care a patient is admitted or is being treated in a mental health licensed facility may approve the patient's temporary absence from that facility.[1234] In this situation, the patient would still be bound by any terms of involuntary admission and any conditions of release included in a care plan. If however the involuntarily admitted patient is on approved leave from a mental health licensed facility but 'fails to observe the conditions of the release specified in the care plan',[1235] a Conveyance Order may be issued for police assistance to return that patient to the mental health licensed facility if s/he refuses to return to the facility after being recalled by the responsible psychiatrist or a delegated member of the multidisciplinary team with the help of the responsible carer. The second option under the Mental Health Act regulating the compulsory treatment of a person with a mental disorder outside a mental health licensed facility involves a Community Treatment Order (CTO) whereby that person is 'compulsorily treated in the community under a care plan that helps the person to live and integrate in the community'.[1236] Indeed, a patient with a mental disorder who is eligible for a CTO cannot be subject to involuntary admission in a mental health licensed facility since it is a less restrictive alternative that allows 'for treatment, care and management of a person with a mental disorder to be provided in the community by healthcare professionals as nominated in the care plan'.[1237] That care plan, which must accompany every application for a CTO, is formulated by the psychiatrist under whose care the patient is being treated in collaboration with other healthcare professionals and with the responsible carer. The care plan is to specify 'the medicinal products, appointments and other aspects of care that the healthcare professionals believe are necessary to enable the person to live in the community'[1238] while also specifying 'the names of the healthcare professionals responsible to provide each identified intervention required by the patient'.[1239] The care plan is to furthermore indicate a 'key healthcare professional responsible for coordinating the various interventions and for explaining to the

1232. *Ibid.*, Art. 44 (1).
1233. *Ibid.*, Art. 44 (2).
1234. *Ibid.*, Art. 2.
1235. *Ibid.*, Art. 44 (2)(b).
1236. *Ibid.*, Art. 16 (1).
1237. *Ibid.*, Art. 16 (2).
1238. *Ibid.*, Art. 18 (3)(c).
1239. *Ibid.*, Art. 18 (3)(d).

patient his rights and the care plan in a language that the patient can understand'.[1240] The patient subject to a CTO shall then 'be required to undergo the authorised treatment',[1241] and it is the duty of the key healthcare professional to ensure that the patient is following the prescribed care plan as well as to inform the responsible psychiatrist if that patient is not complying with those obligations in a situation where the responsible carer cannot ensure that the patient complies with the care plan.[1242] In that case, the responsible psychiatrist may issue a Conveyance Order asking the police to bring that patient to him/her for assessment so as to order treatment if necessary, and if that treatment is refused, the patient may also be detained involuntarily in a mental health licensed facility in terms of the Mental Health Act.

219. A CTO is granted by the Commissioner for Mental Health upon an application made by the responsible carer or, in case the responsible carer does not apply or explicitly refuses consent to make the application, by a mental welfare officer. Similarly to the situation of an application for involuntary admission for observation to a mental health licensed facility, even in circumstances where both the responsible carer and the mental welfare officer are of the opinion that the CTO is not justified, the Mental Health Act provides that 'such disagreement shall not prevent or delay the submission of the application to the Commissioner for consideration'.[1243] This is because a CTO is stipulated upon two medical recommendations involving at least one psychiatrist that, if applicable, would preferably be the psychiatrist under whose care the patient is admitted or is being treated in a mental health licensed facility, albeit that the subject of the CTO need not be an inpatient at the time of the application. The second medical recommendation would preferably be made by the medical practitioner, who would ostensibly be following the patient in the community under the supervision of the responsible psychiatrist. When the medical practitioner responsible to provide treatment in the community to the person on a CTO is not one of the medical practitioners who made the recommendation for that CTO, the Mental Health Act binds that medical practitioner to 'signify his agreement to provide the treatment [in the community] on the prescribed form in accordance with the Eighth Schedule and forward it to the Commissioner'[1244] for Mental Health. The CTO may be granted for a maximum period of 6 months, which may be renewed subject to submission of a new application if the Commissioner for Mental Health is satisfied that the four criteria for CTO are all applicable at the time of each application:

> (a) the person has a severe mental disorder that is amenable to treatment in the community; and (b) the responsible specialist has previously authorised treatment for the illness but the person has refused or failed to consistently cooperate with the treatment to an extent that has resulted or may result in relapse

1240. *Ibid.*, Art. 18 (3)(a).
1241. *Ibid.*, Art. 16 (3).
1242. *Ibid.*, Art. 21.
1243. *Ibid.*, Art. 18 (2).
1244. *Ibid.*, Art. 19 (1).

of the mental disorder or inadequate response which has previously led or may lead to involuntary admission to a licensed facility; and (c) the person should be given treatment for the illness in the interest of his own safety or for the protection of others; and (d) the treatment required for the person can be safely provided in the community.[1245]

If any of those criteria are not satisfied, then a CTO is not tenable under the Mental Health Act. It may however be the case that the person is eligible for voluntary or involuntary admission to a mental health licensed facility. That being said, a CTO may also be revoked by the Commissioner for Mental Health prior to the end of the prescribed period following an application submitted by the responsible psychiatrist.[1246] Either way, any decision or order taken by the Commissioner for Mental Health under *any of the provisions* of the Mental Health Act 'shall be subject to appeal to the Court of Voluntary Jurisdiction'.[1247]

220. It is furthermore perfectly tenable for a medical practitioner-patient relationship to exist when that patient has a mental disorder without requiring a CTO or admission to a mental health licensed facility. In that case, a person with a mental disorder is, all else being equal, little different from any other patient. Indeed, the Mental Health Act itself provides that any 'person suffering from a mental disorder shall, as any other citizen, have access to or provision of any available health, educational or social service ... provided by the State and shall have the right to the same quality of treatment, and subject to the other provisions of [the Mental Health Act], to confidentiality and consent to treatment'.[1248] The Commissioner for Mental Health is to then 'take appropriate action against anyone who discriminates, or exploits a person by reason of his mental health status',[1249] which can also relate to disability law.[1250] There are furthermore laws that *inter alia* aim to empower persons with a mental disorder to participate fully as members of the community and promote their self-determination, including in the context of healthcare. By way of example, the Persons within the Autism Spectrum (Empowerment) Act is intended to 'empower persons within the autism spectrum by providing for their health and well-being in society, the betterment of their living conditions, their participation and inclusion in society and to make ancillary and consequential provisions thereto in full adherence to the UN Convention on the Rights of Persons with Disability'.[1251] In turn, Malta's National Autism Strategy was adopted consequent to the latter legislative Act.[1252] Subsidiary legislation arising from the Social Care Standards Authority Act grounding in law regulatory standards for social care services

1245. *Ibid.*, Art. 16 (4).
1246. *Ibid.*, Tenth Schedule.
1247. *Ibid.*, Art. 46.
1248. *Ibid.*, Art. 43 (1).
1249. *Ibid.*, Art. 43 (3).
1250. *See also* Part I Ch. 4 §4.II above.
1251. Autism Spectrum (Empowerment) Act, Ch. 557 of the Laws of Malta.
1252. Ministry for Inclusion and Social Wellbeing – Government of Malta, *Respecting Diversity – Safeguarding equality: Malta's 2021 – 2030 National Autism Strategy* (An Autism State Support Plan in terms of Article 11 of the Persons within the Autism Spectrum (Empowerment) Act).

may also be applicable to persons with mental disorders.[1253] That notwithstanding, it is still the case that an application may be made by eligible parties before a Magistrate asking for authorisation to enter a person's house and to take that person to a mental health licensed facility for immediate assessment when s/he 'is suspected of suffering from a serious mental disorder and is considered to be a danger to himself or others'.[1254] Moreover, a warrant to enter private premises to take a person to a mental health licensed facility will not be required 'in an emergency situation where there is a serious likelihood of immediate physical harm to the patient or to third parties'.[1255]

221. For the purpose of this Part of the monograph addressing the medical practitioner-patient relationship, it is worthwhile briefly noting that the Mental Health Act also includes provisions that specifically address the situation of patients in criminal proceedings in three situations: (i) the situation where the question of a person's mental capacity, be it at the time of the offence or of the proceedings, arises in the course of any proceedings on the charge of a criminal offence;[1256] (ii) the situation where persons may be directed by a court to be kept in custody in a mental health licensed facility consequent to a plea and finding of insanity;[1257] and (iii) the situation of a person who develops a mental disorder while in prison and cannot be adequately treated in prison.[1258] Furthermore, in accordance with Article 412D of the Criminal Code, the court may make a treatment order requiring a person to submit to treatment if it is satisfied that proper arrangements have been made or can be made for that treatment. To be clear, if the person is accused of an offence, 'a treatment order may only be made with the consent of the accused'[1259] but, in the circumstances when a person is convicted of an offence, 'a treatment order by the court may be made with or without the consent of the convicted person'.[1260] The treatment order, which shall remain in force for a period not exceeding five years and can be extended, varied or otherwise revoked by the court,[1261] can include any of the kinds of treatment mentioned in Article 7 (5) of the Probation Act. This includes instances where, in the opinion of the court, 'the mental condition of the offender is such as requires and as may be susceptible to treatment, but not such as to justify other measures or procedures, or where the court is satisfied that – (a) the offender is a drug addict; and (b) that proper arrangements have been or can be made for

1253. *See, for instance*: S.L. 582.05, Social Regulatory Standards for Outreach and Community-Based Services offered to Individuals with Problems Related to Substance Abuse and other Dependencies; S.L. 582.06, Social Regulatory Standards for Residential Services offered to Individuals with Problems Related to Substance Abuse and Other Dependencies.
1254. Mental Health Act, Ch. 525 of the Laws of Malta, Art. 44 (4).
1255. *Ibid.*
1256. *Ibid.*, Art. 36.
1257. *Ibid.*, Art. 37.
1258. *Ibid.*, Art. 38. *See also* S.L. 260.03, Prisons Regulations, r. 61 (1)(h).
1259. Criminal Code, Ch. 9 of the Laws of Malta, Art. 412D (1).
1260. *Ibid.*
1261. *Ibid.*, Art. 412C (9)–(10). *See also* Art. 412D (3).

treatment'.[1262] In those cases, the treatment is to be provided 'by or under the directions of a suitably qualified person with a view to the improvement of the offender's mental condition or with a view to freeing the offender from drug addiction'.[1263] That treatment may be provided by or under the direction of a suitably qualified person as may be specified in the court order, or the treatment may be provided to the person as a resident or non-resident patient in a hospital or other appropriate agency or institution.

§3. The Dying Patient

222. The Ethics of the Medical Profession Regulations provide that a 'doctor must always bear in mind the importance of preserving human life from the time of conception until death'.[1264] Despite this broad requirement accompanied by plenty of academic literature on the topic of the dying patient in Malta,[1265] there is a 'lack of an elaborate legislative framework to regulate end of life issues'.[1266] This signifies limited topic-specific regulation of end-of-life care in Malta. Qualitative research then suggests that medical practitioners in Malta are concerned by 'a lack of a legal framework and possibly, fear … litigation by the relatives',[1267] and it has been contended that medical practitioners 'need guidance – legal and moral – on this subject [of end of life care], in the absence of which, their religion and philosophy of life is used to guide them in this rather difficult area of practice'.[1268] It has furthermore been suggested that 'developing guidelines or protocols'[1269] for medical practitioners in relation to end-of-life decision-making would facilitate the process for those medical practitioners. As such, this section outlines how the situation of the dying patient is implicitly addressed by existing Maltese medical law.

1262. Probation Act, Ch. 446 of the Laws of Malta, Art. 7 (5).
1263. *Ibid.*
1264. S.L. 464.17, Ethics of the Medical Profession Regulations, Sch. A [10].
1265. *See, for instance*: *Bioethical Issues at the Beginning and End of Life: Proceedings of the Conference Organised by the Bioethics Consultative Committee* (Maurice N. Cauchi ed., Malta Ministry of Health 2001); Pierre Mallia, *The Beginning and End of Life: Moral Controversy* (PEG Publications 2002); Kevin Aquilina, *Maltese Law and the End of Life*, in *Contemporary Issues in Medical Ethics & Law: Conference Proceedings 2012 – 2015*, 103–107 (Kevin Aquilina, Pierre Mallia & Bridget Ellul eds, Progress Press 2017); Joseph Dimech, Emmanuel Agius, Julian C. Hughes & Paul Bartolo, *Challenges Faced by Patients, Relatives and Clinicians in End-Stage Dementia Decision-Making: A Qualitative Study of Swallowing Problems*, 47 (12) Journal of Medical Ethics e39 (2021).
1266. Kevin Aquilina, *Foreword by the Dean of the Faculty of Laws*, in *Consensus Document: Faculty of Medicine & Surgery, Faculty of Laws, Faculty of Theology, Bioethics Research Programme and Medicine & Law Programme as part of an Erasmus+ Project of the Bioethics Research Programme of the Medical School, on Harmonisation of end of Life Care (EndCare)* 4 (Pierre Mallia ed., Erasmus+ Endcare 2018).
1267. Jurgen Abela & Pierre Mallia, *Maltese Doctors: Views and Experiences on End of Life Decisions and Care*, 28 (2) Malta Medical Journal 16, 24 (2016).
1268. Jurgen Abela, *GPs and End of Life Decisions: Views and Experiences*, 27 (2) Malta Medical Journal 31, 36 (2015).
1269. Marilyn Harney, *The Role of the General Practitioner in Palliative Care: A Review*, 4 (1) Malta Medical School Gazette 83, 89 (2020).

223. The absence of a topic-specific legal framework is not equivalent to the absence of a legal framework governing end-of-life care and the situation of a dying patient. It is instead often the laws that are applicable to every patient that would be applicable to the situation of the dying patient in circumstances where end of life 'is taken to mean a spectrum of recognition that death will be imminent within one year up to the point where death is imminent within a few days or a few hours'.[1270] Engaging with the law that broadly governs the patient-medical practitioner relationship to address the situation of the dying patient is jurisprudentially sound because, to paraphrase Lord Hope of Craighead, the way one 'chooses to pass the closing moments of [one's] life is part of the act of living'[1271] and that period of one's life may consequently also be safeguarded by the right to respect for private and family life under the ECHR.[1272] It then is noteworthy that, despite the absence of a topic-specific legal framework addressing the situation of the dying patient, the Charter of Patient Rights and Responsibilities provides that one has the right to 'expect an end of life care that is dignified, comforting and supporting relief from any unnecessary suffering'[1273] as well as the right to 'be constantly accompanied by someone of one's choice during an end of life situation, in accordance with the healthcare establishment's rules and policies'.[1274] Given that the Charter of Patient Rights and Responsibilities sets out a summary of rights and responsibilities,[1275] the authority at law grounding those rights lies elsewhere. One can then, in the first instance, refer to laws that have already been addressed in this monograph.

224. For instance, the consent of the dying patient is required in order to establish a medical practitioner-patient relationship and, all else being equal, the informed consent of the dying patient is necessary before treatment is provided.[1276] Patients, including the dying patient, also have the right to refuse treatment, which will then entail the obligation on medical practitioners to withhold or even withdraw treatment once refused by the dying patient. Furthermore, rather than *ipso facto* assuming that the dying patient lacks the capacity to consent to or refuse treatment, s/he may be provided access to the support s/he requires in exercising his/her legal capacity, such as with the support of a guardian who will, in turn, be acting in line with obligations arising from the Civil Code and under the authority of a guardianship order that is duly monitored.[1277] If, however, the dying patient lacks the capacity to consent to or refuse treatment, for instance, due to young age or unconsciousness, the authority to consent to or refuse treatment will be, all else being

1270. *Consensus Document: Faculty of Medicine & Surgery, Faculty of Laws, Faculty of Theology, Bioethics Research Programme and Medicine & Law Programme as part of an Erasmus+ project of the Bioethics Research Programme of the Medical School, on Harmonisation of end of life care (EndCare)* 11 (Pierre Mallia ed., Erasmus+ Endcare 2018).

1271. *Pretty v. Director of Public Prosecutions and Secretary of State for the Home Department* [2001] UKHL 61 para. 100.

1272. *Pretty v. United Kingdom* App. No. 2346/02 (ECtHR – 29/04/2002) para. 67.

1273. Healthcare Standards Directorate – Ministry for Health, *Charter of Patient's Rights and Responsibilities* 15 (2016).

1274. *Ibid.*

1275. *See* General Introduction §3 above.

1276. *See* Part II Ch. 1 §2 above.

1277. *See* Part II Ch. 1 §2.II above.

equal, vested in a substitute decision-maker.[1278] Safeguards embedded in law will, in those circumstances, also be applicable to the dying patient. By way of example, a mandate made by a person in anticipation of his/her incapacity would have to be applicable to the situation of the dying patient in order to have effect in the circumstances of end-of-life care and performance of the mandate 'shall be conditional upon the occurrence of the incapacity and after obtaining the necessary approval from the court of voluntary jurisdiction upon application by the mandatary designated in the act. The court of voluntary jurisdiction may impose those conditions that it may deem necessary'.[1279] It is however possible that, since General Comments issued by the United Nations Committee on the Rights of Persons with Disabilities are to constitute interpretative guidance when interpreting the substantive rights arising from the UNCRPD for the purpose of the United Nations Convention for the Rights of Persons with Disabilities Act and given that this Committee has said that Article 12 of the UNCRPD requires substitute decision-making to be replaced by supported decision-making, then safeguards regarding decision-making at the end of one's life may eventually *inter alia* be grounded in the right of persons with disabilities to access the support they require in exercising their legal capacity.[1280] It is also embedded in the law that it would be an unlawful discrimination against a person with disabilities as defined in the UNCRPD to refuse to administer food and fluids to him/her due to his/her disability, and there is no reason to say that this should be any different in relation to a person with disabilities who is a dying patient.[1281] The criminal law addressing abuse on elderly or dependent persons would moreover be applicable even in the situation of a dying patient who is elderly or dependent, for instance, in circumstances where the person having the care or custody of the elder or dependent adult wilfully causes or permits the elder or dependent adult to be placed in a situation in which his/her person or health may be endangered.[1282] Furthermore, the Specialist Register held by the Medical Council of Malta includes a specialisation in Palliative Medicine,[1283] which is buttressed by the accompanying training programme that includes 'Aspects of the Law Particularly Relating to Palliative Medicine Practice',[1284] and prescription of medicines in palliative care and/or to ease unnecessary suffering, which can include suffering at the end of life, is duly regulated by the pertinent pharmaceutical and drug laws.[1285]

225. There is furthermore increasing acknowledgement in law of the later stages of one's life, especially in respect of senior citizens. In addition to the functions of the Commissioner for Older Persons,[1286] social regulatory standards for residential

1278. *See* Part II Ch. 1 §§1 and 2.II above.
1279. Civil Code, Ch. 16 of the Laws of Malta, Art. 1864A (2).
1280. *See also* Part II Ch. 1 §2.II above.
1281. United Nations Convention on the Rights of Persons with Disabilities Act, Ch. 627 of the Laws of Malta, Fourth Schedule.
1282. *See* Part I Ch. 4 §1.III above.
1283. *See also* Part I Ch. 1 §3.II above.
1284. Palliative Medicine Postgraduate Training Committee, *Postgraduate Training Curriculum for Palliative Medicine* 7 (Sir Anthony Mamo Oncology Centre Malta 2021).
1285. *See also* Part I Ch. 2 above.
1286. Commissioner for Older Persons Act, Ch. 553 of the Laws of Malta, Arts 9–11.

services for senior citizens, understood as persons over the age of 60, for instance, stipulate the responsibilities of the service provider who is a person or organisation that 'provides and operates a residential care home and associated care services to senior citizens on a long-term basis'.[1287] These obligations include issues that touch upon the closing stages of one's life. Thus, for example, in addition to fulfilling any contractual obligations that apply to them, service providers are to 'ensure that residents, their families, and other significant persons close to them are provided with optimal palliative care and support, as well [to] promote care, sensitivity, respect, and dignity during palliative care'.[1288] This standard imposed on the service provider in relation to palliative care should be read in light of the broader aspects of the regulatory standards. Indeed, these Social Regulatory Standards also make provision for a personal care plan 'based on a holistic assessment of the resident that specifies how the resident's needs and aspirations are going to be met'[1289] as well as a personalised portfolio 'that is based on the person's positive and negative experience that will cater for his specific needs'.[1290] In turn, the holistic assessment is 'the process by which staff identifies the needs and aspirations of community members in relation to their health, personal, emotional, spiritual, and psychological care, protection and social networking and family support; which services should be delivered to satisfy these needs and aspirations'.[1291] It then is the responsibility of the service provider to ensure that the interdisciplinary care team involves each resident during the holistic needs assessment process as well as to 'ensure that the personal care plan is implemented, and its implementation is documented and communicated regularly with all stakeholders'.[1292] The residents' choices, as well as the interests of their relatives and representatives, are also taken into account inasmuch as the service provider is bound to 'maximise the residents' capacity to exercise personal autonomy and choice whilst considering their mental capabilities, [and the service provider shall also] ensure that their relatives and legally appointed representatives are aware of their choice, and shall ensure that the residents are given enough time when they need to take a decision'.[1293] In this respect, although the regulatory standards do not target per se the needs of a dying patient given that a senior citizen using residential services is not necessarily a dying patient and neither do they regulate palliative care as such, there is nevertheless a basis in law identifying the entity responsible in the circumstances of senior citizens in a residential care home to ensure that optimal palliative care is provided as well as the process to decide when that care is to be furnished based upon the needs of the person at hand. In short, medical law that has already been addressed in the monograph can, to an extent, be adapted to cater for the dying patient, albeit that it may not cover

1287. S.L. 582.15, Social Regulatory Standards for Residential Services for Senior Citizens, r. 3.
1288. *Ibid.*, Schedule – Standard 1 [7].
1289. *Ibid.*, r. 3.
1290. *Ibid.*
1291. *Ibid.*
1292. *Ibid.*, Schedule – Standard 2 [2].
1293. *Ibid.*, Schedule – Standard 1 [4].

every situation that affects a dying patient as would law that is designed to specifically cater for that patient. For example, the senior citizen who is not in a residential care home falls beyond the scope of the regulatory standards governing those care homes.

226. That being said, there are subjects pertinent to the dying patient that are given little consideration in Maltese law, with limited space to adapt existing law to suit the requirements of the dying patient. By way of example, instructional advance directives, meaning 'instructions given or wishes made by a capable adult concerning issues that may arise in the event of his or her incapacity',[1294] are not evidently regulated in Maltese law even though the extent of their adaptability or otherwise within the domestic legal order in Malta has been considered elsewhere.[1295] Medically assisted suicide and euthanasia are also barely addressed by Maltese law. In this respect, the Criminal Code provides that whosoever 'shall prevail on any person to commit suicide or *shall give him any assistance*, shall, if the suicide takes place, be liable, on conviction'[1296] to a term of imprisonment. Inasmuch as giving assistance to commit suicide constitutes one of the possible material elements of the criminal offence, it is 'clear that whatever the intention, a person helping anyone to commit suicide is … guilty of an offence'.[1297] There is no exception to the latter provision if it is a medical practitioner that gives assistance to a person to commit suicide. Moreover, euthanasia in whatever form is not specifically mentioned in Maltese law, at least in respect of human beings. Neither is there an explicit and definite distinction in Maltese statutory law between extraordinary treatment and ordinary treatment despite the relevance of that distinction for the purpose of ethical and ostensibly lawful withdrawal of treatment.[1298] It has however been suggested that people in Malta are increasingly accepting the possibility of euthanasia and medically assisted suicide in case of individuals who are terminally ill or in great pain.[1299] Indeed, the electoral manifesto of the political party elected to

1294. Council of Europe, Recommendation CM/Rec (2009) 11 of the Committee of Ministers to member states on principles concerning continuing powers of attorney and advance directives for incapacity, 2.3.

1295. Daniel Bianchi, *Regulating Advance Decision-Making in Malta: To What Extent Are Advance Directives Adaptable to the Domestic Legal Order?*, in *Le scelte di fine vita – Choices at the End of Life* (Angelo Viglianisi Ferraro (ed.), Thomson Reuters – Forthcoming); Daniel Bianchi, *Advance Directives: Addressing the Obligations of Support as Part of the Right of a Person with Disabilities to Equal Recognition Before the Law?*, 70 International Journal of Law and Psychiatry 101561, p. 9 (2020).

1296. Criminal Code, Ch. 9 of the Laws of Malta, Art. 213. Emphasis added.

1297. Maurice N. Cauchi, Kevin Aquilina & Bridget Ellul, *Health, Bioethics and the Law* 116 (Malta University Press 2006).

1298. Pierre Mallia, *The Catholic Position on End of Life: Theological Foundations and Philosophical Reasoning*, in *Contemporary European Perspectives on the Ethics of End of Life Care* 117, 121–122 (Nathan Emmerich, Pierre Mallia, Bert Gordijn & Francesca Pistoia eds, Springer 2020).

1299. Renald Blundell, Stefan Nicholas Vella, Tsisia Okropiridze, Joseph Ignatius Azzopardi & Pierre Mallia, *Trends in Public Perception Towards Euthanasia and Physician-Assisted Suicide in the Maltese Islands*, 10(1) The Journal of the Malta College of Family Doctors 25–35 (2021).

government in March 2022 includes a proposal to commence a national discussion addressing the introduction of voluntary euthanasia for persons who have a terminal illness.[1300]

227. It should also be remarked that there are subjects that, although not formally addressed by the legislator in Malta by way of topic-specific legislation, could nevertheless be, in principle, addressed by the broader Maltese medical jurisprudence. By way of example, absent legislative intervention, do not resuscitate orders (DNRs) can fall within the remit of the independent healthcare establishments, provided that the policies set by these establishments do not violate any related laws. DNRs are then 'sometimes written on a patient's hospital notes to indicate that if he or she suffers a life-threatening complication ... of an existing illness, the patient should not be given emergency life-saving treatment such as cardiopulmonary resuscitation'.[1301] Yet, questions may arise regarding the extent to which the patient him/herself, or his/her legal representative, should be involved in the decision to include a DNR in a patient's hospital notes.[1302] In turn, the Health Act states that patients have a right 'to be involved in discussions and decisions about the treatment to be given'.[1303] Although it is not explicitly stated that patients have a right to be involved in discussions and decisions about treatment that will not be given, it is worthwhile recalling that the Charter of Patient Rights and Responsibilities, which sets out a summary of the rights and responsibilities of patients and other relevant persons, engages with the right of persons to participate in decisions about their care and it provides that healthcare professionals 'should refrain from making decisions related to care and treatment without the patient's direct participation except in exceptional cases'.[1304] This could then also include patient participation in changes to one's care or care plan, which is coherent with the broader Maltese medical jurisprudence and could, in principle, cover changes to care by including a DNR in the patient's hospital notes. If so, patients' right to be involved, either in person or through a lawfully appointed representative, in discussions and decisions about a DNR could attach to patients' rights as safeguarded in the Health Act. Be that as it may, it is for the legislator or delegated authorities to clarify these points, and though it is worthwhile highlighting that it is possible that instruments that are not evidently addressed by Maltese law may nevertheless find grounding therein, it is beyond the scope of this monograph to speculate on this matter. As such, the next section engages with specific activities that are addressed in Maltese law.

1300. Partit Laburista (Labour Party – Malta), *Malta Flimkien: Manifest Elettorali 2022*, 182 (Centru Nazzjonali Laburista Malta 2022).

1301. *Black's Medical Dictionary* 192 (Harvey Marcovitch ed., Bloomsbury 43d ed. 2017).

1302. Jurgen Abela & Pierre Mallia, *Maltese Doctors: Views and Experiences on End of Life Decisions and Care*, 28 (2) Malta Medical Journal 16, 23 (2016).

1303. Health Act, Ch. 528 of the Laws of Malta, Art. 27 (1)(c).

1304. Healthcare Standards Directorate – Ministry for Health, *Charter of Patient's Rights and Responsibilities* 12 (2016).

Chapter 3. Specific Activities

228. The first two chapters of this Part of the monograph furnished an overview of the domestic legal order underpinning the relations between patients and medical practitioners, thereby addressing key principles such as informed consent and secrecy in Chapter 1 while considering specific groups of people in Chapter 2, including minor children and persons with a mental disorder. This chapter instead addresses specific topics in the context of medical law in Malta that have not been broached in detail so far in this monograph. In line with the standard outline of the International Encyclopaedia for Medical Law, the following topics will be considered in this order: (i) Abortion, (ii) sterilisation, (iii) in vitro fertilisation, (iv) prenatal diagnosis, (v) psychosurgical interventions, (vi) organ transplants, (vii) experiments on human beings, and (viii) transsexual interventions. The standard outline of the International Encyclopaedia for Medical Law also includes a section in this chapter addressing the topic of 'euthanasia' but, as explained in section 3 of the preceding chapter, there is little Maltese law dealing with 'euthanasia' and that topic has therefore been integrated into the latter section of the monograph.

§1. Abortion

229. Maltese civil law provides that in 'case of abortion, an act of birth shall only be drawn up where the foetus shall have completely assumed the human form'.[1305] This includes instances when abortion occurs naturally, inasmuch as the process of pregnancy is interrupted without external intervention resulting in a miscarriage of the foetus, as well as instances when abortion is procured by the woman herself or by third parties such as medical practitioners. Although abortion and miscarriage are not defined in law, given that an abortion is a case where the law mandates an act of birth, it consequently means that an abortion or miscarriage cannot occur after birth, and the process of an ongoing abortion or miscarriage must occur prior to birth, in the uterine environment. It should however be recalled that medical practitioners are subject to professional and ethical standards, which is significant given that the Ethics of the Medical Profession Regulations provide that a 'doctor *must always bear in mind* the importance of preserving human life *from the time of conception* until death'.[1306] The latter duty thus covers the importance of preserving human life from conception, albeit without mandating the preservation of that human life in any circumstance. The criminal law in Malta then addresses instances when an abortion is procured by the pregnant woman herself or by third parties such as medical practitioners.

1305. Civil Code, Ch. 16 of the Laws of Malta, Art. 283 (3). *See also*: S.L. 458.02, Tariff of Fees Payable to Medical Practitioners Order, Schedule [21]; S.L. 458.04, Midwives Regulations, r. 18 (b)(ii); S.L. 458.05, Tariff of Fees Payable to Midwives Order, Schedule [8]; S.L. 458.23, Licensing of Private Medical Clinics Regulations, r. 10 (6)(d).

1306. S.L. 464.17, Ethics of the Medical Profession Regulations, Schedule A [10]. Emphasis added.

230. It thus is a criminal offence in Malta under Article 241 of the Criminal Code to cause, *by whatsoever means*, the miscarriage of any woman with child. The party who caused the miscarriage and the woman with child herself, if she consented to the use of the means by which the miscarriage is procured, are liable to conviction and imprisonment. It is also a criminal offence under Article 241 for any woman to procure her own miscarriage. The key elements for the offence under Article 241 of the Criminal Code to subsist therefore include that (i) the woman is pregnant with child, (ii) that the accused (who may include the woman herself) knew of the pregnancy while also possessing (iii) consequent intent to cause the miscarriage of that pregnancy, and (iv) that the miscarriage of the woman with child has in fact occurred and (v) that this miscarriage has been caused or procured by the accused. If any of those five elements is missing, a person cannot be held liable in respect of the Article 241 criminal offence of procuring a miscarriage.

231. Article 243 of the Criminal Code moreover provides that any 'physician, surgeon, obstetrician, or apothecary, who shall have knowingly prescribed or administered the means whereby the miscarriage is procured, shall, on conviction, be liable to imprisonment … and to perpetual interdiction from the exercise of his profession'. In order for this offence to be engaged, there must (i) be a member of one of the professions mentioned in Article 243 of the Criminal Code, though anyone else could, in principle, still fall within the remit of the different offence under Article 241 of that Code, (ii) the pregnancy of a woman with child, (iii) the professional's knowledge of that pregnancy as well as (iv) that professional's knowledge that miscarriage will be procured by way of the means s/he prescribed or administered, and (v) the miscarriage must have in fact been procured and specifically (vi) procured by way of the means prescribed or administered by the accused professional. All six features must be present for this offence to subsist, and the professional will not be guilty in terms of the criminal offence arising from Article 243 of the Criminal Code if even one of those elements is missing. It is also worthwhile noting the difference between Articles 241 and 243 inasmuch as the latter provision hones in on the knowledge of particular professions that their actions would cause a miscarriage. For instance, inducing early childbirth or evacuating a uterus from foetal remains or even terminating an ongoing miscarriage are all beyond the scope of the criminal law on abortion because the key element that 'the miscarriage must have, in fact, been procured' is in those situations missing inasmuch as no miscarriage is procured. The offence arising under Article 243 acknowledges that the professionals indicated in that provision would be aware that a miscarriage is to be procured by the means they *knowingly prescribed or administered* with the intention of procuring that miscarriage rather than, for instance, inducing early childbirth. The offence under Article 241 of the Criminal Code is instead grounded on intent to procure the miscarriage without requiring knowledge that the specific means used will, in fact, procure the miscarriage.

232. Given that Articles 241 and 243 of the Criminal Code require the intent or *dolo* of the person to procure the miscarriage but do not address negligence or *culpa*, Article 243A was added to the Criminal Code in 2002 to envelope the circumstances of culpable miscarriage within the possibility of criminal sanction. As such, whosoever 'through imprudence, carelessness, unskilfulness in his art or profession, or non-observance of regulations, causes the miscarriage of a woman with child, shall, on conviction, be liable to imprisonment' or to a fine. The key elements of the latter offence include (i) the pregnancy of a woman with child, (ii) that the miscarriage of that pregnancy has occurred, and (iii) this miscarriage is caused by reason of the accused person's imprudence, carelessness, unskilfulness in his/her art or profession, or non-observance of regulations. All three elements must exist for the offence under Article 243A to subsist, and the absence of just one of those elements will suffice so that a person is not found criminally liable under Article 243A of the Criminal Code. Yet, unlike the key elements of Articles 241 and 243 of the Criminal Code, knowledge of the pregnancy is not a key element of the offence arising from Article 243A. To be clear, provided that criminal liability is demonstrated,[1307] this provision can also cover the circumstances of a medical practitioner who, due to, for instance, his/her imprudence in the exercise of his/her profession, causes the miscarriage of a woman with child even though that medical practitioner had no intention of causing a miscarriage.

233. The Maltese authorities have carefully safeguarded Malta's sovereignty in respect of the laws regarding abortion. An evident example can be drawn from Malta's accession to the EU whereby it was agreed by the High Contracting Parties that '[n]othing in the Treaty on European Union, or in the Treaties establishing the European Communities, or in the Treaties or Acts modifying or supplementing those Treaties, shall affect the application in the territory of Malta of national legislation relating to abortion'.[1308] The latter Protocol is primary law of the EU, which means that Malta grounded in that primary law its right to retain decisional authority in respect of its sovereignty over the regulation and/or criminalisation of abortion within its territory. As such, Maltese law in relation to abortion in Malta will prevail over any EU law on that topic. Furthermore, Maltese authorities have been careful, when entering into international agreements that include reference to abortion, to only do so in a manner that is in line with the Maltese law on abortion. For instance, the Council of Europe's Convention on preventing and combating violence against women and domestic violence was ratified and incorporated into Maltese law, including the obligation to take necessary legislative or other measures to ensure that the intentional conduct of 'performing an abortion on a woman without her prior and informed consent'[1309] is criminalised. Yet, that was already a criminal offence in terms of Malta's criminal law on abortion even prior to Malta's ratification of the Convention at hand. Furthermore, Maltese authorities have also been cautious to furnish interpretative statements when entering into international agreements so as to clarify that a given provision that could be interpreted in a manner

1307. *See* Part I Ch. 4 §4.III above.

1308. Act concerning the conditions of accession of the Czech Republic, the Republic of Estonia, the Republic of Cyprus, the Republic of Latvia, the Republic of Lithuania, the Republic of Hungary, the Republic of Malta, the Republic of Poland, the Republic of Slovenia and the Slovak Republic and the adjustments to the Treaties on which the European Union is founded – Protocol No 7 on abortion in Malta, OJ L 236, 23.9.2003.

1309. Gender-Based Violence and Domestic Violence Act, Ch. 581 of the Laws of Malta, Schedule [Art. 39].

as relates to abortion will not, in the case of Malta, be interpreted in that manner or affect its criminal law on abortion. Thus, for instance, while the UNCRPD was ratified and incorporated into Maltese law, an interpretative statement was made upon ratification in relation to the phrase 'sexual and reproductive health' in Article 25 of the UNCRPD regarding health so as to clarify Malta's understanding that this phrase 'does not constitute recognition of any new international law obligation, does not create any abortion rights, and cannot be interpreted to constitute support, endorsement, or promotion of abortion'.[1310] Maltese authorities have likewise, at least until September 2022, not acceded to attempts to include a debate on abortion on the legislative agenda domestically. By way of example, a 2021 Private Members Bill with the object of deleting Articles 241, 242, 243 and 243A of the Criminal Code regarding abortion was not placed on the agenda of Malta's House of Representatives by its House Business Committee and was therefore not debated in the House even at First Reading.[1311]

234. That being said, debate in respect of abortion in Malta is increasing, especially because the criminal law regarding abortion has no offence-specific exceptions. This means that, so long as the key elements of the criminal offence are all satisfied and subject to the broader domestic law, a person may be found to be criminally liable in the eventuality that s/he causes the miscarriage of a woman with child. Although rarely used and enforced, there have been instances in the twenty-first century when a person who caused the miscarriage of a woman with child,[1312] the woman who consented to the means to procure her own miscarriage,[1313] as well as the woman who attempted to procure her own miscarriage have been found guilty under the provisions of the Criminal Code addressing abortion.[1314] The absence of offence-specific exceptions underpinning the criminal law on abortion has created a relatively recent debate occasioned by at least two different methods to interpret the same law.

235. A first account focuses squarely on the absence of offence-specific exceptions in the criminal law on abortion to maintain that, as a consequence of that criminal law, 'abortion is illegal in all cases under the law in Malta',[1315] which would entail that there is in Malta 'a total ban on abortion, with no exceptions,

1310. United Nations Convention on the Rights of Persons with Disabilities, Ch. 627 of the Laws of Malta, Third Schedule.

1311. House of Representatives Malta, 13th Legislature, Motion 521: *Criminal Code (Amendment) Bill – First Reading – Private Member's Motion* (12 May 2021).

1312. *Il-Pulizija v. Soumia Mansouri*, Court of Magistrates (Criminal Judicature) – 24/11/2014 [Ref: 1127/2014]; *Il-Pulizija v. Mansouri Soumia*, Court of Criminal Appeal (Inferior) – 28/09/2017 [Ref: 505/2014].

1313. *Il-Pulizija v. Raya Sellami*, Court of Magistrates (Criminal Judicature) – 24/11/2014 [Ref: 1126/2014].

1314. *Il-Pulizija v. XYZ*, Court of Magistrates (Criminal Judicature) – 17/12/2007 [Ref: 715/2007].

1315. Committee on the Elimination of Discrimination against Women, *Consideration of reports submitted by States parties under article 18 of the Convention – Concluding Observations: Malta* (CEDAW/C/MLT/CO/4 – 9 November 2010) p. 8. *See also* Committee on the Rights of the Child, *Concluding observations on the combined third to sixth periodic reports of Malta* (CRC/C/MLT/CO/3-6 – 26 June 2019) p. 9.

including when the woman's life is in danger'.[1316] The gist of this 'total legal ban'[1317] or 'blanket ban'[1318] account of the criminal law on abortion then is that 'the law contemplates no exceptions that would allow a woman or any other person to terminate a pregnancy under any circumstance'.[1319] On the basis of the law as it stands in September 2022, there are at least three difficulties that undermine the validity of this account. First, it is an account that ignores the letter of the law and the consequent key elements of the criminal law on abortion. It should then be recalled that there will be no criminal offence if even one of the key elements of that offence is missing. In turn, in order for the criminal offence/s of abortion to subsist, it is indispensable that a miscarriage of a woman with child has been caused or procured by the accused. If, for instance, a miscarriage is already in progress, it signifies that subject to the provisions of the broader medical jurisprudence, including ethical and professional standards, the pregnancy may be terminated (or childbirth induced) without risking sanction under the criminal law of abortion. This can, for example, occur in the circumstances of an ectopic pregnancy 'when a fetus is implanted outside the uterus, most commonly the fallopian tube'.[1320] Second, when faced with the key elements of the criminal law on abortion, exponents of this first account of abortion in Malta have to change or add features to the criminal law so as to render their account intelligible. By way of example, reference is sometimes made in the literature regarding abortion in Malta to a foetal heartbeat, which is not present in the Maltese criminal law on abortion. For instance, in the circumstances illustrated in the popular press of a woman who was reportedly in the process of having a miscarriage of an unviable pregnancy, it was posited that termination of pregnancy was refused because there was a 'heartbeat'.[1321] Yet, just as much as the criminal law on abortion furnishes no offence-specific exceptions to procure a miscarriage, once a miscarriage is in progress, even if it was caused by a third party or by the woman herself, then there is no exception based on the heartbeat of the foetus as to why the criminal law should apply to a medical practitioner who acts in accordance with professional and ethical standards to terminate that pregnancy or to induce early childbirth. Third, by adding terms that are not present in the law, exponents of this first account fail to engage with the key element of intent in terms of Articles 241 and 243 of the Criminal Code. In so doing, exponents of this first

---

1316. Dunja Mijatovic (Commissioner for Human Rights of the Council of Europe), *Report following her visit to Malta from 11 to 16 October 2021*, CommDH (2022)1 (15 February 2022), p. 22.

1317. Andreana Dibben, *Reproductive politics: Policy responses to teenage pregnancy and motherhood*, in *Social welfare issues in Southern Europe* 160, 165 (Maria Brown & Michael Briguglio eds, Routledge 2022).

1318. *Dear Decision Makers: A Story-Telling Campaign for Reproductive Rights in Malta* 3 (Laura Paris, Emily Galea & Break the Taboo Malta eds, 2021). *See also* World Health Organization, *Global Abortion Policies Database – Country Profile: Malta* (22 April 2020), <https://abortion-policies.srhr.org/country/malta/>.

1319. Doctors for Choice Malta, *Position Paper on Abortion and the Implications of Malta's Complete Ban on Abortion on Women, Children, and Their Doctors* 4 (Version 1.0 – February 2020).

1320. *Black's Medical Dictionary* 209 (Harvey Marcovitch ed., Bloomsbury 43d ed. 2017).

1321. Women for Women, *I Almost Lost My Life Because Maltese Doctors Refused to Terminate an Unviable Pregnancy* (26 September 2019), <https://womenforwomenmalta.com/2019/09/26/welcome-to-womenforwomen/>. *See also* Isabel Stabile, *Real fear of prosecution*, Times of Malta (31 Jan. 2022), <https://timesofmalta.com/articles/view/letters-to-the-editor-january-31-2022.930901>.

account risk creating an argument over a law that does not exist in Malta. They thus, for instance, engage with the doctrine of double effect, which is 'a criterion to discern when an action that negatively affects an instance of a human good is not really a violation of nonmaleficence',[1322] signifying in principle that 'if there is a justifiable reason sufficiently grave for the course of action proposed (whether it is a question of medical treatment or something else), then the abortion which follows may be permitted once it is neither intended nor directly caused'.[1323] In response, exponents of the first account contend 'that it is not clear what constitutes "direct" or "indirect" termination, and … the law as it stands does not make this distinction, condemning any form of induced termination of a pregnancy'.[1324] Yet, if the doctrine of double effect is 'an ethical principle and not a law'[1325] and given that it is true that the Criminal Code does not separate direct from indirect abortion, it means that the entire argument on this account simply engages with laws that do not exist and evades engaging with the actual law. Instead, Articles 241 and 243 of the Criminal Code regarding abortion will not be applicable if the accused did not *intend* to procure a miscarriage. Other laws may arguably be applicable, but not those provisions of the criminal law on abortion.[1326] This was sufficiently clear to the legislator since Article 243A, regarding culpable miscarriage, was added to the Criminal Code precisely because intent to cause the miscarriage is a key element for the offences arising from Articles 241 and 243, meaning that negligence was not encompassed by the criminal law on abortion until the addition of Article 243A.[1327] It consequently means that treatment to address an aggressive form of cancer can be provided to a pregnant woman, and it would not, all else being equal and provided that medical practitioners have not been negligent in their diagnosis, lead to criminal liability even if that treatment causes a miscarriage. As such, rather than there being an unclear criminal law on abortion, it is arguably the use of terms by exponents of this first account that are not familiar to the law or even the erroneous application of the law that makes the law unclear.

236. A second account instead grounds the criminal law of abortion upon the personhood of the foetus so that, if that criminal law is breached, 'the right violated is consequently that of life'[1328] of the foetus or unborn child. This relies on the fact that the criminal law on abortion in Malta is one of the 'Crimes against the Person' and, inasmuch as an offence must then be directed against a person, it would, on this account, be the person of the foetus. On that basis, exponents of this second

---

1322. Alfonso Gomez-Lobo & John Keown, *Bioethics and the Human Goods* 59 (Georgetown University Press 2015).
1323. Anthony J. Mamo, *Notes on Criminal Law: Revised Edition* 288 (1954–1955). Original parentheses.
1324. Gilbert Gravino & Liza Caruana-Finkel, *Abortion and Methods of Reproductive Planning: The Views of Malta's Medical Doctor Cohort*, 27 (1) Sexual and Reproductive Health Matters 287, 297 (2019).
1325. *Ibid.*
1326. *See, for instance*: Criminal Code, Ch. 9 of the Laws of Malta, Art. 218 (1)(c).
1327. House of Representatives Malta – Office of the Clerk, *Kumitat Permanenti għall-Kunsiderazzjoni ta' Abbozzi ta' Liġi (Rapport Uffiċjali u Rivedut),* 9th Legislature: Meeting no. 100 (10 Oct. 2001) 12–13.
1328. Anthony J. Mamo, *Notes on Criminal Law: Revised Edition* 277 (1954–1955).

account might be critical of my observation in the previous paragraph that the criminal law on abortion does not cover situations when one of the key elements at law of that offence is missing because, on this second account, 'Maltese law recognises and protects fetal life from its very conception as is made clear by the Criminal Code in … Articles 241 – 244A'.[1329] The unborn child would then have a right to life that is in part safeguarded by the law on abortion that 'makes no allowance for abortion of whatsoever nature',[1330] albeit that a criminal offence may ostensibly be justifiable or excusable depending on the broader criminal law.[1331] It is indisputable that the unborn child has an important place in Maltese law[1332] and the Civil Code, for instance, also refers to 'any person unborn'[1333] as well as to a 'child, born or unborn'.[1334] While it is beyond the scope of this monograph to discuss the personhood or otherwise of the unborn child in Malta,[1335] this second account of the criminal law on abortion is either way also problematic for at least three reasons. First, it is not clear that the legislative authorities that shaped the Criminal Code had considered the unborn child as the subject of the criminal offence on abortion. By way of example, a jurist involved in the process of codification in the mid-nineteenth century in Malta identified the pregnant woman as 'the unfortunate subject of the offence'[1336] of abortion and not the unborn child. On this basis, that jurist posited that punishment is also accorded to the pregnant woman if she consents to the use of the means to procure the miscarriage because in 'crimes attended with violence to the person, no consent can extenuate'[1337] even if the subject of the offence consents to that violence. Indeed, as noted by the ECtHR, albeit in relation to the ECHR, the 'determination of the level of harm that should be tolerated by the law in situations where the victim consents is in the first instance a matter for the State concerned since what is at stake is related, on the one hand, to public health considerations and to the general deterrent effect of the criminal law, and, on the other, to the personal autonomy of the individual'.[1338] Significantly, Article 242 of the Criminal Code grounds the subject of the criminal offence in the pregnant woman by stipulating that if 'the means used shall cause the death *of the woman*, or shall cause a serious injury to *her person, whether the miscarriage has taken place or*

1329. George Gregory Buttigieg, *Optimising Maltese obstetric medico-legal dynamics: Volume I* 54 (Lambert Academic Publishing 2020).

1330. Kevin Aquilina, *Constitutional Law in Malta* 235 (Kluwer Law International 2018).

1331. *See, for instance:* Giovanni Bonello, *Abortion – Self-defence*, Times of Malta (29 November 2021), <https://timesofmalta.com/articles/view/letters-to-the-editor-november-29-2021.917482>; Giovanni Bonello, *Correct reading of the criminal law*, Times of Malta (15 Jan. 2022), <https://timesofmalta.com/articles/view/letters-to-the-editor-january-15-2022.927769>.

1332. Conferentia Episcopalis Melitensis, *Legislation regulating assisted human reproduction: A position paper* 13–17 (2015). *See also*: *Kaczmarek Marta noe v. Antonel Dobre*, Civil Court First Hall – 16/12/2015 [Ref: 242/2015].

1333. Civil Code, Ch. 16 of the Laws of Malta, Art. 42 (1)(c).

1334. *Ibid.*, Art. 128A (1). *See also* Art. 170 (1).

1335. Parliamentary Ombudsman Malta, *Case Notes 2018* (Edition 38): 'Department of Health states that a baby in utero is not recognised as a person at law', 92–94.

1336. Andrew Jameson, *Report on the proposed Code of Criminal Laws for the Island of Malta and its Dependencies* 122 (Government Printing Press Malta 1844).

1337. *Ibid.*, 49.

1338. *Laskey and others v. United* Kingdom, App. Nos 21627/93, 21628/93, 21974/93 (ECtHR, 19/02/1997) para. 44.

not, the offender shall, on conviction, be liable to the punishment applicable to wilful homicide or wilful bodily harm, diminished by one to three degrees'.[1339] If the unborn child is not the subject of the criminal offence/s of abortion, then the reasoning of this second account has to be reconsidered so as to be intelligible. Second, even if the unborn child were the subject of the criminal offence of abortion, 'a criminal law prohibiting the practice of abortion within a defined territorial jurisdiction will not necessarily protect the life of the unborn child'[1340] in all circumstances or even ground a right to life for that unborn child. Indeed, the legislator acknowledged this point in practice in 2002 when, as was noted in the House of Representatives' Consideration of the Bills Committee, it was not until then a criminal offence to cause the miscarriage of a woman with child through negligence.[1341] Just as much as the legislator had to then intervene since the key element of negligence was missing from the Criminal Code's provisions regarding abortion, legislative authorities would similarly have to, if they so wish, act again to safeguard the unborn child by way of the criminal law on abortion in instances when one of the key elements of the criminal offence is missing. Until that is done, any circumstances falling beyond the scope of the criminal law on abortion will not be subject to sanctions arising from that criminal offence. By way of example, even though it is an offence to procure the miscarriage of any woman with child, and it is clearly an offence to kill the child after birth, the legislator has not so far acted to envelop by way of the criminal law of (intentional) abortion the period during the process of birth or during the course of an ongoing miscarriage even if that child is vital or may yet be born alive. Third, the broader Maltese medical jurisprudence hones in on the distinction between an abortion that is procured and one that has not been procured. An old but still relevant example, albeit not part of the law per se, is the index of the original version of the Criminal Code in Malta that identified, in the original Italian language, 'aborto procurato', meaning procured abortion as the criminal offence at hand. This would then exclude from the ambit of the criminal law abortions that have not been procured by the accused or the situation of a woman who is in the process of undergoing a miscarriage or giving birth. A second more recent example involves the interpretative statement that was made upon Malta's ratification of the UNCRPD, which is now incorporated in Maltese law. This provides that: 'Malta's national legislation considers the termination of pregnancy through *induced* abortion as illegal'.[1342] Inasmuch as an 'induced abortion' is illegal, inducing childbirth or terminating an ongoing abortion or an ongoing miscarriage is not, all else being equal, unlawful in Malta on the basis of the criminal offence/s of abortion.

1339. Emphasis added.

1340. Daniel Bianchi, *Termination of pregnancy: Does the criminal law protect the unborn child?*, 24 *Law & Practice* 25 (2010).

1341. House of Representatives Malta – Office of the Clerk, *Kumitat Permanenti ghall-Kunsiderazzjoni ta' Abbozzi ta' Ligi (Rapport Ufficjali u Rivedut)*, 9th Legislature: Meeting no. 100 (10 October 2001) 12–13.

1342. United Nations Convention on the Rights of Persons with Disabilities, Ch. 627 of the Laws of Malta, Third Schedule. Emphasis added.

237. I hasten to add that even in circumstances falling beyond the scope of the criminal law of abortion, medical practitioners are still subject to the special supervision of the Medical Council. This means supervision of the professional and ethical standards prescribed by that Council, including that medical practitioners are to always bear in mind the importance of preserving human life from the time of conception. This should arguably be of more concern to medical practitioners than the criminal law on abortion when terminating a pregnancy or inducing childbirth that is beyond the scope of the criminal law of abortion. It would have been intriguing had an interpretation presented before the Court of Criminal Appeal in Malta, albeit in a case unrelated to abortion, taken root in Maltese medical jurisprudence. This suggested that the 'death' of the foetus could be understood as that moment when the foetus loses the capacity to have an independent extra-uterine existence.[1343] In that case, if the pregnancy were not viable inasmuch as the foetus has no possibility of an independent and extra-uterine life, then that foetus, though still vital in the sense of living in the uterine environment, would have been considered 'dead' and the uterus could consequently be lawfully evacuated of the foetal remains. Although this interpretation may not have taken root in Maltese medical jurisprudence, the pregnant woman would arguably still be miscarrying if the foetus has no avenue towards an independent and extra-uterine existence, meaning that terminating that pregnancy or inducing early childbirth would not be procuring a miscarriage in terms of the Criminal Code and would consequently not be a criminal offence under the criminal law regarding abortion in Malta.

238. Four relatively recent developments are also worthwhile noting at this stage. First, given that it is not a criminal offence to procure a miscarriage outside the territory of Malta, a woman who consents to procure the miscarriage in another jurisdiction can lawfully receive medical follow-up in Malta.[1344] Second, emergency contraception has been permissible in Malta since 2016, and the drug Misoprostol is sold or distributed at pharmacies.[1345] Third, an application was made in September 2022 asking the First Hall of the Civil Court to declare the criminal law regarding abortion in violation of the Constitution of Malta and the ECHR.[1346] Fourth, as of September 2022, it was reported in the local media that the Government would soon present proposals so that, while 'ensuring we don't open doors to abortion, we will be ensuring that medical staff still carry out their duties'.[1347] Be

1343. *Il-Pulizija v. Garmela Galea*, Court of Criminal Appeal (Inferior) – 27/06/1959.

1344. *See also* S.L. 528.03, Cross-Border Healthcare Regulations, r. 13.

1345. Parliament of Malta: Social Affairs Committee, Health Committee, Family Affairs Committee, *Emergency Contraception* (Joint report of the 12th Legislature – October 2016). *See also*: *Sciberras Miriam Dr Noe v. Is-Suprintendent ghas-Sahha Pubblika*, Civil Court First Hall – 27/01/2022 [Ref: 494/2017].

1346. *Dimitrijevic Avukat Dr Lara v. L-Avukat Tal-Istat et.*, Civil Court First Hall (Constitutional Jurisdiction) [Ref: 499/2022] Registered 20/09/2022.

1347. *Government to propose change in law, but will not 'open door to abortion': Health Minister Chris Fearne says the changes will be presented by October 3*, Times of Malta (2 September 2022), <https://timesofmalta.com/articles/view/government-propose-change-law-open-door-abortion.978197>.

that as it may, the laws and practices in Malta at the time of writing have grounded a situation where there have been no cases of maternal mortality in Malta for over a decade.[1348]

§2. STERILISATION

239. The National Sexual Health Policy in Malta makes no reference to sterilisation in any form.[1349] While this policy is scheduled to be updated, the sterilisation of women and of men conducted by medical practitioners is nevertheless an available option in Malta.[1350] As such, the Health Promotion and Disease Prevention Directorate within the Department for Health Regulation at the Ministry for Health stipulates, within its sexual health online portal, that counselling prior to the sterilisation procedure is very important.[1351] The Maltese courts however ruled, in a case where a pregnancy ensued despite the sterilisation procedure of tubal ligation, that there is no obligation arising from the law that binds medical practitioners to inform patients undergoing tubal ligation that there is a possibility that pregnancy may ensue in spite of that sterilisation procedure.[1352] The Court of Appeal instead ruled that medical practitioners in that situation are only bound to provide the information that generally accepted medical practice indicates that medical practitioners should furnish to their patients.[1353] This rationale would presumably also be applicable in the situation of other sterilisation procedures. The onus of proof in court settings will depend on the nature of the medical practitioner-patient relationship inasmuch as, in liability suits in contract, the onus of proof would lie on the medical practitioner to demonstrate that s/he provided information in line with accepted medical practice, whereas in liability suits in tort, that onus of proof may rest on the claimant.[1354] Either way, all else being equal, a person can consent to undergo a sterilisation procedure, provided s/he has the capacity to consent to it. An exception in this respect arises from the Mental Health Act, which provides that no sterilisation shall be carried out on persons under the age of eighteen years.[1355] No leeway is afforded to the circumstances where the latter person has sufficient maturity and understanding to consent to the sterilisation.

240. As to sterilisation absent patient consent, Malta is a State Party to the Council of Europe's Convention on Prevention and Combating of Violence against

1348. National Obstetrics Information System, *Maternal Mortality Indicators* (2021).
1349. Ministry for Health, the Elderly and Community Care, *Sexual Health Policy for the Maltese Islands* (2010).
1350. *See, for instance*: Charles Savona-Ventura, *Contraception use in Malta* 24 (2) Malta Medical Journal 27, 28 (2012)
1351. Sexual Health Malta, *Surgical methods*, <https://sexualhealth.gov.mt/content/surgical-methods>.
1352. *Zerafa Frankie et. v. Avramov Olga et.*, Civil Court First Hall – 30/01/2006 [Ref: 1000/2002] 7; Court of Appeal (Civil Superior) – 30/05/2008 [Ref: 1000/2002/1] 10.
1353. *Ibid.*, 12. *See also* Part II Ch. 1 §2.I above.
1354. *See* Part I Ch. 4 §1.I above.
1355. Mental Health Act, Ch. 525 of the Laws of Malta, Art. 31 (2). *See also* Part II Ch. 2 §2 above.

Women and Domestic Violence.[1356] Article 39 of that Convention obliges States Parties to take necessary legislative or other measures to ensure the criminalisation of the following intentional conduct: 'performing surgery which has the purpose or effect of terminating a woman's capacity to naturally reproduce without her prior and informed consent or understanding of the procedure'. This requirement to obtain prior informed consent before a procedure of sterilisation is, in practice, extended to all people, not just women, in the provision of the Criminal Code that criminalises enforced sterilisation. Yet, the criminal law furnishes an exception to that offence if sterilization is performed *for medical reasons* without the full and informed consent of the subject of the procedure. Thus, Article 251F of the Criminal Code provides that:

> Any person who for *non-medical reasons*, by force, deceit, bribery or threats surgically removes or disables a person's reproductive organs without that person's full and informed consent, leading to sterilization, shall be guilty of enforced sterilization and shall, unless the fact constitutes a more serious offence under any other provision of this Code, be liable on conviction to imprisonment for a term from four to ten years.[1357]

That being said, even though the Convention on Prevention and Combating of Violence against Women and Domestic Violence makes no exception on the basis of medical reasons to permit forced sterilisation without the subject's full and informed consent, the Group of Experts on Action against Violence against Women and Domestic Violence did not make reference, in their report on Malta, to any exception based on medical reasons for enforced sterilisation in Malta's Criminal Code. It was instead commented that '[f]orced sterilisation is criminalised under Article 251F of the Criminal Code in line with the convention'.[1358] Also, reference to 'non-medical reasons' would at most exempt a medical practitioner from criminal liability on the basis of Article 251F of the Criminal Code so long as sterilisation without full and informed consent is performed for medical reasons but, all else being equal, informed consent would still be required so that an individual receives that treatment and it would also still be the right of every patient to refuse treatment.

241. Furthermore, Malta is a State Party to the Rome Statute of the International Criminal Court, which engages with enforced sterilisation so that the International Criminal Court can have jurisdiction over that offence in given circumstances.[1359] Those crimes have been reproduced in the Schedule of the International Criminal Court Act in Malta so that enforced sterilisation is identified as a crime against

1356. (2011) CETS 210.

1357. Criminal Code, Ch. 9 of the Laws of Malta, Art. 251F. Emphasis added.

1358. Group of Experts on Action against Violence against Women and Domestic Violence (GREVIO), *GREVIO's (Baseline) Evaluation Report on legislative and other measures giving effect to the provisions of the Council of Europe Convention on Preventing and Combating Violence against Women and Domestic Violence (Istanbul Convention)* – Malta, GREVIO/Inf(2020) 17, p. 53.

1359. Rome Statute of the International Criminal Court (Adopted 17 July 1998, entered into force 1 July 2002) 2187 UNTS 3.

humanity when committed as part of a widespread or systematic attack directed against any civilian population with knowledge of the attack, as well as being identified as a war crime and as a serious violation of the laws and customs applicable in armed conflict, regardless whether of an international character or otherwise, within the established framework of international law.[1360]

§3. In Vitro Fertilisation

242. The Embryo Protection Act is one of the main laws in Malta regulating in vitro fertilisation (IVF) and medically assisted procreation in general while also protecting human embryos.[1361] It is thus the Embryo Protection Act that established the Embryo Protection Authority with functions akin to a regulatory authority for the purpose of medically assisted procreation in Malta.[1362] The Protocol established by the Embryo Protection Authority also arises from the Embryo Protection Act, and it is now embedded in its subsidiary law.[1363] That Protocol consists of regulatory principles and guidance notes in respect of the use and storage of human gametes and human embryos for human application.[1364] Those regulatory principles are to then be followed by the Embryo Protection Authority in carrying out its functions under the Embryo Protection Act.[1365] Yet, the process leading to the adoption of the Embryo Protection Act in 2012 was fraught with debate[1366] wherein 'the main concern was in fact the protection of the embryo'.[1367] This concern also entailed that the Embryo Protection Act, from its outset, made it possible for a healthcare professional to be exempted, as a matter of conscience, from participating 'in any procedure or activity specifically and necessarily directed towards the implementation of the technique or procedure leading to a medically assisted procreation but does not exempt him from providing assistance before or after the said procedure of activity'.[1368] However, the Embryo Protection Act, which originally largely prohibited the cryopreservation of embryos and also prohibited third-party gamete

1360. International Criminal Court Act, Ch. 453 of the Laws of Malta.
1361. *See also*: S.L. 452.114, Leave for Medical Assisted Procreation National Standard Order.
1362. Embryo Protection Act, Ch. 524 of the Laws of Malta, Arts 3–4. *See also* General Introduction section 2.II above.
1363. *Ibid.*, Art. 23 (1)(d).
1364. S.L. 524.02, Embryo Protection Authority (Protocol) Regulations (not yet in force).
1365. Embryo Protection Act, Ch. 524 of the Laws of Malta, Art. 4 (1)(i).
1366. *See, for instance*: Social Affairs Committee – Malta House of Representatives, 10th Legislature, *Use of Biotechnology: Genetic Technology and Assisted Procreation – Recommendations* (Approved on 11 July 2005, Tabled on 26 September 2005); Social Affairs Committee – Malta House of Representatives, 11th Legislature, *Follow-up on the latest ethical and moral teachings on assisted procreation: Evaluation of the report published in the 10th Legislature* (September 2009); Select Committee on Medically Assisted Procreation – Malta House of Representatives, 11th Legislature, *Report of the Select Committee on Medically Assisted Procreation* (October 2010).
1367. Pierre Mallia, *Developments in IVF legislation in a Catholic Country*, 16 *Medicine, Health Care and Philosophy* 385, 389 (2013).
1368. Embryo Protection Act, Ch. 524 of the Laws of Malta, Art. 20 (3). *See also* S.L. 524.02, Embryo Protection Authority (Protocol) Regulations, r. 3.13–3.17 (not yet in force).

donation,[1369] has been subject to major amendments since 2012 that have broadened the scope of lawful and regulated medically assisted procreation in Malta. After defining the meaning of medically assisted procreation in Maltese law, this section of the monograph illustrates the scope and ethos of the Embryo Protection Act, the person/s who shall have access to medically assisted procreation, safeguards to protect the life and dignity of the human embryo including the possibility of cryopreservation and adoption of that embryo, as well as the regulation of third-party gamete donation in Malta.

243. Medically assisted procreation in the Embryo Protection Act means 'all treatments or procedures that include the in vitro handling of human oocytes, spermatozoa or embryos for *establishing a pregnancy*'.[1370] The possibility of establishing a pregnancy is therefore a key criterion of lawful medically assisted procreation in Malta, and it is an offence under the Embryo Protection Act to cause 'a human fertilised egg to develop further outside the body for any purpose other than in order to bring about a pregnancy',[1371] to create human embryos 'for the purpose of research or experimentation or for any other purpose not permitted under the'[1372] Embryo Protection Act, or even simply to artificially fertilise 'any egg cell for any purpose other than that of bringing about the pregnancy of the prospective parent'.[1373] It is furthermore the case that establishing a pregnancy by way of medically assisted procreation relates solely in Maltese law to the prospective parent/s and not to the pregnancy of any other person unless otherwise stipulated in the Embryo Protection Act. As such, surrogacy is unlawful in Malta inasmuch as whosoever 'carries out an artificial fertilization of, or transfers a human embryo into, a woman who is prepared to give up her child permanently after birth (surrogate mother)'[1374] shall be guilty of an offence. Likewise, the procedure of uterine lavage to recover in vivo embryos is also unlawful in Malta since whosoever 'removes an embryo from a woman before the completion of implantation in the womb in order to transfer the embryo to another woman'[1375] shall be guilty of an offence as would any removal from the uterine environment of any embryo produced outside the body before the completion of implantation in the womb.[1376] Furthermore, whosoever 'disposes of, hands over or acquires a human embryo produced outside the body'[1377] other than for the purpose of implantation in a woman as authorised by the Embryo Protection Act would also be guilty of an offence. Consequently, any child born as a result of any medically assisted procreation 'shall be considered to be the child of the prospective parent or prospective parents … and shall for all

1369. Act XXI of 2012 – Embryo Protection Act, 2012 [Government Gazette of Malta No. 18,996 – 04/12/2012].
1370. Embryo Protection Act, Ch. 524 of the Laws of Malta, Art. 2. Emphasis added.
1371. *Ibid.*, Art. 8 (2).
1372. *Ibid.*, Art. 15 (2).
1373. *Ibid.*, Art. 6 (a).
1374. *Ibid.*, Art. 6 (f). Original parentheses.
1375. *Ibid.*, Art. 6 (d).
1376. *Ibid.*, Art. 8 (1).
1377. *Ibid.*

intents and purposes of law be deemed to have been naturally born of the same prospective parent or prospective parents without the intervention of any'[1378] medically assisted procreation. As such, the child born of medically assisted procreation is also, for all effects and purposes of law, the direct descendent of the prospective parent/s.

244. The term 'prospective parent' is defined in the Embryo Protection Act to mean 'any person regardless of gender or sexual orientation, who has attained the age of majority [18 years of age] and is a receiver or user of the medically assisted procreation techniques regulated under'[1379] that Act. In turn, any person 'who provides, or assists in, any medically assisted procreation procedure to a person other than a prospective parent shall be guilty of an offence'[1380] albeit that a medical practitioner will be exempt from criminal liability 'where he shows that he took reasonable care to determine that the person on whom the procedure was performed or attempted was entitled to access to such procedure'.[1381] Yet, considering that establishing pregnancy is a pediment of lawful medically assisted procreation, the Embryo Protection Act also stipulates that the latter procedures 'may only be resorted to where there is a reasonable chance of success and the procedures do not entail any known undue risk to the health of the woman or the child, beyond those already well known as inherently associated with the procedure itself'.[1382] The risk involved in the procedure is *inter alia* reflected in the law's engagement with age limits, but while the Embryo Protection Act establishes the minimum age of a prospective parent, it is the Protocol established by the Embryo Protection Authority that sets the maximum permissible age for a prospective parent to have an embryo transferred to her uterus.

245. The imposition of a maximum age limit was the subject of a lawsuit claiming a violation of the right to respect for private and family life and a violation of the prohibition from discrimination under the ECHR and the European Convention Act by prohibiting access to medically assisted procreation to persons who exceed a given age. The courts in Malta ruled that entitlement to medically assisted procreation does not have to be vested in the prospective parents alone but that, instead, the State also has a legitimate role in safeguarding public health, which it could lawfully fulfil in the situation at hand by *inter alia* setting maximum age limits if those limits are justifiable by way of tangible medical evidence.[1383] That being said, the ECtHR ruled that, inasmuch as the imposition of a maximum age to access medically assisted procreation is an interference with the right to respect for private and family life safeguarded under Article 8 of the ECHR, that interference has to be

1378. *Ibid.*, Art. 18 (1).
1379. *Ibid.*, Art. 2.
1380. *Ibid.*, Art. 5 (2).
1381. *Ibid.*
1382. *Ibid.*, Art. 5 (1).
1383. *Lia Gilbert et. v. Avukat Generali et.*, Civil Court First Hall (Constitutional Jurisdiction) – 28/09/2018 [Ref: 11/2017] 52; *Lia Gilbert et. v. Avukat Generali et.*, Constitutional Court – 27/09/2019 [Ref: 11/2017/1] 22–23.

done 'in accordance with a law of sufficient quality'[1384] so as to accord with a lawful interference under Article 8 (2). In this particular case, the ECtHR held that there was a violation of Article 8 of the ECHR since the impugned domestic provision, which had stated that it was 'desirable' that a person be below a certain age to access medically assisted procreation, was not sufficiently foreseeable to justify by way of a law of sufficient quality, an interference with the rights arising from Article 8 (1) of the ECHR. Indeed, although the domestic courts considered that provision not to be mandatory, the Embryo Protection Authority instead treated it as mandatory, which meant that 'the way in which the judicial and administrative authorities involved interpreted and applied the impugned legal provision … was incoherent and thus lacked the required foreseeability'.[1385] The revised Protocol now *inter alia* stipulates that the 'maximum permissible age of the prospective parent for implantation of embryos shall be 48 years in all cases'[1386] while also identifying who among the prospective parent/s that fall within the qualifying age-bracket/s will be referred to treatment, which includes broadly those who have '[i]dentified causes of infertility amenable to treatment by IVF'.[1387] Yet, even if a person is, in principle, eligible to receive medically assisted procreation, a tissue establishment may still refuse treatment and may even be bound to refuse that treatment, for instance, if it 'concludes that any child who may be born or any existing child of the family is likely to be at risk of significant harm or neglect',[1388] in which case that decision is to be reported to the Embryo Protection Authority.

246. Thus, in addition to establishing a pregnancy, an equally important feature of the Embryo Protection Act is the special status of the embryo,[1389] which must be respected by tissue establishments when conducting licensed activities while also taking into account 'the welfare of any child who may be born as a result of treatment services, and any other child who may be affected by the birth'.[1390] For the purpose of the Embryo Protection Act, an embryo means 'the human organism that results from the fertilisation of a human egg cell by a human sperm cell which is capable of developing and shall further include each totipotent cell removed from a human embryo or otherwise produced, that is assumed to be able to divide and to develop as a human being under the appropriate conditions'.[1391] Cloning is then prohibited in Malta inasmuch as any 'intervention seeking to create a human being genetically identical to another embryo, *foetus*, or human being, whether living or dead, is prohibited',[1392] and whosoever transfers an embryo of this nature into a woman will also be liable to sanction. It is nevertheless an offence to wilfully cause the death of any embryo, even if that embryo is a clone.[1393]

1384. *Lia v. Malta*, App. No. 9709/20 (ECtHR, 05/05/2022) para. 68.
1385. *Ibid.*, para. 67.
1386. S.L. 524.02, Embryo Protection Authority (Protocol) Regulations, r. 7.6 (not yet in force).
1387. *Ibid.*, r. 7.5 (a).
1388. *Ibid.*, r. 10.19 (a).
1389. *Ibid.*, Regulatory principles.
1390. *Ibid.*, r. 10.2.
1391. Embryo Protection Act, Ch. 524 of the Laws of Malta, Art. 2.
1392. *Ibid.*, Art. 11 (1). Original emphasis.
1393. *Ibid.*, Art. 16.

247. The special status of the embryo, including the prohibition to cause the death of an embryo, then also directs the type of medically assisted procreation that can be provided to prospective parents depending upon whether they consent or otherwise to the cryopreservation of any supernumerary embryos as well as whether they consent to the donation/adoption of any embryos in cryopreservation that will not be transferred to the prospective parent. Thus, when the prospective parent/s 'do not give their consent to the cryo-preservation of any supernumerary embryos and to the donation of fertilised eggs if necessary, the medical practitioner in charge of the procedure shall only fertilize up to a maximum of two eggs'.[1394] The purpose of this provision is to transfer the maximum permissible 'two embryos into the prospective parent within each treatment cycle'[1395] without requiring the cryopreservation of supernumerary embryo/s. Yet, in case there are embryos that cannot be transferred into the prospective parent within a treatment cycle, the Embryo Protection Act mandates that these embryos 'shall be cryo-preserved in licensed tissue establishments for future use by that prospective parent'.[1396] To be clear, if the prospective parent/s give their consent to the cryopreservation of any supernumerary embryos, this consent 'may only be withdrawn in writing by the prospective parent or prospective parents before fertilisation'[1397] inasmuch as the resulting embryo is safeguarded by law. However, once that consent is provided by the prospective parents, the medical practitioner in charge of the medically assisted procreation may, in consultation with the multidisciplinary team and with the permission of the Embryo Protection Authority, 'decide to fertilize more than two egg cells within one (1) treatment cycle provided that this is done in accordance with the Protocol'[1398] established by the Embryo Protection Authority. An application is thus made to the Embryo Protection Authority that will then determine the permissible number of eggs cells that can be fertilised in each individual case with the consent of the prospective parent, up to a maximum of twelve egg cells as indicated in the Protocol, or to otherwise refuse permission to fertilise more than two egg cells per treatment cycle.[1399] In circumstances where the Embryo Protection Authority grants permission to fertilise more than two egg cells, the medical practitioner in charge of the procedure is nevertheless bound to 'implant up to a maximum of two embryos'.[1400] That notwithstanding, the Embryo Protection Authority 'requires tissue establishments to have a documented strategy to minimise multiple births and should have documented standard operating procedures for egg and embryo transfer'.[1401] Yet, if there are embryos that are cryopreserved, the Embryo Protection Act mandates that 'no more egg cells can be fertilized until all the cryo-preserved embryos have been

1394. *Ibid.*, Art. 18 (1).
1395. *Ibid.*, Art. 6 (c).
1396. *Ibid.*, Art. 7 (3).
1397. *Ibid.*, Art. 18 (1)
1398. *Ibid.*, Art. 6 (b). Original parentheses.
1399. S.L. 524.02, Embryo Protection Authority (Protocol) Regulations, r. 9.8 (not yet in force).
1400. Embryo Protection Act, Ch. 524 of the Laws of Malta, Art. 18 (1).
1401. S.L. 524.02, Embryo Protection Authority (Protocol) Regulations, r. 8.1 (not yet in force).

implanted in the prospective parent from whom they originate from any prior medically assisted procreation treatments except in those instances which may be specified in the Protocol and with the prior authorisation of the'[1402] Embryo Protection Authority. This can then relate to pre-implantation genetic diagnosis, which is considered later in this monograph.

248. The possibility of an increasing quantity of supernumerary embryos being indefinitely stored in cryopreservation is in part addressed in Malta by way of embryo adoption,[1403] which refers in the Embryo Protection Act to instances 'whereby embryos that are not transferred are gratuitously donated to the prospective parent or prospective parents'.[1404] The adopting parent/s would have to be prospective parents in terms of the Embryo Protection Act inasmuch as the process of embryo donation and adoption is a form of medically assisted procreation. As such, embryo adoption does not produce the same effects as adoption under the Civil Code but, instead, results from embryo donation that 'means the transfer of an embryo resulting from gametes … that did not originate from the prospective parent or prospective parents'.[1405] The Embryo Protection Authority may thus give embryo/s for adoption to a third party who qualifies for medically assisted procreation procedures, provided that 'the simultaneous implantation of embryos originating from different persons in a prospective parent during the same cycle is prohibited'.[1406] The Embryo Protection Act foresees the possibility of embryo adoption in the following cases: (i) when the original prospective parent, who is a woman, dies after the fertilisation of the egg cells but before the implantation of the embryos into her womb; (ii) the implantation of the embryo into the womb of the prospective parent cannot take place for any other reason, including where the prospective parent refuses the implantation; (iii) the prospective parent has reached the maximum permissible age for the implantation as identified in the Protocol established by the Embryo Protection Authority; and (iv) the prospective parent/s fail to renew the contract with the licensee of the tissue establishment where the cryopreserved embryos are being stored.[1407] The Protocol established by the Embryo Protection Authority furthermore binds the tissue establishment to ensure that, before prospective parents consent to embryos being stored, they are told 'the options available if a person providing gametes or resulting embryos dies or becomes mentally incapacitated'[1408] and that Protocol also takes into account the possibility that the prospective parent/s may, before reaching the permissible age of transfer, wish to give their embryos for adoption by making a request in writing to the Embryo Protection Authority.[1409] Indeed, in those cases where the cryopreserved embryo is awaiting adoption, the Embryo Protection Authority 'shall be deemed to be curator

1402. Embryo Protection Act, Ch. 524 of the Laws of Malta, Art. 6 (b).
1403. Daniel Bianchi, *The adoption of embryos in Malta: Acting in the interest and welfare of a child in embryonic form?*, 19 (3) Medical Law Review 401–429 (2011).
1404. Embryo Protection Act, Ch. 524 of the Laws of Malta, Art. 2.
1405. *Ibid.*
1406. *Ibid.*, Art. 4 (3).
1407. *Ibid.*, Art. 4 (2).
1408. S.L. 524.02, Embryo Protection Authority (Protocol) Regulations, r. 16.24 (not yet in force).
1409. *Ibid.*, r. 17.5.

of the embryo for all intents and purposes of the law and the Authority shall immediately and during the duration of the curatorship inform and consult with the prospective parent or parents, or in their absence their legal heir, on the decisions which need to be taken on the embryo'.[1410] It is also the Embryo Protection Authority that has the function of determining the eligibility and suitability of prospective adoptive parent/s while ultimately being responsible for authorising the adoption of cryopreserved embryos on the application of a prospective parent or parents. This is subject to certain conditions, including: (i) that the prospective adopting parent/s have been declared physically fit by a medical practitioner for the transfer of an embryo; (ii) that there is a favourable recommendation issued by the Adoption Board in accordance with the Adoption Administration Act on the eligibility and suitability of the prospective (adoptive) parent/s;[1411] and (iii) in circumstances when both the prospective parents of the embryo can still be consulted, the Embryo Protection Authority shall respect their wishes insofar as possible within the parameters of the Embryo Protection Act.[1412] That being said, the Embryo Protection Act provides that any person having a juridical interest, or their legal heir, may within 20 days from the date of the decision of the Embryo Protection Authority regarding the adoption of the embryo/s 'file a sworn application in the Civil Court (Family Section) to enquire into the validity of the decision of the Authority and there shall be a right of appeal therefrom to the Civil Court (Family Section) before the Court of Appeal by means of an application filed within twenty days from the date of the decision of the Civil Court (Family Section)'.[1413] Once the adoption is final, the Embryo Protection Act makes it clear that there shall be no link of filiation between the child born from the adopted embryos and the persons from whom those adopted embryos originated.[1414]

249. The Embryo Protection Act furthermore forms part of the regulatory framework underpinning the storage and use of reproductive or germ line cells, which means 'all egg and sperm cells which may lead to the resultant human being'.[1415] Regulations transposing EU law into domestic law had, even prior to the Embryo Protection Act, already engaged with selection criteria and biological tests that are incumbent on tissue establishments to undertake for donors of reproductive cells.[1416] It is however the Embryo Protection Act that now prohibits the wilful alteration in an artificial way of the genetic information of a human germ line cell while also prohibiting the use of that altered human germ line cell for fertilization, provided that no offence arises against a medical practitioner carrying out the medically assisted procreation procedure 'where the alteration of the genetic information of a germ line cell is the unintended consequence of inoculation, radiation or chemotherapeutic or treatment'.[1417] It is also the Embryo Protection Act that frames if

1410. Embryo Protection Act, Ch. 524 of the Laws of Malta, Art. 4 (4).
1411. Adoption Administration Act, Ch. 495 of the Laws of Malta, Art. 4 (h).
1412. Embryo Protection Act, Ch. 524 of the Laws of Malta, Art. 4 (3)–(4).
1413. *Ibid.*, Art. 4 (4). Original parentheses.
1414. *Ibid.*, Art. 19 (2).
1415. *Ibid.*, Art. 2.
1416. S.L. 483.01, Tissues and Cells (Quality and Safety) Regulations, rs 13–14.
1417. Embryo Protection Act, Ch. 524 of the Laws of Malta, Art. 13 (3).

and how germ line cells can or cannot be stored or used. This will then depend upon whether a person is storing his/her own germ line cells or whether s/he instead donated those germ line cells.

250. It is thus possible for a third party to donate germ line cells for the purpose of medically assisted procreation, which shall not entail a link of filiation between the embryo fertilised using the donated germ line cells and the donor by way of a confidential agreement between that donor and the licensee of the tissue establishment.[1418] It then is the responsibility of the licensee of the tissue establishment 'receiving donor germ line cells to verify the eligibility and suitability of the donor and the prospective parent to whom the germ line cells are donated'.[1419] The eligibility requirements of donors are in part set out in the Embryo Protection Act, which provides that it is not permissible for this donation to occur by an ascendant to a descendant, by a descendant to an ascendant, or from sibling to sibling regardless of whether they are siblings of the full or half-blood.[1420] Other criteria of eligibility include: (i) the donor must be over 18 years of age;[1421] (ii) the donor must be under 36 years of age but the Embryo Protection Authority may authorise a donor above that maximum age limit in exceptional circumstances specified in the Protocol it establishes;[1422] (iii) the donor must have the legal capacity to contract;[1423] (iv) the donor must be of good mental and physical health;[1424] (v) the donor must satisfy any criteria specified in the Protocol established by the Embryo Protection Authority;[1425] (vi) the donor can only make one donation of germ line cells for the purpose of medically assisted procreation, which shall be used in one prospective parent only;[1426] (vii) with the exception of donors of egg cells who may be compensated for the costs and expenses of the stimulation treatments, a donor is not entitled to any consideration for the donation of germ line cells and no person shall pay that consideration to the donor or to any other person to arrange for the services of a donor or offer to pay that consideration;[1427] and (viii) it is not lawful to extract and commence the cryopreservation of egg cells after the death of the person from whom they originate.[1428]

251. Amendments made to the Embryo Protection Act in 2018 ostensibly enable the person making the donation to determine if his/her germ line cells can be used

1418. *Ibid.*, Art. 9 (1).
1419. *Ibid.*, Art. 9 (6).
1420. *Ibid.*, Art. 2.
1421. *Ibid.*, Art. 9 (2).
1422. *Ibid.*, Art. 9 (3). *See also* S.L. 524.02, Embryo Protection Authority (Protocol) Regulations, r. 12.4.
1423. *Ibid.*, Art. 9 (2).
1424. *Ibid.*
1425. *Ibid. See also* S.L. 524.02, Embryo Protection Authority (Protocol) Regulations, r. 12.
1426. *Ibid.*, Art. 9 (5).
1427. *Ibid.*, Art. 9 (8).
1428. *Ibid.*, Art. 7 (2).

before and/or after his death,[1429] and it is, in turn, an offence to knowingly artificially fertilise 'an egg cell with the sperm of a man before or after his death, except in the case where the deceased has donated his sperm'[1430] or to knowingly artificially fertilise 'an egg cell of a woman before or after her death, except in the case where the deceased has donated her egg cells'.[1431] Yet, the Embryo Protection Act also makes it clear that it does not impede 'for medical reasons and according to accepted medical norms, the taking and freezing of sperm or eggs of a person with the aim of making use of that same sperm or egg at a later stage for the generation of an embryo'.[1432] In turn, the Protocol established by the Embryo Protection Authority states that cryopreservation and storage of gametes will be allowed for: '(a) Supernumerary gametes resulting from IVF cycles, (b) Oncology Cases, (c) Fertility Preservation, (d) Transgender persons prior to starting hormone therapy'.[1433] Storage of gametes in those circumstances is not open to donation to third parties unless otherwise stipulated. Instead, the Embryo Protection Act provides that sperm cells 'may be cryo-preserved in authorized tissue establishments during the lifetime of the person from whom they originate'[1434] whereas egg cells 'may be cryo-preserved in authorized tissue establishments up to the maximum permissible age for the fertilisation and transfer thereof into the prospective parent unless they are donated in terms of'[1435] the Embryo Protection Act.[1436]

§4. Prenatal Diagnosis

252. Maltese law distinguishes prenatal diagnosis based upon whether there is an existing pregnancy or otherwise. In the latter case, Maltese law also separates the circumstance when there is not yet an embryo, as defined in the Embryo Protection Act, from circumstances when that embryo is already present. This section addresses those different circumstances in turn.

253. Pre-natal screening programmes of pregnant women 'are aimed at screening for birth defects throughout pregnancy via regular ultrasound scanning, with a detailed fetal anomaly scan at 18+ weeks gestation, together with amniocentesis and chorionic villus sampling in specific cases where necessary'.[1437] That prenatal

1429. House of Representatives Malta – Office of the Clerk, *Kumitat Permanenti ghall-Kunsiderazzjoni ta' Abbozzi ta' Ligi (Rapport Ufficjali u Rivedut),* 13th Legislature: Meeting no. 33 (13 June 2018) 34. *See also* S.L. 524.02, Embryo Protection Authority (Protocol) Regulations, r. 6.19 (b) (not yet in force).
1430. Embryo Protection Act, Ch. 524 of the Laws of Malta, Art. 12 (1)(c).
1431. *Ibid.*, Art. 12 (1)(d).
1432. *Ibid.*, Art. 12 (2).
1433. S.L. 524.02, Embryo Protection Authority (Protocol) Regulations, r. 16.1 (not yet in force).
1434. Embryo Protection Act, Ch. 524 of the Laws of Malta, Art. 7 (1).
1435. *Ibid.*, Art. 7 (2).
1436. *See also* S.L. Embryo Protection Authority (Protocol) Regulations, r. 6 (not yet in force).
1437. Kristina Cassar & Miriam Gatt, *World Birth Defects Day 3 March 2022: Many birth defects, one voice* 5 (Malta Congenital Anomalies Register, Directorate for Health Information and Research 2022).

screening and diagnosis are subject in Malta to the laws that have already been covered in this monograph. This includes that a medical practitioner must always bear in mind the importance of preserving human life from the time of conception[1438] but also that civil[1439] or criminal liability may accrue if, for instance, the medical practitioners cause, through their negligence, the miscarriage of the woman with child.[1440] That being said, it may fall within the professional activities of a midwife, rather than a medical practitioner, to, in the first instance, diagnose pregnancies and monitor normal pregnancies, to carry out 'the examinations necessary for the monitoring of the development of normal pregnancies',[1441] to prescribe or advise 'on the examinations necessary for the earliest possible diagnosis of pregnancies at risk',[1442] to care for and assist the mother during labour as well as to monitor 'the condition of the foetus in utero by the appropriate clinical and technical means'.[1443] The professional activities of the midwife however also include 'recognising the warning signs of abnormality in the mother or infant which necessitate referral to a doctor and assisting the latter where appropriate'.[1444] To be clear, although some pregnant women in Malta receive prenatal diagnoses and antenatal care in private healthcare settings while undergoing childbirth in the public health service,[1445] each individual pregnancy is to, either way, be managed on a case-by-case basis while observing the law. There is also scope for topic-specific provisions in Maltese law regarding prenatal care, for instance, in the case of a pregnant woman held in prison when 'arrangements shall be made for prenatal care and for their transfer to a hospital for their confinement and the delivery of the child'.[1446]

254. Diagnosis and selection of embryos, especially outside the uterine environment, is otherwise largely regulated by the Embryo Protection Act as well as subsidiary law arising there from. It is, in this respect, in the first instance, an offence to select or discard 'an embryo for eugenic purposes'.[1447] Nevertheless, there were 'no specific regulations'[1448] in Maltese law addressing pre-implantation genetic diagnosis until amendments were effectuated to the Embryo Protection Act in 2022.[1449] Those amendments included the addition of a proviso to the offence regarding the selection or discarding of embryos for eugenic purposes:

1438. *See* Part II Ch. 3 §1 above.
1439. *See* Part I Ch. 4 §1.1 above.
1440. *See* Part II Ch. 3 §1 above.
1441. Health Care Professions Act, Ch. 464 of the Laws of Malta, Art. 23 (5)(b).
1442. *Ibid.*, Art. 23 (5)(c).
1443. *Ibid.*, Art. 23 (5)(e).
1444. *Ibid.*, Art. 23 (5)(g). The term 'doctor' here refers to a medical practitioner.
1445. George Gregory Buttigieg, *Optimising Maltese obstetric medico-legal dynamics: Volume I* 363 (Lambert Academic Publishing 2020).
1446. S.L. 260.03, Prisons Regulations, r. 38 (1).
1447. Embryo Protection Act, Ch. 524 of the Laws of Malta, Art. 6 (e).
1448. Committee on Bioethics (DH-BIO) – Council of Europe, *Background document on pre-implantation and prenatal genetic testing: Clinical situation – legal situation*, DH-BIO/INF (2015) 6 (October 2021 update) p. 17. The Committee on Bioethics is now the Steering Committee for Human Rights in the fields of Biomedicine and Health.
1449. Act XI of 2022 – Various Laws relating to Assisted Procreation (Amendment) Act, 2022 [Government Gazette of Malta No. 20,898 – 27/07/2022].

> Provided that the Protocol may specify that certain exceptional circumstances shall not constitute selection of embryos for eugenic purposes; provided, however, also that the medical experts as listed in the Protocol shall provide information and explanations relating to the testing of human egg cells (oocytes) and other testing which is available to the prospective parent or prospective parents and the said prospective parent or prospective parents shall decide which testing shall be carried out after consulting with the medical experts.[1450]

255. The latter proviso added in 2022 then furnishes a basis in law for regulating pre-implantation genetic testing directly on embryos. Yet, the Embryo Protection Act directs that the final decision as to whether to undertake that test or whether to otherwise test and select egg cells will lie with the prospective parent/s. The Embryo Protection Act also mandates that medical practitioners identified in the Protocol that is established by the Embryo Protection Authority are to provide the prospective parent/s with information and explanations regarding the testing of human egg cells prior to engaging in the testing and selection of embryos. Indeed, other than consolidating topic-specific regulatory measures, the testing of human egg cells would have required little to no change to the Embryo Protection Act. It is also, and has always been, lawful under the Embryo Protection Act for a medical practitioner to select sperm cells with the aim of preventing any child resulting from medically assisted procreation 'from falling ill with a sex-linked genetic illness'.[1451] While it is otherwise an offence to artificially fertilise a human egg cell with a sperm cell that is selected for the sex chromosome contained in it,[1452] a combination of sperm cell selection to avoid sex-linked genetic illness, as well as testing and selection of oocytes to detect maternally derived chromosomal aneuploidies and translocations in oocytes, would have on some accounts largely identified and excluded inheritable genetic disease/s prior to fertilisation and the presence of new embryos.[1453] The obligation to inform prospective parent/s about those options thus also aims to avoid unnecessary testing of the human embryo and the possibility of the indefinite cryopreservation of an embryo that bears genetic disease.

256. That being said, the amendments effectuated to the Embryo Protection Act in 2022 led to changes in the Protocol established by the Embryo Protection Authority so as to regulate pre-implantation genetic testing *of embryos* for monogenic diseases (PGTM). Indeed, the Embryo Protection Act now specifies that its provisions should not be construed as prohibiting clinical interventions deemed permissible in terms of the Protocol[1454] and neither does it prohibit prospective parents, in instances specified in the Protocol and with the prior authorisation of the Embryo Protection Authority, from fertilising more egg cells until all the cryopreserved

1450. Embryo Protection Act, Ch. 524 of the Laws of Malta, Art. 6 (e). Original parentheses.
1451. *Ibid.*, Art. 10 (2).
1452. *Ibid.*, Art. 10 (1).
1453. Archdiocese of Malta, *Embryo Protection Act (Amendment) Bill No. 5: A position paper* (2022).
1454. Embryo Protection Act, Ch. 524 of the Laws of Malta, Art. 15 (3).

embryos have been implanted in the prospective parents.[1455] As such, the Protocol, as amended in 2022 and embedded in the subsidiary law, now specifies that the eligible prospective parent/s who fall within the established age-bracket/s can *inter alia* be referred to treatment if they have 'a family history of monogenic diseases which is listed as one of the diseases in the Guidance Notes 11 for Pre-implantation Genetic Diagnosis for Monogenic diseases'[1456] contained in the Protocol. Indeed, PGTM is only to be used for the 'detection of serious genetic conditions as approved by the[1457] Embryo Protection Authority', which now maintains a list of conditions for which PGTM has been approved, including Finnish nephrotic syndrome, gangliosidosis, Huntington's disease, Joubert syndrome, Maple Syrup urine syndrome, nemaline myopathy, spinal muscular atrophy, Tay-Sachs disease, and Walker-Warburg syndrome. In order for a new condition, which is not included in the existing list, to be considered for PGTM testing approval, 'a couple must have a licensed PGTM clinic apply to the[1458] Embryo Protection Authority on their behalf'.

257. Thus, so long as the condition in question is included in the Protocol or the Embryo Protection Authority approves, on application from the PGTM licensed clinic, a condition for PGTM approval, the first step towards conducting PGTM will involve the clinical team of the tissue establishment determining, in agreement with the prospective parents who should sign written informed consent for all procedures they undergo, that the condition is sufficiently serious as to warrant PGTM. An application must then be made to the Embryo Protection Authority. This application must include a report providing details outlined in the Protocol, and[1459] it 'is only after an approval is granted that a PGTM can go ahead'.[1460] This permission will be issued 'if the condition is listed in the approved conditions'[1461] identified in the Protocol. The situation of prospective parents undergoing PGTM is furthermore one of those instances where permission may also be granted by the Embryo Protection Authority to fertilise more than two embryos up to twelve embryos, *inter alia* depending on the prospective parent/s age,[1462] and the embryo biopsies are to then only be carried out by embryologist/s practitioner/s who have been designated and named on the clinic's licence.[1463]

258. The Protocol established by the Embryo Protection Authority makes it clear that embryos 'from which biopsies have been taken or resulting from gametes from which biopsies have been taken, should not be transferred with any other (non-biopsied) embryos in the same treatment cycle'.[1464] Significantly, it is also dictated

1455. *Ibid.*, Art. 6 (b).
1456. S.L. 524.02, Embryo Protection Authority (Protocol) Regulations, r. 7.5 (e) (not yet in force).
1457. *Ibid.*, r. 11.4.2.
1458. *Ibid.*, r. 11.3.
1459. *Ibid.*, r. 11.14.
1460. *Ibid.*, r. 11.15.
1461. *Ibid.*
1462. *Ibid.*, r. 11.15. *See also* r. 9.8.
1463. *Ibid.*, r. 2.25.
1464. *Ibid.*, r. 11.20.

that embryos 'that after biopsies have been carried out result that they have a gene that will develop a serious disease, *cannot be discarded*'.[1465] The latter embryos must instead 'be cryopreserved in a dedicated storage facility, separate from embryos not diagnosed with the disease'.[1466] While this does not apply to embryos that 'are not diagnosed with the disease being tested for but might be carriers of that disease',[1467] which can be transferred into the prospective parents and are to be cryopreserved with embryos that are not diagnosed with diseases, the cryopreserved embryos known to have a gene of a serious disease have two options that can result in transfer to a prospective parent's uterine environment with the possibility of a live birth. First, the prospective parents from whose gametes that embryo resulted may give their consent, after receiving adequate information, to transfer the embryo into the uterine environment. However, this is not a right vested in the prospective parents, and it is instead 'subject to consideration of the welfare of any resulting child and should have approval from the[1468] Embryo Protection Authority'. Second, embryos known to have a gene of a serious disease can be placed for adoption by the Embryo Protection Authority. However, the Protocol dictates that this is only permissible 'once an effective treatment for same disease has been found'.[1469]

259. The Protocol also sets out the requirements and obligations of the tissue establishment and other parties involved in the PGTM. Thus, for instance, a 'senior clinical geneticist should be involved in the decision-making process when deciding whether a patient should receive treatment involving embryo testing',[1470] which should ultimately be discussed between the prospective parents and the clinical team. It is however the responsibility of the tissue establishment to consider whether PGTM is appropriate in particular cases while considering factors listed in the Protocol, which include the likely degree of suffering associated with the condition as well as the availability of effective therapy now and in future.[1471] The tissue establishment is to also ensure that people seeking PGTM are given appropriate information about the treatment as indicated in the Protocol, which includes 'that sophisticated genetic tests can reveal additional genetic information about an embryo(s) and that the clinical effect of these findings on a child born may not be known'.[1472] Yet, the tissue establishment may also offer PGTM and, subject to the patient's consent, withhold the patient's test results.[1473]

1465. *Ibid.*, r. 11.21. Emphasis added.
1466. *Ibid.*
1467. *Ibid.*, r. 11.23.
1468. *Ibid.*, r. 11.24. *See also* Part II Ch. 3 §3 above.
1469. *Ibid.*, r. 11.25.
1470. *Ibid.*, r. 2.26. *See also* r. 11.6.
1471. *Ibid.*, r. 11.11.
1472. *Ibid.*, r. 11.16 (c). Original parentheses.
1473. *Ibid.*, r. 11.12.

§5. Psychosurgical Interventions

260. Treatment and surgery in Malta are underpinned by the laws outlined throughout this monograph. The Mental Health Act however lays topic-specific conditions so that a patient with a mental disorder can lawfully undertake therapeutic interventions that are considered to be invasive or irreversible treatments for mental illness. These treatments are indicated by regulations made by the Minister responsible for health and then exhaustively listed in the 14th Schedule of the Mental Health Act.[1474] The latter Schedule stipulates that:

> Only the following therapeutic invasive or irreversible interventions for mental illness, as determined by the Minister [responsible for health], may be carried out on a patient with a mental disorder: Stereotactic Ablative Anterior Capsulotomy for severe refractory Major Depressive Disorder, Stereotactic Ablative Anterior Capsulotomy for severe refractory Obsessive Compulsive Disorder, Stereotactic Ablative Anterior Cingulotomy for severe refractory Major Depressive Disorder, and Stereotactic Ablative Anterior Cingulotomy for severe refractory Obsessive Compulsive Disorder.[1475]

261. The special treatments listed in the 14th Schedule of the Mental Health Act can only be carried out on a person with a mental disorder if three conditions are met. First, the patient with a mental disorder must give free and informed consent to undertake that treatment. Indeed, the responsible psychiatrist must certify in the application that s/he must submit to the Commissioner for Mental Health in accordance with the 14th Schedule of the Mental Health Act that 'the patient has the mental capacity to give, and has given, informed consent to undergo such treatment'[1476] while also certifying in that application that the patient consented in writing. That written and signed consent must then accompany the application that the responsible psychiatrist will submit to the Commissioner for Mental Health. To be clear, if it is the opinion of the responsible psychiatrist that the patient with a mental disorder either lacks the mental capacity to give consent or is a minor who lacks sufficient maturity and understanding to consent to treatment, then free and informed consent is to be obtained from the responsible carer.[1477] The second condition in order to lawfully furnish to a patient with a mental disorder any special treatment listed in the 14th Schedule of the Mental Health Act involves the responsible psychiatrist submitting an application to the Commissioner for Mental Health in accordance with that Schedule. As such, in addition to the certification regarding the patient's mental capacity and consent to treatment, the responsible psychiatrist must also certify in the application that 'there is sufficient evidence-based knowledge about this treatment; [that] the treatment benefits the health needs of the patient;

1474. L.N. 206 of 2017 – Mental Health Act (Amendment of Fourteenth Schedule) Regulations, 2017 [Government Gazette of Malta No. 19,848 – 18/08/2017].
1475. Mental Health Act, Ch. 525 of the Laws of Malta, Fourteenth Schedule, Part I.
1476. *Ibid.*, Fourteenth Schedule, Part II.
1477. *Ibid.*, Art. 33 (2)(a).

[and that] every available alternative treatment that could reasonably be regarded as likely to produce a sufficient and lasting benefit has been given to this patient without a sufficient and lasting benefit'.[1478] The application must then also feature a clinical report on the recommended treatment, including the 'patient's treatment history; proposed treatment; reasons for such treatment; evidence-based knowledge about this treatment; and benefits for this patient'.[1479] The third and final condition involves the approval of the Commissioner for Mental Health. Thus, after receiving the pertinent application and provided that the Commissioner for Mental Health 'is satisfied that consent is free and informed and that there is sufficient evidence based knowledge that the procedure benefits the health needs of the patient',[1480] that Commissioner may approve the treatment for the patient at hand. All else being equal, it would be unlawful to provide any treatment listed in the 14th Schedule of the Mental Health Act to a patient with a mental disorder if the Commissioner for Mental Health does not approve it. Either way, the decision taken by the Commissioner for Mental Health is subject to appeal to the Court of Voluntary Jurisdiction.[1481]

262. The Mental Health Act also lays topic-specific requirements for the purpose of administering electro-convulsive therapy. This can only be administered based on the prescription of the responsible psychiatrist and after obtaining the second opinion of another psychiatrist confirming the appropriateness of electro-convulsive therapy.[1482] Furthermore, the patient's informed consent will also be required before furnishing electro-convulsive therapy.[1483] If it is the opinion of the responsible psychiatrist that the patient with a mental disorder either lacks the mental capacity to give consent or is a minor who lacks sufficient maturity and understanding to consent to treatment, then informed consent is to be obtained from the responsible carer.

263. More broadly, the Mental Health Act provides that 'no major medical or surgical procedure shall be carried out on a patient suffering from a mental disorder unless such person gives written informed consent'.[1484] Yet, if it is the opinion of the responsible psychiatrist that the patient with a mental disorder either lacks the mental capacity to give consent to treatment or is a minor who lacks sufficient maturity and understanding to consent to treatment, then consent shall be given by the responsible carer.[1485] The Mental Health Act however provides that the requirement of obtaining written informed consent from the patient suffering from a mental disorder or from the responsible carer in the circumstances indicated in Article 32 (b) 'shall not be applicable in an emergency where the patient's life is at risk'.[1486] All else being equal, this entails that unwritten consent from the patient him/herself will

1478. *Ibid.*, Fourteenth Schedule, Part II.
1479. *Ibid.*
1480. *Ibid.*, Art. 33 (2)(b).
1481. *Ibid.*, Art. 46.
1482. *Ibid.*, Art. 33 (3)(a).
1483. *Ibid.*, Art. 33 (3)(b).
1484. *Ibid.*, Art. 32 (a).
1485. *Ibid.*, Art. 32 (b).
1486. *Ibid.*, Art. 32 (c).

suffice if his/her life is at risk and that if the patient also lacks mental capacity or is a minor patient who lacks maturity and understanding to consent to treatment, then the major medical or surgical procedure can proceed only when it is not possible to obtain the consent of the responsible carer due to the emergency at hand when the patient's life is at risk.

§6. Organ Transplants

264. Organ transplants in Malta are broadly addressed in three related but different statutory instruments engaging with the eligibility of as well as the process towards lawfully procuring and donating human organs, the quality and safety of human organs intended for transplantation, and the criminal offence of trafficking in human organs. These three instruments will be considered in turn.

265. The Human Organs, Tissues and Cell Donation Act (HOTCDA) applies 'to all human organ, tissue and cell donations by persons residing in Malta'.[1487] The terms 'human organ' and 'organ' as used in the HOTCDA mean:

> A differentiated part of the human body, formed by different tissues, that maintains its structure, vascularisation and capacity to develop physiological functions with a significant level of autonomy: Provided that a part of an organ is also considered to be an organ if its function is to be used for the same purpose as the entire organ in the human body, maintaining the requirements of structure and vascularisation.[1488]

The term 'tissues' in the HOTCDA means 'all constituent parts of the human body formed by cells'.[1489] In turn, the term 'cells' in the HOTCDA means 'individual diploid human cells or a collection of diploid human cells when not bound by any form of connective tissue',[1490] thereby excluding haploid cells such as gametes that are regulated elsewhere.[1491] Donation of human organs, tissues and cells 'for research'[1492] also falls outside the scope of the HOTCDA and, by way of example, medical schools in Malta make use of a bequeathal form in order for a person to indicate that s/he intends his/her body to be donated to the academic institution after his/her demise.[1493] That being said, the HOTCDA may, in practice, be applicable in regard to consent or authorisation to remove human organs, tissues or

1487. Human Organs, Tissues and Cell Donation Act, Ch. 558 of the Laws of Malta, Art. 2 (2).
1488. *Ibid.*, Art. 3.
1489. *Ibid.*
1490. *Ibid.*
1491. *See* Part II Ch. 3 §3 above.
1492. Human Organs, Tissues and Cell Donation Act, Ch. 558 of the Laws of Malta, Art. 2 (3).
1493. *See, for instance*: Department of Anatomy, Faculty of Medicine & Surgery – University of Malta, *Bequeathal Form* (2020); Queen Mary University London in Malta, *Body Donation*, <https://www.qmul.ac.uk/malta/community-hub/body-donation/>.

cells from living or deceased donors to be used for any purpose, including research, as a consequence of provisions that relate to the trafficking of human organs in the Criminal Code.[1494]

266. The HOTCDA thus furnishes the basis in law for both live organ donation and cadaveric organ, tissue and cell donation. However, the latter type of donation can only be considered after patients 'are certified brain dead by a clinician',[1495] who is 'a health professional being a doctor or consultant whose practice is based on direct observation and treatment of a patient'.[1496] That clinician is to refer to updated and peer-reviewed guidelines maintained by the Superintendent of Public Health 'for the diagnosis of brain death for the purposes of organ, tissue and cell donation'.[1497] These guidelines are however not publicly available at the time of writing.

267. The HOTCDA then grounds in law the National Human Organ and Tissue Donation Register, which is maintained by the Superintendent of Public Health. That Register is used in practice to draw consent for the purpose of cadaveric organ, tissue and cell donation, and it is the only register 'having legal validity for the purpose of a donation under'[1498] the HOTCDA. As such, next of kin are not to be approached to declare whether they consent to the cadaveric donation of organs, tissues and cells 'where the deceased has registered his wish not to be a donor'.[1499] Furthermore, while it is not explicitly stated in the law, a decision to donate organs, tissues and cells that is formally indicated by the donor in the National Human Organ and Tissue Donation Register is, in practice, applied in such a manner that it cannot be overturned by third parties such as relatives even after the donor has died[1500] and only a clinician as defined in the HOTCDA has 'the right to decide that the organ or tissue object of the donation [from the deceased person on the Register] is unfit or unsuitable for transplantation'.[1501] The National Human Organ and Tissue Donation Register thus records the following:

> (a) details of persons residing in Malta who wish to donate their organs, tissue or cells following their demise; (b) details of persons residing in Malta who expressly declare that they do not wish to donate their organs, tissues or cells

1494. Criminal Code, Ch. 9 of the Laws of Malta, Art. 248CA.
1495. Human Organs, Tissues and Cell Donation Act, Ch. 558 of the Laws of Malta, Art. 12 (1).
1496. *Ibid.*, Art. 3. The terms 'clinician' and 'doctor' in the English language version of the law are translated to/from the word 'tabib' in the Maltese language version of the law, which refers to a medical practitioner.
1497. *Ibid.*, Art. 12 (2).
1498. *Ibid.*, Art. 4 (3).
1499. *Ibid.*, Art. 10 (1).
1500. *See, for instance*: House of Representatives Malta – Office of the Clerk, *Dibattiti tal-Kamra Tad-Deputati (Rapport Uffiċjali u Rivedut),* 12th Legislature: Sitting No. 383 (2 May 2016), 120. *See also* Organ Donation, <https://organdonation.gov.mt/>.
1501. Human Organs, Tissues and Cell Donation Act, Ch. 558 of the Laws of Malta, Art. 11.

following their demise; (c) any particular organ, tissue and cell a person chooses to donate; and (d) any particular organ, tissue and cell a person chooses not to donate.[1502]

268. In order to include in the National Human Organ and Tissue Donation Register a person requesting to become a donor, the Superintendent of Public Health must be satisfied that the person has attained 16 years of age and is including his/her name in that Register 'voluntarily, out of his own free will'.[1503] The Superintendent of Public Health must also be satisfied that the person requesting to become a donor 'has had adequate information on the meaning and consequences of registration as a donor under'[1504] the HOTCDA. In this respect, a clinician, as defined in the HOTCDA and who is involved in the donation process, 'must ascertain and certify that the donor fully understands the nature and consequences of the donation'.[1505] The Superintendent of Public Health cannot register a person requesting to become a donor prior to receiving the latter certification, which the law directs should not be provided in case of 'any donor who due to mental incompetence cannot understand the nature and consequences of the donation'.[1506] The HOTCDA also binds the Superintendent of Public Health to only register a person requesting to become a donor after having satisfied him/herself that the person 'is not suffering from any mental disorder which renders him incapable of taking care of his own affairs'.[1507] Once registered on the National Human Organ and Tissue Donation Register, a person is nevertheless entitled to retract his/her choice by applying for de-registration to the Superintendent of Public Health, who is bound to remove the name of that person from the Register.[1508]

269. If a person dies without any entry on the National Human Organ and Tissue Donation Register, then the next of kin of the deceased person may be approached to declare whether they consent to the donation taking place. It is either a clinician, as defined in the HOTCDA or a transplant coordinator, which 'means a health care professional who coordinates activities related to organ donation and transplantation',[1509] that approaches the next of kin of the deceased person.[1510] The transplant coordinator can be either a donor coordinator, which 'means a person who confirms that the donor has the medical characteristics that ensures a successful transplantation'[1511] or a recipient coordinator, meaning 'a person who ensures

1502. *Ibid.*, Art. 4 (2).
1503. *Ibid.*, Art. 5 (1)(c).
1504. *Ibid.*, Art. 5 (1)(d).
1505. *Ibid.*, Art. 14 (1).
1506. *Ibid.*, Art. 14 (2).
1507. *Ibid.*, Art. 5 (1)(b).
1508. *Ibid.*, Art. 7.
1509. *Ibid.*, Art. 3.
1510. *Ibid.*, Art. 10 (1).
1511. *Ibid.*, Art. 3.

that the patient is in a suitable state to accept a successful transplant'.[1512] If the clinician or transplant coordinator obtains consent from the next of kin, the HOTCDA stipulates that 'the donation shall take place and the said person shall be deemed to have been a registered donor for the purposes of'[1513] that Act. That being said, if the deceased is a person who at the time of death is still under 16 years of age, which means that s/he was *ipso jure* never eligible to enter his/her name in the National Human Organ and Tissue Donation Register, the HOTCDA stipulates that 'the parents or legal guardians shall be consulted with regards to an organ, tissue or cell donation taking place'.[1514]

270. It is also lawful in Malta for a person to donate an organ while s/he is still alive. This is however subject to four limitations. First, a clinician, as defined in the HOTCDA, is only to approve donation from a living person under the age of 16 years in case of 'transplantation of regenerative hematopoietic stem cells for blood relatives'.[1515] While this imposes an obligation on clinicians involved in the certification process preceding registration or donation, the remaining three limitations impose obligations on procurement organisations that are authorised by the Superintendent of Public Health to undertake or coordinate the procurement of organs and on transplantation centres that are authorised by the latter Superintendent to undertake transplantation of organs, tissues and cells. As such, procurement organisations and transplantation centres are bound to have a framework that is approved by the Superintendent of Public Health in order to assess all potential live organ donors and to decide whether the organ transplant should be approved based on the criteria laid out in the HOTCDA. These criteria depend on the relation between donor and donee as follows:

> (a) in the case of donation between blood relatives and family members who are not blood relatives, an organ must be donated to an identified recipient; (b) in other non-related donations a pre-existent close emotional link has to be present between the donor and the recipient for such a donation to be acceptable; and (c) in the case of non-directed altruistic organ donation the principle of distributive justice shall be adopted by which a donated organ shall be allocated to a recipient according to his medical needs. Such a decision shall be taken by the Superintendent [of Public Health].[1516]

271. It consequently means that directed altruistic donation is not foreseeable in Malta other than in the situation of a donation between blood relatives and family members or otherwise in cases involving a pre-existent close emotional link. Any other donation has to be non-directed, and the donor has little option to make the donation conditional on criteria of his/her choosing, such as the exclusion of certain

1512. *Ibid.*, Art. 3.
1513. *Ibid.*, Art. 10 (2).
1514. *Ibid.*, Art. 9.
1515. *Ibid.*, Art. 14 (3). *See also* S.L. 483.01, Tissues and Cells (Quality and Safety) Regulations, Schedules II and III.
1516. *Ibid.*, Art. 13.

people from receiving his/her organ, but the allocation of that non-directed altruistic organ donation is instead made by the Superintendent of Public Health according to the recipient's medical needs after the procurement organisation and transplantation centre assess the potential live organ donor/s to decide whether the transplant should be approved. Indeed, procurement organisations and transplant centres are bound to ensure that living donors are selected on the basis of their health and medical history by suitably qualified or trained competent professionals, which may ultimately 'provide for the exclusion of persons whose donation could present unacceptable health risks'.[1517]

272. In addition to the HOTCDA, EU law transposed into domestic law addresses the standards of quality and safety of human organs intended for transplantation. That EU law sets a minimum standard and, given that the competence of the EU to adopt measures setting high standards of quality and safety for organs and substances of human origin, blood and blood derivatives do 'not prevent any Member State from maintaining or introducing more stringent protective measures',[1518] domestic authorities can adopt their own standards so long as they do not undermine the standards arising from EU law.[1519] In addition to organs,[1520] there then is also related legislation addressing tissues and cells,[1521] as well as blood cells and blood components of human origin,[1522] although medicinal products based on human blood constituents are addressed in separate legislation.[1523] The Organ Transplants (Quality and Safety) Regulations, which transpose into Maltese law Directive 2010/53/EU on standards of quality and safety of human organs intended for transplantation,[1524] are particularly relevant to this section of the monograph addressing organ transplants. Indeed, these Regulations ground in law the place where the procurement of organs is performed, by whom medical activities underlying procurement are undertaken as well as obligations incumbent on the medical team, the characterisation of organs and related tests, where and how the transplantation of organs takes place, the traceability of human organs as well as a reporting system and management in case of serious adverse events, the process to follow up organ recipients and living organ donors, while also listing functions incumbent on the Licensing Authority. The Regulations then identify the Superintendent of Public

1517. S.L. 483.06, Organ Transplants (Quality and Safety) Regulations, r. 15 (2).
1518. Treaty on the Functioning of the European Union, OJ C 326, 26.10.2012, Art. 168 (4)(a).
1519. *See, for instance*: Superintendence of Public Health, *National Standards for Blood Transfusion* (2012; Reviewed 2018).
1520. *See also* Human Blood and Transplants Act, Ch. 483 of the Laws of Malta; S.L. 483.07, Information Procedures for the Exchange, between Member States, of Human Organs intended for Transplantation Regulations.
1521. *See, for instance*: Human Blood and Transplants Act, Ch. 483 of the Laws of Malta; S.L. 483.01, Tissues and Cells (Quality and Safety) Regulations; S.L. 483.04, Human Tissues and Cells (Coding, Processing, Preservation, Storage and Distribution) Regulations; S.L. 483.08, Equivalent Standards of Quality and Safety of Imported Tissues and Cells Regulations.
1522. *See, for instance*: Human Blood and Transplants Act, Ch. 483 of the Laws of Malta; S.L. 483.02, Blood (Quality and Safety) Regulations; S.L. 483.03, Traceability Requirements and Notification of Serious Adverse Reactions and Events Regulations.
1523. *See, for instance*: Medicines Act, Ch. 458 of the Laws of Malta.
1524. Directive 2010/53/EU of the European Parliament and of the Council of 7 July 2010 on standards of quality and safety of human organs intended for transplantation, OJ L 207, 6.8.2010.

Health as the Licensing Authority duly indicating functions in relation to the quality and safety of human organs intended for transplantation, which include establishing conditions that are applicable to procurement organisations and transplantation centres while also issuing appropriate 'guidance to healthcare establishments, professionals and other parties involved in all stages of the chain from donation to transplantation or disposal'.[1525] Procurement organisations and transplantation centres are moreover bound 'to have in place a framework for quality and safety that covers all stages of the chain from donation to transplantation or disposal'[1526] that provides operating procedures for matters as listed in the Regulations at hand.

273. The Organ Transplants (Quality and Safety) Regulations also ground in law the norm that donations of organs from deceased and living donors 'shall be voluntary and unpaid'[1527] and that the procurement of organs 'shall be carried out on a non-profit basis'.[1528] An exception to this rule relates to living donors who may receive compensation that 'is strictly limited to making good the expenses and loss of income related to the donation'.[1529] Unless specifically designated by the Superintendent of Public Health, it is furthermore 'illegal to advertise the need for, or availability of, organs where such advertising is with a view to offering or seeking financial gain or comparable advantage'.[1530] These principles underpinning the regulation of organ donation and transplants in Malta are particularly significant in view of the criminal law in relation to that sector, which also renders it a criminal offence to solicit or recruit 'an organ donor or a recipient for financial gain or comparable advantage'.[1531]

274. The Criminal Code relates both to the HOTCDA and to the Organ Transplants (Quality and Safety) Regulations. Indeed, it is a criminal offence to remove a human organ, tissue or cell from living or deceased donors in any of the following circumstances:

> (a) where the removal is not performed under the [HOTCDA] with the free, informed and specific consent of the living or deceased donor, or, in the case of the deceased donor, with the removal being authorised under the [HOTCDA]; (b) where, in exchange for the removal of organs, tissues or cells the living donor, or a third party, has been offered or has received a financial gain or comparable advantage; (c) where in exchange for the removal of organs, tissues or cells from a deceased donor, a third party has been offered or has received a financial gain or comparable advantage.[1532]

1525. S.L. 483.06, Organ Transplants (Quality and Safety) Regulations, r. 3 (2)(i).
1526. *Ibid.*, r. 4 (1).
1527. *Ibid.*, r. 13 (1).
1528. *Ibid.*, r. 13 (5).
1529. *Ibid.*, r. 13 (2).
1530. *Ibid.*, r. 13 (3).
1531. Criminal Code, Ch. 9 of the Laws of Malta, Art. 248CA (2)(c).
1532. *Ibid.*, Art. 248CA (1).

Reference in this paragraph to 'financial gain or comparable advantage' does not include 'compensation for loss of earnings and any other justifiable expenses caused by the removal or by the related medical examinations, or compensation in case of damage which is not inherent to the removal of organs'.[1533]

275. In addition to the person/s removing the organs, any person who makes use of those illicitly removed organs, tissues or cells in the circumstances listed in the previous paragraph is also guilty of an offence. The Criminal Code specifies that this applies 'for purposes of implantation *or other purposes than implantation*'.[1534] This is significant in respect of the use of human organs, tissues and cells that fall outside the scope of the HOTCDA, such as human 'organ, tissue and cell donation for research'.[1535] By way of the Criminal Code, the obligations of consent or authorisation to lawfully remove human organs, tissue and cells arising from the HOTCDA, as well as the voluntary and unpaid nature of that donation, are in practice extended to human organ, tissue and cell donation for research lest removing organs, tissues and cells absent consent or authorisation under the HOTCDA results in a criminal offence even by the persons using those illicitly removed organs, tissues or cells. To be clear, that outcome may not have been foreseen by the legislator, but the wording of the law leaves little room for interpretation.[1536] Indeed, a person is also committing a criminal offence if s/he 'prepares, preserves or stores illicitly removed human organs, tissues or cells'[1537] in the manner described in the preceding paragraph of this section of the monograph or if s/he otherwise 'transports, transfers, receives, imports or exports illicitly removed human organs, tissues or cells'[1538] in the manner described in the previous paragraph of this section of the monograph. A person is furthermore committing a criminal offence in circumstances where the implantation of human organs, tissues or cells from living or deceased donors is not performed under the HOTCDA or if the implantation in any way breaches the HOTCDA.[1539]

276. Malta is also a State Party to the Council of Europe's Convention against Trafficking in Human Organs. Indeed, many of the criminal offences addressed in this section of the monograph, in practice, reflect wording similar to that contained in the latter Convention. Although ostensibly less relevant to medical law per se, trafficking of persons for the purpose of exploiting them in the removal of any organs is also a criminal offence,[1540] and the Convention against Trafficking in

1533. *Ibid.*, Art. 248CA (4).
1534. *Ibid.*, Art. 248CA (2)(a). Emphasis added.
1535. Human Organs, Tissues and Cell Donation Act, Ch. 558 of the Laws of Malta, Art. 2 (3).
1536. House of Representatives Malta – Office of the Clerk, *Dibattiti tal-Kamra Tad-Deputati (Rapport Ufficjali u Rivedut),* 12th Legislature: Sitting No. 383 (2 May 2016), 123.
1537. Criminal Code, Ch. 9 of the Laws of Malta, Art. 248CA (2)(d).
1538. *Ibid.*, Art. 248CA (2)(e).
1539. *Ibid.*, Art. 248CA (2)(b).
1540. Criminal Code, Ch. 9 of the Laws of Malta, Arts 248C and 248D.

Human Organs can, all else being equal, furnish 'a legal basis for extradition'[1541] with another State Party with which it shares no extradition treaty in respect of offences under that Convention.

§7. Experiments on Human Beings

277. The Charter of Patient Rights and Responsibilities stipulates, under its principle 4 concerning shared decision-making and informed consent, that one has a right to 'receive a detailed explanation of the nature and consequence of any *research or clinical trials* that one might be invited to take part in, before it is conducted, and to obtain and document one's consent or refusal to participate'.[1542] Although the latter Charter is mainly relevant to the public health service, it is at this stage significant that the Charter distinguishes clinical trials from any other research. This is also noted under principle 3 regarding information in that, while one has the right to 'expect to receive all the relevant information related to *clinical trials* of any form that one may be subjected to',[1543] one also more broadly has the right to 'participate and discuss ethical matters that may arise in the course of one's care including treatment, participation in *research or educational projects*'.[1544] As such, research can but does not have to include clinical trials, whereas clinical trials are a form of research. In turn, experimentation on human beings in Maltese medical jurisprudence can be considered in relation to, respectively, clinical trials and the broader clinical, medical and scientific research framework.

278. Clinical trials on medicinal products for human use conducted in Malta are subject to Regulation (EU) 536/2014, which is EU law that is directly applicable without requiring transposition into Maltese law. It is therefore best addressed in the monograph regarding EU health law.[1545] It is however worthwhile, for the purpose of this monograph on medical law in Malta, to clarify the scope of Regulation (EU) 536/2014 by way of some definitions to frame its remit so as to then briefly consider the broader Maltese law, beyond clinical trials alone, regarding experiments on human beings.

279. Regulation (EU) 536/2014 applies to all clinical trials conducted in the EU, but it does not apply to non-interventional studies meaning clinical studies other than clinical trials. Indeed, a clinical trial is a type of clinical study, which means 'any investigation in relation to humans intended: (a) to discover or verify the clinical, pharmacological or other pharmacodynamic effects of one or more medicinal products; (b) to identify any adverse reactions to one or more medicinal products; or (c) to study the absorption, distribution, metabolism and excretion of one or more

1541. Convention against Trafficking in Human Organs (2015) CETS 216, Art. 17 (3).
1542. Healthcare Standards Directorate – Ministry for Health, *Charter of Patient's Rights and Responsibilities* 12 (2016). Emphasis added.
1543. *Ibid.*, 10. Emphasis added.
1544. *Ibid.* Emphasis added.
1545. Herman Nys, *European Union Health Law* 155–177 (Kluwer Law International 2d ed. 2021).

medicinal products'.[1546] In turn, a clinical trial for the purpose of Regulation (EU) 536/2014 means a clinical study which fulfils any of the following conditions:

> (a) the assignment of the subject to a particular therapeutic strategy is decided in advance and does not fall within normal clinical practice of the Member State concerned; (b) the decision to prescribe the investigational medicinal products is taken together with the decision to include the subject in the clinical study; or (c) diagnostic or monitoring procedures in addition to normal clinical practice are applied to the subject.[1547]

280. To be clear, in terms of Regulation (EU) 536/2014, a subject 'means an individual who participates in a clinical trial, either as recipient of an investigational medicinal product or as a control'.[1548] Significantly, Regulation (EU) 536/2014 has repealed Directive 2001/20/EC.[1549] The latter Directive was largely transposed into Maltese law by way of the Clinical Trials Regulations, which grounded in Malta's domestic law, the Health Ethics Committee.[1550] That Committee is a pivotal cog in relation to the authorisation of a clinical trial as well as other research.[1551]

281. Broader Maltese law in relation to clinical trials, as well as other clinical studies and medical and scientific research on human beings, is spread across the statute book. Regardless of its nature, medical practitioners involved in experiments on human beings would thus, for instance, be bound by the ethical and professional standards of their profession as well as other legislation, such as data protection law, that may be applicable to the research at hand. There additionally are provisions in the domestic legal order addressing experimentation on particular groups of human beings. By way of example, the Prisons Regulations stipulate that prisoners 'may not be submitted to any medical experiments'.[1552] Adopting a more moderate tone, the Mental Health Act creates additional safeguards if a person subject to a clinical trial or other medical or scientific research has a mental disorder or lacks the mental capacity to give free and informed consent.[1553] It is thus provided in the Mental Health Act that, in addition to the free and informed consent of the person with a mental disorder and the approval of the Health Ethics Committee, the Commissioner for Mental Health is to appoint an independent psychiatrist to examine the

1546. Regulation (EU) No 536/2014 of the European Parliament and of the Council of 16 April 2014 on clinical trials on medicinal products for human use, and repealing Directive 2001/20/EC, OJ L 158, 27.5.2014, Art. 2 (2).
1547. *Ibid.*
1548. *Ibid.*
1549. Directive 2001/20/EC of the European Parliament and of the Council of 4 April 2001 on the approximation of the laws, regulations and administrative provisions of the Member States relating to the implementation of good clinical practice in the conduct of clinical trials on medicinal products for human use, OJ L 121, 1.5.2001.
1550. S.L. 458.43, Clinical Trials Regulations, r. 7.
1551. *See also* Part I Ch. 4 §4.III above.
1552. S.L. 260.03, Prisons Regulations, r. 36 (1).
1553. *See* Part II Ch. 1 §2.II above.

person with a mental disorder who may not then be subjected to clinical trials or other medical or scientific research unless that independent psychiatrist 'certifies in the clinical records that in his opinion the person is capable to give free and informed consent and that the expected benefits of the trials or research are likely to outweigh any potential harm to that person'.[1554] Even so, the person subject to the clinical trial or other research has the right to at any time withdraw his/her consent to participate in the trial or research. The Mental Health Act furthermore stipulates that no person who lacks the capacity to give free and informed consent may be subjected to clinical trials or other medical or scientific research unless, in addition to the approval of the responsible carer and of the Health Ethics Committee, the Commissioner for Mental Health is also first satisfied 'after assessment by two independent experts, one of whom shall be a specialist in mental health, that the expected benefits of the trials or research are likely to outweigh any potential harm to that person'.[1555] Also, in case of the person who lacks mental capacity to give free and informed consent, it is the responsible carer who has the right to any time withdraw consent for participation in any clinical trials or medical or scientific research. Moreover, if a clinical trial or other medical or scientific research is proposed on a minor suffering from a mental disorder, in addition to requirements regarding consent and/or refusal to participate, the Mental Health Act stipulates that this shall not proceed unless the Commissioner for Mental Health is also satisfied, after an independent review by two psychiatrists, that:

> [T]he expected benefits of the trials or research are likely to outweigh any potential harm to that minor. Such trials or research shall be subject to ethical or any other additional safeguards that may be applicable. Furthermore, the Commissioner shall appoint an appropriate independent [psychiatrist] to monitor the minor during such trials or research.[1556]

282. In respect of experimentation on human beings, the Embryo Protection Act makes it clear that '[a]ny experimentation on human embryos is prohibited'.[1557] However, clinical interventions on a human embryo 'are allowed on condition that said interventions pursue an exclusively diagnostic and, or therapeutic purpose related to the embryo and are in the interest of the health and development of the embryo itself',[1558] and clinical interventions may even be permissible under the Protocol established by the Embryo Protection Authority.[1559] It is furthermore an offence to unite 'embryos with different genetic material to a cell conglomerate using at least one human embryo'[1560] or to join 'a human embryo with a cell that contains genetic information different from the embryo cells and induces them to

1554. Mental Health Act, Ch. 525 of the Laws of Malta, Art. 35 (1)(b).
1555. *Ibid.*, Art. 35 (2)(a).
1556. *Ibid.*, Art. 31 (3).
1557. Embryo Protection Act, Ch. 524 of the Laws of Malta, Art. 15 (1).
1558. *Ibid.*, Art. 15 (3).
1559. *See* Part II Ch. 3 §3 above.
1560. Embryo Protection Act, Ch. 524 of the Laws of Malta, Art. 14 (1)(a).

develop further'[1561] or to 'fertilize a human egg cell with the sperm of an animal or [to fertilize] an animal's egg cell with the sperm of a man, with the intention of generating an embryo capable of development'.[1562] It is likewise an offence to transfer an embryo arising from any of the latter three procedures to a woman or to an animal or to otherwise transfer a human embryo into an animal.[1563]

283. In addition to EU law and any domestic law regulating clinical trials or other medical and scientific research,[1564] as well as other related domestic laws such as laws regulating the processing and production of cannabis for medicinal and/or research purposes,[1565] research institutions in Malta can also shape codes of practice grounding research conducted in their facilities and by their staff. By way of example, the University of Malta is a tertiary education institution in Malta, and its functions and powers include setting up and properly maintaining 'libraries, laboratories and other facilities required for teaching, research, experimentation, or diffusion of knowledge and sciences as well as the establishment of academic audit and quality assurance schemes'.[1566] The University of Malta then has a Research Code of Practice that 'provides guiding principles and standards of good practice in research … [that] applies to all those undertaking research on the University's premises using its facilities, or on behalf of the University, including staff, students, visiting or affiliate staff, associates, contractors and consultants'.[1567] Any of these researchers thus applies to conduct research (involving human beings) by completing a Research Ethics and Data Protection Form that serves as a self-assessment exercise in the first instance. That then indicates if further review is warranted and Research Ethics Committees are established in each Faculty (FREC) at the University of Malta to review those applications unless the proposed research involves special categories of personal data in terms of the GDPR[1568] or if, otherwise, ethics or data protection issues cannot be resolved by the FREC with the researcher. In the latter two cases, the FREC reviews the application for any consideration related to ethics and makes a recommendation to the University Research Ethics Committee (UREC) that will be responsible for dealing with the application and duly inform the FREC.[1569] Either way, so long as self-assessment indicates review by the

1561. *Ibid.*, Art. 14 (1)(b).
1562. *Ibid.*, Art. 14 (1)(c).
1563. *Ibid.*, Art. 14 (2).
1564. *See also* Patent and Designs Act, Ch. 417 of the Laws of Malta; S.L. 427.56, Good Laboratory Practice Regulations; Medicines Act, Ch. 458 of the Laws of Malta; S.L. 458.47, Good Clinical Practice and Requirements for Manufacturing or Import Authorisation of Investigational Medicinal Products (Human Use) Regulations; S.L. 585.01, Basic Safety Standards for Ionising Radiation Regulations.
1565. Production of Cannabis for Medicinal and Research Purposes Act, Ch. 578 of the Laws of Malta.
1566. Education Act, Ch. 327 of the Laws of Malta, Art. 72 (g).
1567. University of Malta, *Research Code of Practice* 1 (Approved by the Senate of the University of Malta on 20 September 2017 and amended by Senate on 21 March 2019).
1568. Regulation (EU) 2016/679 of the European Parliament and of the Council of 27 April 2016 on the protection of natural persons with regard to the processing of personal data and on the free movement of such data, and repealing Directive 95/46/EC, OJ L 119, 4.5.2016, Art. 9.
1569. University of Malta, *Research Ethics Review Procedures* 2 (Approved by the Senate of the University of Malta on 20 September 2017 and amended by Senate on 21 March 2019).

research ethics committee, which will always occur if the study involves human participants, then research cannot be undertaken until the Research Ethics and Data Protection Form is approved by the pertinent research ethics committee.

§8. Transsexual Interventions

284. The standard outline of the International Encyclopaedia for Medical Law refers to 'transsexual interventions', which has been defined in some Maltese jurisprudence as an 'older and medicalised term used to refer to people who identify and live in a different gender'.[1570] It then is a term that is not typically used in Maltese statutory law if only because a 'person shall not be required to provide proof of a surgical procedure for total or partial genital reassignment, hormonal therapies or any other psychiatric, psychological or medical treatment to make use of the right to gender identity'.[1571] Indeed, it is the right of every Maltese citizen to request the Director of the Public Registry to change their recorded gender and/or first name 'in order to reflect that person's self determined gender identity',[1572] and the Director of the Public Registry will only require as evidence a declaratory public deed drawn up by a Notary Public who 'shall not request any psychiatric, psychological or medical documents for the drawing up of the declaratory public deed'.[1573] The focus in Maltese law thus is on a person's own self-affirming gender identity and gender expression without requiring any medical intervention to certify that identity and/or expression. Thus, rather than 'transsexual', the term 'transgender' is used in some Maltese jurisprudence as follows:

> An inclusive umbrella term referring to people whose gender identity and/or gender expression differ from the sex/gender they were assigned at birth. It may include but is not limited to: people who identify as transsexual, transgender, transvestite/cross-dressing, androgyne, polygender, genderqueer, agender, gender variant, gender non-conforming, or with any other gender identity and/or expression which does not meet the societal and cultural expectation placed on gender identity.[1574]

285. To be clear, gender identity is safeguarded under Maltese law. Although the Mental Health Act stipulates that no 'implantation of hormonal or other invasive devices to modify sexual and, or emotional and, or behavioural changes arising from mental illness shall be carried out on minors'[1575] under 18 years of age, it is

1570. Office of the Deputy Prime Minister of Malta – Ministry for Health, *Transgender Healthcare* 19 (2019).
1571. Gender Identity, Gender Expression and Sex Characteristics Act, Ch. 540 of the Laws of Malta, Art. 3 (4).
1572. *Ibid.*, Art. 4 (1).
1573. *Ibid.*, Art. 5 (2).
1574. Office of the Deputy Prime Minister of Malta – Ministry for Health, *Transgender Healthcare* 19 (2019).
1575. Mental Health Act, Ch. 525 of the Laws of Malta, Art. 31 (2).

the Gender Identity, Gender Expression and Sex Characteristics Act (GIGESCA) that grounds the right of all citizens of Malta to: '(a) the recognition of their gender identity; (b) the free development of their person according to their gender identity; (c) be treated according to their gender identity and, particularly, to be identified in that way in the documents providing their identity therein; and (d) bodily integrity and physical autonomy'.[1576] In turn, gender identity in the GIGESCA refers to:

> [E]ach person's internal and individual experience of gender, which may or may not correspond with the sex assigned at birth, including the personal sense of the body (which may involve, if freely chosen, modification of bodily appearance and, or functions by medical, surgical or other means) and other expressions of gender, including name, dress, speech and mannerisms.[1577]

286. In this respect, the 'gender identity of the individual shall be respected at all times'.[1578] Yet, while recalling that the situation of a person who has not yet attained the age of 16 years in relation to *inter alia* sex assignment treatment was illustrated earlier in this monograph,[1579] medical interventions are also safeguarded in the GIGESCA itself inasmuch as it provides that all 'persons seeking psychosocial counselling, support and medical interventions relating to sex or gender should be given expert sensitive and individually tailored support by psychologists and medical practitioners or peer counselling. Such support should extend from the date of diagnosis or self-referral for as long as necessary'.[1580] This is also based on the premise that gender affirmation 'is a key determinant of transgender health'.[1581] Thus, although conversion practices, which aim to change, repress and/or eliminate a person's sexual orientation, gender identity and/or gender expression, are largely prohibited in Malta,[1582] that prohibition does not exclude the following gender-affirming services:

> (a) any services and, or interventions related to the exploration and, or free development of a person and, or affirmation of one's identity with regard to one or more of the characteristics being affirmed by [the Affirmation of Sexual Orientation, Gender Identity and Gender Expression Act] through counselling, psychotherapeutic services and, or similar services; or (b) any healthcare service related to the free development and, or affirmation of one's gender identity

1576. Gender Identity, Gender Expression and Sex Characteristics Act, Ch. 540 of the Laws of Malta, Art. 3 (1).
1577. *Ibid.*, Art. 2. Original parentheses. *See also* Affirmation of Sexual Affirmation, Gender Identity and Gender Expression Act, Ch. 567 of the Laws of Malta, Art. 2
1578. *Ibid.*, Art. 3 (3).
1579. *See* Part II Ch. 2 §1 above.
1580. Gender Identity, Gender Expression and Sex Characteristics Act, Ch. 540 of the Laws of Malta, Art. 15 (1).
1581. Office of the Deputy Prime Minister of Malta – Ministry for Health, *Transgender Healthcare* 7 (2019).
1582. *See* Part I Ch. 3 above.

and, or gender expression of a person; and, or (c) any healthcare service related to the treatment of a mental disorder.[1583]

287. The Fifth Schedule of the Social Security Act, which lists the diseases and conditions in respect of which a person may be entitled to free medical aid available within the national public health service, then includes in that list 'Gender Identity and Sex Characteristics Related Conditions'.[1584] Indeed, a Gender Wellbeing Clinic has been established in Malta that, in addition to initial assessment and psychosocial as well as family support, offers services that include hormone prescription, communication therapy, orchiectomy, and hysterectomy.[1585] A multidisciplinary team has, in that respect, been set up within the public health service to address the needs of transgender persons. This team includes professionals from the fields of 'endocrinology, urology, gynaecology, plastic surgery and psychiatry together with psychologists, social workers, family therapists, speech language pathologists and a nurse coordinator… [,] paediatric experts … [while being] led and supported by public health medicine specialists in the service planning and implantation stages'.[1586]

288. The Embryo Protection Authority (Protocol) Regulations furthermore acknowledge that since 'feminising/masculinising hormone therapy limits fertility it is important for patients to make decisions concerning fertility such as cryopreserving of gametes, before starting hormone therapy or undergo surgery to remove/alter their reproductive organs'.[1587] In this respect, while tissue establishments are typically not to obtain gametes for treatment from anyone under the age of 18, an exception is made if 'those gametes are intended for the patient's own treatment in … transgender persons'.[1588] In turn, cryopreservation and storage of gametes will *inter alia* be allowed for fertility preservation and for '[t]ransgender persons prior to starting hormone therapy'.[1589] It is thus recognised in Maltese law that trans patients, read as an umbrella term referring to all trans identities,[1590] may store their gametes so long as this complies with the requirements of the Embryo Protection Act, which provides that nothing in its provisions 'shall be construed or interpreted in a way as to impede, for medical reasons and according to accepted medical norms, the taking and freezing of sperm or egg of a person with the aim of making use of that same sperm or egg at a later stage for the generation of an embryo'.[1591]

1583. Affirmation of Sexual Affirmation, Gender Identity and Gender Expression Act, Ch. 567 of the Laws of Malta, Art. 2. *See also* Part II Ch. 2 §2 above.
1584. Social Security Act, Ch. 318 of the Laws of Malta, Fifth Schedule, Part II [17].
1585. Human Rights Directorate (Malta), *Live it out: Health Services for Trans and Gender Queer Communities* (2021).
1586. Office of the Deputy Prime Minister of Malta – Ministry for Health, *Transgender Healthcare* 15 (2019).
1587. S.L. 524.02, Embryo Protection Authority (Protocol) Regulations, r. 4.17 (not yet in force).
1588. *Ibid.*, r. 14.7 (a).
1589. *Ibid.*, r. 16.1 (d).
1590. *Ibid.*, r. 5.8.
1591. Embryo Protection Act, Ch. 524 of the Laws of Malta, Art. 12 (2). *See also* Part II Ch. 3 §3 above.

Indeed, the Protocol established by the Embryo Protection Authority then notes that 'if a trans person is visiting the clinic after gender reassignment they may be seeking ways to use their preserved tissue, eggs or sperm in treatment with a partner, or extend their storage periods due to premature infertility'.[1592] Tissue establishments are, in turn, bound to ensure that they take account of the particular need of trans patients and 'make appropriate changes to relevant processes and practices to accommodate their needs'[1593] while acting in line with the law, including the laws safeguarding the human embryo.

1592. S.L. 524.02, Embryo Protection Authority (Protocol) Regulations, r. 5.9 (not yet in force).
1593. *Ibid.*, r. 3.6.

Part III. The Physician in Relation to the Healthcare System

289. Part III of the monograph is split into three chapters addressing collegial relationships within the medical profession, the relationship between medical practitioners and other healthcare providers, and the relationship between medical practitioners and healthcare institutions. This follows the standard outline of the International Encyclopaedia for Medical Law, with the exception that the section regarding healthcare centres in Chapter 1 of the standard outline was instead integrated into section 1 of Chapter 3 regarding hospitals.

Chapter 1. Collegial Relationships

§1. Associations

290. The Health Care Professions Act stipulates that a professional association 'means an organization consisting wholly of health care professionals and which fulfils'[1594] conditions for recognition as laid out in the Fourth Schedule of that Act. For the purpose of medical practitioners, those conditions include that the minimum fifteen full members of each association are registered as specialists with the Medical Council and that the association 'follows the guidelines issued from time to time by the European Union of Medical Specialists or the Union of European General Practitioners, as applicable'.[1595] Some examples of the associations of medical practitioners recognised in Malta for the purpose of the Fourth Schedule of the Health Care Professions Act include the Association of Anaesthesiologists of Malta, the Malta College of Family Doctors, the Malta College of Obstetricians and Gynaecologists, the Maltese Association of Psychiatrists, the Maltese Paediatric Association, and the Medical Association of Malta (MAM).

291. Among the conditions so that a professional association can be recognised under the Fourth Schedule of the Health Care Professions Act, there are two conditions that are worthwhile identifying for the purpose of this Part of the monograph regarding medical practitioners in relation to the healthcare system. First, it is a condition for recognition that the association 'actively participates in post-graduate education and continuing professional development'.[1596] The significance of this condition to the medical profession was already, to an extent, addressed earlier when discussing 'training of physicians' in Part I of the monograph.[1597] Indeed, the SAC in Malta will 'issue certificates of completion of specialist training of the specialities listed in the relevant part of the Fifth Schedule [of the Health Care Professions Act], upon the *fulfilment of the criteria recommended by the relevant professional associations listed in the Fourth Schedule*'.[1598] This relates to the role of the professional associations underpinning the training programmes that, upon successful completion as indicated by the pertinent association, lead to the issuance of the certificate of completion of specialist training. In light of this, the SAC, in relation to medical practitioners, includes in its composition one member appointed by each of the relevant professional associations, albeit that the selected member/s of the association/s sitting on the latter Committee cannot also be member/s of the Medical Council during their tenure on the SAC.[1599] Also, the Medical Council's function to levy fees from its registered medical practitioners for initial registration,

1594. Health Care Professions Act, Ch. 464 of the Laws of Malta, Fourth Schedule, Part I [1].
1595. *Ibid.*, Fourth Schedule, Part I [1 (f)].
1596. *See* Part I Ch. 1 above.
1597. Health Care Professions Act, Ch. 464 of the Laws of Malta, Fourth Schedule, Part I [1 (c)].
1598. *Ibid.*, Art. 30 (6)(a)(i). Emphasis added.
1599. *Ibid.*, Art. 30 (2)(d).

as well as yearly retention fees, may be prescribed 'in consultation with those associations representing the majority of medical practitioners ... and any other body which is deemed appropriate by the Council'.[1600]

292. A second condition for recognition of a professional association under the Fourth Schedule of the Health Care Professions Act that is pertinent to this section is that the association is to be 'regulated by a statute which is available to the public in general'.[1601] This statute may then lay out the objectives of the professional association. By way of example, the statute of the MAM stipulates that the 'principle purpose of the MAM shall be to regulate relations between members in the profession and between members and their employers or employers' associations in accordance with the Laws of Malta'.[1602] The MAM is then, in addition to a professional association under the Health Care Professions Act, also a registered trade union[1603] for its members,[1604] and it thus enters into sectoral agreement/s with the Ministry for Health addressing conditions for medical practitioners who work in the public health service. The ancillary objects of the MAM ground its role as a trade union inasmuch as those objects include 'to provide advice and assistance to its members in their mutual relations, in their relations with State or other authorities and organisations whether individual or as a profession'[1605] and 'to provide spokesmen for any member seeking the assistance of the MAM'.[1606] Yet, the ancillary objects of the MAM, as listed in its statute, also stipulate a possible basis for collegial relationships within the medical profession. Indeed, those ancillary objects include uniting 'all members of the medical profession and to safeguard their interests',[1607] promoting the 'ethical, scientific, professional, cultural, social and economic interests of the medical profession',[1608] and strengthening 'the position and unanimity of the medical profession in order to maintain the highest standards of education, ethics and patient care'.[1609] In addition to its role in the context of the sectoral agreement and collegial relationships within the medical profession, the ancillary objects of the MAM moreover relate to the law more broadly by aiming towards securing medical practitioners' 'freedom of practice in the interests of the patient individually and of the community as a whole'.[1610] Inasmuch as this freedom of practice may entail an objective leading towards a tradition of self-regulation that can only occur in Malta subject to and within the limits of the law and MAM's statute also notes that, in fulfilling its objectives, 'the MAM shall be guided by the established sociocultural and ethical principles of the Maltese medical profession'.[1611]

1600. *Ibid.*, Art. 10 (1)(i).
1601. *Ibid.*, Fourth Schedule, Part I [1 (b)].
1602. Medical Association of Malta, *Statute*, Art. 2 (i).
1603. *See also* Employment and Industrial Relations Act, Ch. 452 of the Laws of Malta.
1604. Department of Industrial and Employment Relations (Malta), *List of Trade Unions and Employers' Associations* (2021).
1605. Medical Association of Malta, *Statute*, Art. 2 (ii)(b).
1606. *Ibid.*, Art. 2 (ii)(c).
1607. *Ibid.*, Art. 2 (ii)(a).
1608. *Ibid.*, Art. 2 (ii)(d).
1609. *Ibid.*, Art. 2 (ii)(f).
1610. *Ibid.*, Art. 2 (ii)(e).
1611. *Ibid.*, Art. 2.

§2. Professional Duties Towards Colleagues

293. Professional and ethical standards in the Health Care Professions Act 'includes standards relating to the general conduct of a member of a health care profession, including … the behaviour of such member *towards other members of his profession* and towards members of other health care professions'.[1612] As such, professional duties of medical practitioners towards other medical practitioners, as well as towards members of other healthcare professions,[1613] are *inter alia* part of the professional and ethical standards that are prescribed and maintained by the Medical Council. This has, to an extent, been considered earlier in the monograph, for instance, when addressing the duties of medical practitioners acting in an official capacity when visiting an employee under the instructions of his/her employer.[1614] Be that as it may, the duties of medical practitioners towards other medical practitioners may, in the first instance, be prescribed in the Ethics of the Medical Profession Regulations, and it is indeed those Regulations that, for example, stipulate that no medical practitioner 'shall for the purpose of being engaged by patients or of promoting his own professional advantage … (c) procure or acquiesce in the publication of notices commending or drawing attention to his own professional skill, knowledge, qualifications or services or depreciating those of other practitioners'.[1615] It, in turn, is the Ethics of the Medical Profession Regulations that address at least three situations as to how medical practitioners should engage with patients who are already under the care of another medical practitioner and who may, for instance, be seeking a second opinion.

294. First, if a medical practitioner is consulted in his/her own office, s/he is under no obligation to ask the patient if s/he is under the care of another medical practitioner.[1616] In that case, the medical practitioner can exercise his/her profession, and even if the patient is in fact under the care of another medical practitioner, the medical practitioner consulted at his/her own office owes no particular professional duty towards his/her colleague, all else being equal. Second, in circumstances when a medical practitioner is 'called upon in an emergency to visit a patient who, under ordinary circumstances, would have been attended to by another practitioner, [s/he] shall, after the emergency has been provided for, retire in favour of the ordinary medical attendant'.[1617] There is no particular definition of emergency in the Ethics of the Medical Profession Regulations, but the medical practitioner can only act in the latter circumstances within the confines of and as required to deal with the emergency situation in the patient's interest. Third, barring consultation at the office of the medical practitioner or in the eventuality of an emergency, if a medical practitioner is otherwise requested to attend to a patient who is already under the care of another medical practitioner, s/he is to decline to do so until one

1612. Health Care Professions Act, Ch. 464 of the Laws of Malta, Art. 2. Emphasis added.
1613. *See also* Part III Ch. 2 below.
1614. *See* Part II Ch. 1 §1 above.
1615. S.L. 464.17, Ethics of the Medical Profession Regulations, r. 5 (1)(c). Emphasis added.
1616. *Ibid.*, Sch. A [13 (c)].
1617. *Ibid.*, Sch. A [13 (b)].

of two conditions are fulfilled depending upon whether the medical practitioner caring for the patient agrees or otherwise to the second consultation. In the latter case, the medical practitioner caring for the patient must first be informed, 'preferably in writing, that his services are no longer desired'.[1618] However, the Ethics of the Medical Profession Regulations also stipulate that a 'doctor shall not hesitate to propose or to accept consultation with a professional colleague when, for any reason, this appears to be desirable in the interest of the patient'.[1619] In the case of agreed consultation, the attendance of the consulting practitioner shall cease when the consultation is concluded unless another appointment is arranged by the medical attendant. To be clear, when 'a consultant sees a patient in his rooms at the request of his medical attendant, it is his duty to write to the latter stating his opinion on the case and the mode of treatment which he thinks should be adopted'.[1620] If there then is an irreconcilable difference of opinion between the two medical practitioners, the Ethics of the Medical Practitioners Regulations provide that 'the circumstances should be frankly and impartially explained to the patient or his relatives either by the consultant or by the medical attendant in the presence of the former'.[1621]

295. In addition to the Ethics of the Medical Profession Regulations, Codes of Conduct issued by the Medical Council also indicate medical practitioners' professional duties towards their colleagues. By way of example, the Code of Ethics on Advertising and Financial Conduct by Medical/Dental Practitioners stipulates that any advertising material by medical practitioners should not 'claim superiority to other practitioners in their field or superiority of qualifications, qualities, experience or skill',[1622] while the Regulations on Advertising and the Provision of Information to the Public provides that comparative advertising 'commending or drawing the attention to one's own professional skills, knowledge, qualifications or services, even if not prima facie appearing to depreciate those of others in the same field, is not permissible'.[1623] The Code of Ethics for the Use of Social Media by Doctors and Dentists furthermore provides that care 'must be taken not to resort to harm the reputation of the profession, colleagues or patients in any online posting or communication with patients'.[1624] Medical practitioners' professional duties towards their colleagues may also relate to sources other than the Medical Council. For example, the Code of Ethics in the Statute of the MAM asserts that a medical practitioner shall 'behave towards his colleagues as he would have them behave towards him'[1625] and s/he 'shall not entice patients from his colleagues'.[1626]

1618. *Ibid.*, Sch. A [13 (a)]. *See also* Healthcare Standards Directorate – Ministry for Health, *Charter of Patient's Rights and Responsibilities* 10 (2016).
1619. *Ibid.*, Sch. A [11 (a)].
1620. *Ibid.*, Sch. A [11 (b)].
1621. *Ibid.*, Sch. A [11 (c)].
1622. Medical Council of Malta, *Code of Ethics on Advertising and Financial Conduct by Medical/ Dental Practitioners* 6 (2010).
1623. Medical Council Malta, *Regulations on advertising and the provision of information to the public* 4 (2017). Original emphasis.
1624. Medical Council Malta, *Code of Ethics for the use of social media by doctors and dentists* 7 (2020).
1625. Medical Association of Malta, *Statute*, Appendix 4. The Statute uses the term 'physician'.
1626. *Ibid.*

296. The Statute of the MAM furthermore indicates that a medical practitioner is to 'strive to expose those physicians deficient in character or competence, or who engage in fraud or deception'.[1627] Yet, the manner by which one medical practitioner exposes the behaviour of another medical practitioner can also draw on the professional duties owed by medical practitioners towards their colleagues. It has, for instance, been noted by the Medical Council that looking after colleagues 'is an integral element of professional conduct'.[1628] As such, if a medical practitioner becomes aware that another medical practitioner is behaving inappropriately, including towards a fellow medical practitioner, this should be discreetly drawn to their attention in the first instance. A report or complaint can also be made internally within the structures of the employment framework in which the medical practitioner works.[1629] For instance, a medical practitioner as a public officer in the context of the public health service may be liable to disciplinary proceedings under the Public Service Commission Disciplinary Regulations for misconduct that includes '(a) unprofessional or unethical behaviour; (b) *behaviour disrespectful to colleagues*, superior officers or members of the public; and (c) neglect or dereliction of duty'.[1630] That being said, it is ultimately within the functions of the Medical Council to investigate allegations of professional misconduct or breach of ethics.[1631] In this respect, the Medical Council may also investigate allegations of professional misconduct occasioned by the actions of one medical practitioner that risk negatively affecting the professional integrity of a second medical practitioner. In one such case, a medical practitioner, who was also the chief executive officer (CEO) of a private hospital, suspended another medical practitioner from rendering his services at that hospital due to the excessive professional fees he was charging patients. The document informing the latter medical practitioner of his suspension was however also transmitted to the MAM and to other members of the medical profession. The medical practitioner CEO of the private hospital was even interviewed by Maltese media outlets in relation to this case. The Medical Council found the medical practitioner CEO who gave the interviews and transmitted correspondence to parties other than the pertinent medical practitioner guilty of professional misconduct inasmuch as he ostensibly sought to diminish a medical practitioner's integrity in the medical profession, thereby lessening the quantity of work that would be referred to him.[1632] Although this case was successfully challenged before the domestic courts on the basis that the Medical Council did not conclude the inquiry within the time period stipulated by law,[1633] the point at hand is that, even if it is within the remit of the licensee of licensed healthcare premises to ensure that

1627. *Ibid.*
1628. Medical Council Malta, *Code of Ethics for the use of social media by doctors and dentists* 8 (2020).
1629. *See also* Part I Ch. 4.3 above.
1630. S.L. Const. 03, Public Service Commission Disciplinary Regulations, r. 4 (1). Emphasis added. *See also* Office of the Principal Permanent Secretary – Office of the Prime Minister, *Manual on Disciplinary Procedures in the Public Service* (26 July 2022).
1631. *See* Part I Ch. 4 §4.I above.
1632. Medical Council Malta, Case No. MC/D/262.
1633. *Portelli Dr Frank M.D. FRDC v. Farrugia Dr Josella noe et.*, Civil Court First Hall – 25/04/2014 [Ref: 1110/2009]; *Portelli Dr Frank M.D. FRDC v. Farrugia Dr Josella noe et.*, Court of Appeal (Civil, Superior) – 19/07/2019 [Ref: 1110/2019/1].

excessive fees are not charged within those premises,[1634] the related claim of overcharging without corroborating evidence in circumstances where the CEO of a private hospital was also a practising medical practitioner rendered the matter subject to investigation and appropriate penalty by the Medical Council. This would also be the case in other circumstances of professional misconduct or breach of ethics by one medical practitioner towards another medical practitioner.

297. It is worthwhile noting in this section of the monograph that the profession of dental surgeon is itself regulated by and subject to the special supervision of the Medical Council. In spite of this, a dental surgeon is, all else being equal, not the same as a medical practitioner. Thus, no person 'shall practise as a dental surgeon unless he holds a license for that purpose issued by the President of Malta'[1635] and, in order to qualify for that license, one must *inter alia* have his/her 'name entered in the Register of Dental Surgeons'[1636] held by the Medical Council. The latter Register is different and separate from the Medical Register. It is however possible for a person to fulfil conditions to enter both the Medical Register and the Register of Dental Surgeons, and the Specialist Register held by the Medical Council indeed includes a list on Oral and Maxillo-Facial Surgery that features individuals who, among other qualifications they hold, are qualified as medical practitioners and as dental surgeons. For the purpose of this section of the monograph regarding professional duties towards colleagues, it is noteworthy that the Ethics of the Medical Profession Regulations provide that when 'a practitioner has reason to believe that a patient is suffering from a condition arising from, or in connection with, dental treatment, it is the duty of the practitioner concerned to recommend to the patient to permit him to communicate with a dental practitioner'.[1637] This duty is owed to the patient rather than to the dental surgeon per se. Indeed, if the patient refuses that proposal, 'the practitioner may give such treatment as may be necessary to deal with the emergency condition'.[1638] That being said, and recalling that the term 'practitioner' in the Ethics of the Medical Profession Regulations 'means a medical practitioner or a dental surgeon registered under the[1639] [Health Care Professions] Act', there are circumstances when a medical practitioner bears professional duties towards a dental surgeon. For instance, a medical practitioner may not necessarily indicate the treatment that s/he considers should be given by a dental surgeon inasmuch as this would fall within the professional competence of that dental surgeon rather than within the professional competence of the medical practitioner. Thus, if the patient is not being followed by a dental surgeon, 'it is acceptable, following the specific request of the patient, for the medical practitioner to indicate the name of a dental practitioner *without indicating the treatment which he considers should be given by the dental practitioner*'.[1640] Another duty that may be incumbent on a medical practitioner towards a dental surgeon relates to informing him/her, subject

1634. *See also* General Introduction §2.III above.
1635. Health Care Professions Act, Ch. 464 of the Laws of Malta, Art. 8 (1)
1636. *Ibid.*, Art. 8 (2)(c).
1637. S.L. 464.17, Ethics of the Medical Profession Regulations, r. 26 (1).
1638. *Ibid.*, r. 26 (2).
1639. *Ibid.*, r. 2.
1640. *Ibid.*, r. 26 (4)(a). Emphasis added.

to the patient's permission, of proposed actions and subsequent outcomes. Thus, so long as his/her patient agrees, the medical practitioner may 'communicate with the dental practitioner and if the medical practitioner requires a further medical or dental opinion, a pathological or radiological report from a third party, or a reference to hospital, *he shall inform the dental practitioner concerned of the proposed action and of the subsequent outcome*'.[1641] Furthermore, that medical practitioner 'shall not refer the patient to a second dental practitioner unless he obtains from the patient permission to disclose this fact to the first dental practitioner'.[1642] Likewise, a dental practitioner may have a professional duty to, for instance, 'inform the patient's medical practitioner [if that patient is under medical care] of any proposed operation requiring an anaesthetic'.[1643]

1641. *Ibid.*, r. 26 (4)(b). Emphasis added.
1642. *Ibid.*, r. 26 (3).
1643. *Ibid.*, r. 26 (5).

Chapter 2. Relationship with Other Health Care Providers

§1. PHARMACISTS

298. In accordance with the Health Care Professions Act, '[n]o person shall practise the profession of pharmacist unless he holds a licence for that purpose issued by the President of Malta',[1644] and no person will qualify for that licence to practise as a pharmacist unless his/her name is *inter alia* 'entered in the Register of Pharmacists'[1645] that is kept by the Pharmacy Council. The Health Care Professions Act, duly transposing the list indicated in Article 45 (2) of Directive 2005/36/EC into domestic law, lists the minimum activities that persons registered as pharmacists shall gain access to and pursue subject to the requirement, where appropriate, of supplementary professional experience.[1646] The Pharmacy Council furthermore keeps the Register of Pharmacy Technicians[1647] and the Register of Qualified Persons,[1648] which *inter alia* relates to the licence of a manufacturer of medicinal products inasmuch as the application to grant that licence must include 'the name of at least one qualified person who shall be professionally responsible for the activity'.[1649] The functions of the Pharmacy Council then include prescribing and maintaining 'professional and ethical standards for pharmacists and pharmacy technicians and qualified persons'.[1650] The Code of Ethics for the Pharmaceutical Profession, in turn, 'sets out the principles that are mandatory on registered pharmacists, qualified persons and pharmacy technicians in their professional and personal conduct'.[1651] In relation to the definition of 'pharmacist', which is being addressed in this section of the monograph, the latter Code usefully notes:

> The term 'pharmacist' encompasses, but is not limited to, the following areas of practice: managing pharmacist, community pharmacist, locum pharmacist, clinical pharmacist, hospital pharmacist, pharmacist working in the advertising and marketing of medicinal products including medical representation, responsible pharmacists in wholesale distribution of medicinal products, pharmacists working in industry not including qualified persons, pharmacists practising in regulatory affairs, administration, policy making, academia and in research and development.[1652]

A pharmacist can additionally work over the internet leading the Pharmacy Council to publish a directive aimed at ensuring that pharmacists 'are aware of their

1644. Health Care Professions Act, Ch. 464 of the Laws of Malta, Art. 13 (1).
1645. *Ibid.*, Art. 13 (2)(c).
1646. *Ibid.*, Art. 13 (3).
1647. *Ibid.*, Art. 17.
1648. *Ibid.*, Art. 18A.
1649. Medicines Act, Ch. 458 of the Laws of Malta, Art. 38 (1)(e).
1650. Health Care Professions Act, Ch. 464 of the Laws of Malta, Art. 16 (1)(d).
1651. Pharmacy Council, *Code of Ethics for the Pharmaceutical Profession* 1 (2008).
1652. *Ibid.*, 2.

responsibilities to ensure that online digital activity is consistent with their professional role'.[1653] Given their varied areas of practice, the relationship between medical practitioners and pharmacists will then depend in part on the area of practice of the pharmacist at hand.

299. To be clear, a medical practitioner cannot hold a licence to open or keep a pharmacy, and it shall not be lawful for any medical practitioner 'to enter into any agreement with any pharmacist or any other person for any share in the profits of a pharmacy, or to have any direct or indirect interest of whatever nature in any pharmacy'.[1654] This then separates the role of parties who are authorised to issue prescriptions in terms of Maltese law, including medical practitioners, from those preparing and dispensing medicinal products that normally fall within the remit of a pharmacist.

300. The general rule thus is that, unless otherwise provided by or under the Medicines Act, 'a medicinal product shall only be prepared or dispensed from a pharmacy or by a pharmacist'.[1655] There are exceptions provided at law to this rule that engage both with the location where a medicinal product may be prepared or dispensed[1656] and who can prepare and dispense that medicinal product, which may then also cover medical practitioners. By way of example, the Provision of Medicinal Products through the Genito Urinary Clinic within the Government Health Services Rules includes in its Schedule a list of medicinal products that are to be provided by the consultant who is responsible for the clinic to patients attending or who have been referred to that clinic. In this respect, that consultant is to 'keep an updated, written and agreed procedure with the hospital pharmacy supplying the medicinal products'.[1657] Also, free samples of medicinal products can lawfully be provided on an exceptional basis to persons qualified to prescribe them, which includes medical practitioners.[1658] Moreover, a medical practitioner may furnish a starter pack that means:

> [S]mall packs for which a marketing authorisation has been granted, designed to provide sufficient medicine for a prescriber to initiate treatment in such circumstances where there might be undesirable or unavoidable delay in having

1653. Pharmacy Council, *Directive for Digital Activity* 1 (June 2020).
1654. S.L. 458.16, Pharmacy Licence Regulations, r. 3 (2).
1655. Medicines Act, Ch. 458 of the Laws of Malta, Art. 76 (1).
1656. *See, for instance*: S.L. 458.45, Authorisation of Dispensing of Medicinal Gases from Premises other than a Pharmacy Rules; S.L. 458.52, Dispensing of Medicinal Products (Foundation for Social Welfare Services) Rules; S.L. 458.56, Authorisation for Dispensing and Delivery to Patients of Parenteral Nutrition Solutions and Ambulatory Dialysis Solutions from Premises other than a Pharmacy Rules; S.L. 458.62, Authorisation for Preparation and Dispensing of Medicinal Products by Automated Means from Designated Premises at Central Procurement and Supplies Unit (CPSU) Rules.
1657. S.L. 458.55, Provision of Medicinal Products through the Genito Urinary Clinic within the Government Health Services Rules, r. 4 (h).
1658. S.L. 458.32, Medicinal Products (Advertising) Regulations, r. 11.

a prescription dispensed, where immediate commencement of treatment is necessary, or where the prescriber feels that the use of such presentation is indicated in the interests of the patient.[1659]

Also, the administration by or under the direct personal supervision of a medical practitioner of a drug covered by the Internal Control of Dangerous Drugs Rules 'shall not be deemed to be supplying the drug within the meaning of these Rules'.[1660]

301. A pharmacist is to typically prepare or dispense any medicinal product against the presentation of a prescription made by, for instance, a medical practitioner[1661] so long as the prescription has not surpassed the time frame of its validity as set in law.[1662] Verbal instructions by a medical practitioner over the telephone may be accepted, except in respect of narcotic or psychotropic substances,[1663] if the pharmacist is satisfied that the instructions are being furnished by a person authorised to prescribe in terms of the Medicines Act who 'by reason of an emergency is unable to furnish a prescription immediately'[1664] and that the prescriber undertakes to furnish the pharmacist with a prescription that otherwise complies with law within 48 hours of the verbal instruction. That being said, unless the Medicines Authority deems that a medicinal product does not require a medicinal prescription[1665] entailing that the dispensing pharmacist will assume full responsibility for dispensing that product,[1666] it shall not otherwise be lawful for a pharmacist to dispense any medicinal product except on the prescription of a person authorised to prescribe under the Medicines Act, including a medical practitioner.[1667] This includes, in line with the requirements of Directive 2011/24/EU,[1668] prescriptions made by medical practitioners in another EU Member State provided that the pharmacist can ascertain that the medical practitioner in question 'is licensed to practice his profession in the member state of origin'.[1669] Yet, unless the prescribing medical practitioner requests a particular branded product by writing 'branded' or '®' on the prescription, the pharmacist 'can dispense the medicinal product prescribed *or an equivalent medicinal product* having the same chemical entity, dose, dosage form

1659. *Ibid.*, r. 2.
1660. S.L. 101.02, Internal Control of Dangerous Drugs Rules, r. 5.
1661. *See, for instance*: Medicines Act, Ch. 458 of the Laws of Malta, Art. 80 (1); S.L. 458.24, Prescription Forms for Free Medicinals Rules, r. 4; Drug Dependence (Treatment not Imprisonment) Act, Ch. 537 of the Laws of Malta, Art. 10 (5).
1662. S.L. 458.49, Prescription and Dispensing Requirement Rules, r. 4.
1663. *See, for instance*: S.L. 31.18, Drugs (Control) Regulations, r. 8; S.L. 101.02, Internal Control of Dangerous Drugs, r. 7; S.L. 101.06, Methadone Rules, r. 7.
1664. S.L. 458.49, Prescription and Dispensing Requirement Rules, r. 4 (3)(a).
1665. S.L. 458.34, Medicines (Marketing Authorisation) Regulations, r. 27.
1666. Medicines Act, Ch. 458 of the Laws of Malta, Art. 80 (4).
1667. *Ibid.*, Art. 81 (1).
1668. Directive 2011/24/EU of the European Parliament and of the Council of 9 March 2011 on the application of patients' rights in cross-border healthcare, OJ L 88, 4.4.2011, Art. 11. *See also* S.L. 528.03, Cross-Border Healthcare Regulations, r. 7 (1)(d)(ix).
1669. Medicines Act, Ch. 458 of the Laws of Malta, Art. 81 (3).

and dosage frequency as the medicinal product indicated on the prescription'.[1670] The Medicines Act also stipulates that a pharmacist is not bound to dispense a medicinal product if s/he 'has a justified reason of concern that the prescription is false, that the person is misusing the prescribed medicinal product, or that the medicinal product is not available or if he has professional reasons for not preparing or dispensing the prescription'.[1671] In those cases or when the dosage regime indicated on the prescription goes beyond what can be considered a safe and therapeutic dose, 'the pharmacist is bound to draw the attention thereto of the person prescribing the same and may require such person to write out in ink or in other indelible manner on the prescription a statement assuming responsibility for the prescription'.[1672] Even so, the Code of Ethics for the Pharmaceutical Profession provides that members of the pharmaceutical profession 'have no obligation to offer or provide a professional service in ways which conflict with their own personal, moral or religious beliefs'[1673] and furthermore that members of that profession 'must preserve their professional autonomy and exercise professional judgement in the interests of patients and society, within the parameters of their responsibilities, after taking into account all the relevant circumstances'.[1674]

302. Subject to observance of pertinent law and/or guidelines, a pharmacist may however prepare and dispense medicinal products in different forms. Thus, a magistral formula means 'any medicinal product prepared in a pharmacy in accordance with a medical prescription for an individual patient',[1675] and an officinal formula means 'any medicinal product which is prepared in a pharmacy in accordance with the prescriptions of a pharmacopoeia and is intended to be supplied directly to the patients served by such pharmacy'.[1676] The Medicines Act provides that the 'preparation of magistral and officinal formulas, and the division of authorised packs into smaller units, reconstitution, dispensing and administration of medicinal products and any other activity related to medicinal products and their use shall be in accordance with such standards as may be established under this Act'.[1677] The Pharmaceutical Unit, which falls under the Department for Health Regulation, furthermore has guidelines in respect of the supply of medicinal products through processes that are not covered by the Medicines Act, subsidiary legislation arising there from or other relevant laws such as the regulation of clinical trials. These guidelines provide that a request for the latter type of unlicensed medicinal product must be made by a medical practitioner or dentist registered in Malta on one of the pertinent forms made available by the Pharmaceutical Unit that must *inter alia* 'indicate the hospital/clinic or community pharmacy from which it will be supplied and the pharmacist responsible for the supply, preparation (if required) and dispensing to the

1670. *Ibid.*, Art. 80 (2). Emphasis added.
1671. *Ibid.*, Art. 80 (1).
1672. *Ibid.*, Art. 80 (3).
1673. Pharmacy Council, *Code of Ethics for the Pharmaceutical Profession* 1 (2008).
1674. *Ibid.*, 3.
1675. Medicines Act, Ch. 458 of the Laws of Malta, Art. 2.
1676. *Ibid.*
1677. *Ibid.*, Art. 87.

patient'.[1678] The form is to be submitted via the Pharmaceutical Unit to the Superintendent of Public Health, who, if appropriate, 'authorizes the doctor to prescribe and the wholesale dealer and pharmacist to supply the requested unlicensed product as approved'.[1679] Clinical responsibility for this type of prescription rests with the prescriber, but the dispensing pharmacist must ensure that 'the prescriber is fully aware of the unlicensed status of the product'.[1680]

§2. Nurses and Midwives

303. The Health Care Professions Act establishes that nurses and midwives fall under the special supervision of and are regulated by the Council for Nurses and Midwives. It is also the case that nurses and midwives are among two of the professions employed within the public health service that are represented by the Malta Union of Midwives and Nurses, acting as a trade union. That being said, nurses and midwives are two related but not identical professions in Malta.[1681]

304. Indeed, no person is to practice the midwifery profession 'unless he holds a licence for that purpose issued by the President of Malta'[1682] and, in order to obtain that licence, one must *inter alia* be listed in the Register of Midwives that is kept by the Council for Nurses and Midwives. Yet, the Health Care Professions Act provides that no person shall practise the nursing profession unless his/her name 'is entered in any part of the Register of Nurses'[1683] that is kept by the Council for Nurses and Midwives. Part I of the latter Register regards first level registered nurses, which *inter alia* relates to the professional activities of nurses responsible for general care. Part II of the Register of Nurses lists second-level registered nurses who may not practise their profession 'unless under the supervision of a first level registered nurse or, in the absence of a first level registered nurse, under the direction of a medical practitioner'.[1684] The Register of Nurses also consists of 'Special Parts in respect of nurses trained in the different special areas recognized by the Council for Nurses and Midwives'.[1685] This ostensibly relates to subsidiary legislation originally arising from the Medical and Kindred Professions Ordinance and presently grounded under the Medicines Act that, while referring to the register of nurses trained in adult nursing, also refers to nurses for the mentally sick, nurses for

1678. Pharmaceutical Unit – Superintendence of Public Health (Malta), *Guidelines for the supply of medicinal products for human use through processes which are not covered by the Medicines Act, 2003 and its subsidiary legislation (unlicensed medicinal products)* 3 (DH Circular 270/06 – September 2006). Original parentheses.

1679. *Ibid.*, 4. The term 'doctor' here refers to a medical practitioner.

1680. *Ibid.*, 5.

1681. *See, for instance*: the following that are still formally part of the statute book: S.L. 458.13, Training School for Midwives Regulations; S.L. 458.20, Training School for Registered Nurses Regulations; S.L. 458.21, Training School for Enrolled Nurses Regulations.

1682. Health Care Professions Act, Ch. 464 of the Laws of Malta, Art. 19 (1). *See also* S.L. 458.04, Midwives Regulations, r. 2.

1683. *Ibid.*, Art. 20 (1)(c).

1684. *Ibid.*, Art. 20 (2)(a).

1685. *Ibid.*, Art. 24 (1)(c).

the mentally handicapped, and nurses for sick children.[1686] The Health Care Professions Act then specifies that it 'shall not be lawful for a person whose name is entered in a special part, but not in Part I of the Register of Nurses, to practise the nursing profession except in the special area in respect of which he is registered or as a second level registered nurse outside the special area in respect of which he is registered'.[1687] A licence to practice the profession of a nurse is, in turn, granted by the President of Malta on the recommendation of the Council for Nurses and Midwives to those first-level nurses and nurses in the Special Part of the Register who hold a degree in nursing granted by the University of Malta or an equivalent nursing qualification obtained from a university, college or nursing school recognised by the Council for Nurses and Midwives, and who have been registered with the latter Council for a minimum period of 2 years and 'have been practising their profession of nurse on a full-time basis for two years or their equivalent'.[1688] If a first-level nurse or a nurse in the Special Part of the Register does not fulfil these criteria but is in possession of a diploma in nursing granted by the University of Malta or an equivalent nursing qualification obtained from a university, college or nursing school recognised by the Council for Nurses and Midwives, 'the licence shall only be granted after five years from their registration with the Council and after practising the profession of nurse on a full-time basis for five years or their equivalent'.[1689]

305. In light of these professional qualifications, a nurse and/or a midwife can, in some circumstances, lawfully exercise professional services rendered by a medical practitioner. To be clear, the general rule is that no medical practitioner is to 'enable an unqualified person to exercise his profession, attend in any manner to any matter requiring professional knowledge and skill, issue or procure the issue of any professional document or otherwise act as if he were duly qualified or registered'.[1690] However, this general rule 'shall not apply when the practitioner is supervising over any person so employed and retains personal responsibility for the professional services rendered in the case of: … (b) the legitimate employment of nurses, midwives, physiotherapists and other persons trained to perform specialised functions relevant to different professions'.[1691] This does not however mean that a nurse or midwife must blindly follow any instruction furnished by a medical practitioner, even if the latter practitioner retains personal responsibility for the professional services rendered. It was thus noted in a judgment concerning the civil liability of healthcare professionals that nurses have independent obligations towards patients, including the obligation not to harm their patients,[1692] which means that nurses cannot exculpate themselves from liability solely on the basis that

1686. S.L. 458.17, Register and Roll of Nurses (Special Parts) Regulations.
1687. Health Care Professions Act, Ch. 464 of the Laws of Malta, Art. 20 (2)(b).
1688. S.L. 464.15, Nurses Profession (Licence to Practise) Regulations, r. 4 (1)(c).
1689. *Ibid.*, r. 4 (2).
1690. S.L. 464.17, Ethics of the Medical Profession Regulations, r. 18 (1).
1691. *Ibid.*, r. 18 (2)(b).
1692. *Maggur Briffa Alfred et. v. The Golden Shepherd Group Limited noe et.*, Civil Court First Hall – 31/10/2013 [Ref: 2651/2000/1] 37–38.

they follow the instructions furnished by medical practitioners.[1693] In this respect and provided that the criteria for liability are established, it is possible for a nurse to be held liable in circumstances when s/he follows the instructions of a medical practitioner, even if it is the latter practitioner who, for instance, prescribes the medication that is administered to the patient by the nurse that occasions damages to the patient.[1694] Instead, as noted in the tentative job descriptions of a staff nurse and of a midwife, while they should collaborate with directions of other professionals, those nurses and midwives should also 'have the ability to challenge decisions made by others if they are against policy or not in the best interest of the client'.[1695]

306. The relationship between medical practitioners and nurses or midwives will then also depend on the specific profession in view of the competencies of the professional at hand, establishing which activities s/he is responsible for and/or when and how to liaise with medical practitioners. The professional activities of a midwife are covered in part by Article 42 (2) of Directive 2005/36/EC, which has been transposed into Maltese law via the Health Care Professions Act, and include 'carrying out treatment prescribed by doctors'[1696] as well as 'recognising the warning signs of abnormality in the mother or infant which necessitate referral to a doctor and assisting the latter where appropriate'.[1697] The midwife is to furthermore take 'the necessary emergency measures in the doctor's absence, in particular the manual removal of the placenta, possibly followed by manual examination of the uterus'.[1698] The Midwives Regulations, though not regularly engaged with, are also still formally part of the body of law grounding the professional relationship between midwives and medical practitioners. These Regulations, which were promulgated in the early 1950s under laws then in force, thus stipulate that in cases where a medical practitioner has been called, the midwife is to 'await his arrival and faithfully carry out his instructions'.[1699] Situations listed in the Midwives Regulations when a midwife is to immediately call a medical practitioner include cases where the child is born but is in danger of death[1700] and in a situation when the foetus is born apparently dead, in which case, in addition to calling a medical practitioner, the midwife is to 'persevere in the treatment till his arrival or for not less than an hour after the child has ceased to give any signs of life'.[1701] Circumstances included in the Midwives Regulations in which a midwife is to insist on calling a medical practitioner include instances when the child develops any irritation or redness of the eyes, and in case the parents refuse to call a medical practitioner, then

1693. *See also* Part I Ch. 4 §4.II above.

1694. *See, for instance*: *Cassar Emanuel v. Tabib Principal tal-Gvern et.*, Civil Court First Hall – 01/03/2022 [Ref: 1032/2017].

1695. Nursing Services Directorate Malta, *Job Description: Staff Nurse (SN)* 3 (2021); Nursing Services Directorate Malta, *Job Description: Midwife* 6 (2021).

1696. Health Care Professions Act, Ch. 464 of the Laws of Malta, Art. 23 (5)(j). The term 'doctor' in this provision refers to a medical practitioner.

1697. *Ibid.*, Art. 23 (5)(g).

1698. *Ibid.*

1699. S.L. 458.04, Midwives Regulations, r. 10.

1700. *Ibid.*, r. 16.

1701. *Ibid.*, r. 14.

the midwife is to inform 'the medical officer of health ... and meanwhile the washing of the eyes should be frequently repeated'.[1702] The Midwives Regulations furthermore provide for instances when the midwife cannot act, attend or continue to attend except under the direction of a medical practitioner, including in respect of vaginal irrigations,[1703] possession of any oxytoxic drugs or giving injections or drugs except a simple asperient,[1704] and in 'all cases of illness of the patient or of the child, or of any abnormality occurring during pregnancy, labour or lying-in'.[1705] This includes circumstances such as abortion, whether actual or threatened, as well as multiple pregnancy.

307. Moreover, the Council for Nurses and Midwives has the function 'to prescribe and maintain professional and ethical standards for the nursing and midwifery professions'.[1706] Thus, in addition to statutory law, the 'Code of Ethics and Standards of Professional Conduct for Nurses and Midwives' together with the 'Midwives Code of Practice' issued by the Council for Nurses and Midwives, also provide for the professional relationship between midwives and medical practitioners. The latter Code indeed provides that in 'an emergency, or where a deviation from the norm, which is outside her current sphere of practice, becomes apparent in the mother or baby during the antenatal, intranatal and postnatal periods a practising midwife shall call a registered medical practitioner who may reasonably be expected to assist her'.[1707] The Midwives Code of Practice furthermore indicates that in circumstances when a midwife is attending a home birth, 'the midwife should find out whether or not a registered medical practitioner [who will normally be an obstetrician] is available for referral, to attend or to be on call if required'.[1708] That being said, the Health Care Professions Act also, in principle, stipulates 'the specialities in respect of which the Specialist Accreditation Committee for midwives shall issue certificates of completion of specialist training',[1709] which include: neonatal, obstetrics, perinatal mental health, primary and community care, public health and reproductive health.

308. The Health Care Professions Act furthermore, in principle, lists the 'specialities in respect of which the Specialist Accreditation Committee for nurses shall issue certificates of completion of specialist training',[1710] which includes, among others: geriatrics, paediatrics, oncology and psychiatry. That being said, the Minimum Training Conditions (Health Care Professions) Regulations, duly transposing

---

1702. *Ibid.*, r. 15.
1703. *Ibid.*, r. 6.
1704. *Ibid.*, r. 7. *See also* r. 22, and: Council for Nurses and Midwives, *Midwives Code of Practice* 6 (2005).
1705. *Ibid.*, r. 18.
1706. Health Care Professions Act, Ch. 464 of the Laws of Malta, Art. 22 (1)(d).
1707. Council for Nurses and Midwives Malta, *Midwives Code of Practice* 4 (2005).
1708. *Ibid.*, 7.
1709. Health Care Professions Act, Ch. 464 of the Laws of Malta, Fifth Schedule, Part D.
1710. *Ibid*, Fifth Schedule, Part C.

Article 31 (3) of Directive 2005/36/EC into domestic law, lists the minimum competencies that the formal qualification as a nurse responsible for general care provide evidence of for the purpose of the professional who obtained that qualification. These competencies include the 'competence to comprehensively communicate professionally and to cooperate with members of other professions in the health sector'[1711] and the 'competence to work effectively with other actors in the health sector'.[1712] In turn, the Council for Nurses and Midwives non-exhaustively recommends the basic competencies that a nurse is expected to be capable of performing, the acts that are only to be performed pursuant to an order by a third party who is authorised by law to perform or to order that act, and the acts that nurses themselves can determine are required and can carry out but which does not exclude the possibility of a third party ordering that act. In the latter case, which can involve instructions from a medical practitioner, 'nurses may make the decision to initiate the act, within the parameters of the order, and they are competent to perform it independently'.[1713] This can include administration, but not necessarily prescription, of intravenous drugs. That notwithstanding, a nurse 'must be aware and honour the fact that he or she is fully accountable for all aspects of her or his professional practice'[1714] while acknowledging that nurses (and midwives) 'should accept and value the diversity of co-workers and acknowledge the need for non-discriminatory interpersonal and interprofessional relationships'.[1715]

309. Statutory law itself distinguishes instances when the presence of a medical practitioner is required from instances when the presence of a nurse or of a midwife is required. By way of example, the Licensing of Private Medical Clinics Regulations establishes duties incumbent on the licensees of private clinics, which 'includes a private hospital and a day care medical clinic, but does not include a medical practitioner's consulting room'.[1716] Those duties include the number and type of nurses required to ensure proper care of the patients in the clinic[1717] and, while it is also the duty of the licensee to ensure that there is resident medical coverage when in-patients are receiving treatment at the clinic, the Licensing of Private Medical Clinics Regulations lists the surgical operations carried out at that clinic where 'the presence of a registered nurse shall be sufficient'.[1718] The Licensing of Private Medical Clinics Regulations furthermore provide that the person in charge of the clinic, who must be either 'a medical practitioner or a registered nurse',[1719] must 'make certain that adequate general and specialist medical cover is provided

---

1711. S.L. 451.04, Minimum Training Conditions (Health Care Professions) Regulations, r. 3 (7)(g).
1712. *Ibid.*, r. 3 (7)(b).
1713. Council for Nurses and Midwives Malta, *The Scope of Professional Practice 2002*, 6 (Updated in 2018).
1714. *Ibid.*, 9.
1715. Council for Nurses and Midwives Malta, *Code of Ethics and Standards of Professional Conduct for Nurses and Midwives* 16 (2020).
1716. S.L. 458.23, Licensing of Private Medical Clinics Regulations, r. 2.
1717. *Ibid.*, r. 9.
1718. *Ibid.*, r. 8.
1719. *Ibid.*, r. 7 (2)(a).

as needed'[1720] wherever antenatal, intranatal or postnatal care is given at the clinic. The person in charge may also be a 'registered midwife',[1721] but only in respect of midwifery services and, in any case, 'a practising midwife shall be present on duty at all times maternity care is provided'.[1722]

§3. Paramedical Professionals

310. The term 'paramedical professionals', which is used in the standard outline of the International Encyclopaedia for Medical Law, is not defined in Maltese law. It is therefore a term that is sparsely used in Malta, restricted to brief reference in relation to the prison medical service,[1723] to sports law,[1724] and to an instance when EU law was transposed verbatim into domestic law.[1725] The Health Care Professions Act engages instead with the professions complementary to medicine. It is thus provided that '[n]o person shall practise any of the professions complementary to medicine unless his name is entered in the respective register kept by the Council for Professions Complementary to Medicine'[1726] in accordance with the provisions of the Health Care Professions Act and a 'licence shall be granted by the President of Malta to those persons whose name is entered in one of the registers held by the Council [for Professions Complementary to Medicine] and on the recommendation of [that] Council'.[1727] The professions complementary to medicine then include acupuncture, audiologists, dietetics, physiotherapy, dental hygiene, chiropractic, nutrition, optometry, orthoptics, osteopathy, speech language pathology, clinical perfusion, podiatry, radiography, environmental health, dental technology, occupational therapy, medical laboratory science, medical physicists, and nutritional therapists.[1728] In addition to medical practitioners, dental surgeons, midwives, nurses, pharmacy technicians and pharmacists, it is the persons authorised to practice one of the professions complementary to medicine that are typically, unless otherwise provided at law, referred to as healthcare professionals in Malta. An example of an instance when Maltese law extends the definition of healthcare professional can be drawn from the Mental Health Act, which provides that a healthcare professional in that Act 'means a professional registered with the relevant Council under the Health Care Professions Act *or under any other Act regulating the professions of social work and, or psychology*'.[1729] Professions involved in healthcare that are not regulated under the Health Care Professions Act include social workers, counsellors,

1720. *Ibid.*, r. 10 (2)(a).
1721. *Ibid.*, r. 10 (1).
1722. *Ibid.*
1723. S.L. 260.03, Prisons Regulations, r. 31 (5).
1724. *See, for instance*: S.L. 455.13, Anti-doping Regulations, r. 2; Prevention of Corruption in Sport Act, Ch. 593 of the Laws of Malta, Art. 2; Sports Governance and Integrity Act, Ch. 626 of the Laws of Malta, Art. 2.
1725. S.L. 451.03, Recognition of Professional Qualifications Regulations.
1726. Health Care Professions Act, Ch. 464 of the Laws of Malta, Art. 25 (1).
1727. S.L. 464.16, Professions Complementary to Medicine Regulations, r. 3.
1728. Health Care Professions Act, Ch. 464 of the Laws of Malta, Third Schedule.
1729. Mental Health Act, Ch. 525 of the Laws of Malta, Art. 2. Emphasis added.

psychologists and psychotherapists.[1730] That being said, the Allied Health Care Services Directorate within the Ministry for Health, which addresses the public health service, denotes allied health professionals that are not restricted to persons regulated in terms of the Health Care Professions Act, extending instead to *inter alia* include psychologists and social workers.

311. Maltese law is increasingly engaging with the concept of multidisciplinary teams in healthcare, which are composed of individuals from different healthcare and other professions, each addressing the treatment and care of patients within their remit and competence. That being said, the relationship between medical practitioners and any one of the professions complementary to medicine, as well as the other professions related to healthcare but that are not regulated under the Health Care Professions Act, will depend on which individual profession is involved in that relationship. In respect of the professions complementary to medicine, it is the 'duty of such persons who have been issued a licence, or who have been registered to have a licence issued to them under [the Professions Complementary to Medicine Regulations], to abide by the conditions and to satisfy the requirements laid down by the Code of Practice for their profession'.[1731] These Codes can then address the relationship with medical practitioners, albeit with nuanced or even stark differences between the different Codes depending on the profession to which the particular Code relates. By way of example, it is acknowledged that optometrists 'examine the eyes and the associated visual system to detect the presence of any abnormality or disease which may require referral to a medical practitioner'[1732] and, indeed, the Code of Practice of Optometry indicates that, unless the optometrist is of the opinion that the condition does not merit medical investigation, 'the patient and a letter of referral must be sent to a registered medical practitioner'.[1733] By comparison, the Code of Practice of Physiotherapists stipulates that they 'should communicate effectively with registered medical practitioners, other health professionals and relevant outside agencies to provide effective and efficient service to the patient'.[1734] There then is a little formal restriction to the practice of physiotherapy based on referral by or to a medical practitioner, and while a physiotherapist is to cooperate with medical practitioners in the diagnosis and management of patients, it is noted in the Code of Professional and Ethical Conduct for the Professions Complementary to Medicine that this 'rule is not intended to restrict physiotherapists from practising their profession independently from a referral by any medical practitioner'.[1735]

1730. *See also* General Introduction §2.II above.
1731. S.L. 464.16, Professions Complementary to Medicine Regulations, r. 5.
1732. Council for the Professions Complementary to Medicine Malta, *Benchmarking Document: Optometry* 2 (2021).
1733. Council for the Professions Complementary to Medicine Malta, *Code of Practice: Optometry* 4 (2020).
1734. Council for the Professions Complementary to Medicine Malta, *Code of Practice: Physiotherapy* 3 (2020).
1735. Council for the Professions Complementary to Medicine Malta, *A Code of Professional and Ethical Conduct for the Professions Complementary to Medicine* 93 (2019).

312. A question that can arise regards the extent to which a member of the professions complementary to medicine can alter the treatment recommended by a referring medical practitioner. This has been discussed by the inquiring board of the pertinent regulatory body in relation to physiotherapists, finding that a physiotherapist is entitled to recommend treatment different to the treatment recommended by the referring medical practitioner 'given that a physiotherapist may, after assessing a patient, come to a conclusion as to the cause of a patient's symptoms and perform appropriate physiotherapy'.[1736] The physiotherapist must however communicate with the medical practitioner 'as liaison with the referrer in the diagnosis and management of patients is paramount',[1737] and the minimum expected would be a note informing the medical practitioner that the recommended treatment is being changed. It is also the case that a physiotherapist 'is bound and has the right to decline to carry out any treatment that his/her professional training and expertise suggests is actively harmful to the patient',[1738] and it has then been noted, in the context of palliative treatment, that if 'it is clear that the request for treatment is not appropriate or cannot be justified in the circumstances, the referring medical practitioner is to be approached and the responsibilities of the therapist explained'.[1739] That being said, so long as the conditions for pursuing a given regulated healthcare profession have not been harmonised under EU law, it is tenable for the Maltese domestic authorities to mandate particular healthcare professionals to pursue their profession subject to collaboration with, for instance, a medical practitioner or a dental surgeon provided that this is itself in line with the obligations undertaken by Malta under the EU Treaties. This is the case, for example, in relation to dental technologists who are not authorised to work in Malta in direct contact with patients other than through a dental surgeon.[1740]

1736. Board for the Professions Supplementary to Medicine, *Report of Board of Inquiry in respect of Mr Pierre Caruana Senior Physiotherapist* (30/12/2002). *See also*: *Caruana Pierre v. Bord tal-Professjonijiet Supplimentari tal-Medicina*, Court of Appeal (Civil, Superior) – 14/02/2006 [Ref: 6/2003/2].

1737. *Ibid.*

1738. Council for the Professions Complementary to Medicine Malta, *A Code of Professional and Ethical Conduct for the Professions Complementary to Medicine* 95 (2019).

1739. *Ibid.*, 95–96.

1740. *See, for instance*: C-125/16, *Malta Dental Technologists Association and Others v. Superintendent tas-Sahha Pubblika, Kunsill tal-Professjonijiet Kumplimentari ghall-Medicina*, EU:C:2017:707; *Malta Dental Technologists Association et. v. Superintendent tas-Sahha Pubblika et.*, Civil Court First Hall – 31/05/2022 [Ref: 424/2012].

Chapter 3. Relationship with Health Care Institutions

§1. Hospitals

313. The Licensing Authority in Malta distinguishes between public hospitals, rehabilitation hospitals, and private hospitals. The latter licensed hospitals would not, unless otherwise stipulated, be part of the public health service, whereas the other two types of hospitals can fall within the public health service. That being said, the 'Maltese government entered into a public-private partnership to transfer responsibility for the development and management of three public hospitals [which includes one rehabilitation hospital within the public health service] to a private contractor'.[1741] In this case, while those three hospitals in practice remain part of the public health service in that health services remain free at point of use subject to entitlement criteria and all 'Government workers in the three hospitals will remain Government employees',[1742] management is otherwise transferred to a private contractor: Steward Health Care. Also, to be clear, there are establishments within the public health service in Malta that, while using the name 'hospital', presently hold other licenses. Thus, Mount Carmel Hospital is a mental health licensed facility, and Sir Paul Boffa Hospital is licensed as a Long-term Care facility. Furthermore, Sir Anthony Mamo Oncology Centre, although licensed as an Oncology centre, is physically located within the footprint of and connected to Mater Dei (public) hospital, whereas health centres spread across Malta and Gozo furnish primary healthcare services within the public health service but are separate from hospitals.

314. There are, of course, laws and obligations that are incumbent on or relate to medical practitioners vis-à-vis hospitals regardless of the type of licensed hospitals with which they are or were affiliated. By way of example, the Ethics of the Medical Profession Regulations stipulate that the signs exhibited in connection with a practice should not exceed what is reasonably necessary to those who are seeking it, which also entails that 'the names of hospitals where one has studied or held appointments shall not appear on a nameplate'.[1743] This is significant inasmuch as it is medical practitioners who are ultimately 'responsible for all signs, plates and notices which are directly or indirectly related with [their] practice and which are situated in the public part of the pharmacy or premises'.[1744] Moreover, a medical practitioner 'may not accept a commission for the introduction of a patient or a client to a consultant, to a private hospital or other institution, or to a medical practitioner, or to a dental surgeon or dentist, to a veterinary surgeon, apothecary, nurse, midwife or any other person or company'.[1745] The Prevention of Sharp Injuries in

1741. OECD/European Observatory on Health Systems and Policies, *Malta: Country Health Profile 2021, State of Health in the EU* 8 (OECD Publishing 2021).
1742. Natasha Azzopardi-Muscat, Stefan Buttigieg, Neville Calleja & Sherry Merkur, *Malta – Health system review*, 19 (1) Health Systems in Transition 1, 97 (2017).
1743. S.L. 464.17, Ethics of the Medical Profession Regulations, r. 8 (7).
1744. *Ibid.*, r. 8 (10).
1745. *Ibid.*, r. 21 (2).

Hospitals and Health Care Establishments Order is likewise applicable 'to all workers in the hospital and healthcare sector, and all who are under the managerial authority and supervision of an employer'.[1746] The breadth of the latter Order is necessary since its purpose is to achieve:

> [T]he safest possible working environment for health care workers by preventing injuries caused by medical sharps, including needle-stick injuries, protecting all workers at risk through the establishment of policies in risk assessment, risk prevention, training, information, awareness raising and monitoring and putting in place response and follow up procedures.[1747]

There thus are duties on the employer, which include promoting 'a no blame culture focusing incident reporting procedures on systematic factors rather than individual mistakes'[1748] as well as duties on the workers that include making 'use of the resources supplied by the employer to minimise the risk of occupationally acquired injuries or infections'.[1749]

315. That being said, it is also the case that the relationship between medical practitioners and hospitals can be affected depending upon whether the hospital at hand falls within the public health service or is otherwise a private hospital. It has thus already been considered throughout this monograph how, in addition to any other medical law, the rights and obligations of medical practitioners in relation to the public health service are also embedded in laws pertinent to public service and/or otherwise arise from agreements made by or for medical practitioners.[1750] Inasmuch as 'Government health-sector employees are civil servants',[1751] the People Management Division within the Ministry for Health is largely responsible for the human resources strategies in relation to medical personnel, while the Department for Healthcare Services advises upon the allocation of those human resources 'between public health service providers',[1752] though the actual duties of individual medical practitioners are addressed at the micro-level within the individual hospital/s. Medical practitioners working as public officers within hospitals in the public health service are also subject to the exercise of disciplinary control under the public service.[1753] This covers those public officers performing duties at the hospitals under the public-private partnership agreement entered into between the Government of Malta and Steward Health Care. The Prime Minister of Malta has, however,

1746. S.L. 465.11, Prevention of Sharp Injuries in Hospitals and Health Care Establishments Order, r. 4.
1747. *Ibid.*, r. 3.
1748. *Ibid.*, r. 5 (e).
1749. *Ibid.*, r. 6 (c).
1750. *See* Part III Ch. 1 §1 above.
1751. Natasha Azzopardi-Muscat, Stefan Buttigieg, Neville Calleja & Sherry Merkur, *Malta – Health system review*, 19 (1) Health Systems in Transition 1, 60 (2017).
1752. S.L. 528.04, Functions and Responsibilities of Department of Health Services Regulations, r. 3 (2)(h).
1753. S.L. Const. 03, Public Service Commission Disciplinary Regulations.

acting on the recommendation of the Public Service Commission, delegated that disciplinary authority to entities as listed in the instrument of delegation.[1754]

316. The laws and regulations underpinning private hospitals and hospitals in the public health service are in some respect similar. Indeed, liability may accrue if there is a failure by the hospital authorities to provide adequate equipment and/or personnel, regardless of whether that occurs in a public or private hospital.[1755] The Department for Health Regulation in the Ministry for Health moreover has the function 'to monitor and ensure the maintenance of public health standards and regulations in licensed premises and other entities as appropriate'.[1756] Yet, these and other obligations are, to an extent, also embedded in law in relation to private hospitals via the Licensing of Private Medical Clinics Regulations, which even engages with medical practitioners in relation to private hospitals. It is, for instance, a condition in order to grant, transfer or renew the licence for the running of a private hospital that it is 'in the charge of a medical practitioner or a registered nurse'[1757] and it shall be the duty of the licensee of the private hospital 'to ensure that at all times in-patients are receiving treatment at the clinic, there is available resident medical coverage for such patients to the satisfaction of the Superintendent [of Public Health], taking into consideration the number and condition of such patients and the service being provided',[1758] albeit that nursing coverage may sometimes suffice as explained earlier in the monograph.[1759] Furthermore, where antenatal, intranatal or postnatal care is given, the Licensing of Private Medical Clinics Regulations stipulate that the medical practitioner or nurse in charge of the private hospital 'should make certain that adequate general and specialist medical cover is provided as needed'[1760] and that adequate arrangements 'exist for obtaining obstetric, paediatric, anesthetic and any other necessary help in an emergency situation'.[1761] It is also provided that, where epidural anaesthesia is to be offered to women in labour, 'this should be carried out by an anesthetist trained in this procedure'[1762] and there should be '[q]ualified and fully trained staff able to react and operate the cardiac emergency equipment, if so required, … on duty 24 hours a day'.[1763] The hospital is to also keep proper records of the patients treated there, which includes 'the name and address of the patient's medical practitioner'[1764] and the name of any medical practitioner who performed or assisted in the performance of any surgical operation. To be clear, the performance or non-performance of obligations incumbent on the licensee of the private hospital should not negatively affect the obligations of

1754. Office of the Principal Permanent Secretary – Office of the Prime Minister, *Manual on Disciplinary Procedures in the Public Service* (26 July 2022), Appendix A.
1755. *See* Part I Ch. 4 §1.II above.
1756. S.L. 528.05, Functions and Responsibilities of the Department of Health Regulation Regulations, r. 3 (2)(f).
1757. S.L. 458.23, Licensing of Private Medical Clinics Regulations, r. 7 (2)(a).
1758. *Ibid.*, r. 8.
1759. *See* Part III Ch. 2 §2 above.
1760. S.L. 458.23, Licensing of Private Medical Clinics Regulations, r. 10 (2)(a).
1761. *Ibid.*, r. 10 (2)(b).
1762. *Ibid.*, r. 10 (2)(c).
1763. *Ibid.*, Third Schedule.
1764. *Ibid.*, r. 11 (1)(a).

medical practitioners towards their patients, and it is thus, for instance, stipulated in the Licensing of Private Medical Clinics Regulations that, when surgical operations can be performed at a private hospital, 'the prudent exercise of clinical judgement by the surgeon and the anesthetist, faced with an individual problem and *particularly when faced with non-ideal facilities*, is mandatory'.[1765]

§2. Preventive Healthcare

317. Preventive healthcare in Malta is broadly part of public health, which is a specialisation in the specialist register kept by the Medical Council and in the Public Health Act 'means the physical and mental well being of the community'.[1766] It then is one of the functions of the Department for Health Regulation, which is headed by the Superintendent of Public Health, 'to prevent communicable and non-communicable diseases and carry out surveillance and control in order to protect the general public from such diseases'.[1767] The latter Superintendent is responsible for public health in Malta and is to *inter alia* 'develop and implement strategies to promote and improve public health'.[1768] Strategies that have been issued by the Superintendence of Public Health have covered matters such as the healthy weight of people[1769] as well as the prevention and control of non-communicable diseases.[1770] It is also the case that national strategies or policies that are related to preventive healthcare can but do not have to emanate exclusively from the office of the Superintendence of Public Health per se.[1771] In this respect, the adoption of the Healthy Lifestyle Promotion and Care of Non-Communicable Diseases Act is noteworthy inasmuch as it is to be administered by the Superintendent of Public Health, and its purpose is to 'establish and ensure inter-ministerial lifelong approach favouring physical education and healthy balanced diets for a healthy lifestyle reducing the level of non-communicable diseases throughout all age groups'.[1772] The functions of the Advisory Council on Health Lifestyles that is to be established under the latter Act then include encouraging 'a lifelong approach, from intrauterine life till old

1765. *Ibid.*, Second Schedule, Part I. Emphasis added.
1766. Public Health Act, Ch. 465 of the Laws of Malta, Art. 2.
1767. S.L. 528.05, Functions and Responsibilities of the Department of Health Regulation Regulations, r. 3 (2)(i).
1768. Public Health Act, Ch. 465 of the Laws of Malta, Art. 4 (b).
1769. Superintendence of Public Health – Ministry for Health, the Elderly and Community Care Malta, *A Health Weight for Life: A National Strategy for Malta 2012 – 2020* (Health Promotion and Disease Prevention Directorate 2012).
1770. Department of Health Promotion and Disease Prevention, Public Health Regulation Division – Ministry for Health, the Elderly and Community Care, *A Strategy for the Prevention and Control of Noncommunicable Disease in Malta* (Progress Press 2010).
1771. *See*, *for instance*: Ministry for the Family, Children's Rights and Social Solidarity Malta, *National Alcohol Policy 2018 – 2023* (2018); Ministry for Health Malta, *Building resilience, transforming services: A mental health strategy for Malta 2020 – 2030* (2019).
1772. Healthy Lifestyle Promotion and Care of Non-Communicable Diseases Act, Ch. 550 of the Laws of Malta, Art. 3. Not yet in force.

age, to physical activity and a healthy lifestyle'.[1773] A first target is food consumption in schools.[1774] This approach to health can also eventually touch on the duties of medical practitioners. Indeed, the Ethics of the Medical Profession Regulations, for instance, stipulate that practitioners shall not 'publicly associate themselves with any product, such as a tobacco product, which clearly affects health adversely since such action may give an inappropriate message to the public'.[1775]

318. In addition to the above, the Public Health Act is a central piece of the domestic legal order for the purpose of public health. Thus, in respect of preventive healthcare, it is, for instance, by way of the Public Health Act that the Superintendent of Public Health may make, vary or revoke orders 'ensuring the protection of the public by immunisation against particular diseases'.[1776] This includes prescribing those diseases against which immunisation of humans is compulsory and publishing schedules regarding compulsory or recommended immunisations, resulting in the national immunisation schedule. An Advisory Committee on Immunisation Policy then has duties that include advising 'the Superintendent of Public Health with respect to vaccination programme priorities in the short, medium and long term'[1777] as well as to 'develop written recommendations for the routine administration of vaccines'.[1778] Thus, while employers of workers in the hospital and healthcare sector are bound to offer them vaccination if a risk assessment reveals that there is a risk to their health and safety due to exposure to biological agents for which effective vaccines exist, that '[v]accination and, if necessary, re-vaccination shall be carried out in accordance with the schedules and recommendations established by the Superintendent of Public Health'.[1779] As such, it is the latter schedules and recommendations that ground in practice the extent to which vaccination and immunisation will be compulsory or otherwise recommended in Malta. By way of example, all else being equal, immunisation against seasonal influenza and even immunisation against COVID-19, though recommended, have not to date been made compulsory in Malta.[1780] That being said, the regulation of immunisation is also still formally grounded, in addition to the Public Health Act and its subsidiary law, in the Prevention of Disease Ordinance that *inter alia* stipulates the procedure for the compulsory vaccination of children,[1781] even though the latter Ordinance is in principle subject to repeal.[1782] It is furthermore relevant that, while approval may be required to advertise any medical or health service or treatment, this is not the

1773. *Ibid.*, Art. 5 (2)(e).
1774. *Ibid.*, Art. 6 (b). *See also* S.L. 550.01, Procurement of Food for Schools Regulations.
1775. S.L. 464.17, Ethics of the Medical Profession Regulations, r. 7 (1)(b).
1776. Public Health Act, Ch. 465 of the Laws of Malta, Art. 27 (d).
1777. S.L. 465.05, Advisory Committee on Immunisation Policy Regulations, r. 3 (c).
1778. *Ibid.*, r. 3 (d).
1779. S.L. 465.11, Prevention of Sharp Injuries in Hospitals and Health Care Establishments Order, r. 10 (2).
1780. *See also* S.L. 465.65, Vaccination against COVID-19 Certificate Order.
1781. Prevention of Disease Ordinance, Ch. 36 of the Laws of Malta, Arts 54–67. *See also* S.L. 36.07, Typhoid fever regulations; S.L. 36.29, Forms for Immunisation Regulations; S.L. 36.31, Vaccination for Rubella Regulations; S.L. 36.35, Infectious or Contagious Diseases (Extension) Order.
1782. Public Health Act, Ch. 465 of the Laws of Malta, Art. 45.

case with 'a service provided by Government',[1783] which justifies and enables vaccination campaigns by the Government subject to the power of the Superintendent of Public Health to make, vary or revoke orders 'controlling advertisements that may affect public health'.[1784]

319. The Superintendent of Public Health may furthermore make, vary or revoke orders 'prescribing measures to guard against or to control dangerous epidemics or infectious disease'.[1785] This authority includes orders to regulate 'the provision of medical aid, the distribution of medicine, the establishment of hospitals, the promotion of cleansing, ventilation and disinfection and otherwise for guarding against the spread of disease and for the treatment of persons suffering therefrom'[1786] and more broadly includes 'prescribing such other matter as the Superintendent [of Public Health] may deem expedient for the prevention or mitigation of such disease'.[1787] Cleansing can also relate to persons or their clothing given that if 'it appears to the Superintendent [of Public Health] that a person is so dirty or, on a report by a medical practitioner, that a person or his clothing are verminous, and that person does not consent or is unable to consent to be cleansed, the Superintendent [of Public Health] may cause such person, including his clothing to be cleansed'.[1788] There are furthermore instances when action must be taken by a medical practitioner, including, for example, in the case of notifiable diseases inasmuch as any 'medical practitioner who treats or examines any person for a notifiable disease shall report such notifiable disease to the Superintendent [of Public Health] on the prescribed certificate'.[1789] This reporting obligation is also vested in the 'person in charge of a laboratory that receives a primary specimen or sample that yields a positive result indicating that the patient who supplied the specimen is suffering from a notifiable disease'.[1790] That being said, there is also, in principle, a general obligation of *any person* 'who becomes aware of any fact or situation which he reasonably ought to believe to be a public health risk or a potential public health risk [to], as soon as he becomes aware of such risk, inform the Superintendent'.[1791]

320. The Public Health Act then empowers the Superintendent of Public Health to, if s/he is satisfied, declare a public health emergency specifying the nature of the emergency and the area to which it applies.[1792] A public health emergency was, for instance, declared in April 2020, with effect from 7 March 2020,[1793] following the COVID-19 pandemic and applied to Malta, lasting until the end of June 2020.[1794] Although the measures that may be taken once a public health emergency is

1783. Medical and Kindred Professions Ordinance, Ch. 31 of the Laws of Malta, Art. 90A.
1784. Public Health Act, Ch. 465 of the Laws of Malta, Art. 27 (b).
1785. *Ibid.*, Art. 27 (c).
1786. *Ibid.*, Art. 27 (c)(iii).
1787. *Ibid.*, Art. 27 (c)(v).
1788. *Ibid.*, Art. 30.
1789. *Ibid.*, Art. 31 (1). *See also* Part II Ch. 1 §1 above.
1790. *Ibid.*, Art. 31 (2). *See also* S.L. 458.25, Licensing of Private Medical Diagnostic Laboratories.
1791. *Ibid.*, Art. 18 (1).
1792. *Ibid.*, Art. 14.
1793. S.L. 465.36, Declaration of a Public Health Emergency Order.
1794. S.L. 465.45, Second Repealing Regulations, r. 2 (x).

declared do not greatly differ from the broad authority that the Superintendent of Public Health holds in respect of notifiable diseases, including, for instance, ordering 'that any person undergo a medical examination',[1795] it is the scale of the measures that can differ in practice as considered necessary by the Superintendent of Public Health to reduce, remove or eliminate the threat to public health.

§3. Health Insurance

321. Healthcare benefits under the public healthcare system furnish broad coverage of health insurance in Malta, which has, to an extent, already been covered in the General Introduction to this monograph. The Health Act thus stipulates that, without prejudice to any other law, 'only an insured person may qualify for free healthcare benefits provided by, or on behalf of, the public healthcare system'[1796] and the Minister responsible for health is to 'from time to time, determine through regulations made under [the Health] Act who shall be deemed to be an insured person'[1797] for the purpose of entitlement to free healthcare benefits under the public healthcare system. In this respect, the insured person in the Health Act 'means a person included in the list established by regulations made under'[1798] the Health Act. In turn, any person who is not an insured person as defined in the Health Act 'shall be subjected to pay the full fees and, or costs for benefits, services, interventions or treatment as they result from the register'[1799] established in that Act. This is a register kept by the Permanent Secretary of the Ministry for Health that includes 'all the benefits, services, interventions and treatments provided by the public healthcare system, and the cost and, or fees corresponding to each such benefit, service, intervention and treatment'.[1800] Even so, there presently is no subsidiary law arising from the Health Act that stipulates who is deemed to be an insured person under that Act and the register of benefits under the public healthcare system, which is kept by the Permanent Secretary of the Ministry for Health but maintained by the Advisory Committee on Healthcare Benefits and updated by the Department of Policy in Health, is being updated at the time of writing. That being said, the broader legal framework regarding health insurance and the healthcare system also ostensibly feeds into the basis of that insurance. By way of example, subsidiary law arising from the Fees Ordinance, while arguably outdated, furnishes a list of categories of persons to whom those regulations, which establish fees for the care and treatment of patients 'in any hospital or other institution of the Department of Health',[1801] do not apply and are therefore furnished without fee at point of service. Furthermore, without prejudice to any law or regulation, the Minister responsible

1795. Public Health Act, Ch. 465 of the Laws of Malta, Art. 15 (1)(e).
1796. Health Act, Ch. 528 of the Laws of Malta, Art. 24 (1).
1797. *Ibid.*, Art. 24 (2).
1798. *Ibid.*, Art. 2.
1799. *Ibid.*, Art. 25 (4).
1800. *Ibid.*, Art. 25 (1).
1801. S.L. 35.14, Hospital Fees for Foreign Patients Regulations; S.L. 35.28, Healthcare (Fees) Regulations.

for health 'may approve for the partial, or full, waiver of fees and, or costs due by any person, not being an insured person, in exceptional circumstances and, or on humanitarian grounds'.[1802]

322. It should also be noted that Article 17 of the Constitution of Malta provides that workers 'are entitled to reasonable insurance on a contributory basis for their requirements in case of accident, illness, disability, old-age and involuntary unemployment' and every citizen 'incapable of work and unprovided with the resources necessary for subsistence is entitled to maintenance and social assistance'. In turn, the Social Security Act regulates social insurance contributions and benefits as, to an extent, explained earlier in this monograph.[1803] The Social Security Act thus *inter alia* grounds in law sickness benefits and medical assistance, which covers sickness assistance, leprosy assistance, tuberculosis assistance, milk grant, and free medical aid.[1804] This medical aid is subject to the provisions of the Health Act in addition to the provisions of the Social Security Act. For instance, a person suffering from a disease or condition as indicated in the Social Security Act 'shall be entitled to such Free Medical Aid as in the opinion of the Chief Medical Officer to Government are indicated in his case according to protocols which may be issued by him from time to time and are available within the national health service'.[1805] As such, while the Social Security Act establishes the diseases and conditions covered by the latter norm, the prescription forms to be used by medical practitioners to prescribe medicinal products or medical aids under the Social Security Act (or upon being discharged from hospital), as well as the actual benefits, services, interventions, and treatments that are available within the public health service may be governed by other laws including the Health Act and the laws underpinning the medicinal products that are covered by the Government Health Services. By way of example, the Government Formulary List, which covers products that can but need not only be medicinal products in terms of the Medicines Act, shall include:

> [C]onditions specific to coverage within the Government Health Services in terms of entitlement to free medicines, supply within the Government Health Services (primary and secondary care, use in specific clinics or hospitals), prescriber criteria and use within the Government Health Services (specific prescribers, conditions for prescribing, protocols, therapeutic guidelines or clinical guidelines).[1806]

323. Private health insurance cover is separate from the public health service and is *inter alia* governed by the Insurance Business Act and the Insurance

1802. Health Act, Ch. 528 of the Laws of Malta, Art. 25 (5).
1803. *See* General Introduction §2.III above.
1804. Social Security Act, Ch. 318 of the Laws of Malta, Part III.
1805. *Ibid.*, Art. 23 (3).
1806. S.L. 458.31, Availability of Medicinal Products within the Government Health Services Regulations, r. 5 (3). Original parentheses. *See also* S.L. 123.112, Deductions and Tax Credits (Pharmacy of Your Choice) Rules; S.L. 458.24, Prescription Forms for Free Medicinals Rules.

Distribution Act.[1807] The competent authority in relation to that sector is the Malta Financial Services Authority.[1808] Private insurance in Malta is largely stipulated upon the individual insurance policy, which is subject to medical underwriting as well as risk-based premiums, and unless otherwise specified, often relates to treatment furnished by medical practitioners as opposed to other healthcare professionals. A typical claim form then requires a medical statement that must be completed by the medical practitioner in general practice, who in turn refers the patient/s to a specialist medical practitioner who must also complete the pertinent medical statement in the claim form. That being said, while private health insurance can include a full refund of fees, this may be limited by the insurer to what is customary and reasonable. Yet, medical practitioners are not bound by the fees that the insurance company considers to be customary and reasonable. Instead, oversight of fees charged by medical practitioners lies elsewhere, including with the licensee of the private hospital/clinic and the Medical Council.

324. Private insurance is also available for medical practitioners as professional indemnity insurance. This is significant in relation to the Indemnity Insurance for Healthcare Professionals Regulations, which transpose into Maltese law a requirement arising from Article 4 of Directive 2011/24/EU. As such, it is the 'duty and responsibility of every healthcare professional providing healthcare to patients in Malta to ensure that he is covered by a professional indemnity insurance policy, or a guarantee or similar arrangement that is equivalent or essentially comparable as regards its purpose, which is appropriate to the nature and extent of the risk which he undertakes when providing healthcare services to patients'.[1809] This effectively entails a 'policy of insurance against all risks of professional liability arising from the exercise of one's profession'[1810] as a medical practitioner. That being said, this obligation to obtain professional indemnity insurance 'shall not apply to public healthcare provided by healthcare professionals, but only insofar as the services they provide within the public healthcare system of Malta are concerned'.[1811] This is because the latter services proffered by medical practitioners and other healthcare professionals will fall within the Government indemnity cover.

1807. Chapter 487 of the Laws of Malta.
1808. Insurance Business Act, Chapter 403 of the Laws of Malta, Art. 2.
1809. S.L. 528.02, Indemnity Insurance for Healthcare Professionals Regulations, r. 3 (1).
1810. *Ibid.*, r. 2.
1811. *Ibid.*, r. 3 (2).

Selected Bibliography

Aquilina Kevin, Mallia Pierre & Ellul Bridget (eds), *Contemporary Issues in Medical Ethics & Law: Conference Proceedings 2012–2015* (Progress Press 2017).

Azzopardi-Muscat Natasha, Buttigieg Stefan, Calleja Neville & Merkur Sherry, *Malta – Health System Review* 19 (1) Health Systems in Transition 1–137 (2017).

Azzopardi-Muscat Natasha, Melillo Tanya & Cauchi Daniel (eds), *Public Health in Malta 1999 – 2019* (Malta Association of Public Health Medicine 2019).

Bianchi Daniel, *Termination of Pregnancy: Does the Criminal Law Protect the Unborn Child?*, 24 *Law & Practice* 25–37 (2010).

Bianchi Daniel, *The Adoption of Embryos in Malta: Acting in the Interest and Welfare of a Child in Embryonic Form?*, 19 (3) Medical Law Review 401–429 (2011).

Bianchi Daniel, *Advance Directives: Addressing the Obligations of Support as Part of the Right of a Person with Disabilities to Equal Recognition Before the Law?*, 70 International Journal of Law and Psychiatry 101561 (2020).

Bianchi Daniel, *European Association of Health Law Covid-19 Legislative Survey – Malta*, European Association of Health Law Newsletter 27–29. ISSN: 2708-2784 (2020 Issue no. 2).

Bianchi Daniel, *European Association of Health Law Covid-19 Legislative Survey Second Edition: Malta*, European Association of Health Law Newsletter 56–60. ISSN: 2708-2784 (2020 Issue no. 3).

Bianchi Daniel, *Regulating Advance Decision-Making in Malta: To What Extent Are Advance Directives Adaptable to the Domestic Legal Order?*, in *Le scelte di fine vita – Choices at the End of Life* (Angelo Viglianisi Ferraro ed., Thomson Reuters – Forthcoming).

Buttigieg George Gregory, *Optimising Maltese Obstetric Medico-Legal Dynamics: Volume I* (Lambert Academic Publishing 2020).

Cassar Kevin & Piscopo Tonio, *The Malta Foundation Programme: Time to Act*, 21 (1) Malta Medical Journal 5–7 (2009).

Cauchi Maurice N. (ed.), *Patients' Rights, Reproductive Technology, Transplantation: Proceedings of a Symposium* (The Bioethics Consultative Committee Malta 2000).

Cauchi Maurice N., Aquilina Kevin & Ellul Bridget, *Health, Bioethics and the Law* (Malta University Press 2006).

Emmerich Nathan, Mallia Pierre, Gordijn Bert & Pistoia Francesca (eds), *Contemporary European Perspectives on the Ethics of End of Life Care* (Springer 2020).

Selected Bibliography

Footman Katherine, Knai Cécile, Baeten Rita, Glonti Ketevan & McKee Martin, *Cross-Border Health Care in Europe* (World Health Organization 2014).

Government of Malta – Ministry for Health, *Building Resilience, Transforming Services: A Mental Health Strategy for Malta 2020 – 2030* (2019).

Government of Malta – Ministry for Health, the Elderly and Community Care, *Sexual Health Policy for the Maltese Islands* (2010).

Government of Malta – Ministry for Inclusion and Social Wellbeing, *Freedom to live: Malta's 2021 – 2030 National Strategy on the Rights of Disabled Persons* (2021).

Government of Malta – Ministry for Inclusion and Social Wellbeing, *Respecting Diversity – Safeguarding equality: Malta's 2021 – 2030 National Autism Strategy* (An Autism State Support Plan in terms of Article 11 of the Persons within the Autism Spectrum (Empowerment) Act) (2021).

Government of Malta – Ministry for Social Justice and Solidarity, the Family and Children's Rights, *Mandatory Reporting Guidelines for Professionals in terms of the Minor Protection (Alternative Care) Act, CAP. 602 of the Laws of Malta* (Technical Committee 2020).

Government of Malta – Office of the Deputy Prime Minister of Malta: Ministry for Health, *Transgender Healthcare* (2019).

Government of Malta – Parliamentary Secretariat for Health, *A National Health Systems Strategy for Malta 2014–2020: Securing our Health Systems for Future Generations* (2014).

Grassi Pietro & Zammit Raymond (eds), *La Bioetica e i cinque sensi: Tra practica clinica e metafore* (Tau Editrice 2021).

Grech Kenneth, Podesta Maya, Calleja Antoinette & Calleja Neville, *Report on the Performance of the Maltese Health System, 2015* (Ministry for Energy and Health Malta 2015).

Healthcare Standards Directorate – Ministry for Health, *Charter of Patient's Rights and Responsibilities* (Malta 2016).

Mallia Pierre, *Problems Faced with Legislating for IVF Technology in a Roman Catholic Country*, 13 Medicine, Health Care and Philosophy 77–87 (2010).

Mallia Pierre, *Developments in IVF legislation in a Catholic Country*, 16 Medicine, Health Care and Philosophy 385–390 (2013).

Mallia Pierre, *Malta*, in *Handbook of Global Bioethics* 1289–1304 (Henk A M J ten Have & Bert Gordign eds, Springer 2014).

Mallia Pierre, Laferla Godfrey, Aquilina Kevin & Agius Emmanuel, *University of Malta Bioethics Research Programme – Consensus Statement on End of Life Ethico/Legal Issues* (Erasmus+ EndCare Project 2017).

Mallia Pierre (ed.), *Consensus Document: Faculty of Medicine & Surgery, Faculty of Laws, Faculty of Theology, Bioethics Research Programme and Medicine & Law Programme as part of an Erasmus+ project of the Bioethics Research Programme of the Medical School, on Harmonisation of end of life care (EndCare)* (Erasmus+ EndCare Project 2018).

Mamo Anthony J., *Notes on Criminal Law: Revised Edition* (1954–1955).

Nys Herman, *European Union Health Law* (Kluwer Law International 2d ed. 2021).

Scherpe Jens, Dutta Anatol & Helms Tobias (eds), *The Legal Status of Intersex Persons* (Intersentia 2018).

Index

The numbers here refer to paragraph numbers.

Index

Index

www.ingramcontent.com/pod-product-compliance
Lightning Source LLC
Chambersburg PA
CBHW071434230926
51846CB00001B/228
9789403549668